BACK TO
AFRICA

BENJAMIN COATES

AND THE

COLONIZATION MOVEMENT IN AMERICA

1848–1880

BACK TO AFRICA

EDITED BY

Emma J. Lapsansky-Werner
Margaret Hope Bacon

WITH

Marc Chalufour
Benjamin B. Miller
Meenakshi Rajan

THE PENNSYLVANIA STATE UNIVERSITY PRESS
UNIVERSITY PARK, PENNSYLVANIA

Library of Congress
Cataloging-in-Publication Data

Back to Africa : Benjamin Coates and the colonization movement in America,
1848–1880 / edited by Emma J. Lapsansky-Werner, Margaret Hope Bacon ; with
Marc Chalufour, Benjamin B. Miller, Meenakshi Rajan.
p.   cm.
Includes bibliographical references and index.
ISBN 0-271-02684-7 (cloth : alk. paper)
1. Coates, Benjamin—Correspondence.
2. African Americans—Colonization—Africa—Sources.
3. Abolitionists—Correspondence.
4. Abolitionists—Biography.
5. Back to Africa movement—History—Sources.
6. Antislavery movements—United States—History—19th century—Sources.
7. United States—Race relations—History—19th century—Sources.
8. American letters.
I. Lapsansky-Werner, Emma J. (Emma Jones), 1945– .
II. Bacon, Margaret Hope.

E448.B114 2005
304.8′66008996073—dc22
2005025500

CONTENTS

PREFACE

The United States is a nation of immigrants. Beginning—we believe—with immigration from Asia tens of thousands of years ago, continuing with immigration from Europe and Africa several centuries ago, then picking up velocity in the eighteenth, nineteenth, and twentieth centuries, a diverse collage of peoples and cultures have created a heterogeneous mix on the North American continent. But for at least the last few centuries, immigration and emigration have been contentious subjects, shaping Americans' notion of race, landownership, and the management of social problems. Though Americans have not always been welcoming to newcomers, the Statue of Liberty remains the symbol of our conviction that relocation can relieve the tired, poor, and huddled masses from the pain of social oppression. This volume highlights one subtheme that is part of that conviction. It explores the relationship between the abolition of slavery and the establishment of a black colony in West Africa, as seen through the essays and correspondence of one resolute Quaker, Benjamin Coates. Coates, a businessman with international connections, described himself as "a thorough abolitionist, [who] could not be such without being a Colonizationist" (Letter 87, Benjamin Coates to William Coppinger, June 6, 1866). In pursuit of this single-minded mission, Coates made friends with Joseph Jenkins Roberts, Liberia's first black president. He also kept up a brisk correspondence with others across the world that he hoped to enlist in these causes.

   In 1998, Haverford College purchased the collection of the more than 100 letters that form the nucleus of this volume. These letters were written by various nineteenth-century abolitionists to Philadelphia Quaker Benjamin Coates, one of the best-known nineteenth-century white supporters of African colonization. But Coates was more than a Quaker and a supporter of colonization; he was a dedicated, lifelong member of the Religious Society of Friends, and it was this dedication that shaped his deep connection to Haverford

College. Haverford was the first college established by the Religious Society of Friends, and Coates served as a member of the college's governing board and probably helped to support several of his nephews while they studied at Haverford in the 1850s and 1860s. The Coates family, which included noted Philadelphia business people and philanthropists, were members of the Friends Meeting at Fourth and Arch streets. From the early nineteenth century, the Coates family owned a number of residential and business properties near their meeting house. In 1937, when one of these properties was sold, Coates's voluminous correspondence was stored in the attic of a descendant. There it languished for more than six decades before the abolitionist segment of the materials was offered to Haverford College.

Three summers were devoted to annotating the letters *to* Coates and to locating and annotating letters *from* Coates between 1848 and the end of Coates's active life in the racial justice movement of his day. The year 1848 marks the beginning of Coates's friendship with Roberts, when Roberts was president of Liberia and when the west African country was becoming an independent republic. The friendship and correspondence between the two men is, ironically, predicated on their agreement that they should live in separate societies, and the correspondence presented here—though by no means limited simply to the interchange between these two colonizationists—mirrors that shared conviction. The result is the compilation of 162 letters included in this volume.

Coates was interested in colonizing African Americans in West Africa, and the correspondence gathered here focuses on that aspect of his life. Though the correspondence with Roberts begins when Coates is middle-aged—forty years old—it is clear that he had been involved in various African American reform organizations at least a decade earlier. Through the succeeding years, his writings reveal his development as a politically aware and economically astute mediator of abolitionist ideas and personalities. His open letter to Frederick Douglass (Letter 3, June 27, 1850) is clear evidence of the nimbleness of his mind, and several of his letters are apologetically autobiographical, but the clearest statement of the subtlety of this thinking is his pamphlet on why and how cotton should be grown in Africa, published in 1858 when he was fifty years old.

Editing these documents and piecing Coates's story together was a wonderful exercise in collaboration. With the generous support of Haverford College, a team was created consisting of the Curator of Special Collections, an independent scholar with expertise in Philadelphia Quakerism and abolitionism, and three students who had been trained in documentary editing through the Haverford College History Department's Seminar in Historical

Evidence. Each team member possessed different expertise, energy, and perspective, allowing a kind of synergy in the detective work of locating additional letters and information at sites outside Haverford College Special Collections: the Friends Historical Library at Swarthmore College, the Historical Society of Pennsylvania, the Library Company of Philadelphia, the Library of Congress, and the present-day Delaware Valley Quaker communities. In all this, the help and enthusiasm of Elisabeth Potts Brown, Diana Franzusoff-Peterson, and Joelle Bertolet of Haverford College Special Collections were invaluable. We also received wonderful support from Christopher Densmore of Friends Historical Library, Swarthmore College, from Phillip Lapsansky at the Library Company of Philadelphia, and from Osborn Cresson. Gary B. Nash and Thomas Hamm read portions of the manuscript and steered us away from some of the more glaring errors. Peter Potter and Peter Ripley assured us that an enthusiastic readership awaited the publication of this volume. Several other scholars, including Julie Winch and John Stauffer, read the manuscript at various stages and offered crucial criticisms. We hope that the result will excite other readers as it excited us.

The materials reproduced here are an introduction to a compelling story. Benjamin Coates was a man of many involvements—and many words— and there is a great deal more correspondence between him and his family and friends, but that is the subject of another volume. He was active in Philadelphia's Quaker business community, and he supported schools and charities—as did his cousin, Benjamin *Hornor* Coates, with whom he is often confused. The letters in this volume, then, represent a narrow but important segment of Coates's life, one that invites us to hope that other letters, still buried in private collections, will come to light. For example, we have found no correspondence between Coates and Martin Delany, who was Coates's contemporary and who was the premier black proponent of relocating African Americans to West Africa. Coates was never shy about writing to anyone who shared his interests, or who might be persuaded to share them, and Delany's traveling companion on his 1859 trip to Africa in search of a resettlement site was Robert Campbell, who was Coates's correspondent over many years. Were there letters from Coates among the effects that were destroyed in the fire at Delany's home in Wilburforce, Ohio, that wiped out Delany's artifacts from his Africa trip? Are there letters from Delany *to* Coates still stored away in another attic? Are there additional exchanges between Campbell and Coates? Is there a rich colonization correspondence between Coates and others waiting to be brought forth? It is our hope that this volume will stimulate the search for more of Coates's correspondence, which would help scholars more fully understand his mind and his work.

ABBREVIATIONS

AAS	American Anti-Slavery Society
ACS	American Colonization Society
ACS Papers	Papers of the American Colonization Society, Library of Congress, Washington, D.C.
AFUC	American Freedmen's and Union Commission
ANB	John A. Garraty and Mark A. Carnes, eds. *Dictionary of American National Biography*, 24 vols. New York: Oxford University Press, 1999
Appleton's	James Grant Wilson, ed. *Appleton's Cyclopaedia of American Biography*, 10 vols. New York: D. Appleton, 1887–1924
BAP	C. Peter Ripley, ed. *The Black Abolitionist Papers*, 5 vols. Chapel Hill: University of North Carolina Press, 1985–1992
CMS	Church Missionary Society
FHL	Friends Historical Library, Swarthmore College, Swarthmore, Pennsylvania
HCSC	Haverford College Special Collections, Haverford, Pennsylvania
HDL	D. Elwood Dunn and Svend E. Holsoe, eds. *Historical Dictionary of Liberia*. Metuchen, N.J.: Scarecrow Press, 1985
HSP	Historical Society of Pennsylvania, Philadelphia
PAS	Pennsylvania Abolition Society (itself short for the Pennsylvania Society for Promoting the Abolition of Slavery; the Relief of Negroes Unlawfully Held in Bondage; and for Improving the Condition of the African Race)
PAS Minutes	Pennsylvania Abolition Society Minutes, Haverford College Special Collections, Haverford, Pennsylvania
QC	Quaker Collection, Haverford College, Haverford, Pennsylvania

BENJAMIN COATES: A CHRONOLOGY

1808   Born on February 16 to George Morrison and Rebecca Hornor. Born
        into Northern District Meeting. His parents transfer membership to
        Philadelphia Monthly Meeting (Arch Street) on March 22
1827   Hicksite schism separates him from family and William Penn Char-
        ter schoolmates.
1831   Early philanthropy: Joins Union Benevolent Association
ca. 1835 Becomes active in the Pennsylvania Abolition Society (PAS) and the
        American Colonization Society (ACS)
1839–82 Institute for Colored Youth (ICY)
             Board of Managers: 1854–81/82 (appointed a manager in 1854)
             Board of Education: 1853 (?)–77 (?)
             Vice President: 1858–87
             Library Committee: 1870–72
             Supplies Committee: 1870–77
             Visiting Committees: 1866–80 (all members served in visiting
                 committees; in an 1881 report, Coates's name was crossed out in
                 pencil and replaced by "S. Allen")
1855   Library Company of Philadelphia:
             Subscriber ($2/month): 1855–65
             Life Member ($25): 1866–87
1857   Becomes vice president of the PAS
1858   Published "Cotton Cultivation in Africa," first as an article and then
        as a pamphlet
1859   Established Coates Bros. wool merchants with brother, George M.
        Coates
1862–64 Haverford College Board of Managers (trustees)

1863   Portrait painted by Thomas Sully as "a present to the Colonization Society"

Joins Friends' Freedmen's Association (he attended 8 of 12 meetings 1873–74, 8 of 28 meetings 1874–76, and after around that time he stopped altogether)

    Conference Committee: 1863

    Executive Board: 1863–78 (?)

    Instruction Committee: 1863–66

    Committee on Stores: 1864

    Publication Committee: 1864–65 (resigned)

    Committee on Nomination of New Members: 1865

    Subcommittee on Appointment and Transportation of Teachers: 1866

    Committee on Circulation of Holy Scriptures, &c.: 1866–73

1864   Joins Pennsylvania Freedmen Relief Association

1869   Establishes Porter & Coates publishing house with brother, George M. Coates, which eventually becomes Henry T. Coates Co.

1877   Publication Fund of the Historical Society of Pennsylvania

    Subscriber: 1877–83 (no list after 1883)

1887   Dies on March 7. Buried at Laurel Hill Cemetery, Philadelphia

STATEMENT ON EDITORIAL POLICIES

We followed the editorial standards set forth in Mary-Jo Kline, *A Guide to Documentary Editing*, 2nd ed. (Baltimore: Johns Hopkins University Press, 1998). We also used, as models, the rationale and conventions set forth in similar publications of nineteenth-century abolitionist papers, including C. Peter Ripley, ed., *The Black Abolitionist Papers*, 5 vols. (Chapel Hill: University of North Carolina Press, 1985–92); John W. Blassingame, ed., *The Frederick Douglass Papers: Series One: Speeches, Debates, and Interviews*, 5 vols. (New Haven: Yale University Press, 1979–92); and John W. Blassingame, ed., *The Frederick Douglass Papers: Series Two: Autobiographical Writings*, 5 vols. (New Haven: Yale University Press, 1999). In all of these collections, the emphasis has been on preserving the context and format as well as the content of original documents.

After much deliberation, we chose to arrange the letters chronologically rather than by correspondent, subject, and so forth, because we feel this arrangement will allow the reader to develop the clearest picture of how Coates experienced the development of his contemporaries' differing thoughts on the subject of colonization. Each letter (and its accompanying contents, if any) is numbered sequentially for ease of reference. On the assumption that social historians will be as interested in the weather, health concerns, and local gossip as in politics and economics, each letter has been reproduced in its entirety. Irregular spelling and grammar have been retained and are unmarred by the presence of "[*sic*]." We have not completed words, and we have retained the correspondents' spelling. Illegible words or letters are indicated by a two-em dash (———). Alternate spellings, expanded abbreviations, page breaks, details of text placement, indications of smudged words, and guesses at what a word actually is are in brackets ("[Coates]"); a question mark following the word indicates significant uncertainty ("[Coates?]"). We describe each letter's significance through detailed footnotes rather than headnotes, and sources are listed at the ends of footnotes, with microfilm referenced as reel:volume:frame numbers where available. Where possible, biographical notes are taken from standard biographical reference sources, and these are also briefly cited in footnotes. For more obscure people or references, we have included more detailed citations for biographical materials. For Quaker individuals, we have drawn heavily on the typescript of the *Dictionary of Quaker Biography*, compiled by William Bacon Evans between 1959 and 1970 and available at the Haverford College Special Collections, the Friends Historical Library at Swarthmore College, and the Library of Friends House, London. We have also relied on obituaries in various Friends' periodicals and meeting records.

Individuals, places, publications, or other references in the letters are explored only in the letter where the reference first appeared. Subsequent letters are footnoted to refer to the previous letter. A subject index allows the reader to cross-reference letters on similar topics. Nineteenth-century abbreviations have not been explained if their meaning is obvious (for example, "J^{no}" for Jonathan, "rcpt" for receipt, and so forth). We have reproduced the format of letters, placing date, greeting, and signature as the correspondent placed it. Correspondents' corrections have been indicated by strikethrough marks. The titles of some sources are abbreviated, with a list of abbreviations appearing with the endnotes.

Unless otherwise noted, the letters *to* Benjamin Coates are from the Benjamin Coates Collection, Haverford College Special Collections, Haverford, Pennsylvania. The letters *from* Coates are from the American Colonization Society Papers, Library of Congress, Washington, D.C., which is designated as "ACS Papers;" followed by microfilm reel, volume, and frame numbers; and noted in the first footnote of each letter. Likewise, letters from the Historical Society of Pennsylvania are noted as "HSP" in the first footnote of individual letters.

Edward Wilmot Blyden, Robert Campbell, Mary Ann Shadd Cary, Alexander Crummell, Frederick Douglass, Henry Highland Garnet, James T. Holly: their names are familiar to anyone interested in the history of black Americans. Creative and restless, cantankerous and charismatic, they were among the dozens of men and women whose imaginations, activities, and personalities dominated the struggle to end slavery and to achieve respect for nineteenth-century African Americans. Their lectures, pamphlets, books and political organizing shaped the vision of two generations of black and white American reformers.

Some two dozen black men and women, and an equal number of their white allies, are the focus of this volume, which illuminates some of the exchanges between them and one white man, Philadelphia Quaker Benjamin Coates. They all shared a passion for racial justice—and Coates was single-minded in his notion of how to define and secure it. Although many of his black correspondents held diverse and ever-changing opinions about how to effect a better life for slaves and ex-slaves, Coates never wavered in his conviction that a new colony in West Africa, populated by black Americans, was the best strategy for ending slavery and giving African Americans a positive new start. Out of this conviction Coates forged an enduring alliance with African American Joseph Jenkins Roberts, who emigrated to Liberia in 1829 and became a stellar example of the personal, financial, and economic opportunities that could be had in Africa. From the 1840s until Roberts's death in 1876, Coates and Roberts collaborated on their mission—their "view to encourage emigration"—and consistently advised their black correspondents to emigrate and encouraged their white associates to help them do so. Coates's perspective was shaped by many forces in his local environment—his Quaker commitment to nonviolence, his economic concerns, the turmoil in the Friends' communities, and the abolitionist networks around him.

Although there is no evidence that Coates traveled abroad, his connections to philanthropists and social activists across the United States, Canada, England, and Africa broadened his horizons, enlarging his story beyond the confines of his Philadelphia community. He also read widely, from the local Quaker press to publications of black and white intellectuals around the world, and in his sometime role as publisher, he brought to print the writings of missionaries and social reformers—especially if they were interested in Africa. Black and white correspondents inevitably brought their own hopes, wounds, suspicions, and agendas into their communications with Coates. Yet the central pivot of Coates's interactions with his world remained his unshakeable belief that if he could convince black Americans to adopt a "view to encourage emigration," many of the ills of several societies—in the American North and South, in communities white and black, and in Africa itself—would be alleviated.

But of course neither Coates nor his correspondents strategized in a vacuum. National and international economic and political forces inevitably affected their plans. This was especially true throughout the 1850s, as efforts such as the Underground Railroad intensified and as the tension rose between abolitionists and pro-slavery advocates. As southern cotton crop prices rose to more than half the dollar value of American exports,[1] Coates's struggle to separate his own need for cotton from the brutality of the slavery that produced it became almost an obsession. Over the course of his life, Coates also came to envision emigration as a powerful tool for developing the economy of the entire Atlantic world. His correspondence suggests that he intended to expand American capitalism globally by using the morality of abolition to help black people become a competitive part of that world. He could thus increase his own opportunities to benefit from market competition and ally himself with like-minded entrepreneurs in England. If better, cheaper cotton could be had in an international market, the South's pernicious chattel system and its stranglehold on the world's cotton market could be destroyed. For Coates, moral purity, capitalist development, and black progress were a seamless goal.

Joseph Jenkins Roberts' story, equally dramatic, begins in Virginia but takes him and his family abroad to West Africa by 1829, and then on an upward trajectory through successful entrepreneurship, to become the president of the newly independent Liberia in 1848. In this ascent, Roberts courted and counted on the support of a community of philanthropists in the United States and Britain. Among this group Coates was a well-known and respected figure, and his efforts to promote emigration in general, and Liberia in particular, are the focus of this volume.

Abolition, Colonization, and Assimilation: The Search for a Strategy

Benjamin Coates saw the abolition of slavery as the catalyst for worldwide change, because he viewed slavery as a problem that plagued his religious community, his business relationships, his country's political system, the world's

1. Michael Tadman, *Speculators and Slaves: Masters, Traders, and Slaves in the Old South* (Madison: University of Wisconsin Press, 1989), 116.

economy—and his Quaker conscience. His business enterprises involved tex-
tiles—especially cotton—and he was laboring under the weight of a long-
standing Quaker prohibition against exploitation and violence. In America,
cotton was produced with slave labor, and slavery implied both exploitation
and violence. Some Quakers skirted this issue by arranging their economic
lives to avoid contact with the corruption of slavery. Other white Quakers
even went so far as to relocate from North Carolina to Indiana or Illinois in
order to put distance between themselves and the moral pollution of slavery.[2]
Coates's religious convictions led him to a different strategy, the elements of
which he developed through numerous discussions with his white Quaker
family and friends and through frequent exchanges with black abolitionists.

Benjamin Coates was born in Philadelphia in 1808—the year Congress enacted the end of the African slave trade—into a Quaker family that
raised him to believe in the principles of the Religious Society of Friends. A
Christian sect that developed out of the teachings of seventeenth-century
English men and women, the Friends aimed to "make their lives speak" their
convictions, to make their religious beliefs permeate all of their daily behav-
iors. Coates's ancestors had been among the seventeenth-century settlers who
joined William Penn[3] in shaping Pennsylvania into a commonwealth based
upon these utopian Quaker principles. "True Godliness," Penn had admonished his followers, "don't turn men out of the world."[4] Rather, said Penn,
true faith encouraged men to engage the world more deeply, to "endeavor to
mend it." For Coates's generation, the central problem that required mend-
ing was slavery: whether and how to end it and how to conceive of abolition's aftermath. Throughout his adult life Coates was engaged with these
challenges.

By the time of Coates's birth, the Friends had been concerned about
the problem of slavery for more than one hundred years. In 1688, members of
Germantown Meeting (containing both Quakers and Mennonites) published
the first known declaration against slavery of any religious group. In this document they proclaimed that slavery violated the Golden Rule. Although some
Quakers (including William Penn) owned slaves, the Friends struggled over
the morality of slavery for many years, prodded by critics such as Benjamin

2. Thomas D. Hamm, *God's Government Begun: The Society for Universal Inquiry and Reform, 1842–1846* (Bloomington: Indiana University Press, 1995), 43–56.
3. Mary Coates, *Family Memorials and Recollections, or Aunt Mary's Patchwork* (Phila-delphia: Author's Family, 1885).
4. William Penn, *No Cross, No Crown*, ed. Ronald Selleck (1669; reprint, Richmond, Ind.: Friends United Press, 1981), 36.

Lay, Anthony Benezet, and John Woolman.[5] These reformers reasoned that in addition to promoting violence, slavery resulted in the twin evils of preventing the enslaved man or woman from being free to answer whatever call God might send them and encouraging moral flabbiness among slave owners. Also, some Quaker anti-slavery activists argued, keeping a group of people dressed in shabby clothing and confining them to menial labor would make society forget that their souls were equal before God.[6] By 1773 the New England Yearly Meeting of Quakers had ruled that any member who continued to own slaves could be "disowned" (that is, expelled) by the Religious Society of Friends. Philadelphia Yearly Meeting made the same move in 1776, and other yearly meetings soon followed suit.[7] As a young man, Coates was exposed to these ideas, and they informed his adult life.

In addition to freeing *themselves* from slave-owning, the Friends became active in the wider movement for the abolition of slavery. On April 14, 1775, ten Quakers, spurred by the plight of a free Afro-Indian woman who had been sold as a slave, met at Sun Tavern in Philadelphia to form the Society for the Relief of Negroes Unlawfully Held in Bondage. This group met four times before the Revolutionary War temporarily suspended their momentum. In 1784, when the group reorganized, it included others besides Quakers, and it was renamed the "Pennsylvania Society for Promoting the Abolition of Slavery, the Relief of Negroes Unlawfully Held in Bondage; and for Improving the Condition of the African Race." The first such organization in the world, the Pennsylvania Abolition Society (PAS), attracted such prominent men as Benjamin Franklin and Benjamin Rush, lobbied for the exclusion of slavery from the new nation at the time of the Constitutional Convention, and pushed for laws abolishing slavery in Pennsylvania and other northern states. The PAS sponsored the development of sister organizations in a number of states, including some in the South, and it joined the successful lobby to abolish the slave trade in 1808.[8] But the PAS members were divided about what should follow abolition, and the contours of that division would deeply influence Coates's life and work.

5. Jean Soderlund, *Quakers and Slavery: A Divided Spirit* (Princeton: Princeton University Press, 1985).

6. Soderlund, *Quakers and Slavery.*

7. Thomas E. Drake, *Quakers and Slavery in America* (New Haven: Yale University Press, 1950), 79–84.

8. Margaret Hope Bacon, *History of the Pennsylvania Society for Promoting the Abolition of Slavery; the Relief of Negroes Unlawfully Held in Bondage; and for Improving the Condition of the African Race* (Philadelphia: Pennsylvania Abolition Society, 1959).

Like his fellow Quakers, Coates had broad concerns, ranging from his dismay about the fate of slaves themselves, to his anxiety about the souls of slaveholders, to his distress over the divisiveness of the slavery and anti-slavery controversies. The abolitionist communities were united in their goal—the ending of slavery—but they were much less unified about what might be the future of free African Americans. Some of the divisions were evident among Quakers. Most abolitionists did not envision a biracial society, and most Friends shared this opinion. Some thought that assimilating black people into white America was an unrealistic goal, and instead favored providing free black people with colonies where they could live in separate communities in Canada, in the Caribbean, or in Africa. Philadelphia Quaker abolitionist John Hepburn believed that relocation of African Americans would automatically follow emancipation. Eighteenth-century white Quaker reformer Benjamin Lay agreed, because he was convinced that assimilation was not possible. Lay's contemporary, Anthony Benezet, invested considerable time and energy in teaching black children in his school, but he also believed that black people should be relocated away from white society—perhaps in the western territories of North America. In the early nineteenth century, Benjamin Lundy—who published America's first abolitionist newspaper, *The Genius of Universal Emancipation*—also traveled widely looking for suitable sites to segregate the objects of his philanthropy, even as he simultaneously spoke of absorbing black Americans as equal citizens. Even Elias Hicks of Long Island, New York, widely known as a fiery abolitionist, favored colonization. In the 1820s, Hicks argued that, instead of raising money to support the Greeks in their war for independence, Americans should raise funds to buy the freedom of the slaves and to settle them in the Southwest.[9]

Few Friends imagined that by providing schools and religious instruction they could help to "elevate" black people to play an equal role in society. In 1816, when a group of southern planters established the American Colonization Society (ACS) to relocate freed African Americans to Africa, the idea had wide appeal and many Quakers saw its merit. Lacking a sophisticated knowledge of Africa, many ACS supporters only perceived "foreign" language in their midst and concluded that speakers of these languages should be sent "home." By the time Benjamin Coates was a teenager, when the ACS had transported its first black settlers to Monrovia (the town in West Africa named

9. Drake, *Quakers and Slavery in America*, 121; Elias Hicks Papers, Miscellaneous Fragments, Box 30, Friends Historical Library, Swarthmore College, Swarthmore, Pennsylvania (hereafter FHL); Merton L. Dillon, *Benjamin Lundy and the Struggle for Negro Freedom* (Urbana: University of Illinois Press, 1966).

for James Monroe, a founder of the ACS),[10] many white Americans, including some Quaker abolitionists, favored "returning" black people to Africa. This general goal, however, was an umbrella for many diverse objectives and concerns. Some supporters of the ACS were southern planters like Monroe, worried that free African Americans would cause unrest among slaves. Other ACS members were southerners beset by guilt, or drawn into the rising evangelical argument that releasing slaves was tantamount to relinquishing sin, and that it was a necessary prerequisite to Christian salvation. Some white reformers focused on the need to rid white America of the sin inherent in the slave system: the temptation to sloth and lust, and the invitation to violence and excess to which slaves subjected white Americans, thereby degrading the quality of life for *white* Americans. Some saw unpaid slave labor as potentially depressing the wages of white workers. Many northern Quaker merchants, while abhorring slavery, were sympathetic to the problems its end would cause for southern planters—who were, as often as not, relatives and business partners of northern Quakers. Others hoped that colonization would promote "the work of giving civilization and Christianity to Africa."[11]

Most white reformers were unclear about how to respond to free black people like James Forten, a wealthy and well-respected black Philadelphia sailyard owner who early voiced his conviction that to relocate to Africa was not to "return" to anything. His home, he asserted, as well as his commercial ties and loyalties were here in America. It was hard to make a case that a successful businessman like Forten, who had contributed much to the community and economy of Philadelphia, would be better off in Africa, or that Philadelphia's white society would be well served by his absence.[12] Yet the ACS aggressively pursued the goal of encouraging all black people to leave. Until the late 1820s, Forten even considered this possibility, and he helped several of his employees to relocate to Haiti. When these emigrants returned, disappointed, to the United States, Forten completely abandoned his interest in expatriation.[13]

After 1816, the PAS was frequently approached by the ACS for an endorsement, but PAS members were never able to agree to support the ACS. At first, PAS leader Roberts Vaux denounced the ACS, saying it "originated in

10. Philip J. Staudenraus, *The African Colonization Movement, 1816–1865* (New York: Columbia University Press, 1961).

11. Letter 149, Tracy to Coates, March 10, 1869.

12. Forten owned a large shipyard, where he employed a number of black and white workers. He also gave generously—both time and money—to philanthropic causes. Julie Winch, *A Gentleman of Color: The Life of James Forten* (New York: Oxford University Press, 2002).

13. Winch, *A Gentleman of Color*, 193, 209–20.

the bosom of the slave state as a scheme for strengthening slavery." Later, however, Vaux joined the ACS and became a strong supporter. Another PAS member, Thomas Shipley, worked closely with black leaders such as James Forten and Forten's son-in-law, Robert Purvis, and remained staunchly opposed to colonization. In 1827, at a meeting of the PAS, he proposed a resolution: "Whereas the objects of this Society are declared in the constitution to be to promote the abolition of Slavery and the relief of free negroes unlawfully held in bondage and to improve the condition of the African race, and whereas the project of colonization is wholly unconnected with said objects therefore: resolved that this society will take no part in the colonization society."[14]

Eventually, however, the PAS gave up trying to discern what might be the best strategy: the question was too divisive of its own membership. In 1829, when the subject came up again, Thomas Earle suggested a motion: "Resolved that it is inexpedient at this time to express in the address to the convention any opinion favorable or adverse to the colonization of people of color." But the attempt at conciliation failed; Elliott Cresson, a strong advocate of colonization, resigned later in the same meeting.[15]

In fact, beginning as early as the 1780s, colonization had had a vocal following, and not just in Philadelphia. The most important Quaker to inspire the colonization movement was himself an African-American. Paul Cuffe (1758–1817) was born on the island of Cuttyhunk, off the Massachusetts coast, and was the son of an African father and Wamponoag Indian mother. He moved to the mainland with his family in 1766, and he spent most of his life at Westport, Massachusetts, engaging in trade as the captain of a coastwise schooner. A civic-minded citizen, he sued for his right as a taxpayer to vote, became a member of the Acoaxet Friends Meeting, and started a school for black and white children.[16]

Despite his own privileged circumstances, Cuffe felt that opportunities for advancement for black people were limited in America, and he became interested in African colonization. In 1811 Cuffe sailed his brig *Traveller* to Sierra Leone to investigate the African coast. The trip convinced him that if trade could be established between England, the United States, and Africa, there would be less incentive for black Africans to engage in the internal slave trade, selling their captives to European slavers at the coast. Upon his return

---

14. Pennsylvania Abolition Society Minutes (hereafter PAS Minutes), General Meeting, June 28, 1827, microfilm.

15. PAS Minutes, General Meeting, November 26, 1829, microfilm.

16. Rosalind Cobb Wiggins, *Captain Paul Cuffe's Logs and Letters, 1808–1817* (Washington, D.C.: Howard University Press, 1996), 45–55.

to the United States, he traveled from city to city, setting up African Institutes among free black people dedicated to advance his scheme. The institutes were supposed to raise money, and to recruit free people interested in resettling in Africa. His plans were interrupted by the War of 1812, but when it was over he transported thirty-eight African Americans from Boston to Sierra Leone, most at his own personal expense.[17]

At first, it appeared that Cuffe had the support of many free African Americans, including James Forten, who agreed to head up the African Institute in Philadelphia. But by 1816, when the ACS was formed, black people began to feel uneasy about the real motives of its organizers. By December of that year, when Forten assembled a meeting of the African Institute to hear about Cuffe's plans for colonization, the large audience of black people denounced the scheme, saying that they preferred to remain citizens of the United States and work for equality. At the end of the gathering, the group issued a statement: "We never will separate ourselves from the slave population of this country, they are our brethren by ties of consanguinity, suffering and of wrongs."[18] Through the 1820s, a few black Americans emigrated to Haiti. Several hundred followed the lead of John Russwurm, America's first black newspaper publisher, who moved to Liberia in 1829. Russwurm—who was also America's first black college graduate, receiving a degree from Bowdoin College in 1826—railed at the fact that in America, African Americans were "shut out and excluded from any share in the administration of government." But most black Americans agreed with New York Episcopal minister Peter Williams, who proclaimed in 1826, "we are natives of this country . . . we have toiled to cultivate it; we ask only . . . to enjoy the fruits of our labor."[19]

Cuffe's pessimism about prospects for black people in America was certainly well-founded, for even among reform Quakers, interracial friendships seem to have been rare. Ironically, Cuffe's own relationship with Stephen Gould, a white watch repairman, exemplifies the complexities of such friendships. Gould visited and corresponded with Cuffe, encouraged his education, and regarded the black sea captain as a spiritual teacher. But when Cuffe—one of only a handful of African Americans who had membership and leadership in a Quaker meeting—died in 1817, there is no evidence that Gould

---

17. Wiggins, *Captain Paul Cuffe's Logs and Letters, 1808–1817*, 62–67.

18. *Resolutions and Remonstrances for the People of Colour of Philadelphia, Against the Colonization on the Coast of Africa* (n.p., 1818). Winch, *A Gentleman of Color*, 191.

19. Philip S. Foner, *Lift Every Voice: African American Oratory, 1787–1900* (Tuscaloosa: University of Alabama Press, 1998), 101, 115.

ever made friends with another African American.[20] It is almost as if Cuffe was an anomaly in Gould's life, and the nature and mutuality of that relationship remains murky. Several Quaker families in the New England, New York, and Philadelphia Yearly Meetings made conscious efforts to draw black people into their social circles, visiting the homes of their black friends, and inviting these friends to their own social events. Noteworthy among these were Philadelphians James and Lucretia Mott, who included the black Forten and Purvis families in their family events, and the Hopper family in Philadelphia, who were on intimate terms with black school teacher Sarah Mapps Douglass. Abby Kelly Foster of Massachusetts was also on close terms with Mapps Douglass. But such relationships were the exception, and they were often frowned upon by local Quaker meetings.[21]

There are tantalizing scraps of evidence pointing to the difficulties in trying to assess Quakers' attempts to build interracial communities, but the nature, depth, and duration of the relationships between black and white settlers remains problematic. For example, throughout the 1830s and 1840s, Augustus Wattles and his brother John made repeated attempts to establish interracial communities on the western frontier. But in 1846, when John set up his Brotherhood of Spiritualists community in Clermont County, Ohio, the settlement consisted of six families and three African American carpenters. Were the carpenters unmarried workmen, not part of any family? Were they full participants in the life of the community, or only paid employees?[22] Such descriptions of community life also raise the question of class. Even Lucretia and James Mott, the best-known of those Quakers who befriended their black neighbors, seem to have restricted their social relationships to middle-class, urban, sophisticated black people, not those newly out of slavery. The absence of evidence of any antebellum marriages between white Quakers and African Americans reinforces the implication that what passed for "equal" in nineteenth-century terms would not be so considered today.

Hence, through the early decades of the nineteenth century, colonization of African Americans was, for many white Americans, an attractive alternative to either slavery or to free black people in America, and the debate

---

20. Rosalind Cobb Wiggins, "Paul and Stephen, Unlikely Friends," *Quaker History* 90, no. 1 (Spring 2001): 8–27.

21. Margaret Hope Bacon, "The Motts and the Purvises: A Study in Interracial Friendship," *Quaker History* 92, no. 2 (Fall 2003): 1–18; Paul Goodman, *Of One Blood: Abolitionism and the Origins of Racial Equality* (Berkeley and Los Angeles: University of California Press, 1998).

22. For this insight I am indebted to Timothy C. Westcott, who shared with me his unpublished essay, "'No Message but Peace': The Utopian and Abolitionist Encounters of John Otis Wattles" (June 2004).

over whether it was desirable for America and/or for African Americans for black people to relocate to Africa absorbed Benjamin Coates's energies for most of his life. "Colonization" versus "assimilation"—as the controversy would come to be known—absorbed the attention of black leaders as well.

Abolitionism and the Hicksite Schism: Tension in the Quaker Communities

In 1827, when Benjamin Coates was nineteen and graduating from the William Penn Charter school, the Philadelphia Yearly Meeting of the Religious Society of Friends split into two factions: the "Orthodox" Friends, who saw themselves as defenders of the old Quaker traditions, and the emerging group of Hicksites, followers of Long Island minister and abolitionist Elias Hicks. A number of issues were involved, including matters of religious orthodoxy, the power of the elders to regulate the how and when Friends might speak in worship gatherings, the degree to which the issue of slavery should be raised in meeting for worship, and what were acceptable strategies for effecting social reform. Hicks, a champion of rural Friends and a strong abolitionist, attacked a number of prominent Philadelphia Friends on their business dealings with slave owners in the South. He argued that many urban Quaker businessmen were too sluggish and conservative in their reform efforts and too willing to accept a gradual phasing-out of slavery. Many "Orthodox" Friends were fiscally conservative urban businessmen who were wary of breaking society's rules and norms. While they shared the Hicksites' concern for social reform, they were less likely to advocate aggressive flaunting of tradition. Also, whereas the Hicksites tended to stress the authority of the Inward Light or individual conscience, conservatism often led the Orthodox Friends to revere the authority of the Bible over the potentially anarchic value of individual morality.

The majority of members of Philadelphia Yearly Meeting became Hicksites, perhaps 17,000 in all, while about 9,000 remained Orthodox. In the city of Philadelphia itself, however, the balance was reversed, with the Orthodox retaining the loyalty of about 3,000 members, as opposed to some 1,500 adult Hicksite members.[23] The leadership of Arch Street Monthly Meeting, to which the Coates family belonged, was busy disowning members who sided

23. H. Larry Ingle, *Quakers in Conflict: The Hicksite Reformation* (Knoxville: University of Tennessee Press, 1986), 218; J. William Frost, "Years of Crisis and Separation: Philadelphia Yearly Meeting, 1790–1860," in *Friends in the Delaware Valley*, ed. John M. Moore (Haverford, Pa.: Friends Historical Association, 1981), 57–102.

with the Hicksite faction, and the sons of Hicksites were encouraged to withdraw from William Penn Charter School. The schism divided families and
caused increasingly bitter feelings, with some of Coates's distant cousins—his
classmates and friends—becoming prominent Hicksites.[24]

The Hicksite schism coincided with the emergence of a similar strident disagreement between abolitionists in the wider network: their urgency
about cleansing sin from both individuals and society corresponded also to the
growing mood of romanticism that spawned such movements as the Second
Great Awakening and Transcendentalism. Historians are still puzzling about
the philosophical underpinnings of the new reformers emphasis on ending
slavery "immediately" and "unequivocally," but it is clear that the frenetic, no-
holds-barred evangelicalism that developed among some abolitionists in the
antebellum period contained a moral message about slavery as mortal sin that
was new in American discourse. As scholars decode the rhetoric, there is con-
sensus that the concept of "immediate" was not about *time*—about the *sched-
uling* of slavery's demise—but about a willingness to adopt an aggressively
confrontational posture about the abolition of slavery/sin.[25] Among Quakers,
it was more likely to be Hicksites than Orthodox who embraced this unyield-
ing position.

The schism was surely a blow to the young Coates, who had until
then been a part of a cozy and nurturing extended family and community, with
traditions and relationships that had deep roots. Both maternal and paternal
ancestors had come to the Philadelphia area at the time of the Quaker colony's
founding. Benjamin's father, George Morrison Coates, had been educated at
the Penn Charter School, established by the founding Friends to educate their
children to the Quaker way of life and to give them a career start with those
who shared their values. At age twenty-one, George Coates had entered the
hardware business in the Market Street store of Benjamin Hornor, a Quaker
merchant. After George had spent some years with Hornor, his father gave
him money to buy merchandise to establish his own business, specializing in
seeds and in pottery. He traveled to England to requisition the goods and to
establish relationships with Quaker merchants there, and he then spent several
months in Germany buying goods, boarding with a German Quaker family, and

24. Frost, "Years of Crisis and Separation."
25. See, for example, David Brion Davis, "The Emergence of Immediatism in British
and American Antislavery Thought," *Mississippi Valley Historical Review* 49, no. 2 (September
1962): 209–30; Anne C. Loveland, "Evangelicalism and 'Immediate Emancipation' in American
Antislavery Thought," *Journal of Southern History* 32, no. 2 (May 1966): 172–88.

learning the language.[26] Returning to the United States, he married Rebecca Hornor, the daughter of his former employer, on May 19, 1807, in the Philadelphia Monthly Meeting for the Northern District, on Keys Alley. The two set up house on Market Street, between Front and Second, next door to the Hornor store. Here, on February 16, 1808, their first son, Benjamin, was born.[27] Thus George Coates had been sheltered within a Quaker world through childhood, education, his early career, and his marriage. His son Benjamin would live a life similarly sheltered within the confines of Quaker communities.

Near the Coates' home stood the old Quaker meeting house, called the Greater Meeting house, which had served many generations of Quakers. But a new meeting house had been built in 1804 at the corner of Fourth and Mulberry (now Arch) and the old building was torn down in 1808, the year of Benjamin's birth. George Coates transferred his family's membership to the Orthodox monthly meeting, which now met at the new meeting house, in 1808, and there Benjamin belonged all his life.[28] The Hicksite schism, however, surely challenged his loyalties, for while commitment to philanthropy toward—but separation from—African Americans was common among Orthodox Friends, the single-minded fervor for reform—"immediatism"— was more characteristic of Hicksites. Benjamin Coates, then, straddled the line between the Hicksite fervor for reform driven by individual Inward Light, and the Orthodox reluctance to break society's rules.

The Arch Street Meeting always prided itself on being the original monthly meeting of Philadelphia. Its official name, Monthly Meeting of Friends of Philadelphia, is the one given it in 1682 at the time of its establishment. As Quaker families moved farther from the local meeting house, a number of fledgling meetings grew up under its aegis, and by 1816 it had been joined by four additional city meetings, South Meeting on Pine, North Meeting, on Noble, Western Meeting on 12th Street, and Green Street, all under the care of the Philadelphia Quarterly Meeting. In subtle ways however, the Arch Street Meeting continued to feel itself the center of the small Quaker universe. At the time of the split between the Orthodox and Hicksite reformers, the Arch Street Meeting remained Orthodox, and although, across Philadelphia, the Orthodox managed to hold onto all of the scattered monthly meetings except Green Street, Arch Street Meeting maintained its status as the most prestigious Orthodox Meeting. Twenty-eight years later, when the

26. Coates, *Family Memorials and Recollections*, 59.
27. Coates, *Family Memorials and Recollections*, 59, attached genealogical chart.
28. Coates, *Family Memorials and Recollections*, 59, attached genealogical chart; Membership Records, Philadelphia Monthly Meeting.

Orthodox Quakers split again—into the Gurneyite, or progressive, and Wilburite, or conservative wings—Arch Street Meeting remained both conservative and powerful. Membership in this august body was not received or given up lightly.[29] That Coates's closest business associates were part of this meeting surely added to what were probably divided loyalties between Orthodox Quakers' goals for gradual and negotiated abolition and the urgency espoused by many Hicksites.

The Coates family—with its numerous branches and many members—held a revered place in the Arch Street community. Following the birth of Benjamin Coates, his mother, Rebecca H. Coates, continued to have babies at regular intervals. Josiah Langdale was born in November 1809, but he died in infancy. A third son, not named, also died. There followed Beulah, born 1813; Mary, 1815; George Morrison, 1817; twin girls who lived only a few hours; Joseph Potts Hornor, 1821; and Sarah Hornor, 1825.[30]

Benjamin grew up playing with his sisters and his many cousins. In fact, George Coates's older sister, Mary, married Benjamin Hornor Jr., George's wife's older brother, creating a family of double cousins. In addition, his uncle, Samuel Coates, had married a second wife, Amy Hornor, a sister to Rebecca Hornor Coates. Samuel and Amy's second son, born in 1797, was Benjamin Hornor Coates, who became a well-known doctor and was sometimes confused with Benjamin Coates, the abolitionist.[31]

Benjamin was equally close to his maternal cousins. His mother's brother, Joseph P. Hornor, and his wife and children were near neighbors, and the children grew up playing together, exploring Pewter Platter Alley behind their house, skating on the Delaware River, which was regularly frozen over in the winter, listening to the bells of Christ Church, visiting the remnants of Benjamin Franklin's presses nearby, and enjoying the excitement of market days, when the shambles along Market Street were full of produce from the country.[32]

Uniquely "Quaker" family configurations resulted from the development of Friends' communities, affecting everything from inheritance practices to education to attitudes about how to treat African Americans. Such huge, closely interconnected families were one manifestation of Philadelphia Quakers' family traditions. The prohibition against marrying someone who was

29. Frost, "Years of Crisis and Separation," 60.
30. Coates, *Family Memorials and Recollections*, attached genealogical chart.
31. Coates, *Family Memorials and Recollections*, 60–63. Edwin Wolf II, *Philadelphia: Portrait of an American City* (Philadelphia: Library Company of Philadelphia, 1990), 123–41.
32. Coates, *Family Memorials and Recollections*, 61–62, attached genealogical chart.

not a Friend—the grievous sin of "marrying out"—also forced Quakers to be endogamous. In addition, there was a natural tendency to find mates within one's own monthly, quarterly, or yearly meeting. This tendency was reinforced by the Hicksite-Orthodox separation of 1827, which left the Orthodox Friends in the minority in the Philadelphia region. Yet Quakers enforced strict laws against the marriage of first cousins, and widowers were not allowed to marry their former wife's sisters, or vice versa.[33]

Limited by these restrictions and enabled by economic independence, a very high rate of Quaker women, as well as men, remained single. In the late colonial period, this number may have risen to 10 percent.[34] By the end of the nineteenth century, forty percent of Quaker women did not marry.[35] Benjamin's grandfather was one of ten children, of whom two died in infancy, four married, and four remained single; his father was one of fourteen, of whom seven died in infancy, three married, and three did not. Benjamin continued this tradition by remaining single, becoming a dutiful son, and from age forty-two also assuming the care of a widowed sister-in-law and her children. We can only speculate about how he viewed his family goals and commitments, but apparently he took them seriously,[36] making his home with his sisters Beulah, Mary, and Sarah at 814 Arch Street for a number of years, before moving to 1616 Arch Street in 1863. Their mother, Rebecca, died in 1853, and their father, George Morrison, in 1868. The latter was partially blind in his old age, and he evidently needed some help. In addition, there was Joseph's widow, Eliza, and her two sons, George Morrison and Edward Hornor, who needed fatherly care. Both of these boys attended Haverford College, perhaps aided by Benjamin.[37]

Large and close-knit families and communities such as Coates enjoyed made it quite unnecessary for family members to go beyond their Quaker circles for friends, education, or employment. Not only did they have many cousins to play with and go to school with every day, but at the time of gatherings, of quarterly and yearly meetings, other cousins would come up to the city from the country, and stay with their relatives. These were times of high excitement in Quaker families, and often led to further inbreeding, as

33. Philip S. Benjamin, *The Philadelphia Quakers in the Industrial Age, 1865–1920* (Philadelphia: Temple University Press, 1976), 156; Ingle, *Quakers in Conflict*, 218; Minutes, Philadelphia Monthly Meeting for the Western District, September 1874, June 15, 1926, microfilm.

34. J. William Frost, *The Quaker Family in Colonial America* (New York: St. Martin's Press, 1973), 168 n. 3.

35. Benjamin, *The Philadelphia Quakers in the Industrial Age*, 159.

36. Coates, *Family Memorials and Recollections*, 69, attached genealogical chart.

37. Coates, *Family Memorials and Recollections*, 64–65, attached genealogical chart.

young Quakers discovered new relatives to admire. But events were mostly confined to Quaker neighborhoods and Quaker people. At the time of Benjamin's attendance at the William Penn Charter School, in the 1820s, it was located at Fourth and Chestnut Streets, not far from his family's home. A few very wealthy and worldly Quaker families sent their sons to the University of Pennsylvania or even to Harvard at the time, but the Coateses were strict Friends and would not allow their son such mingling with "the world's people." Not until the founding of Haverford College in 1833 would many young Quaker men be afforded the opportunity for higher education.[38] In such a restricted world, surely Benjamin felt the loss of whole segments of the community when the Hicksite and Orthodox Quakers were split asunder, and his abolitionist posture—a blend of Hicksite fervor for radical religious witness on the one hand and Orthodox caution about rule-breaking on the other— probably reflected his immersion in those two worlds and his relative isolation from other perspectives. This relative isolation may also help explain his passion for letter-writing, for it seems that only his correspondence took him over the Quaker walls that hedged him in.

When the schism came, Coates's mother's distress was surely visible to Benjamin, who, throughout his entire life, not only resided with or near his family or origin, but also vacationed with or near other Friends. Some measure of the feeling among this family toward the Hicksites is revealed in a letter Rebecca Coates wrote to her daughter Beulah in July 1831, while Benjamin was still living with his mother and frequently adding his addenda to his mother's letters to other children who were away from home. Rebecca had been to visit her uncle Ellis Yarnall, whose son, Ellis Horner Yarnall, was married to Eliza Coffin, sister of Lucretia Coffin Mott. The Yarnalls remained Orthodox while Lucretia was a Hicksite and an outspoken abolitionist who socialized with black friends.

> I drank tea with Uncle Ellis the day before yesterday. I sat a while with cousin Eliza where I found Lucretia Mott. She mentioned that her daughter Anna and Martha Biddle had gone to spend a week with John Comly. I felt right sorry to find that our dear little Martha was exposed to what I consider dangerous company. Poor child, however sound her sentiments may have been, I fear they became by degrees

38. William F. Gummere, *Old Penn Charter* (Philadelphia: William Penn Charter School, 1973).

injured. It is hard for a young person to keep in the right
path where there are so many holding out the hand of sub-
tly to draw them aside.[39]

There is clear evidence that Coates felt it difficult to part with young
friends who became Hicksite. In a letter to his sister dated July 10, 1829, he
mentions calling on a friend Joseph Pryor, now a Hicksite, and seeing "two
or three of those dear young Hixities" ("Hixities" was a term the Orthodox
used in derision). In July 1831 he wrote again to Beulah, who was staying with
the Potts family in Trenton, and mentioned that he was "[c]orresponding frequently, and that the subjects may not be confined to politics, that they were
sometimes perhaps interesting I am free to acknowledge—he [George Potts]
knows I go to see someone. I will make the offer to him of being my grooms-
man in case I should be married first."[40]

Later in the letter came a hint: "I called to see Sarah Pugh—she
mentioned that Sally Whitall expects to bring this celebrated teacher from
Hartford home with her. So I suppose our friends the Longstreths will not
see her. Rachel Price has gone out of town and she expects to go shortly. The
balance of the conversation I would not like to repeat now—suffice it to say it
was very interesting to _me_."[41]

It seems likely that Coates was romantically interested in a young
protégé of family friend Sarah Pugh, possibly a teacher at Pugh's Water Street
school, and undoubtedly a Hicksite. Rebecca Coates was interested in this
school and visited it in 1829. In 1830 she called on Sarah Pugh and reported
to Benjamin that "she seemed pleased to see me and desired her love be sent
to thee when I write."[42] Nevertheless, it is unlikely that the Coates family
would have condoned a courtship with a Hicksite, and after 1831, all references
to romance disappear from the Coates correspondence, and with it a certain
note of gaiety in Benjamin's letters. Marriage between Hicksite and Orthodox
Quakers led to immediate disownment for both participants in the highly

39. Rebecca Hornor Coates to Beulah Coates, c/o William Potts, July 29, 1831, Coates
Family Papers, Free Library of Philadelphia Collection, #1184, Quaker Collection, Haverford
College, Haverford, Pennsylvania (hereafter QC). John Comly was a well-known Hicksite.
40. Benjamin Coates to Dear Sister, July 10, 1829; Benjamin Coates to Dear Sister, July
31, 1831; Coates Family Papers, Special Collections, Haverford College Library, Haverford, Pennsylvania (hereafter HCSC).
41. Benjamin Coates to Dear Sister, July 10, 1829; Benjamin Coates to Dear Sister, July
31, 1831; Coates Family Papers, HCSC.
42. _The Memorial of Sarah Pugh: A Tribute of Respect from Her Cousins_ (Philadelphia:
J. B. Lippincott, 1888). Rebecca Hornor Coates to Benjamin Coates, August 28, 1829; and Benjamin Coates to Beulah Coates, July 23, 1830; Coates Family Papers, HCSC.

charged atmosphere following the schism. It was a choice between the joys of marriage and the pain of cutting all ties with one's religious community. Few Philadelphia Quakers were courageous enough to undertake the latter. While family letters reveal that many families managed to bridge the gap between Hicksite and Orthodox members and still keep in close touch, in others the breach became irreconcilable.[43] It seems that Coates was never entirely reconciled to the loss of the woman of his choice. A descendant, still alive in the twenty-first century, holds a portrait of Coates as a young man. Attached to the picture is a note, written by a late nineteenth-century relative: "Uncle Benjamin Coates. He never married, He asked the lady he's been in love with for forty years to marry him, but she said, 'No, it's too late.'"[44] The energy Coates might have lavished on a wife and children was diverted instead to his focus on emigration.

In these and other ways, Coates's life fits the profile described by one historian as the model for the typical "immediatist." Frustrated in traditional career goals and lacking a parental role, many immediatists found "concrete meaning" in "benevolence . . . sin, and repentance." Pragmatic action marked the lives of such reformers.[45] Coates's enduring and focused "view to encourage emigration"—as he described his own perspective—fits this model.

In Philadelphia, the Hicksite schism, which sundered communities, Quaker meetings, families, and business relationships, and even brought some Friends to fisticuffs, created painful tears in Coates's safe Quaker canopy. This tension in his family and religious community may have accounted for the fact that, in his role as reformer, Coates was in many ways a man in the middle, unwilling to embrace either religious or political extreme, constantly struggling to mediate between opposing views, or, when this was not possible, excusing himself from the controversy. Although a lifelong member of the Orthodox wing of the Religious Society of Friends, he sometimes worked with and supported Hicksite Friends in their anti-slavery endeavors, which often included means and goals that were more radical than those of Orthodox abolitionists. He also worked with Hicksites after the Civil War in establishing schools for newly freed black people. Within the Orthodox wing of Quakerism, he

43. The records of the Fair Hill Burial Ground list Sarah Pugh as a member of Green Street. For disownments for marrying out see minutes of Arch Street Meeting and Green Street Meeting, FHL.

44. Interview with Coates's great-nephew Osborne Cresson, June 30, 2001. This portrait and note are now in HCSC.

45. Loveland, "Evangelicalism and 'Immediate Emancipation' in American Antislavery Thought," 180.

sided with those interested in ecumenical social action, rather than those who held themselves aloof. Although a man of strong, sometimes rigid, opinions, he managed to maintain good relations with persons whose views differed from his. Faced with conflict, as in the case of the Pennsylvania Colonization Society and its domination by Elliott Cresson, a man whom he disliked, Coates withdrew rather than continuing to battle.[46]

If Philadelphia Friends were pained by the Hicksite schism, Quakers in New York—Elias Hicks's home territory and where Coates spent his summers—were equally so. There too, differences of opinion about anti-slavery activity helped fuel the divisions. Both Hicksites and Orthodox agreed that in New York, the Hicksites—more outspoken and aggressive about their beliefs and social conscience—were in the majority (though each side differed about the actual percentage). And in the religious-revival atmosphere of northwestern New York, Hicksite Quakers were often more willing than the Orthodox to demonstrate their convictions by welcoming fugitives to live among them. But the prevailing view among both groups of New York Quakers was not supportive of colonization.[47] Clearly, if Benjamin Coates were to remain within the Quaker community, he had to temper his passion for colonization with a tolerance for Friends who held other views.

"A View to Encourage Emigration": Benjamin Coates Encounters Race and Radicalism

Just a block from the Coates residence on Arch Street lived a prominent African American family. Robert Douglass, a hairdresser active in African American affairs, and Grace Bustill Douglass, a milliner and schoolteacher, had six children, of whom five survived. Sarah Mapps Douglass, born in 1806, and Robert Douglass, born in 1809, were close in age to Benjamin Coates. Moreover, the Douglass children attended Arch Street Meeting with their mother, who had been raised in Quaker ways. Grace Douglass, however, was never admitted to membership in the Religious Society of Friends, and at Arch Street she was always encouraged to sit in a separate bench reserved for "colored people."[48]

46. *Friends Intelligencer and Journal* 44, no. 19 (1887): 300.
47. Hugh Barbour and others, ed., *Quaker Crosscurrents: Three Hundred Years of Friends in the New York Yearly Meetings* (Syracuse: Syracuse University Press, 1995), 68–75, 100–130.
48. Maria J. Lindhorst, "Sarah Mapps Douglass: The Emergence of an African American Educator/Activist in Nineteenth Century Philadelphia" (Ph.D. diss., Pennsylvania State

If Benjamin Coates ever played with the Douglass children growing up in his neighborhood, no record of this survives. It is more likely that he did not mingle with these darker-skinned neighbors. The Friends' testimony on race did not at this time include interracial mingling. Although the Friends ran schools for black children, they did not admit them to their own select schools, and although they theoretically accepted black people as members, most meetings discouraged black people from applying and seated them separately, as with the Douglass family. So common was this custom in American meetinghouses that it passed without notice for the most part. In 1837, Angelina and Sarah Grimke, two sisters from South Carolina wedded to the anti-slavery cause, deliberately sat with Grace and Sarah Douglass in protest to the exclusion. This became a widely publicized case. Many years later, two sisters, Rebecca White and Hannah White Richardson, lifelong members of Arch Street, befriended Sarah Douglass and eased the restrictions. But there is no mention in Sarah Douglass's papers of any interest shown in the Douglasses by any member of the Coates family. Later in life, Benjamin Coates came to know Sarah Douglass as a teacher at the Institute of Colored Youth, and Robert as a young black man interested in colonization. Coates even left Sarah $100 in his will. However this was more likely an act of charity than of friendship, for Sarah received no pension and was apparently nearly destitute in her later years.[49]

If Coates was not friendly with his middle-class black neighbors, he surely was not unaware of other black residents in his community. In the 1840s and 1950s, the popular press was filled with stories about the city's 15,000 black residents. And most of the stories would surely have confirmed Coates's conviction that black Americans could not flourish economically or morally in America's cities. But the cities are where most free African Americans headed. There a small percentage of them became prosperous citizens. Most, however, had difficulty finding work and quickly fell dependent upon social services such as orphanages and almshouses. Others—and this must have grated on Coates's Quaker sensibilities—turned to the bawdy houses, bars, and brothels that proliferated along the fringes of the city, just a few blocks from the Coates

---

University, 1995); Ann Bustill Smith, "The Bustill Family," *Journal of Negro History* 10, no. 4 (1925): 638–44; Dorothy Sterling, ed., *We Are Your Sisters; Black Women in the Nineteenth Century* (New York: Norton, 1984), 110–12, 114–15, 126–33, 413, 435.

49. Last will and testament of Benjamin Coates, 1872. Coates was probably one of several members of the Board of Managers of the Institute for Colored Youth (ICY), which purchased a cabinet of minerals from Sarah Douglass after she resigned from teaching in 1877. ICY Minutes, November 11, 1878.

family home. In these establishments, gambling, dancing, gaming, prostitution, and interracial socializing caught the attention of commentators like George W. Foster, who in 1852 published an exposé titled "Philadelphia in Slices."[50] Foster, who wrote of similar activity in New York, must have helped shape Coates's conviction that African Americans were better off where they could be immersed in Christianity and inspired by the likes of Liberian entrepreneur Joseph Jenkins Roberts.

But social isolation from their black neighbors led many white Quakers (along with many Methodists, Presbyterians, Episcopalians, Baptists, and other denominations) to an insensitivity to the needs, wishes, desires, and opinions of the black community. In 1810, shortly after Coates was born, there were 9,500 African Americans in Philadelphia out of a total population of 92,000, or a little over 10 percent. By 1820, the total population grew to 113,000, while the black community increased to 12,000, one of the largest concentrations of black inhabitants in the United States, and it included a sizeable prosperous and educated black elite, to which the Douglass family belonged. Most of these families shared James Forten's view that, having helped build America's wealth, they were entitled to share in it. Had families such as the Coateses come to know their black neighbors, they might have been more sympathetic to the feelings of African Americans about such issues as colonization.[51]

Ironically, when Benjamin Coates finally formed a friendship with a man of color, it was with one who lived some four thousand miles away. Joseph Jenkins Roberts became lieutenant governor of the Liberian colony in 1839, and governor in 1841. In 1847, when Liberia became independent, he became its first president. In this capacity, he came to Coates's attention, and the two began a correspondence which endured until Roberts's death in 1876. The tone of the letters was warm, and when Roberts was visiting in the United States he and his family were often guests in Coates's home. Coates never ceased to be Roberts's loyal supporter. Not only did he write warmly to Roberts, he also wrote kindly *about* him, praising Roberts and his leadership of Liberia,[52]

---

50. See Emma J. Lapsansky, "'Since They Got Those Separate Churches': African Americans and Racism in Jacksonian Philadelphia," in *African Americans in Pennsylvania: Shifting Historical Perspectives*, ed. Joe William Trotter Jr. and Eric Ledell Smith, 93–120 (University Park: Pennsylvania State University Press, 1996).

51. U.S. Census Bureau, Third Census (1810) and Fourth Census (1820). Julie Winch, *Philadelphia's Black Elite: Activism, Accommodation, and the Struggle for Autonomy, 1787–1848* (Philadelphia: Temple University Press, 1988); and Winch, *A Gentleman of Color*.

52. See Letter 6, Coates to McLain, September 5, 1850.

and sending laudatory letters to the ACS on Roberts's behalf.[53] Roberts, whose mother had worked her way out of Virginia slavery, came from a family accustomed to hard work and leadership. After the death of her husband, Roberts's mother moved to Liberia with her sons in 1829. One of his brothers, after receiving a medical education in the United States, returned to Liberia to open a thriving practice. A second brother became a bishop in Liberia's Methodist Episcopal Church.

Joseph Jenkins Roberts, who established a flourishing trade in hides, ivory, and the exotic red lumber of the camwood tree while doing business with merchants in New York and Philadelphia, was convinced that the financial prospects in Africa could offer to all African Americans were superior to any to be had in America. The possibilities of a profitable international trade with Africa, in which he would have the inside track, could not have been lost on the enterprising Coates, whose father had studied business practices in Germany. Hence, Coates's first—and arguably his only—close relationship with a man of color was predicated on their mutual agreement about the economic value of racial segregation. In succeeding years, Coates carried on intermittent correspondence with other African Americans who sometimes shared his vision. But only with Roberts—the Liberian aristocratic businessman—was the correspondence consistently cordial and of long duration.

Perhaps together Coates and Roberts—the two capitalists—developed the concept of growing cotton in Africa, a scheme that seemed to have advantages for both. In any case, their visits and letters reveal a relationship of mutual respect, which included cordial exchanges between not only them, but also Roberts's wife and Coates's siblings. Still, the real substance of Roberts's relationship with Coates is unclear. Perhaps Coates hosted the black man on his visits to America only because a traveling black person would have had a difficult time finding lodging. Perhaps they saw each other as equals and as friends. Roberts was certainly among the most esteemed of the wide network of black and white abolitionists to whom Coates sent persuasion, money, and reading material in hopes of enlisting them—or keeping them loyal to—the cause of colonization. Supported by the ACS, Roberts's view on colonization differed widely from those of most prominent members of the Philadelphia

---

53. Thomas Slaughter's *Bloody Dawn: The Christiana Riot and Racial Violence in the Antebellum North* (New York: Oxford University Press, 1991) chronicles the story of the Christiana, Pennsylvania, incident in 1851. Albert Von Frank's *The Trials of Anthony Burns: Freedom and Slavery in Emerson's Boston* (Cambridge: Harvard University Press, 1998) tells of a similar standoff in Boston in 1854.

black elite.[54] Yet Roberts and Coates shared a mission—a "view to encourage emigration"—expressed in the 1869 letter from Roberts to Coates.[55]

If Coates and Roberts, with their alliance based on colonization, represented one axis of the colonization/assimilation debate, New England reformer William Lloyd Garrison was the boldest spokesperson for the assimilation argument. As Garrison became more strident in his statements, the abolitionist movement fragmented around him. The split created by Garrison in the anti-slavery movement was in some ways as profound as that by Elias Hicks in the Religious Society of Friends. Garrison first came to public notice when he founded his newspaper, the *Liberator*, in Boston in 1831, and published an attack on the colonization movement, *Thoughts on Colonization*, in 1832. A member of the Unitarian Church, he had been converted from support of colonization several years earlier when he met William Watkins and some other members of the black community in Baltimore where he was working as a journalist. Garrison had absorbed their fear that colonization was an excuse to rid the United States of free black people and of their radicalizing influence on their enslaved brothers and sisters.

Garrison's pamphlet, supported financially by wealthy Philadelphia black people such as James Forten and his son-in-law, Robert Purvis, converted many abolitionists from support of colonization. Abby Kelley, a Quaker from Lynn, Massachusetts, felt that she had been duped by the colonization scheme after hearing Garrison speak. John Greenleaf Whittier, also a member of the Religious Society of Friends, wrote a pamphlet, *Justice and Expediency*, in 1833, pointing out that in the sixteen years since the organization of the ACS, only 613 manumitted slaves had been transported to Africa, while the number of slaves in the United States had increased by over half a million. James and Lucretia Mott were the leaders of a circle of anti-slavery Hicksite Friends associated with Garrison.[56]

Coates, meanwhile, deepened his commitment to colonization. Like most Friends, both Hicksite and Orthodox, he probably saw Garrison as a

54. A. Doris Banks Henries, *The Life of Joseph Jenkins Roberts (1809–1876) and His Inaugural Address* (London: Macmillan and Company, 1964).

55. Letter 142, Roberts to Coates, January 30, 1869.

56. William Lloyd Garrison to Robert Purvis, May 12, 1832, and May 30, 1832, in Boston Public Library, Boston, Massachusetts. See Walter Merrill, *Against Wind and Tide: A Biography of William Lloyd Garrison* (Cambridge: Harvard University Press, 1963); *Liberator*, August 18, 1832; John Greenleaf Whittier, *Justice and Expediency* (1833; reprinted in *Against Slavery: An Abolitionist Reader*, ed. Mason Lowance, 149–55 [New York: Penguin Books, 2000]); Margaret Hope Bacon, *Valiant Friend: The Life Of Lucretia Mott* (New York: Walker, 1980); *Liberator*, August 18, 1832.

troublemaker whose rabble-rousing was incompatible with Quaker values. Moses Shepherd, a wealthy Hicksite from Baltimore and a supporter of the colonization movement, was so strongly opposed to Garrison and his influence on some Friends that he hired a private investigator to find information to discredit Garrison.[57]

As anti-slavery agitation grew more vocal in the mid-1830s, and riots against the abolitionists and black people occurred in northern cities, the majority of Friends, both Hicksite and Orthodox, shrank further from involvement in what they came to regard as a confrontational political campaign. Those who held to the anti-slavery position were encouraged to hold their own meetings, establishing small Friends Anti-Slavery Associations. Hicksites who associated publicly with Garrison were often threatened with disownment or actually disowned for their radicalism. Urban Hicksites in Baltimore, Philadelphia, and New York were particularly concerned to rid themselves of the radicals. Isaac Hopper and his son-in-law James Gibbons were disowned, as was Abby Kelley, Arnold Buffum of Providence, Rhode Island, and a handful of others. In Philadelphia, Lucretia Mott was disciplined by the elders of her meeting and threatened with disownment for preaching her Garrisonian views in Quaker meeting. Some rural Friends even withdrew from the Hicksite meetings over the suppression of anti-slavery discussion in the meeting, splintering into separate meetings such as the Longwood Yearly Meeting in Pennsylvania or the Congressional Friends in upper New York State, for which anti-slavery protest was a defining characteristic.[58] Often it was the activities of these groups that led to the mistaken public impression that all Quakers were radical abolitionists.

In 1840, the American Anti-Slavery Society split over the election of a woman, Abby Kelley, to a committee.[59] Behind the split was a growing dissatisfaction among more conservative abolitionists with Garrison's desire to mingle the anti-slavery cause with a number of other issues: women's rights, nonresistance (including no cooperation with government), and communitarian projects. This split affected Quaker abolitionists, further isolating the Garrisonians. The attitude of Orthodox Quakers toward the Garrisonians is summed up by an entry in the journal of wealthy merchant Thomas P. Cope:

57. Moses Shepherd Papers, Record Group 5, Series 2, FHL.

58. Drake, *Quakers and Slavery in America*, 158–62, 174–76. See Maria Childs, *Issac Hopper: A True Life* (Boston: John. P. Jewett and Company, 1853); Dorothy Sterling, *Ahead of Her Time: Abby Kelley and the Politics of Anti-Slavery* (New York: Norton, 1991); Christopher Densmore and others, "After the Separation," in Barbour and others, *Quaker Crosscurrents*.

59. Sterling, *Ahead of Her Time*, 104–5.

"October 21, 1850: A call from a man producing the recommendation of William Lloyd Garrison & Jas. Mott, two madcaps of the anti-slavery school This man , it would seem had been engaged in running away with slaves— had been detected & mulct of a large sum. His object is to collect by sub- scription an amount to replace the sum. I declined to contribute."[60]

If Coates's friendship with one of the teachers at Sarah Pugh's school had survived the chasm created by the Hicksite separation, it might have foundered over anti-slavery politics. As a close friend of Lucretia Mott's, Pugh became allied with the radical anti-slavery movement led by Garrison. After 1835 she joined and became active in the Philadelphia Female Anti-Slavery Society, which included Coates's black neighbor Grace Douglass and her daughter Sarah. Later Pugh was an officer in the Pennsylvania Anti-Slavery Society. In 1840 she went to London with Lucretia and James Mott and sev- eral others, as a delegate to the World Anti-Slavery Convention.[61] Coates was probably appalled by Garrison, and would surely have quarreled with radicals like Pugh over their support of the movement. Nevertheless, his brief in- volvement with Pugh and her protégés may have had a profound influence on his life, explaining his lifelong interest in supporting both Orthodox and Hicksite anti-slavery efforts, and in being supportive of Hicksite philanthro- pies in his will.[62]

Businessman, Quaker, Philanthropist

Beginning in the 1830s, Coates social reform interests were intertwined with his economic life. After serving an apprenticeship in his father's store, Benja- min in 1835 established his own dry goods store at 210 Mulberry Street (Arch), where the family had moved in 1833. Because the textile trade inevitably led its participants to cotton production, Coates was constantly connected to slave labor. He later moved his store to a property on Market Street owned by his father. Meanwhile, his younger brother, George Morrison, opened a seed business next door on Market. Joseph, the youngest son, took over their father's business in 1846. Unfortunately, Joseph was ill with tuberculosis, and he died four years later at age twenty-nine, leaving a widow and two children.[63] As

60. Eliza Cope Harrison, ed., *The Diary of Thomas P. Cope, 1800–1851* (South Bend, Ind.: Gateway Editions, 1978), 603.
61. *Memorial of Sarah Pugh.*
62. Last will and testament of Benjamin Coates, 1872.
63. *McElroy's Philadelphia City Directory* (Philadelphia: A. McElroy and Company, 1835–1859).

the activities and needs of his family swirled around him, surely Benjamin struggled to balance his ethical and religious concerns with his need for a substantial income.

In 1852 Coates shifted his business, becoming a wool merchant in partnership with another Orthodox Philadelphia Quaker, Walter Brown (whose family was caught up in its own version of the Quaker schism, because Brown was married to the niece of outspoken Hicksite agitator Lucretia Mott). During the financial panic of 1857, George Morrison became bankrupt. Benjamin survived, but he parted company with Walter Brown in order to team up with his own brother in what would become a very successful wool business. A decade later, the two brothers joined in the publishing house of Porter & Coates, with offices on Sansom Street, which also became extremely prosperous.[64] But once again, the need for cast-off cotton rags to produce paper brought Coates up against the dilemma of how to procure materials for his business without encouraging slavery.

Besides being a devoted brother and uncle, and a successful, if restless, businessman, Coates was a philanthropist, as his father had been before him. He became an early member of the Union Benevolent Association, a nondenominational group of Philadelphia businessmen, organized in 1831 after the poor of the city had experienced a particularly bad winter. This group gave food, clothes, and fuel to the "worthy poor," without regard to race, and it attempted to teach them to become self-supporting and useful members of society. He also took an interest in the maintenance of libraries and historical collections; he was a lifelong member of the Apprentice's Library Company of Pennsylvania and of the Historical Society of Pennsylvania. He took an interest in the development of Haverford College in the 1830s, and he served on its Board of Managers from 1862 to 1864.[65]

Coates was a faithful member of the Arch Street Monthly Meeting to which he belonged, but he never played an active role in this meeting. His main religious interest was religious education, an activity of which Arch Street Meeting long disapproved. His commitments to many nondenominational philanthropic groups also ran counter to the prevailing spirit of Arch Street, which emphasized the importance of maintaining strict Quaker

64. *The Biographical Encyclopedia of Pennsylvania in the Nineteenth Century* (Philadelphia: Galaxy Publishing Company, 1874), 156; J. Thomas Scharf and Thompson Westcott, *History of Philadelphia, 1609–1884*, vol. 3 (Philadelphia: L. H. Everts and Company, 1884), 233.

65. Apprentices' Library Company of Philadelphia, *Annual Reports, 1823–1880* (Philadelphia: Author); *Pennsylvania Magazine of History and Biography* 8, list of life members; Board of Managers of Haverford College, May 1862–1864, QC.

ways, and isolation from "the world's people." While members of the other city Orthodox Meetings, especially Twelfth Street, were much influenced by Joseph John Gurney, an evangelical Quaker from England who visited this country in the 1830s, and urged Friends to improve their schools, to initiate First Day Schools (Sunday schools), and to be more active in philanthropic enterprises, Arch Street was closer to the position of John Wilbur, a Rhode Island Friend who distrusted Gurney's worldly views. Following a split in New England Yearly Meeting between Gurneyite and Wilburite Friends in 1845, Philadelphia Yearly Meeting had the problem of deciding which branch to recognize. Twelfth Street urged acceptance of the Gurneyite group, while Arch Street recommended recognition of the Wilburite faction. Rather than splitting the yearly meeting, the elders, in 1855, decided to communicate with neither group.[66]

As a result of this split, Twelfth Street Friends were more apt to be found in the leadership of philanthropic enterprises than Arch Street Friends, and hence Coates's most intimate community included few radical reformers. There were, however, important exceptions. Josiah White, a coal merchant, was the founder of White's Institutes, for the education of black people and of Native Americans. White's daughters, Rebecca White and Hannah White Richardson, all members of Arch Street, served on the board of the Woman's Hospital of Philadelphia and ran a school for black children at the House of Industry. Josiah's concern for Native Americans was one which Coates shared. Nevertheless, Coates, now finding most of his colleagues to be members of Twelfth Street Meeting, experienced another instance of straddling conflicting factions.[67] At his meeting, he probably heard the ministry of Eli and Sybil Jones, evangelical missionaries from New England, who traveled the world—including Israel, Nova Scotia, and Liberia—in their efforts to spread Quakerism. When the Jones's biography was written in the 1880s, the Coates publishing house printed it.[68]

While he was active in city enterprises, Coates's real energy was focused on the cause to which he devoted himself, the abolition of slavery and the education of Africans. As a boy he had heard the evils of slavery discussed at home and in his Quaker meeting, and had read Thomas Clarkson's *History*

66. Frost, "Years of Crisis and Separation," 82–83.
67. White Family Papers, QC.
68. Rufus Matthew Jones, Sybil's nephew, wrote their biography, *Eli and Sybil Jones: Their Life and Work* (Philadelphia: Porter and Coates, 1889). Although it was published in 1889, after Benjamin Coates's death, it seems likely that editorial policies would still have reflected Coates's values.

of the African Slave Trade. At the same time, he developed an early interest in Africa and Africans. In 1834 he joined the Philadelphia Branch of the Young Men's ACS, and his devotion to the cause of the education of Africans became a guiding interest in his life.[69]

The Religious Society of Friends in Philadelphia, which had long operated schools for African Americans, opened a new school in 1837, the Institute for Colored Youth (ICY), which was established according to the will of Richard Humphries. In 1839, Coates became an active supporter of the ICY, was elected to its advisory body in 1842 and to its board of managers in 1854, and remained active until the late 1870s. Board members took turns visiting the school regularly, thereby becoming well acquainted with the teachers. One outstanding teacher was Robert Campbell, who later traveled to Africa. Another was Sarah Douglass, a member of the black family that had lived on Arch Street, near the Coates family, during Benjamin's youth. Through the school Coates may have met Sarah Douglass's brother Robert, an artist, who also was interested in colonization for a time and who traveled to Haiti and Jamaica with a view to emigration. Robert Douglass was originally scheduled to go to Africa with Robert Campbell, but dropped out due to lack of funds.[70]

Coates's chief responsibilities in the ICY were to arrange a speaker for the annual examination exercises for graduates and to set up a series of forums, which the Institute conducted in the course of the year. Among forum speakers whom Coates secured in 1862, for example, were Frederick Douglass, Alexander Crummell, James Wilson (a black teacher), William Douglass (a black Episcopal minister), and Sarah Mapps Douglass (now William's wife). Though the intellectual Crummell was the only committed colonizationist among the group, these contacts undoubtedly sharpened Coates's respect for African Americans and strengthened his belief in the power of education to develop leadership among black people.[71] Coates's correspondence with Crummell, begun as early as 1857, and continuing for more than a decade, peaked in 1862, the year Crummell published—with Coates's encouragement

69. Benjamin Coates to William Coppinger, May 24, 1866; Papers of the American Colonization Society (hereafter ACS Papers), vol. 183, 142 (hereafter cited as reel[where available]:volume:part[where available]:page[s]).

70. *A Brief Sketch of the Schools for Black People and Their Descendants Established by the Religious Society of Friends in 1770* (Philadelphia: Friends Book Store, 1867); ICY Minutes, General Meeting, 1839; Corporation, 1842–; Board of Managers, 1854–; FHL. Sarah Douglass to Rebecca White, fragment, possibly December 1858, White Family Papers, QC.

71. ICY Managers Minutes, 1862, FHL.

and advice—an optimistic vision of Africa's future as a cultural and economic leader in the world.[72]

The ICY was always close to Coates's heart. After becoming a partner in Porter & Coates, Coates provided the ICY with school supplies from the publishing firm at a large discount, and he became a member of the supply committee, in charge of purchasing all school supplies. He also continued his interest in libraries by serving on the ICY's library committee. After the Civil War, his interest and attendance began to dwindle, because he turned his attention more and more to southern schools for newly freed slaves.[73]

Another of Coates's consuming interests was the PAS and its Clarkson Hall school, which the organization ran for local African Americans. Joining the PAS himself in 1842, Coates was elected to the Education Committee, a post he held for several decades. Joining the PAS at the same time as Coates was Robert Purvis, the wealthy African American abolitionist and the first black member of the PAS. Purvis, husband of James Forten's daughter Harriet, was Philadelphia's most ardent opponent of colonization. Though no records have come to light in which Purvis speaks positively of Coates, Coates reported that Purvis eventually grew to admire Coates for his contributions toward African American education.[74]

After 1858, as one of two vice-presidents of the PAS, Coates frequently manifested his ecumenical interest in the education of African Americans. Coates had engaged in heated debate with Frederick Douglass, who opposed colonization. Yet in 1860, he helped arrange for Douglass to become a corresponding member of the PAS, the second black person to be elected to the organization. He also arranged for Robert Campbell to speak to the group about his recent trip to the Yoruba region of west Africa (part of present-day Nigeria) to visit lands where cotton could be grown. Campbell, who wrote to Coates from Africa in 1859, extolled the cotton growing capacity of the land but did not urge the organization to support colonization efforts.[75]

Yet another of Coates's interests was the Free Produce Movement, an effort on the part of abolitionists to boycott the products of slavery, such as cotton, sugar, and dyes. By refusing to use slave products, abolitionists felt they were keeping their own hands clean from slavery, while at the same time

72. Alexander Crummell, *The Future of Africa: Being Addresses, Sermons, Etc., Etc., Delivered in the Republic of Liberia.* (New York: Charles Scribner, 1862).

73. ICY Managers Minutes, 1870–1879, FHL.

74. PAS Minutes, 1843–1878; PAS Minutes June 30, 1842; Benjamin Coates to William Coppinger, June 6, 1866; ACS Papers 98:166.

75. PAS Minutes, January 13, 1858; June 6, 1860; September 27, 1860; September 29, 1870; June 29, 1871; Minutes, Committee of Employment, 1862–1867.

undermining the market for slave goods and thus reducing the necessity of slave power. Though Hicksite Friends were the first to be involved in Free Produce, Philadelphia Orthodox Friends solidified the idea, organizing the Free Produce Association of Friends in 1845, which soon developed a national membership.[76]

Benjamin Coates and African Americans

Consistent with his mediator posture, Coates tried to hold a middle-ground position on race, even as he threw himself wholeheartedly into the colonization cause. He opposed slavery and strongly favored education for African Americans, believing them to be as capable as whites. But he was also passionate about the welfare of Africans, and he was convinced that only through colonization could both African Americans *and* Africans make real social, economic, and political progress. He described himself as a "true abolitionist," desiring to end slavery not only in the United States but also in Africa. In a rare burst of egotism, for which he later apologized, he said that "he was probably the only man in America who has held this position [advocacy for Africans *and* African Americans] in the same degree."[77]

Coates was eager to interest prominent African Americans in the cause of colonization, and he corresponded with such immediatist leaders as Frederick Douglass, arguing that the cause of colonization and of anti-slavery were one.[78] No record exists of many of his efforts to persuade local African Americans, because most of his communications with them were verbal. But he never tired of trying to recruit African American leaders to his cause, and he was quick to spot any inconsistencies or weaknesses in a black leader's position. Thus when Frederick Augustus Hinton, a member of the Philadelphia black elite and a foe of colonization, helped to recruit a shipload of emigrants for the island of Trinidad, which was desperate for workers, Coates protested to a black leader—it may have been James Forten—the inconsistency of this action.

Writing to an officer of the ACS, Coates reported, "One of the influential men (colored) told me the other day when I asked him how he reconciled

76. Drake, *Quakers and Slavery in America*, 171–73. See Ruth Ketring Nuermberger, *The Free Produce Movement: A Quaker Protest Against Slavery* (Durham: Duke University Press, 1942).

77. Letter 84, Coates to Coppinger, May 24, 1866. ACS Papers 98:183:142, microfilm.

78. Douglass to Coates, April 17, 1856. William M. Coates Collection, Historical Society of Pennsylvania, Philadelphia (hereafter HSP).

it [the Trinidad scheme] in those who opposed colonization in Africa. . . . 'I cannot, sir, I agree with you it is very inconsistent."[79]

Because of these constant efforts to enlist African Americans in his cause, he was frequently critical of the ACS for its refusal to take a firm stand against slavery and the slave trade in the United States, and against the deference it paid to its southern members. If the ACS would take such a stand, argued Coates, leaders like Frederick Douglass and others might be won over to the cause.[80] In 1834, at age 26, Coates, admiring Elliott Cresson for his "young man's zeal," had joined the Young Men's ACS, organized by Cresson. But by 1837, when this organization became part of the Pennsylvania Colonization Society, Coates, weary of tangling with the combative and manipulative Cresson, became inactive in the group.

Nevertheless, Coates maintained his interest in the ACS and in its colonies in Africa. He kept up a correspondence with the ACS leadership, hoping to bring them around to his point of view. He worried constantly about any move on the part of the ACS that might alienate potential black supporters. When a new settlement near Bassa Cove was named Cresson in 1851, he wrote to protest, suggesting the name Buchanan instead. Cresson, he said, "is decidedly the most unpopular man ever connected with the Colonization cause, and..despite all his zeal, has done more to injure it in this city than all its enemies combined."[81] Following this debacle, presumably hoping to assure his own continued influence in Liberia, Coates wholeheartedly pursued his relationship with Roberts, sending him literature, raising funds, and soliciting the support of other philanthropists in Liberia's behalf.

Despite the potential for parochialism in his Philadelphia Orthodox Quaker community and his own focus on colonization, Coates's reach into the wider world is reflected not only in the list of his correspondents, but also in the references within the content of the letters. From the black side, his world was broadened by the brilliant and embittered Edward Blyden, the staunchly American Frederick Douglass, the restless educator Robert Campbell, the mercurial minister Henry Highland Garnet, and shoemaker-orator James T. Holly—who was promoting black settlement in Haiti. Through these black correspondents he was informed of the ideas of those outside his immediate circle, including Charleston black leader Francis Cardozo, Liberian statesman

79. Benjamin Coates to Samuel Wilkeson, November 27, 1839. ACS Incoming Correspondence, November 27–December 31, 1839, ACS Papers, microfilm. Winch, *A Gentleman of Color*, 316.
80. Letter 36, Coates to Gurley, January 13, 1859.
81. Letter 8, Coates to McLain, May 16, 1851. ACS Papers 122:2:170.

Edward J. Roye, and New England black photographer Augustus Washington. The exchanges among the members of this circle included news of African places and peoples; New England towns and Quaker meetings; Canadian society and politics; the Catholic church; schools and colleges in Liberia; Washington, D.C.; Philadelphia, Ohio, and New York; and businesses, charities, and political or lobbying organizations in England, France, Africa, New England, and the West. Books and newspapers were freely circulated, and the intellectual resonance was electric. Coates's correspondence, and his economic generosity, placed him at the hub of it all.

While energetically pursuing connections with black leaders, Coates simultaneously remained connected with the myriad influential white reformers: Thomas Chase and Annie Heacock, businessman Alfred Cope and journalist Edmund Morris, and philanthropist Henry Hartshore. They shared concerns not only about African Americans, but also about the integrity of Quaker practices to keep the work centered in its religious context. ACS leader William Coppinger kept Coates on his mailing list, frequently thanking him for contributions and expressing his concern that Coates receive current information. Those concerned with race relations who were not among Coates's correspondents showed up in the content of the letters. The actions and ideas of Abraham Lincoln, Henry Ward Beecher, John C. Fremont, and Caleb Clothier were part of the conversation that spun around Coates. So, too, did letters arrive at Coates's door by the circuitous route of having correspondents forward to Coates letters that were not originally intended for him, but that contained information assumed to be of interest to him.[82] In the spring of 1869, for instance, Coates received, by way of John Pinney, letters written by Edward Blyden and D. B. Warner, which were not originally intended for Coates at all.[83] Thus Coates was kept in the information circle.

In 1858, after ten years of interest and study of the matter, Coates wrote and published a pamphlet, "Cotton Cultivation in Africa, Suggestions on the Importance of the Cultivation of Cotton in Africa, in Reference to the Abolition of Slavery in the United States. . . ."[84] On the basis of research done by the Cotton Supply Association of Manchester, England, which had demonstrated that a high grade of cotton could be grown inexpensively in

82. See Letter 150, Blyden to Pinney, March 12, 1869, and Letter 152, Tracy to Coates, March 18, 1869.

83. See Letter 150, Blyden to Pinney, March 12, 1869.

84. The pamphlet was printed in Philadelphia by C. Sherman and Son. A copy of it is in the FHL, and it may be viewed at the library's Web site: http://www.swarthmore.edu/Library/friends.

"Yoruba," Coates's pamphlet advocated the development of this industry to provide Africans with the means of competing successfully with the American South on the world market. The possible results: the decline of the cotton trade in the United States and the subsequent elimination of the need for slaves, as well as the enrichment of free Africans.[85]

To promote African cotton production, Coates proposed the creation of a new organization, the African Civilization Society. He may have been inspired by an earlier society, the African Education and Civilization Society, organized in 1839 by Sir Thomas Buxton, an English abolitionist with ties to Quakerism. Buxton, a supporter of Free Produce, was opposed to the ACS, because he felt that it soothed slave owners into believing that slavery was a necessary evil and that it used coercive measures in forcing migration of black people to Africa. But Buxton supported the *voluntary* colonization of black people.[86]

The original African Civilization Society had languished, perhaps due to Buxton's death in 1845, but it was rejuvenated in 1858 when New York black minister Henry Highland Garnet, who was interested in the Free Produce Movement, read Coates's pamphlet, was inspired by it, and took leadership in promoting the idea and developing the new organization.[87] Coates hoped the new organization would appeal to many Friends who longed to do something to end slavery, but were put off by the political nature of both the anti-slavery movement and the colonization movement:

> There are in the Religious Society of Friends, many who deeply feel the wrongs of slavery, and who would gladly avail themselves of an opportunity for more extended usefulness, but who have not deemed it their duty to take an active part in the political conflict that the slavery question has engendered. Such will probably see in this quiet and peaceful, yet most effective mode of overcoming the principal obstacle to our national prosperity, the way made clear for extending more enlightened view of governmental policy to the nations of the world, some of whom have been

85. Benjamin Coates, *Cotton Cultivation in Africa: Suggestions on the Importance of the Cultivation of Cotton in Africa, in Reference to the Abolition of Slavery in the United States, Through the Organization of an African Civilization Society* (Philadelphia: C. Sherman and Son, 1858).

86. *Dictionary of Quaker Biography*, typescript, QC.

87. See Joel Schor, *Henry Highland Garnet: A Voice of Black Radicalism in the Nineteenth Century* (Westport, Conn.: Greenwood Press, 1977).

deterred from adopting our professed principles from the inconsistency of our practice, in continuing an institution at variance with both the obvious precepts of Christianity and our boasted republicanism.[88]

Coates also hoped that the new organization, and the fact that it had a well-respected black leader, would appeal to prominent African American leaders, who had opposed the ACS. He sent his pamphlet and materials on the African Civilization Society to Frederick Douglass, hoping that Douglass might see it as a middle ground. Douglass, however, did not budge. Coates also pursued Charles L. Remond and Robert Purvis, and mailed literature on the project to a number of publications either published by, or aimed at, an African American audience. The new spirit of nationalism, unleashed by the revolutions of 1848 and by Louis Kossuth's visit to the United States, was affecting some African Americans, instilling a new sense of pride in their African ancestry. Coates hoped to build on that pride.[89]

While Coates promoted the new group, it was Garnet who became its first president and principal spokesperson. Coates worked hard to elicit financial support, and he attempted to support and nurture those black people who chose to go to Africa under the aegis of the African Civilization Society to raise cotton or conduct schools. Much of his voluminous correspondence after 1858 was devoted to the development of the new organization.[90] Yet even with Garnet's able leadership, the Society faced criticism from influential black Americans. The newspaper, the *Weekly Anglo-African*, undertook a survey of black attitudes toward the Society in 1861. Robert Purvis responded with typical scorn, saying that he regarded the new group as a euphemism for the old enemy, colonization: "The best judgment of the colored people today is to remain in this country for reasons as good—nay better than that of any other class remains."[91]

Although Coates could be consumed by the colonizationist cause, firing off pages of reasoned prose about it to colleagues and would-be colleagues, he also was capable of assuming a contradictory posture and a different epistolary style. From the 1830s through the 1860s, Coates seems to have escaped the oppressive Philadelphia weather nearly every summer, traveling to

88. Coates, *Cotton Cultivation in Africa*, 15.
89. See, for example, Letter 87, Coates to Coppinger, June 6, 1866. ACS Papers 183:166, microfilm; and Coates with Frederick Douglass, Mary Ann Shadd, and Henry Highland Garnet.
90. Schor, *Henry Highland Garnet*, 155–56.
91. *Weekly Anglo-African*, April 21, 1860.

Mackinac, Michigan; St. Paul, Minnesota; Geneva and Utica, New York; the Great Lakes region; and New Bedford, Massachusetts.[92] From these places he wrote home to his father and sisters letters that were warm, gossipy, and filled with reports of the scenery, weather, and his own well-being. His style was casual, his language relaxed and unguarded. Although he sometimes reported having attended Quaker meeting, and his letters were often dated as if it was his habit to use his Sunday afternoons to catch up on correspondence, there is much to suggest that he used these summer vacations to throw off some of his Quaker restraint. Unlike many of his Quaker peers, he includes minimal discussion of theology, and his use of Friends "plain speech"—"thee" and "thy" and numbers for days of the week—is mixed liberally with the designation for days and months that was common in the larger society.

Coates also may have used these summers to distance himself somewhat from the colonization work. Although his travels took him through the most active Underground Railroad regions, during some of its most turbulent times, his letters home did not speak of abolition or of the steady parade of African American fugitives moving through these regions. Instead, he chronicled his social life and sightseeing. Parties and meals and the architectural tastes of his well-off hosts dominated his reports, with only his careful attention to the landscaping and gardening reflecting his interest in horticulture, and his seed business. Sometimes he reported exchanging seeds with people he encountered in his travels. He kept a close eye on the progress of the epidemics that swept through America in the summers, and he regularly reported on his own robust health, complaining only of the loss of two front teeth because it might make him "appear an old man."[93] (He was forty-seven when he wrote this.) Apparently these trips invigorated him: his letters are filled with commentary on how exhilirated and healthy he felt, and how he was unsure when he would return to Philadelphia—it would not be soon.

But Coates's life and philanthropy, and his persistent focus on wooing black supporters, were based in Philadelphia, and he always eventually returned. There, the furious and curious, supplicants and detractors, and merchants and politicians consulted him in person or by mail, seeking his wisdom, inspiration, and financial support. His correspondence seemed to invigorate him, too, offering a chance to expand his limited universe and to test his ideas

92. See, for example, Coates to Beulah Coates, July 31, 1831; July 5, 1832; June 27, 1851; July 17, 1854; June 2, 1855; July 17, 1855. Coates Family Papers, Free Library of Philadelphia Collection, #1184, QC.

93. Coates to Beulah Coates, July 5, 1832; Coates to George Morrison Coates, June 2, 1855. Coates Family Papers, Free Library of Philadelphia Collection, #1184, QC.

against other active minds. He allied himself with countless organizations, supporting them generously with time and money for as long as they pleased him, withdrawing from them when he felt compromised by their policies, or when their internal dissension tried his patience. His account book from 1885 suggests that his contributions to various organizations reflected his commitment to his causes. His biggest donation that year—$300—went to his friend Henry Hartshorne to support the work of the weekly *Friends Review*, the Orthodox Quaker publication that consistently touted his colonization ideas. One of his several $100 gifts went to the Friends' Freedmen's Association, and there were a number of donations to Philadelphia's Bedford Street Mission, which offered shelter to homeless people, and to city soup societies and animal rescue organizations. He sent money—as well as seeds[94]—to Midwestern Quaker Indian schools, but to the Quaker Bible societies he made only nominal donations.[95] Always his largest and most frequent donations were to key figures and programs in the grand scheme of African colonization.

For a businessman, Coates was remarkably cavalier about the costs and financing of his plans. It is hard to believe that he was unaware of the rapid increase in the slave population, which tripled between 1820 and 1860. Yet his correspondence does not include any estimate of how much time, money, and organization it would require if any significant number of black Americans were to request assistance to relocate. Perhaps he was sanguine that he could enlist the support of other white Quakers to underwrite the project.

Cotton Cultivation in Africa

It was probably through his correspondence with Joseph J. Roberts that Coates became interested in growing cotton in Africa. By 1858, concluding that an American black colony in Africa was the prescription for healing the ills of slavery and the slave trade for both Americans and Africans, Coates published *Cotton Cultivation in Africa*,[96] which laid out his argument for international social reform. He tried to appeal to the multiple issues that were stirred by the question of slavery. Colonization, Coates argued, would accomplish a number of important goals. First, it could eradicate southern slavery by providing an alternative cotton supply, grown and harvested by wage-earning

94. Jonathan Richards to Coates, May 5, 1875; J. L. Mohan to Coates, June 18, 1877. Coates Family Papers, Free Library of Philadelphia Collection, #1184, QC.

95. Coates, Ledger Book, 1885. Coates Family Papers, Free Library of Philadelphia Collection, #1184, QC.

96. Coates, *Cotton Cultivation in Africa*.

black people. This system would give African Americans a way to make a living in Africa.

Because it would be more cost-effective than slave products, Coates explained, African cotton would be less expensive than American cotton, and both English and American consumers would therefore prefer it. African societies would flourish, while American slavery, no longer profitable, would simply atrophy. Citing statistics from experiments carried out by British investors over the previous decade, Coates aimed to show that cotton-growing in Africa was both practical and efficient.[97] He pointed to the Gurney family, wealthy British bankers with a long-standing interest in abolition, and to other English statesmen who had supported African experiments in this high-minded endeavor.[98] He reminded his readers that if slavery were allowed to wither in the American South, there would be no need for either violent confrontation or political pressure, both of which were abhorrent to Coates's Quaker sensibilities. This pamphlet, widely read and well received among black and white abolitionists, was the culmination of Coates's years of cogitation and communication about black Americans. It was also the launching of Coates's most intense two years of colonization focus, during which he established his own printing business to get out his message, and he sent bundles of books and periodicals to anyone he thought would read them.

Coates was sure that a cotton enterprise in Africa could also have other benefits. By bolstering the African economy, cotton cultivation could also reduce the slave trade among Africans, who were engaged in it, he believed, because there were few other viable economic alternatives. In addition, developing a cotton industry in Africa could also provide a creative and economically rewarding outlet for talented Americans. With its majority black population, Africa would also offer black Americans opportunities for political leadership. In the right circumstances, even black people who had not shown leadership ability would have a chance to develop it. Alluding to Joseph Jenkins Roberts, who had been president of Liberia since 1848, Coates pointed out that such leadership positions were unavailable to black people in white America. It is likely that Coates would have read the work of black American political philosopher Martin Delany, who, several years earlier, had published his conviction that black people could never have political power in a society where they did not constitute a majority.[99]

97. Coates, *Cotton Cultivation in Africa*, 28.
98. Coates, *Cotton Cultivation in Africa*, 40–41.
99. Martin Robison Delany, *The Condition, Elevation, Emigration, and Destiny of the Colored People of the United States* (1852; reprint, New York: Arno Press, 1968).

Coates's final argument for the benefits of colonizing black Americans in Africa was that such a plan would introduce Christianity—which he equated with "civilization"—into Africa. Black Christian missionaries like Crummell and Edward Blyden, both of whom corresponded with Coates, shared this view. Working in Africa since Liberia's beginnings in 1817, black religious leaders were spearheading the "civilization and Christianization of Africa," which was part of "the great work of the world's redemption."[100] Christianization, argued Coates, would lead to "republican principles, a high degree of prosperity, and . . . an honored and most respectable position among the civilized governments of the world."[101] Coates was sure that all of this could be accomplished if only 10 percent of free black Americans would choose to emigrate.[102]

Since at least the 1830s, when he entered the textile business, Coates had studied the issue of colonization, listening intently to various arguments for and against it, and in his essay he tried to address the variety of objections he had heard from different constituencies. To those white Americans who feared that transporting black Americans to Africa would be too expensive, he promised that the profits would outweigh the investment. To those who worried that Africa could not produce crops equal to those grown in the South, he spoke of the fertility of African soil and the skill of African growers. To southern planters who were anxious about a rise in labor costs when slavery ended, he promised that most African Americans would *choose* to remain in the South and work for wages. To white philanthropists who doubted black peoples' abilities and self-discipline, he offered examples of Africans' and African Americans' skill and ambition. Religious leaders, said Coates, should not be put off by the Africans' paganism: here was an opportunity to cultivate new souls for the Lord. And for Quakers, Coates pointed out that this nonviolent method of ending slavery was consistent with their principles. He reassured black Americans that his plan would not *coerce* anyone into emigrating. Rather, he said, for those black Americans who had the imagination and pent-up ambition to *choose* this alternative, the opportunities would be comparable to those found by prospectors in California or Australia.[103] African coffee and sugar, as well as cotton, could make black planters wealthy, while undercutting slave-grown products in the Americas.[104] It could also help white men of conscience—like Coates himself—obtain the raw materials they needed.

100. Coates, *Cotton Cultivation in Africa*, 11.
101. Coates, *Cotton Cultivation in Africa*, 11–12.
102. Coates, *Cotton Cultivation in Africa*, 12.
103. Coates, *Cotton Cultivation in Africa*, 11.
104. Coates, *Cotton Cultivation in Africa*, 10.

Abolitionist Schemes in Black and White

Black anti-slavery activists often had an uneasy relationship with their white allies, and were distrustful of white plans and motives. Coates, for example, was one of a number of white Quakers who embraced colonization schemes as a solution to resettling ex-slaves, partly because they had found it hard to find homes for freed people in American communities. Some white abolitionists had even resorted to purchasing parcels of land in northern New York, New England, or the West, where they promoted separate black settlements. In a few cases, radical white reformers joined black settlers in such communities.[105] Yet most black Americans remained unconvinced. Among the black resisters was Frederick Douglass, and for more than a decade Coates had tried—through a combination of flattery and appeal to guilt—to convert the influential black orator to the cause. Douglass himself, Coates pointed out, was a talented man who had escaped slavery and was free to use his talents where and how he chose. Why would Douglass not encourage others to leave slavery and choose to live wherever and however they chose, including in Africa? But while Douglass published Coates's correspondence in his paper *The North Star*, he did so with an air of dismissal, remarking that he "deem[ed] it unnecessary to go into a lengthy reply" because "the points raised by [Coates] have been answered satisfactorily in my own mind."[106] Despite continued efforts, and an apparent respect between the two men, Coates was never able to change Douglass's mind on the subject of Liberia, even though, for a short time in the early 1860s, Douglass considered moving to Haiti.[107]

The 1850s exchanges between Douglass and Coates occurred when reformers' morale was at a low point. The Fugitive Slave Act of 1850, which required Northern citizens to help apprehend runaways, was followed by the Kansas-Nebraska Act in 1854, which allowed slaveholders and nonslaveholders to engage in a free-for-all to settle these new territories. The 1857 U.S. Supreme Court's decision in the Dred Scott case, which declared that black Americans were not—nor could they ever be—citizens, had dashed the hope that slavery would be eradicated without a violent crisis. The press was filled with reports of dozens of dramatic confrontations between slave hunters,

105. David M. Gradwohl and Nancy M. Osborn, *Exploring Buried Buxton: Archaeology of an Abandoned Iowa Coal Mining Town with a Large Black Population* (Ames: Iowa State University Press, 1984); Hamm, *God's Government Begun*, 103–60; John Stauffer, *The Black Hearts of Men: Radical Abolitionists and the Transformation of Race* (Cambridge: Harvard University Press, 2002).

106. Letter 3, Coates to Douglass, June 27, 1850, published in *The North Star*.

107. William S. McFeely, *Frederick Douglass* (New York: W. W. Norton, 1991), 83, 276.

fugitives, and abolitionists, underscoring the reality that the crisis was in the North as well as in the South.[108] In this grim climate, abolitionists—black and white—vented their frustration not only at slaveholders, but also at each other. Slavery seemed permanent, no strategy for abolition and/or black citizenship seemed likely to dislodge it, and no strategy could therefore coalesce a unified majority of abolitionist thinkers. For black and white abolitionists, the questions were myriad: how—and whether—black reformers should ally themselves with white sympathizers, and, if so, how should leadership roles be distributed; where should African Americans should take up residence—the United States, Canada, Haiti, Central America, or somewhere in Africa; how to pay for whatever plan would be adopted; who could be trusted to have the larger vision in mind; and who had selfish motives for supporting the abolition movement.[109]

Through their newspapers, and through their correspondence with each other and with Coates, black Americans engaged in spirited debate about these issues, challenging the white Quaker reformer, being challenged *by* him, and using him as their sounding board as they honed their ideas and worked out tensions among themselves. African Civilization Society president Henry Highland Garnet, for example, wrote to Coates about plans for colonization and about his collaboration with British philanthropist Theodore Bourne and others in setting up a British correlate to the Society. But Garnet also wrote about his rift with Frederick Douglass, who could not be swayed from his steadfast opposition to the idea. Complaining that Douglass was the "bitter unrelenting enemy" of the colonization movement, and that Douglass "will endeavour to injure our cause in England as he has done at home," Garnet also raged that Robert Campbell, Coates's emissary to England to raise money for colonization, could not "be relied upon in our cause." Campbell, Garnet reported, was "selfish, selfish!," lacked "steady purpose," and "uses [the colonization cause] just so far as it suits his purpose, and then drops us."[110]

A cantankerous man, Garnet was not above using violence to end slavery, yet Coates, a pacifist, continued to include both Garnet and Campbell in the circle with whom he exchanged letters. Often Coates would also send

---

108. This story is dramatically covered in Henry Mayer's *All on Fire: William Lloyd Garrison and the Abolition of Slavery* (New York: St. Martin's Press, 1998).

109. Benjamin Quarles, *Black Abolitionists* (New York: Oxford University Press, 1969), describes the myriad positions adopted by African American leaders as they sought to design a viable antislavery strategy and community.

110. Letter 41, Garnet to Coates, April 27, 1859; Letter 48, Garnet to Coates, July 17, 1859; Letter 56, Garnet to Coates, September 9, 1859.

reading on abolition, temperance, and other reform issues, and the recipients frequently either reported reading these, or made excuses for why they had not done so.[111] Ever the diplomat, Coates also corresponded with George Stearns, the northern white businessman who helped bankroll John Brown's effort to incite a slave insurrection at Harpers Ferry, Virginia. And he maintained contact with Edward Blyden, a Liberian immigrant who was constantly at odds with Coates's ally Joseph Jenkins Roberts. Likewise, Coates frequently joined Frederick Douglass in criticizing the ACS for the deference it paid to its southern members and for its refusal to take a firm stand against slavery and the slave trade in the United States.

Coates was always concerned about keeping alliances alive that could further colonization. When he became a vice president of the PAS in 1858—the year his cotton cultivation pamphlet brought him international attention—the group was opposed to colonization, but Coates continued to try to convert the members, who were mostly white and Hicksite, to his cause. Coates also hoped for more enthusiasm on the black side, but some of the most influential black thinkers—Martin Delany for example—were interested only in what they called "emigration," by which they meant that African American settlers would choose their own destination. Still, many other black Americans joined forces with Coates and his white colleagues in developing their Liberian plans—at least intermittently. When a working relationship was established between Liberia and the American Missionary Association (AMA), many African American people availed themselves of the funds raised to help people relocate there.

Mary Ann Shadd, a free-born black Pennsylvanian who, with her parents and siblings, had relocated to Ontario, Canada, in the wake of the Fugitive Slave Law of 1850, came slowly to approve the colonization scheme. Early in the 1850s, Shadd had broken ranks with the AMA, partly because of the organization's policies of steering clear of slaves and fugitives and offering assistance only to black Americans who were already free. But in 1858, after reading Coates's pamphlet on cotton cultivation, the fiery and opinionated Shadd wrote to Coates, committing her newspaper, *The Provincial Freeman*, to helping promote colonization.[112] Within a few months, Shadd's sister-in-law also wrote to Coates, saying that she had recruited several potential colonists from near her home in Canada.[113] Likewise enthusiastic about colonization

---

111. See, for example, Letter 42, Douglass to Coates, May 2, 1859.
112. Letter 34, Cary to Coates, November 20, 1858.
113. Letter 45, Bibb Cary to Coates, June 14, 1859.

was William Watkins Jr., a black essayist who had worked with the *Frederick Douglass' Paper*[114] before also moving to Canada in the 1850s. Watkins, however, shared Shadd's concern about excessive white intervention in black affairs, and by 1863, when the Civil War promised to eradicate slavery, both Shadd[115] and Watkins withdrew their support from plans to send African Americans to Africa. Such shifts in perspective and strategy were typical of the era, as black Americans analyzed their shifting political and economic prospects.

Through the 1850s and 1860s, then, there was no dearth of information for Coates, who was an avid reader of abolitionist and Quaker publications. For some years, publishers in England and the United States had flooded the market with treatises from and about slaves and slavery. In the wake of Congress's passage of the Fugitive Slave Law in 1850, the public discourse about slavery reached fever pitch. In addition to black periodicals like Frederick Douglass's paper, Shadd's *Provincial Freeman*, and news sheets by white abolitionists—*The Liberator*, *The National Anti-Slavery Standard*, and others—white reformers like Harriet Beecher Stowe wrote novels and other anti-slavery materials. Stowe's *Uncle Tom's Cabin*, initially published as a serial in the *National Era* in 1851–52, was quickly translated into many foreign languages, and it was followed in 1853 by her *Key to Uncle Tom's Cabin*, in which she defended the accuracy of the first volume.[116] But Stowe herself was in the middle of the colonization debate, because many black abolitionists criticized the pro-colonization ending of her novel.

Black essayists and novelists produced reading that surely would have set Coates to thinking, too. Among the boldest and most colorful writers was Martin Delany. Like Coates, Delany had turned his attention to Africa as early as the 1830s, and his ideas came to full maturity in the 1850s. In 1852, Delany published the first of several pamphlets in which, while he continued to distinguish "emigration" from "colonization," he recommended that African

114. *Frederick Douglass' Paper*, a merger of John Thomas's *Liberty Party Paper* and Douglass's *North Star*, was a weekly that began publication in Rochester, New York, in June 1851. After several iterations and economic struggles, it ceased publication in 1860. C. Peter Ripley, ed., *The Black Abolitionist Papers* (hereafter BAP), vol. 4 (Chapel Hill: University of North Carolina Press, 1991), 90–91 n.

115. Shadd's life and opinions are chronicled in Jane Rhodes, *Mary Ann Shadd Cary: The Black Press and Protest in the Nineteenth Century* (Bloomington: Indiana University Press, 1998).

116. Harriet Beecher Stowe, *Uncle Tom's Cabin: or, Life Among the Lowly* (Boston: J. P. Jewett, 1852); Harriet Beecher Stowe, *A Key to Uncle Tom's Cabin: Presenting the Original Facts and Documents Upon Which the Story is Founded, Together with Corroborative Statements Verifying the Truth of the Work* (Boston: J. P. Jewett, 1853).

Americans consider relocating to West Africa. Like Coates, Delany maintained a lifelong interest in the possibilities of colonization in Africa.[117]

Other black men and women joined Delany in broadcasting their
ideas about the present and future state of African American life in the United
States. In 1855, Frederick Douglass, who had already published several ver-
sions of his life story, wrote an updated edition, entitled *My Bondage and
My Freedom*.[118] Using this work as a platform to argue that there are some
white people who can be trusted and some who cannot, Douglass encouraged
African Americans to orchestrate their own freedom, but he did not recommend emigrating to Africa. Through novels—such as *The Garies and Their
Friends*, written by black Philadelphia novelist Frank J. Webb, with an introduction by Harriet Beecher Stowe[119]—Coates could absorb the mood of contemporary African Americans. Harriet Jacobs and other black women were
working with white Quaker women to get their stories into print.[120]

Coates, a voracious reader, and involved in the publishing business
in the 1850s, surely knew of these contemporary writers and their work. He
struck up a correspondence with James T. Holly, the black shoemaker from
Washington, D.C., who had sought relief from American racism by moving
first to New England, then to Canada. A frequent visitor to Haiti, Holly often
lectured to packed audiences on the appeal of Haiti—not Africa—for black
settlement.[121] Coates's relationship with Edward Wilmot Blyden also reflected
the Quaker philanthropist's capacity for tact. Born in the Virgin Islands,
Blyden had arrived in the United States in 1850, only to be denied admission
to Rutgers Theological Seminary. Forlorn about his prospects here, he moved
on to Africa.[122] But his move to Liberia made him no happier, and his letters

117. Delany, *The Condition, Elevation, Emigration, and Destiny of the Colored People of
the United States*.

118. Frederick Douglass, *My Bondage and My Freedom*, with an introduction by Dr.
James M'Cune Smith (New York: Miller, Orton, and Mulligan, 1855).

119. Frank J. Webb, *The Garies and Their Friends*, with an introductory preface by
Harriet Beecher Stowe (1857; reprint, Baltimore: Johns Hopkins University Press, 1997). Originally published in London in 1857, the book has been reissued, with a new introduction to the
1997 edition by Robert Reid-Pharr.

120. Harriet Jacobs' *Incidents in the Life of a Slave Girl, Written By Herself*, ed. L. Maria
Child (1861; reprint, Cambridge: Harvard University Press, 2000) was actually published in 1861,
but it had been several years in the making, with much correspondence between Jacobs and white
abolitionist Lydia Maria Child. For a fuller discussion of this genre of women's literature, see Jean
Fagan Yellin, *Harriet Jacobs: A Life* (New York: Basic Books, 2004).

121. Foner, *Lift Every Voice*.

122. Gregory U. Rigsby, *Alexander Crummell: Pioneer in Nineteenth Century Pan-
African Thought* (Westport, Conn.: Greenwood Press, 1987), 128–29.

to Coates are filled with his frustration with Roberts. Undaunted, Coates continued his dialogue with both Roberts *and* Blyden.

The Crisis: Slavery, Race, and Civil War

Of course, slavery had its ardent defenders, too. Throughout the 1850s, southern planters and political economists solidified their case about the value of slavery. Building on the ideas raised by Thomas Dew during Virginia's state constitutional debates in 1832 and on the work of John Calhoun, William Harper, James Henry Hammond, and other southern slavery apologists, George Fitzhugh had attracted much attention with his controversial *Cannibals All, or Slaves Without Masters*, published in 1857. In this volume, Fitzhugh claimed that southern slavery was more humane than northern labor systems because it behooved the slave master to take care of all slaves—women, children, and the infirm—in order to maximize his investment. Northern employers, explained Fitzhugh, need have no regard for family members who could not work. Hence, northern industrialists could have "slaves" without having to be "masters"—that is, they could have inexpensive labor without taking on the personal responsibility to which slave owners were subject.[123]

To round out the debate, there were white southerners who believed that slavery was depleting the South of its vitality. Before the 1830s, there had been active anti-slavery societies, encouraged by influential planters like James Monroe. Often these "anti-slavery" advocates were acting out of concern that slave labor would dissipate southerners' ambition, or that slaves might one day unite and stage a revolution, as had occurred in the Caribbean island of Santo Domingo. In fact, the ACS, with which Coates allied himself, was founded by people with just such beliefs. After the case made by Dew in the 1830s, however, membership in southern anti-slavery dried up, and abolition sentiment all but disappeared from the South. When it was resurrected by North Carolinian Hinton Rowan Helper's 1857 publication, *The Impending Crisis of the South; How to Meet It*, there was such a furor that Helper was forced to leave the South.[124] Using statistics from the 1850 census, Helper insisted that

---

123. In *The Ideology of Slavery: Proslavery Thought in the Antebellum South, 1830–1860* (Baton Rouge: Louisiana State University Press, 1981), historian Drew Gilpin has compiled excerpts from pro-slavery writings. A good modern edition of George Fitzhugh's work is *Cannibals all! or, Slaves Without Masters*, ed. C. Vann Woodward (Cambridge: Belknap Press, 1960).

124. Hinton Rowan Helper, *The Impending Crisis of the South; How to Meet It* (New York: Burdick Bros., 1857).

the concentration of wealth, land, and slaves in the hands of a minority of the white planters had resulted in depressed wages and that preferential public policies impoverished non-slaveholding white southerners. Helper was not lobbying for social advancement for African Americans, but for protection of white Americans. Nevertheless, he was ostracized by southerners.

Such was Coates's world in the spring of 1859, when Robert Campbell set out to join Martin Delany's excursion to West Africa in search of a place in West Africa (*not* Liberia) to repatriate African Americans. Campbell was the science teacher from the ICY, of which Coates had been a trustee since 1854. Like Delany, Campbell had grown weary of trying to imagine a life of dignity for a talented black man in America. Delany and Campbell were very excited about this mission, even though less-than-successful fundraising meant that Delany had had to carve down his original design of a scouting party of eight to a committee that included only himself and Campbell. Campbell wrote to Coates during the trip that the journey was slow (it included a stop-over in England to raise more funds) and that it was fraught with frustrations.[125] However, by the end of 1860, Delany and Campbell's "Niger Valley Exploring Party" returned to America having successfully negotiated a treaty inviting them to settle African Americans in lands of the Yoruba people, near the Niger River, some 200 miles east of Liberia. "Africa for the African race, and black men to rule them," was their rallying cry, and they were filled with anticipation. In 1861, Coates published Campbell's journal of his trip, *A Pilgrimage to My Motherland*, in which Campbell explained why he had decided to pack up his family and move to Africa.[126] Delany planned to do the same.

In 1860, however, Campbell and Delany returned to an America that was in crisis. In December, the state of South Carolina seceded, with another ten states following in quick succession. White Americans, smarting under the aftermath of northern abolitionist John Brown's attempt to seize a federal arsenal in southern slave territory,[127] were preparing for civil war.

For their side, black Americans continued their quest for trustworthy white allies—and they continued their willingness to change loyalties if the situation seemed to warrant it. The situation in Chicago was typical. H. O. Wagoner, a well-to-do black Chicago barber, had opposed colonization in the early 1850s. But by 1859, soured by the Chicago black community's unsuccessful

125. Campbell to Coates, July 14, 1859.
126. Robert Campbell, *A Pilgrimage to My Motherland* (Philadelphia: Thomas Hamilton, 1861).
127. Paul Finkleman, ed., *His Soul Goes Marching On: Responses to John Brown and the Harper's Ferry Raid* (Charlottesville: University of Virginia Press, 1995).

attempt to gain franchise in 1855, Wagoner poured out his frustration to Coates: "the fact is, my friend, the colored people have so long been the subjects of so many conflicting views and opinions, both by the government and the people, that it affords just grounds why colored men should be apprehensive."[128] Wagoner was explaining to Coates that many black Americans did not see a difference between Coates's ideas of *voluntary* colonization and the ACS's apparent interest in *enforced* deportation of American black people. Wagoner himself was now thinking that—whatever it might be called—relocation to Africa was the only sensible alternative for African Americans. In Pennsylvania, black businessman William Whipper had had a similar change of heart. Having attacked expatriation in the 1840s, he briefly considered emigration to Canada in the 1850s, in the wake of the Fugitive Slave Law.[129] Even Robert Purvis, whose friendships and business interests were deeply rooted in the black and white communities of Philadelphia, and who had long opposed colonization, briefly considered moving to England in 1856. Indeed, colored people were constantly reacting to many conflicting views and opinions.

The outbreak of the Civil War produced an impending crisis for Quakers interested in abolition. Their longtime commitment to nonviolence prevented many from endorsing the war, yet the hope that the struggle would lead to the emancipation of the slaves made others supportive of the North's cause. A few young Quakers violated the peace testimony and fought in the Civil War, and some of their elders were willing to bend sufficiently to supply goods to the Union Army. (Whether the Coates brothers were in this category, we do not know.) Others were stricter in their refusal to enter into the struggle.[130] But the frustration of anti-slavery Friends during the Civil War was somewhat relieved by the opportunity to be of practical service, by providing material aid and schools for the newly freed slaves behind the Union Army lines. In both the Orthodox and Hicksite meetings, women organized themselves to pack boxes and barrels of food and clothing for the freedmen, and they were later joined by the men. Orthodox Friends organized the Friends Freedmen's Association in late 1863; the Hicksites set up the Association for the Aid and Elevation of the Freedmen in early 1864.[131]

128. Letter 35, Wagoner to Coates, January 8, 1859.

129. Julie Winch, *The Elite of Our People: Joseph Willson's Sketches of Black Upper-Class Life in Antebellum Philadelphia* (University Park: Pennsylvania State University Press, 2000), 137–38.

130. Edwin Bronner, "A Time of Change," in *Friends in the Delaware Valley, 1681–1981*, ed. John M. Moore, 103–137 (Haverford, Pa.: Friends Historical Association, 1981), 114.

131. Friends Freedmen's Association, Executive Board Minutes, QC. Friends Association for the Aid and Elevation of the Freedmen, Executive Board minutes, FHL.

Reconstruction and Reorganization

At war's end, Coates shifted his priorities to place educating the newly freed slaves above his African interests. He suspended his interest in cotton-growing in the Yuroba region of Africa, though he continued to correspond with Joseph Jenkins Roberts. He attended the organizing meeting of the Friends Freedmen's Association, held at 304 Arch Street on November 5, 1863. He joined the executive committee of the organization, which would send teachers to the South to set up black schools. He also served on the supply committee, the publications committee, and a committee to distribute the Bible. At first this group planned to give Bibles only to freedmen, but at a meeting on September 8, 1868, it was agreed to distribute them to poor white people as well, a position that Coates strongly backed.[132]

By 1868, the Friends Freedmen's Association had established twenty-five such schools; by 1870 the number grew to forty-six. But as interest in the freedmen waned after the Civil War, funds to support these schools dwindled. In 1873 Coates joined the special appeal to all Orthodox Friends to support the black schools. It was soon necessary to cut back, however, and the Association began to concentrate on funding Hampton Institute, which concentrated on manual education, and a similar training institute in Christiansburg, Virginia.[133]

Coates remained a faithful member of the Friends Freedmen's Association until 1878. But he was engaged in similar educational work in the South with the PAS, which also sent teachers south to establish schools. In 1875, at the time of the centennial of the organization, the PAS was supporting some sixty schools in the South. Eventually, it also narrowed its focus, concentrating on a school outside of Charleston, South Carolina, established by Civil War nurse Cornelia Hancock. This school came to be known as the Laing School, after Henry Laing, treasurer of the PAS.[134]

Laing was a Hicksite, as were many of the members of the PAS at this time. Nevertheless, as a nonsectarian body, PAS supported both the Friends Freedmen's Association and the Friends Association for the Aid and Elevation of the Freedmen. Coates was always concerned that the funds be equally divided between the two. "When proposing an appropriation to the

132. Friends Freedmen's Association, Executive Board Minutes, QC.
133. Friends Freedmen's Association, Executive Board Minutes, QC.
134. See Margaret Hope Bacon, "The Heritage of Anthony Benezet: Philadelphia Quakers and Black Education," in *For Emancipation and Education: Some Black and Quaker Efforts, 1680–1900*, ed. Eliza Cope Harrison (Germantown, Pa.: Awbury Arboretum Association, 1997).

former [Friends Freedmen's Association] from the funds of the Abolition Society, he always coupled it with a like one to those 'not orthodox,' as he was wont to term our body," James Truman wrote in Coates's obituary in the *Friends Intelligencer*.[135]

Coates also belonged to the Pennsylvania Freedmen Relief Association, originally the Port Royal Association, a nondenominational group with strong representation from both Orthodox and Hicksite Friends, as well as prominent ministers such as Phillips Brooks of Trinity Episcopal Church and William Furness of the First Unitarian Church. All of these groups occasionally cooperated. In 1865, the Pennsylvania Freedmen Association met with the Friends Freedmen Association (Orthodox), the Friends Association for the Aid and Elevation of the Freedmen (Hicksite), and the PAS's Committee of Employ, to create a coalition to try to find homes and jobs for the many newly freed slaves who were pouring into Philadelphia, as well as other northern cities. One of the employees of this group was William Still, an African American coal merchant who had been a leader in the Underground Railroad. As vice president of the PAS, as well as a member of two of the other groups, Coates took an interest in this enterprise.[136]

The Pennsylvania Freedmen Relief Association also operated schools in the South. As in other organizations, Coates was interested in helping men and women regardless of race. In April 1866, he offered a resolution to this group calling for aid to be extended to poor white people in the South as well as former slaves.[137] It was adopted.

While serving on the education committee of all of these groups, Coates still put significant effort into schools run by the African Civilization Society in the South. These schools aimed to prepare African Americans to take economic skills—and Christianity—to Africa. There was an Educational Department of the African Civilization Society, located in Washington, D.C., and a Superintendent of Schools who oversaw the work, under the supervision of Coates and other members of an Education Committee. In the annual report, as of May 1, 1866, the superintendent, Rufus Perry, reported that the African Civilization Society supported thirty-three teachers in twenty-two schools with 1,500 pupils, in Washington, D.C., Georgetown, Frederick City, and Frederick County, Maryland; and in Alexandria, Arlington, and Halifax City, Virginia; as well as St. Catherine's Island, Georgia. In the same annual

---

135. *Friends Intelligencer and Journal* 44, no. 3 (1887): 300.
136. PAS Minutes, Committee of Employment, 1862–67.
137. Letter 84, Coates to Coppinger, May 24, 1866.

report, the superintendent mentioned that, "Miss Emma Amos of Reading sailed for West Africa under appointment as missionary teacher."[138]

Keeping track of all the freedmen schools supported by all these various organizations was a major task. Coates received numerous letters from teachers begging for supplies and for support. He gave money, but he also sent books, supplies and seeds, probably from his brother's former seed business, to all with whom he corresponded, and to several of the schools run by the Hicksites as well.[139]

In March 1868, Coates received a letter from Laura Towne, a teacher at the William Penn School at Port Royal, thanking him for the "your spring blessing—the garden seeds." She reported she had given most of them to the elderly who could not plant field crops, and to school children, as well as sending others on to Martha Schofield in Aiken, South Carolina. She thanked him again, stating: "I know of no such benefaction as giving these seeds; for the people depend more and more upon them every year, and we think we see already much benefit to the health of the children, from greater variety in their food."[140]

The reality of the Civil War, in fact, realigned all Americans' priorities and perspectives. At first there was controversy among black Americans about whether to support a country and war that was not about liberating them and that would not accept their help in defending itself.[141] But by 1863 the Emancipation Proclamation had raised black hopes. Delany, while retaining his interest in emigration, set aside his African plans in order to help raise black troops for the Union cause. Purvis, the leading black member of the PAS, rejoiced that this was not "simply and solely a fight about the black man. It is not merely a war between the North and the South. It is a war between freedom and despotism the world over."[142] Just three years earlier Purvis had railed against "*your* [white American] government . . . that deliberately, before

138. *Annual Report of General Superintendent of Schools—Educational Department of African Civilization Society*, 112 F. Street, Washington, D.C., May 1, 1866, Library Company of Philadelphia.

139. See Letter 107, Schofield to Coates, March 12, 1868; Ezra Johnson to Benjamin Coates, May 3, 1868; Letter 144, Heacock to Coates, February 7, 1869, February 7, 1869.

140. Laura Towne to Benjamin Coates, *American Freedman*, July and August 1868 (New York: American Freedmen's and Union Commission, 1866–1869).

141. James McPherson's *The Negro's Civil War: How American Negroes Felt and Acted During the War For the Union* (New York: Pantheon Books, 1965) is a good source for exploring how African Americans perceived the meaning of the Civil War.

142. Robert Purvis, "The Good Time is at Hand," speech before the thirtieth annual meeting of the American Anti-Slavery Society (AAS), at Cooper Institute (New York City), May 12, 1963. Published in *The Liberator*, May 22, 1863. Reprinted in Philip S. Foner, *Lift Every Voice: African-American Oratory, 1787–1900* (Tuscaloosa: University of Alabama Press, 1998), 392–97.

the world, and without a blush, declares one part of its people . . . disfran-
chised and outlawed."[143] In 1865, Garnet, no longer encouraging emigration,
celebrated the passage of the Thirteenth Amendment that would, as he
phrased it, "let the monster [slavery] perish."[144]

The PAS was interested in problems in Philadelphia as well as in
the South in these years, and Coates lent his support here, too. A campaign
to desegregate the horsedrawn trolley cars had been begun under the leadership of William Still after black families had been discriminated against when
visiting their relatives at Camp William Penn, an army camp for training
black troops located in Chelten Hills, north of Philadelphia. In 1866, Coates
moved that the case of Martin White, a discharged colored soldier who had
been ejected from the passenger cars, be referred to a committee of PAS, which
was given the authority to spend a sum not exceeding $50 to assist White in
his campaign for justice. In 1867, the campaign was brought to a successful
conclusion and Still was elected to the PAS. Coates worked with him on
several issues, and supported the Social and Statistical Association that Still
formed.[145]

When slavery was officially ended, Coates returned his focus of
interest to Africa. Though he still wanted complete political and social rights
for African Americans, he believed that they would never be entirely acclimated to the United States, and many, having been freed and educated, would
want to return of their own volition to Africa or some other area with a
warmer climate. In addition, Coates believed, the arrival of many European
immigrants to compete with them for jobs would hasten this process. In a
letter to William Coppinger of the ACS, Coates emphasized that he did not
wish to rid the United States of African Americans, as had Southern members of the organization; rather, he preferred to disseminate the Christian
religion and democratic values to the nations of Africa.[146]

The arrival of Chinese immigrants in California and Oregon, and
the completion of the Union Pacific Railroad linking the East and West coasts,

143. Robert Purvis, "The American Government and the Negro," speech before the
twenty-seventh anniversary of the AAS (New York), May 8, 1860, and published in *The Liberator*,
May 18, 1860. Reprinted in Foner, *Lift Every Voice*, 331–39.

144. Henry Highland Garnet, "Let the Monster Perish," speech before the United
States House of Representatives, February 12, 1865. Reprinted in Foner, *Lift Every Voice*,
432–43.

145. PAS Minutes, March 29, 1866; List of Members, Centennial Celebration of Pennsylvania Abolition Society, 1875, Library Company of Philadelphia. Letter 87, Coates to Coppinger, June 6, 1866.

146. Letter 92, Coates to Coppinger, April 6, 1867. ACS Papers 187:42, microfilm.

were developments that Coates viewed as complementary to his grand scheme. The competition of Chinese labor would further shrink the labor market for African Americans, causing them to become more interested in emigration. The Chinese themselves could be educated, Christianized, and prepared for the great missionary role of taking Christianity back to Asia, just as the African-Americans were destined to take it to Africa.[147]

"This is not an imaginary theory, but judging from the experience of the past ten years, what we may . . . calculate upon," Coates wrote Coppinger. "In the meantime, the black population among us must be educated and I am glad to say are being rapidly educated, in literature, in politics, or the art of self government, in true religion, and in the arts and sciences belonging to a high civilization, so as to fit them to become intelligent and valuable citizens of our common country, or to qualify them as missionaries to heathen lands."[148]

The end of the war had brought an end to some of the bitterness that had arisen between abolitionists and colonizationists. Coates corresponded with members of the AMA, an organization that had opposed colonization, eliciting their support for schools in Liberia. He also believed himself to be reconciled to such Garrisonians as Robert Purvis, perhaps the most bitter opponent of colonization in the Philadelphia area. While maintaining some affiliation with the ACS, Coates worked with whatever group he believed would forward his concern for African and African American education.[149]

But Coates never gave up his commitment to Africa, continuing to send money, books, and supplies to Liberia, and especially to Liberia College, which was now headed by his friend Joseph Jenkins Roberts. He applauded the United States's diplomatic recognition of Liberia in 1862, and in 1866, even while he continued to be a generous donor to the ICY and the Friends Freedmen's Association, he wrote a long autobiographical letter to the ACS, defending his life's work and reiterating his conviction that colonization was not only a viable alternative to American racial tension, but the best possible opportunity for black economic and political leadership. Many white abolitionists also shared Coates's idea that it would be good to try to persuade already-settled free black Americans to pull up roots and relocate. They seemed never to grasp the idea that black Americans might conceive of the United States as their home, as the place they had built and should not be asked to leave. Coates's admiration for Roberts, and his close friendship with Roberts's family, probably

147. Letter 92, Coates to Coppinger, April 6, 1867. ACS Papers 187:42, microfilm.
148. Letter 92, Coates to Coppinger, April 6, 1867. ACS Papers 187:42, microfilm.
149. Benjamin Coates to William Coppinger, April 6, 1866. ACS Papers 83:166, microfilm. See Letter 123, Whipple to Coates, August 27, 1868.

encouraged him to imagine that *any* black American could make a successful adjustment to a new home in Africa.

Benjamin Coates's Legacy

At any given moment, Coates could not be sure how his black allies viewed his ideas, or him. Hence, much of his letter-writing was apologetic, explanatory—and defensive—designed to try to win, or maintain, the loyalty of men and women who distrusted his motives or denigrated his designs. And the correspondence between Coates and black abolitionists also reflects their attempts to win over Coates from his loyalties to a competing *black* faction. Thus the possibilities for permutations and alliances were endless, and, over the course of years, as white abolitionists squabbled among themselves, black abolitionists argued with each other, and each group bared its teeth across a chasm of racial mistrust, Coates rode the crest of the waves of animosity, penning long theses of reasoned prose, weaving together networks of hostile and frustrated reformers while dispersing books, pamphlets, and packets of hybrid cotton seeds, hoping that, ultimately, his vision would reign triumphant.

Thus is created a complex story centered around the dreams of two men—one white, one black—who were born within a year of each other. Benjamin Coates and Joseph Jenkins Roberts's persistent efforts at African colonization constitute a story that meanders through various organizations, letters and diaries, alliances and rivalries, private frustrations, national and international intrigue, and civil wars. It is a story through which we see political anxieties play out in personal animosities, individuals' beliefs and loyalties bobbing and weaving as the tides of political waters shift with the economic, technological, and ideological winds. Buried in this correspondence are petty jealousies and lofty ideas, banal family illnesses and grand political schemes that invite the reader into the interstices of public and private lives.

The colonization story is, in many ways, a tragic one, reflecting the maelstrom of racial ambivalence, evangelicalism, inflexibility, and limited imaginations that still plague American society. And Coates's correspondence illuminates some of the misapprehensions in the good will of white philanthropists, as well as the bitterness and mistrust between various black factions and white allies. Coates's letters represent this era for what it was: complex, hopeful, anxious, angry, and, ultimately, a disappointment.

In 1875 the PAS celebrated the hundredth anniversary of its founding with a gala gathering in Philadelphia. William Still was in charge of the ceremonies, and all the old abolitionist men of whatever persuasion were invited, including Frederick Douglass and William Lloyd Garrison (who could not come but sent a letter). Several abolitionist women also attended: Lucretia Mott, Abby Kelley Foster, and African American poet Frances Ellen Watkins Harper, who read a poem. The inclusion of women was unusual in that the PAS did not admit women into membership until well into the next century. But this was a special time, a time of celebration and of pouring balm on old wounds. In his role as vice president, Coates had a central place in the ceremonies. As a man who had spent his life seeking the middle ground he must have been gratified,[150] but as an advocate of emigration, he must have seen that his vision was overshadowed by the freedmen and freedwomen's focus on racial justice in America.

Shortly after this, Coates was stricken with a lingering illness, causing paralysis. This might have been Multiple Sclerosis or Parkinson's disease, or it may have been the result of a series of strokes. His sister, Mary, stated in 1885 that he had been incapacitated for some years by ill health, preventing him from active duty in his philanthropies. His correspondence dwindled, and his attendance at his various boards and committees fell off. Records show, however, that he continued to give generously to the causes nearest his heart. On March 3, 1887, he died, leaving an estate of approximately $200,000, providing primarily for his dependents, but including over $17,000 to the concerns to which he gave his life: the Union Benevolent Association; the ICY; Liberia College and Liberian education; the AMA; Friends Freedman's Association; Indian Aid Association (Orthodox); and the Indian Committee of Philadelphia Yearly Meeting (Hicksite).[151] With Coates's death in 1887, thirteen years after Joseph Jenkins Roberts died, dreams of black American colonization to Africa receded. But the lure of an autonomous black political entity—including the possibilities of an African capitalist trade linking many parts of the Atlantic rim—is woven through the lives and careers of later colonization advocates like Marcus Garvey, Chief Sam, and W. E. B. Du Bois.[152]

150. Report, Centennial Celebration of the Pennsylvania Abolition Society, 1875, Library Company of Philadelphia, Philadelphia.

151. Last will and testament of Benjamin Coates, 1872, Philadelphia City Archives. See Appendix I.

152. See, for example, Sterling Stuckey, *Slave Culture: Nationalist Theory and the Foundations of Black America* (New York: Oxford University Press, 1987).

The Colonizationist Correspondence
of
Benjamin Coates

1

"... notice from Mr. McLain": Antebellum Years, 1848–1860

In the period before the Civil War, Benjamin Coates and his correspondents worked frantically to develop a strategy for destroying slavery by undermining its economic base and by developing alternatives for emancipated slaves, fugitives, and free black people. In the sixty-four letters found from these years, colonization is a central focus of their debates, and Rev. William McLain's leadership of the American Colonization Society regarding Liberia figured prominently in Coates's ideas and activities.

Both Coates and McLain developed a strong relationship with Joseph Jenkins Roberts, the African American expatriate who, in 1848, became Liberia's first president. Through more than a dozen exchanges with or about Roberts, Coates revealed his admiration for the black president and his hope for Roberts's success. But Coates was sharply aware that many influential black leaders, notably Frederick Douglass, regarded resettlement in Africa as a pernicious scheme. By disseminating information—and soliciting financial contributions—Coates hoped to build support for what he hoped was the ultimate solution both to the problem of slavery and to the question of African Americans' post-slavery fate.

By soliciting other white philanthropists at home and abroad, and distributing literature promoting black African civilizations and economic potential, Coates aimed to create a groundswell of international interest in African economic development. He hoped also to convince the United States to do what Roberts had convinced England to do: give diplomatic recognition to a free Republic of Liberia. By 1853, Coates was forced to admit that the colonization efforts were "dragging," but he persevered, publishing in 1858 a pamphlet on cultivating cotton in Africa. The pamphlet brought him international renown—and an enthusiastic, if short-lived, response from black Americans.

❊ ❊ ❊

❖ I ❖

New York July 8th. 1848

Dear Sir

Your very kind favor of the 3[d] inst[1] was duly received. I, however, delayed an answer until now hoping about this time to be able to say definitely whether I shall be in Philadelphia or not: it is, however, still doubtful.

I have just received notice from Mr. M[c]Lain[2] that the Executive Committee[3] will meet me, and the Commissioners, here on the 12th. inst; and that the Board of Directors is called to be held in this City on the 18th. inst. So you see I shall be pretty much engaged up to the time of my departure for Europe. I hope to, and, if possible, shall, leave this country by the steamer of the 20th. inst.

Mr Atherbury [Alterbury?], Phelp's son-in-law[4], and myself have been trying to arrange to leave here on Thursday afternoon next for your city to spend a few hours there. We may do so, I cannot say possitively now. If not, will you not take a run [up] here? If not too much engaged, I hope you will, in case you do not see me some time this week or very early in the next. I should hate very much to leave the U.S. without seeing you

---

1. "instant," or present month.
2. The Reverend William McLain became the secretary of the ACS in 1844 and remained an officer for many years.
3. Roberts was probably referring to the executive committee of the ACS.
4. Anson Green Phelps (March 1781–November 1853) was born in Simsbury, Connecticut. In October 1806 he married Olivia Eggleston, and the couple had one son and seven daughters. Phelps was a merchant primarily based in Hartford, Connecticut, with a branch in Charlestown, South Carolina. In 1815 he moved to New York City and became a metal dealer. Much of his money came from real estate investment. He was the president of the New York Blind Asylum, President of the New York Colonization Society, a life director of the ACS, and a member of the American Board of Commissioners for Foreign Missions. He was also involved with the American Bible Society and the Colonization Society of the State of Connecticut. Upon his death, he left $371,000 to charitable institutions, $100,000 to his only son, and $5,000 to each of his twenty-four grandchildren. There was much controversy over his will, and the case went to the Court of Appeals of the State of New York. James Grant Wilson, ed., *Appleton's Cyclopaedia of American Biography* (hereafter *Appleton's*), vol. 4 (New York: D. Appleton, 1887–1924), 751–52; John A. Garraty and Mark A. Carnes, eds., *Dictionary of American National Biography* (hereafter *ANB*), vol. 14 (New York: Oxford University Press, 1999), 525; *African Repository*, February and August 1849.

I regret to learn that your father's[5] health is no good. Please remember me to him and the family. Mrs. R.[6] is very anxious to see you all. She, however, will not visit your city. She begs to be remembered to the family

Very truly Yours ——

J.J. Roberts[7]

Benjm. Coates Esqr

❖ 2 ❖

Philad[a]. June 23rd 1850

Rev[d]. W[m]. M[c]Lain[8]

Dear Sir

Shall I trouble to have the three letters enclosed forwarded to Liberia by the "Packet." After the rect [receipt] of your letter some two weeks in informing me of the non acceptance of the dft [draft] drawn on you in my favor by Jn[o]. N Lewis, I requested the books to have it

5. George Morrison Coates (1779–June 16, 1868) grew blind as he aged and suffered from poor health. He had been a merchant and a member of the Horticultural Society and Wills' Hospital. Coates, *Family Memorials and Recollections*.

6. Jane Waring married Joseph Jenkins Roberts soon after he emigrated to Liberia. She was the daughter of Colstone M. Waring, the pastor of a Baptist church and a wealthy coffee producer. After Roberts's death, Jane moved to England. Henries, *The Life of Joseph Jenkins Roberts*, 10.

7. Joseph Jenkins Roberts (March 15, 1809–1876), was born in Virginia, the second of seven children. His father and older brother died while he was still young. In 1829 he and the rest of the family emigrated to Liberia, where he and his younger brothers became successful merchants. One of his earliest positions in the Liberian government was as High Sheriff, an office that tried to slow the slave trade on the West African coast. In 1839 Roberts became lieutenant governor under Thomas Buchanan. He held this position until Buchanan's death in 1841, when he became the first governor of Liberia who was not 100 percent white. Under his leadership, in response to trade conflicts with British merchants and the lack of support from the American government, Roberts and the ACS began working for Liberian independence. In 1847, when Liberia became independent, Roberts became its first president. Shortly after his election, Roberts traveled to Europe and the United States, where he tried to gain recognition of Liberian independence. He was elected for four two-year terms and was succeeded by Stephen A. Benson. After his presidency, Roberts became president of Liberia College, a position he held until his death. In his role as the head of the college, Roberts traveled to the United States on several occasions to raise money for the institution. In 1871, when international financial troubles helped to end President Edward James Roye's term, Roberts was in England. Roye's vice president completed his term, but Roberts was elected the next year and served two terms. Many of Roberts's critics blamed Roberts for the problems faced by Roye's government. He died shortly after the end of second term. Henries, *The Life of Joseph Jenkins Roberts, 1809–1876*.

8. Reverend William McLain.

returned, but it seems that he either misunderstood or forgot it. I have now directed him to hand the <u>draft</u> to <u>you</u> with the request that you will enclose it to Mr Lewis for me, should you be in Washington when his letter is recd, as I fear it will be too late for me to send it to him from here if it shoud be returned now

The reason for your not honoring the draft I fully understand, although I regret not to get the money, I appreciate the embarrassment that you have to contend with

Yours very truly

Benj^a. Coates

❖ 3 ❖

June 27, 1850

THE NORTH STAR[9]

Rochester, New York

PHILADELPHIA, June 17th, 1850.

FREDERICK DOUGLASS:[10]—I have often thought that I should like to converse with you on a subject on which we seem to differ in opinion

9. Frederick Douglass began publishing *The North Star* on December 3, 1847. He edited this paper with Martin Robison Delany, but Delany left the paper soon after it began. In June 1851 Douglass merged his paper with the Liberty Party Paper and renamed it *Frederick Douglass' Paper*. This paper continued until the summer of 1860, when it was replaced by *Douglass' Monthly*, which in turn lasted until 1863, when Douglass began recruiting black soldiers for the Union army. Published in Rochester, the paper did well financially in the early years because of help from Gerrit Smith, a wealthy abolitionist and politician. In 1853, with the decline of the Liberty Party, the *Frederick Douglass' Paper* began to experience difficulties. Julia Griffiths, a British woman, helped Douglass continue the paper until they were forced to make it a monthly periodical. Penelope L. Bullock, *The Afro-American Periodical Press, 1838–1909* (Baton Rouge: Louisiana State University Press, 1981), 52; *BAP* 4:90 n.

10. Frederick Douglass (1817–1895) was born Frederick Augustus Washington Bailey, the son of a slave mother and an unknown white man who was possibly his master. In 1825 he was sent to Baltimore, where he worked as a domestic servant and a ship's caulker. After his escape in 1838, he fled to New York, where he married a free black woman from Baltimore, with whom he subsequently moved to New Bedford, Massachusetts. His public antislavery career began when he became a lecture agent for the Massachusetts Anti-Slavery Society in 1841, and he proceeded to become one of the most prominent abolitionists of his time. For most of his life he was firmly opposed to colonization, but he briefly considered the idea in 1860 after the *Dred Scott* decision and the execution of John Brown. In 1861 he accepted an invitation to join an expedition to Haiti with James T. Holly, but with the beginning of the Civil War he changed his plans; this marked the end of his support for emigration. Originally, he agreed with William Lloyd Garrison—his mentor—that the abolition of slavery could be effected through politics and "moral [per]suasion,"

very materially; and aware, as I am, of the <u>great prejudice</u> that you entertain (in common with most of your colored brethren, as well as most of the white ——, the subject that I wish to present to with all your prejudice, is African colonization. Were you a less intelligent man than you are, I acknowledge that I should consider the task a hopeless one; but I cannot bring my mind to believe that Frederick Douglass, with his power of judging between cause and effect, can fail to see that the elevation of the colored man, in <u>any part</u> of the world, must have a favorable influence on his race, and that the establishment of an independent republic of colored men on the west coast of Africa, acknowledged by the most powerful and the most civilized nations of Europe, having commercial intercourse with all parts of the civilized world—thus bringing the citizens, through the medium of their commerce, into social communication with the citizens of every clime, and particularly with the United States, as the country from whence they emigrated, whose language they speak, and where *some* of their friends and relations still reside—thus appealing directly and powerfully to the sense of *justice*, and all the nobler feelings of our nature, by *proving* to what the colored man can attain under favorable circumstances, conclusively destroying the *only argument* that many honest and good men entertain, that he cannot take care of himself, and must therefore be kept in slavery; but also, and which perhaps (I am sorry to say it) is of more we ——, appealing to the *self-interest* of the whites, the love of gain, which is a powerful incentive in the American character, and so strong in it as to overcome even the prejudice of color or caste arising from slavery, that this must be the case, and *is* the case already, to some extent, I know, and having seen the evidence myself—having had occasion very often to aid my Liberian friends in their purchases, both in this city and New York, where their money has obtained for them, in many cases, a consideration that their *color alone* would not, and with the increase of Liberia, in the power of her government, and her extended commerce, must naturally flow a much greater intercourse.

Think you not, Mr. Douglass, that the man who may be turned out of a railroad car, or is not allowed to get into an omnibus today, on account of his color, should he return from Africa next year with his camwood, his palm oil, or his gold dust, consigned to his commission merchant, here, and goes

---

but he eventually came to believe that violent intervention would be necessary. Although he was deeply disappointed that the Civil War had ended slavery but not racism, Douglass worked with the federal government in various capacities until his death in 1895. *BAP* 1:173; Floyd J. Miller, *The Search for a Black Nationality: Black Emigration and Colonization, 1787–1863* (Urbana: University of Illinois Press, 1975), 138–39, 140, 154, 239–44; Quarles, *Black Abolitionists*, 222–23; McFeely, *Frederick Douglass*.

out through our cities to make his purchases, is a different man in the estimation of the community from him who is content to stay here and sell old clothes, black boots, or dress fine, and drive the young ladies along Broadway, or, with their white aprons on, make such good servants at our hotels? Which of the two, let me ask you, Mr. Douglass, is doing most for his race, for his brethren in bonds, the servant or the boot-black here, or the freeman, the farmer or merchant of Liberia? I do not ask you to praise the Colonization Society, nor to speak well of those who have sustained it through all its difficulties and embarrassments. If it pleases you best, and accord with your taste and inclination to impute unworthy motives to those outraged in it, do so. I am very willing, for one, to bear my full share of the odium that you may think proper to throw on colonizationists, and for a private individual, my zeal will entitle me to not a very small portion of the wrath that should be visited on the heads of those who have aided (by their exertions, their influence, their money) this most diabolical and wicked scheme, as it has been termed. It is not to deprecate your wrath or your censure that I write, although I believe the time will come, and that before many years, when Frederick Douglass will be convinced, that African colonization is one of the most powerful means not only for regenerating Africa, but for regenerating America, in effecting the abolition of slavery, and aiding largely in the emancipation of the *free* colored population of the United States from the weight of prejudice that keeps them down, paralyses their exertions, and crushes their hopes; and that being so convinced, he will have the manliness and independence to acknowledge that the men who have accomplished this are not *quite* such bad men as he had taken them to be, not altogether such an association of fools and knaves as they are represented. I am fully aware of the difficulties you would encounter after overcoming the deep-rooted prejudice of your own mind in going counter to the general sentiment of your friends, in acknowledging your error and their error in this respect. Had I time, and was it important to my present purpose, I could prove to you that the most zealous colonizationists, those on whom the cause depends for support, and who have sustained it through all its difficulties, are the friends of the colored man in America, as well as in *Africa*; that the most prominent friends of the Colonization cause in one State were among the truest friends of the colored man in advocating his rights to citizenship in Pennsylvania, by resisting the introduction of the word *white*, in our late convention for revising the constitution a few years since.[11] Who

11. In 1838 Pennsylvania revised its constitution to limit suffrage to adult white men. Various efforts to overturn this rule, supported by abolitionists and others, were unsuccessful.

are the friends of the Emancipation cause in Kentucky; and who have labored so hard and persevering to accomplish it the last year, against the proscriptive influence of the pro-slavery party? *Nearly every man of them colonizationists* (the Breckenridges,[12] Young, Cassius M. Clay,[13] and so on.) And in your own State, who has more manfully advocated the right of the colored man than Horace Greeley?[14] I presume that you are ready to say, as I believe you have said before, that there are honorable exceptions, and that in charging upon colonizationists a hatred to the black man, you do not mean to include some good, well meaning men, who have been misled by the scheme. Now, sir, here is where I think you make the mistake. You are accustomed to consider colonization as a southern scheme, got up and sustained by slaveholders, to "*get rid*" of the few colored population, that they may the more securely hold their slaves; and in support of this opinion you will quote from speeches from Southern men, made in favor of African colonization, where the free man of color is spoken of as a "*nuisance*," or "unworthy of —— from the *very men* that colored people are in the habit of calling upon for aid, looking to as their friends at times of difficulty.

As a case in point: I see in the last number of the North Star, of June 13th, a letter from Mr. J.B. Vashon,[15] of Pittsburgh, calling colonization the "twin-sister of slavery, and denouncing every man who allows himself to be colonized in Africa, as an enemy to the slave, and a traitor to the anti-slavery cause." Yet when in Pittsburgh, a few years since, I saw Mr. Vashon, and had a conversation with him on the subject of colonization in the course of which I asked him who he called upon when they wanted to build a church, or for aid to the colored man -whether it was not such men as Hon. Walter Forward,[16]

Robert Purvis, *Appeal of Forty Thousand Citizens Threatened with Disenfranchisement, to the People of Pennsylvania* (Philadelphia: Merrihew and Gunn, 1838).

12. Robert Breckenridge (1800–1871) of Kentucky, a family friend of Thomas Jefferson and a lawyer turned Presbyterian minister, was regarded as colonization's foremost spokesman in Kentucky. Staudenraus, *The African Colonization Movement*, 144.

13. Cassius M. Clay (1810–1903), an abolitionist from Kentucky, ran for governor of the state in 1849 on an antislavery ticket. *The Columbia Encyclopedia*, ed. William Bridgewater and Elizabeth J. Sherwood (New York: Columbia University Press, 1950).

14. Horace Greeley (1811–1872), newspaper editor and reformer, was known for his antislavery stand. Richard Morris, ed., *Encyclopedia of American History* (New York: Harper and Row, 1970).

15. John B. Vashon (1792–1854) was a barber and proprietor of the City Baths in Pittsburgh. He set up the African Education Society in 1832 and founded the Pittsburgh Anti-Slavery Society in 1833. He was a friend and financial supporter of William Lloyd Garrison and the *Liberator*. Quarles, *Black Abolitionists*.

16. The Honorable Walter Forward (1786–1852), a politician from Pittsburgh, served in the U.S. Congress, as U.S. Secretary of Treasury, and as charge d'affaires in Copenhagen. *ANB*.

or Charley Brewer, Esq.? (the only colonizationists that I happened to know.) Yet he said these very men; that his son was then studying law with Mr. Forward, and that Mr. F. had endorsed his note at a bank for several thousand dollars. Mr. Brewer, too, they looked upon as a friend in need. Yet both these men do more for colonization than nineteen-twentieths of the whole population of South Carolina. Mr. Vashon informed me, at the same conversation, that his son intended to emigrate to France or Mexico; and has since then, I learn, gone to, or "suffered himself to be colonized" in, Haiti. Has he thus proved himself "an enemy to the slave," and "an enemy to the anti-slavery cause?" Or is it only going to Africa that makes this great difference!

But I see that you do not make this distinction, as you say in the same paper in reply to Horace Greeley: "To our apprehension, it is far more noble on the part of the free colored people to remain here, struggling against the adverse winds of prejudice and slavery, than selfishly to quit the country with a view of bettering their own condition." You say further, "Let Mr. Greeley complain as much as he may of our determination to remain here. It shall go hard with us, before we shall consent to leave these shores, while three million of our countrymen are in chains. We are resolved to fall or flourish with them."

Well, sir, I can hardly suppose that Horace Greeley, or any other right-thinking man, does wish Frederick Douglass to leave these shores. Such men as yourself, Samuel R. Ward,[17] H.H. Garnet,[18] and a few others, are no

17. Samuel Ringgold Ward was born a slave in 1817 in Maryland. In 1820 his family escaped to New Jersey and six years later moved to New York City. As a child, he attended the African Free School in New York, where Crummell and Garnet were also students. After his marriage to Emily Reynolds in 1838, they moved to upstate New York, where he was the minister for two white churches between 1841 and 1851. He was also an agent for the New York State Anti-Slavery Society in 1839 and became an agent for the AAS in 1840. When the AAS split later that year, Ward joined the American and British Anti-Slavery Society, which opposed Garrison and the AAS. As the vice president of the American Missionary Association (AMA), he campaigned for black suffrage. In 1847 he bought a newspaper and became its editor. The newspaper changed names several times and was dissolved in 1851. That same year, Ward was forced to flee with his family to Canada because of his role in helping a runaway slave, an illegal act strongly enforced by the Fugitive Slave Law of 1850. In Canada he founded a newspaper, the *Provincial Freeman*, in 1853. That year the American and British Anti-Slavery Society sent Ward to England, where he remained for two and a half years, lecturing and publishing his autobiography. In 1855 he and his family moved to Jamaica, where he worked as a minister for five years. He began farming there in 1866, but he died later that year. *BAP* 3:383; *African-American Culture and History*; *ANB* 22:647.

18. Henry Highland Garnet (December 23, 1815–1882) was born into slavery in Maryland. His family escaped to New York City when he was nine years old. Their former owners pursued them for several years, and in 1829 the family was almost returned to slavery. The events of his childhood, such as brushes with slavecatchers and a severe knee injury, marked Garnet for

doubt doing as much good for your race, and probably a good deal more, than if you were in Africa. But is that a reason for preventing those who are not so favorably circumstanced, who have not had the opportunity for displaying their native talents here, and are so situated as not readily to acquire the education necessary thereto, from emigrating to Africa, or any where else, if they desire it, without being denounced as "selfish," as "an enemy to the slave," and "a traitor to the anti-slavery cause?" I think you would hardly like to be judged by your own principles. Were you not born in Maryland? Does not slavery exist there? And have you not left your brethren in bonds, to settle (call it colonize or emigrate, as you please) in Western New York, to breathe the air of freedom, while your brethren are suffering under the lash in Maryland? Was that selfish? Are you thereby an enemy to the slave," and " a traitor to the anti-slavery cause?" I should say, by no means; that although you are enjoying a state of freedom and equality that you could not have done in Maryland, yet you have acquired an education and move in a society that you could not obtain in a slave state. You edit a paper, and can lecture to your countrymen,

---

all of his life. Equally important were his educational experiences. After arriving in the North, Garnet attended the New York African Free School. Among his classmates were Samuel Ringgold Ward, James McCune Smith, and Alexander Crummell. Garnet later attended the Noyes Academy in New Hampshire with Crummell until they were forced to leave. Garnet then studied at Onedia Institute in upstate New York. Garnet's central concerns throughout his life were religion, the antislavery movement, and education, which he viewed as of a piece. He became the first pastor of Liberty Street Presbyterian Church in Troy, New York, in 1840. He was actively involved with the AMA and broke with Frederick Douglass in 1849 over the issue of Bible distribution. Garnet believed that slaves should be given copies of the Bible, while Douglass did not. Garnet first became well known in the black abolitionist community at the 1843 convention in Buffalo, New York. Unlike many other abolitionists, Garnet believed violence might be necessary to end slavery. He was also unusual in his early support for emigration. While he did not emigrate, he supported those who wished to leave the United States. Although he did not condemn others' violence, his own actions were often peaceful. He supported the Liberty Party, which strove to deal with slavery in the political world, and worked with the Free Produce Movement in England in the 1850s. Although he supported emigration, he was well aware of the difficulties faced by many American black people, and he founded a school in Geneva, New York, to attempt to combat such problems. Beginning in 1852, Garnet spent four years in Jamaica. When he returned to the United States in 1856, he became the pastor of Shiloh Presbyterian Church in New York City. Garnet assisted in the formation of the African Civilization Society, an organization that combined his interests in religion, emigration, and free produce. He traveled to England again in 1861 and received a passport despite the recent ruling that black people could not be citizens of the United States. The following year Garnet returned to the U.S. and recruited black soldiers for the Union army. As the Civil War drew to a close, Garnet and the African Civilization Society concentrated less on an African colony and more on education of freedmen. Garnet moved to Washington, D.C., in 1868 and became the pastor of the Fifteenth Street Presbyterian Church. In 1881 he joined the ACS and became the U.S. minister to Liberia. Schor, *Henry Highland Garnet*; BAP 3:336–37.

both white and colored, on the evils of slavery, and accomplish, in this way, a thousand-fold more for your oppressed brethren, than if you had remained in your native State. Is it not so? Is not every colored man who leaves the South when he was born, and when his brother in chains yet remain, enabled to do more for them here, with greater opportunity of acting on public sentiment, than by remaining there? Yet, according to your doctrine, (for the principle is the same precisely,) no one should leave the Southern States, while slavery exists. You not only came away from it yourself, but, if I mistake not, you are willing to aid others in doing the same, even to colonizing in Canada, in a cold, uncongenial climate, and where their efforts cannot so well tell on slavery in the Southern States. All this I by no means object to.—Any condition, in my opinion, is better than slavery. But if you can see the *consistency* of denouncing those who escape from slavery, or from the prejudice arising from slavery, which cramps all their energies to a country where they can enjoy all the rights of man—to a country governed entirely by slaveholders—where they can make themselves respected, and bring all their talents, all their industry, all the influence of their associated force, through the government established by themselves, to bear directly on slavery, and in favor of their oppressed brethren, both bond and free, and be satisfied with yourself for doing the same thing, is more than I can understand.

Do you blame the pilgrims who settled New England, or the followers of Fox and Penn, who, to escape persecution in England colonized Pennsylvania? Would they have accomplished more by remaining in England, where they were oppressed and taxed to sustain what their conscience could not consent to, by colonizing America, and building up a government based on the principles of freedom? I cannot believe that you so think.—And why you should not be willing that your colored brethren should enjoy the privileges that you could accord to *your* white brethren, is to me a mystery. The fact is—allow me to say so—that you do yourself injustice in this matter, as well as your brethren. You have looked at *one side* of the picture so long and so intently, that you cannot see the other. A few weeks since, in publishing the account of the mass meeting of colored men in St. Louis in favor of colonization, when Mr. Bell[19] declared his intention to remove to Liberia, and saying that the few months he spent there was the only *real* freedom that he had known in his life, you asked, "What ails the man?" "Has he been to Africa since he published his pamphlet?" Allow me to say, sir, the error was with

19. Possibly Philip A. Bell, an African American minister in New York City who was prominent in abolitionist affairs.

yourself. You published only part of his remarks, and that part the most unfavorable to Liberia; and in endeavoring to give a wrong view to others, you got a wrong view yourself, and perhaps really convinced yourself that Mr. B. had given a discouraging account of the country. Should you give as an excuse for doing so, that colonizationists gave too flattering an account, and that you only wished to give the other side, I would remind you that two wrongs never make a right, and that the only proper way is, to tell "the truth, the whole truth, and nothing but the truth."

I have spun out a long letter, and spoken my mind very plainly; but I trust that if you do not agree with me in all my views, you will consider the subject of a sufficient importance to the welfare of your race to be a sufficient apology for my writing thus to one that I feel sure is interested in all that concerns the interest, both present and future, of his oppressed brethren.

I am, very respectfully,

BENJAMIN COATES.

❖ 4 ❖

June 27, 1850
THE NORTH STAR
Rochester, New York

The Letter of Benjamin Coates.

————

Having recently given our views on the subject of African colonization, we deem it unnecessary to go into a lengthy reply to the letter of Mr. Benjamin Coates. The points raised by him, have been answered satisfactorily to our own mind, times without number. He seems amazed at the amount of prejudice, which the colored people entertain towards the American colonization society. We assure him that there is something more than prejudice; and it is an intelligent appreciation both of the men composing that society and the measures they proposed. It has created more prejudice in this country against the free colored man—raised against him a greater amount of hostility, than the infant Republic of Liberia will be able to atone for in fifty years. It has taught the nation that we are low, ignorant and besotted, that our elevation in this country is impossible—that Africa, and not America, is our country; and some of its members have gone the scandalous length of recommending the enactment of stringent laws against our rights and liberties, with a view to our coercion and final expatriation. It is not at all surprising that colored men should contemplate that society with other than feelings of complacency.

For ourselves, we look with suspicion on any medium which proposes to free the nation from its unrighteous treatment of the colored people, that does not involve a deep and radical repentance. To remove the objects of American hatred, is not to remove that hatred itself. It is a climbing up some other way, and is therefore to be discarded. We beg and entreat our colonization friends to desist from their colonization scheme, and to allow its sufficient repose or resume that course of steady improvement which has marked and will continue to mark the progress of colored men, in this, the land of their nativity.

For more than two hundred years, we have been the constant companions of the white man, and the joint possessors, with him, of this country; and the readiness with which we adapt ourselves to the circumstances around us, induces the belief that we stand as good a chance of advancement, *here* in all things pertaining to human welfare as we should do, were we instantly transformed to the western coast of Africa.—F.D.

 5

Philad[a] July 9th 1850[20]

Rev[d]. W[m] M[c].Lain

Being absent from the city for a few days I just recd. your favor of 6th inst. enclosing your note dated July 6th 1850 at 4 [mos.] for $620. payable at Bank of Washington in —— of Lewis' dft [draft] for $500. + Dr. Roberts,[21] drawn Jany 2nd 1850 —— 30 days. This shape of settlement is more convenient to me, + for it please accept my thanks.

Yours very truly

Benj[a]. Coates

Private

I am very glad to hear that Roberts has secured the Gallinas,[22] altho' the price is higher than I supposed he could buy it for. An English friend would probably give us a lift if they are not again disgusted + <u>bored</u> by an indiscreet

20. ACS Papers 62:119:37.
21. Joseph Jenkins Roberts.
22. Gallinas, possibly a set of books?

friend[23] of the cause who has again gone over to talk colonization to them. I desired a friend who sailed a few days in advance of him to inform Samuel Gurney[24] that our Philad^a. volunteer is more the <u>embodiment</u> of the Colonization Cause + that the Socy [Society] is not responsible for what he may say + do. B.C

❖ 6 ❖

Rev William McLain [postmark: Boston, Sep 5]
Colonization Room
Washington
D.C.

Philadelphia Sept 5 1850[25]

Rev^d. W^m. McLain

Dear Sir

I received a letter from President Roberts[26] last evening in which he speaks of having written to you to procure for him the appointment of Agent for Recaptured Africans. Of both your inclination and ability to procure this office for him I hardly entertain a doubt, yet as he expresses a wish that I should address you on the subject if I think well of it, which I most certainly do, I have concluded to send you a copy of his letter, both for this object, but more particularly in relation to the subject of Cotton cultivation by the English on the West Coast of Africa as a matter of importance for you to make use of as you may judge best (in case he should not

23. "Indiscreet friend" probably refers to Elliot Cresson (1796–1854), a Philadelphia merchant who served as secretary of the Pennsylvania Colonization Society in 1829 and who developed the Young Men's Colonization Society in 1834. In 1837 he became vice president of the Pennsylvania Colonization Society, a position he retained for the rest of his life. In 1850 he was in Great Britain for the colonization cause. Coates left the Pennsylvania Colonization Society after conflict with Cresson. Letter 8, Coates to McLain, May 16, 1851.

24. Samuel Gurney was an English Quaker born in 1786. He was a banker and interested in antislavery activities. In 1848 J. J. Roberts traveled to England and met Gurney. Gurney corresponded with Roberts throughout the rest of his life and donated money to Liberia, as a colony and as a nation, after it lost much of its support from the ACS as a result of popular opposition to colonization from American black people. As a result of his support for Liberia, a town there was named after him. Gurney died in 1856. His son, also Samuel Gurney, was also involved in antislavery activities and was a member of the British and Foreign Anti-Slavery Society as well as other organizations. *Dictionary of Quaker Biography; Friends' Review* 9, no. 6 (1856): 177; and Mrs. Thomas Geldart, *Memorial of Samuel Gurney* (Philadelphia: Henry Longstreth, 1859).

25. ACS Papers 63:119:230–31.

26. Joseph Jenkins Roberts.

have mentioned it in his letter to you). In relation to the appointment that he desires, I think it very certain that the government could not have a better man, and it will be of some advantage to President Roberts in a pecuniary point of view as he has necessarily to be at great expenses in maintaining the proper dignity of his office as chief magistrate of the Republic besides the advantage that [page break] it will be to the cause ^{by} that kind of friendly relation to the new state from our government. I think that Roberts is much the best man for the station he holds that I know of in Liberia, and I should like to see him re-elected for a third term, six years being not too long to keep a good officer in power, and a precedent of short terms + continual changes is not the best thing for Liberians, in my opinion, however it may suit here. this appointment then I think will enable President Roberts to remain, without too great a sacrifice on his part of what may be due to his family. I trust that you have sufficient influence with the President[27] or Mr Webster[28] to obtain it for him, and no doubt Mr Clay[29] will gladly lend his aid if needed. I had thought of writing to Mr Clay on the subject + enclose him a copy of this letter to me, but did not wish to interfere in any way in what ~~mor~~ properly belongs to you.

The subject of cotton culture in the coast of Africa strikes me as a matter of great importance + if successful, (of which I scarcely have a doubt as it has been raised there in small way for many years) will be a death blow to slavery in the United States, as it will render not only England but the northern states of this Union independent of our cotton growing states and the only interest that sustains slavery. not knowing how the information might affect the interest of the Colonization cause in the recognition of the Independence of Liberia and [page break] the steam ship project now before Congress I thought I would not give my letter publication, before consulting with you on the subject. if it would be likely to awaken a jealousy on the part of Southern members who are at present friendly disposed towards the cause, it will be best to say nothing about it at present. otherwise as a matter of interest, I would give it to one of our papers for publication, or if you think it advisable you may do so. Would it not be well to show Roberts' letter to Mr Clay + consult with him on both subjects? I cannot believe that President Roberts'

27. Coates here refers to the U.S. President, Millard Fillmore (1800–1874), who was in office from 1850 to 1853. Morris, *Encyclopedia of American History*.

28. Daniel Webster (1782–1852) became Secretary of State in 1850. Morris, *Encyclopedia of American History*.

29. Henry Clay (1777–1852), a U.S. Senator from 1849 to 1852. His sponsorship of the Compromise of 1850 earned him the title of "The Great Pacificator." Morris, *Encyclopedia of American History*.

complexion can be an objection to his appointment as an agent of the United States in Africa.

Please let me hear from you.

Yours very truly

Benj^a Coates

[Letter 6, Coates to McLain, September 5, 1850, contains a copy of the following letter: Roberts to Coates, July 18, 1850.]

Government House

My Dear Sir   Monrovia July 18th 1850

We are without new here, nor have I any thing important to write about, yet I am sure you will be gratified to learn that our public affairs are progressing quietly and in order, and that Liberia is decidedly improving. I really think, and the impression is general, that our prospects were never better than at the present time. Every thing is encouraging. Commerce is rapidly increasing, and greater attention than ever is now being paid to agriculture, improvements generally, and of a more permanent character are going on throughout the state.

The following may be an item of interest. There is now here an English agent who has been sent to the Coast by a company of eminent firms in London, Manchester, + Liverpool, to test by practical experiments the possibility of procuring cotton from the West Coast of Africa. He is about commencing operations here under flattering prospects. If he succeeds it will prove of great benefit to the people here, as we have none pecuniarily able to make the experiments that this agent will make. There is no doubt but that cotton will grow well here, still it is found that a little insect, (how generated is not known) injures the plant while budding. These must be disposed of in some way, and the culture here is doubtless somewhat different from the American mode. A great many things with regard to its culture must be demonstrated by experiment. I have written to Mr McLain,[30] requesting him to procure for me, if he can, the appointment of United States agent here for re-captured Africans. If you think well of it will you write him a line on the subject. If not, request him from me to with-hold the application.

With high regard and esteem

I am my dear sir

Benj^a Coates Esqr   Your ob^t serv^t
Philad^a   J.J Roberts.

---

30. Reverend William McLain.

� 7 ✧

January 16, 1851
THE NORTH STAR
Rochester, New York

PHILADELPHIA, Jan. 1st, 1851.

FREDERICK DOUGLASS,—DEAR SIR:—I have intended sub-
scribing for the "North Star" for some time, and have been prevented from
doing so earlier, by the accumulation of newspapers that I already receive,
making it difficult for me to find time to read them all without infringing on
time that should be devoted to my business.

I regard however the fact that *good Newspapers*, so ably edited by
Colored men as the "North Star" and "Impartial Citizen," are, as among the
best vindications of the capacity of colored man to fill respectable positions
in society, creditable to themselves, and to the best interest of the world; and
shall therefore be glad to see all such papers have an extended circulation, not
only among those for whose advancement they were particularly established,
and who, therefore, are most especially bound to support them well, and thus
increase their influence. But also should I like to have them read by those who
need information as to the capabilities of our colored population for other
pursuits besides waiting on table, blacking boots, or wheeling barrow. Their
efforts for mental improvement as exhibited by their Papers, and the talents
they there show themselves to be possessed of, must lead to the successful
assertion of their rights. Desiring to aid in a small way towards spreading
information of this kind, I enclose five dollars, for one year's subscription to the
"North Star" for myself, and the balance you will please appropriate to sending copies of the paper occasionally to *prominent Southern men*, members of
Congress and others, where you think they will do the most good. I forwarded
to you a short time since several of our city newspapers, showing the practical working of the new Fugitive Slave Law, exemplified in the case of Adam
Gibson,[31] arrested as a slave, and sent without a trial, and against evidence, to
a slave State, from whence he was returned as a freeman. This case had aroused
considerable feeling on the subject here, and will no doubt do much good.

I had intended writing to you before this, to thank you for your courtesy, in publishing a letter I addressed to you in the summer on the subject
of Colonization, knowing as I well do the very strong prejudice that you, in

31. Adam Gibson was a slave who was recaptured under the Fugitive Slave Law and
then freed.

common with most of your readers, entertain against this cause. I fully appreciated your liberality in presenting it to your readers. While I have no desire to make myself conspicuous in this way or any other, I yet feel so strong an interest in the prosperity of the young Republic of Liberia,[32] and consider that the successful establishment of an independent and enlightened government on the continent of Africa, conducted entirely by colored men, is so intimately connected with the best interest of the whole race over the world, that I am glad of *every* opportunity of spreading correct information on the subject among the colored population of the United States, even should it come from none other than myself, claiming to be well acquainted with the objects and tendency of measures in which I have taken an active part, and with all the means of information that anyone can possess. I feel well assured that the new Republic, even in its infancy, is already exciting an influence, favorable to the entire race, by whom its government is conducted; and that as it increases in population and extent of territory, with the national augmentation of both physical, and moral power, it must contribute largely to the spread of Anti-Slavery sentiment, over the civilized world. Whether, therefore, you regard the indirect, the reflex influence of a powerful Republican Government on the continent of Africa, conducted on truly enlightened and Christian principles, by colored emigrants from the United States, or whether you view it in its political aspect in successfully competing with America, in the culture of cotton, that one product of our Southern States, the large profits of which have in my opinion been the principal if not the only cause of the continuance of Slavery in the United States, you will have to acknowledge that Liberia is destined to accomplish—yes, *is now* in the full tide of a most important Anti-Slavery work, and for this reason alone should be regarded with especial favor by every true friend of the colored race. That cotton of excellent quality is raised in Africa, has been known for a long time, and now that English capitalists and the British Government have turned their attention to it, I think it will be proved that it can be raised in *any quantity*, and *cheaper*, than in the United States. On this subject, allow me to refer you to President Roberts'[33] letter to Lord Palmerston,[34] and the report of the "Chamber of Commerce,

32. In 1822 the first party of freed slaves arrived at Cape Mesurado under the aegis of the ACS. A white American named Jehudi Ashmun took control over the settlement in 1822 and led it until 1828. Joseph Jenkins Roberts (see Letter 1, Roberts to Coates, July 8, 1848) was Liberia's first black governor, taking office in 1841, and in 1847 he declared it an independent nation, became its first president, and severed its ties with the ACS.

33. Joseph Jenkins Roberts.

34. Lord Palmerston. Henry John Temple (1784–1865) was a British statesman and evidently a supporter of colonization. *ANB*.

and manufacturers of Manchester[35]" in regard to the samples of cotton transmitted to them. Should this new discovery of the process of preparing flax prove successful in lessening the demand for cotton in both Europe and America, and if the information on this subject is correct, flax must supersede the use of cotton to a great degree. Why should not the markets of Great Britain, and the United States, be supplied with cotton entirely from Africa? Slave labor being then *unprofitable*, will not slavery be abolished at once? Will not the *patriotism* and *philanthropy* of the whole people be aroused to denounce, so *anti-republic* and *anti-christian* an institution, "that was forced on us by Great Britain against our wishes, not regarding our emphatic protest against it?" And methinks it will be difficult to find many *who ever approved* of the system. Verily we are in an age of progress, and certainly human Slavery will not prove the only exception to the change that is taking place in the world. Liberia is destined soon to become a joyful Republican Government. The English are laying the foundation of future states south and east of Liberia, and with their colony of Sierra Leone, and the settlement on the Gambia at the north, must ere long be united in a powerful confederacy that shall command the respect of the world; and your children may see the day if you and I shall not, when the United States of Africa, shall be considered as one of the most enlightened and distinguished nations of christendom, rivalling in all that Constitutes true glory, the United States of America. Then may our children, while revering the name of their fathers, be able to point to *his name*, who, once an American Slave, lent the weight of his talent and the power of his press, to aid in consummating so great a work. When you look at the question in all its aspects.—(I care not what you choose to regard as the origin to the Colonization Society—what motives you may still insist on attributing to its founders)—it is impossible that you should not feel a strong interest in the prosperity and rapid progress of the young Republic, that you should not sympathize with your brethren there, identified with yourself in all that pertains to the suffering of the past and the prosperity of the future, many of them like yourself, having experienced the iron rod of Slavery in America, and now with yourself working out the redemption of your race. That you should in *any way* oppose the triumph of the anti-slavery cause, through the aid of the freemen of Liberia, because the Colonization Society should thereby receive a share of the glory, I am entirely unwilling to believe.—It is entirely opposed to true nobleness—inconsistent with that sincere devotion to the

35. Chamber of Commerce and Manufacturers of Manchester. See Coates, *Cotton Cultivation in Africa*.

welfare of your race, which I believe you to possess, and in a word unworthy the name and fame of Frederick Douglass. I shall therefore expect you to give your readers such information as may be interesting to them and affecting any portion of your people, whether in America or Africa, and shall take the liberty of sending to you occasionally documents from Liberia, and will be glad if you will copy into the North Star the last letter from President Roberts to myself, which you will find in the "Colonization Herald." I should also be gratified if you would copy from the "Pennsylvania Freeman" of last week, an article on the subject of the slave-trade, in which Sir Charles Hotham speaks of the agency of Liberia in its suppression.   Yours, very truly,

BENJAMIN COATES.

❖ 8 ❖

Private

Philadelphia May 16th 1851[36]

Revd Wm McLain[37]
Secy. Amn. Coln. Socy.[38]
My dear Sir

I was very much surprised this morning to learn that the Board of Managers of the "Penna Colonization Socy." had thought it ~~worth~~ proper to ask the Executive Committee of the "Amr. Colonization Society" to change the name of the new settlement at Fishtown Bassa County Liberia[39] from Buchanan[40] a name dear to every Colonizationist throughout

36. ACS Papers 65:122:2:170 ½.
37. Reverend William McLain. See Letter 1, Roberts to Coates, July 8, 1848.
38. The ACS provided transportation for free black people to Liberia. Many black people, however, did not support the ACS, believing that the organization's white membership was merely attempting to protect slavery by sending free black people, who could be seen as a threat to the institution of slavery, out of the country.
39. In 1834 the New York Colonization Society and the Young Men's Colonization Society of Pennsylvania together created the Bassa Cove settlement near the mouth of the St. John's River in Liberia. In 1835 it was attacked and destroyed, but the settlers rebuilt on a nearby site within a few years. In 1851 the settlement was expanded and renamed, although not without controversy. *African Repository* (Washington, D.C.: American Colonization Society, 1850–1892), vol. 27, 88, 91, 139, 157, 167, 247; Archibald Alexander, *A History of Colonization on the Western Coast of Africa*, 2nd ed. (Philadelphia: W. S. Martien, 1849), 468–70; D. Elwood Dunn and Svend E. Holsoe, eds., *Historical Dictionary of Liberia* (hereafter *HDL*) (Metuchen, N.J.: Scarecrow Press, 1985), 32; Staudenraus, *The African Colonization Movement*, 234–36.
40. Thomas Buchanan (1808–41) was governor of Liberia from 1839 to 1841. He first went to Liberia as leader of the Bassa Cove settlement in 1836. *HDL* 33; Staudenraus, *The African Colonization Movement*, 241.

this Country + Liberia, and especially endeared to the Friends of the Cause in this City and State, who knew him personally, and laboured with him through the most difficult times and the darkest days that the Society has experienced, and give it the name of one, whom I can safely say is <u>decidedly</u> the most unpopular man <u>ever</u> connected with the Colonization cause, and who despite all his zeal, has done more to injure it in this city than all its enemies combined. You are aware that I have not been connected with our state Socy for many years only because I was unwilling to be responsible for the actions of Mr Cresson[41] and did not wish to be constantly opposing him. Some of the very best friends that the cause has ever had in this city left the [direction] at the same time with myself, and since then others who had come into [to] the Board from their interests for objects of the Socy. have found it impossible to sanction measures calculated more to promote the interests, or gratify the vanity of an individual rather than advance the interest of the Cause, thus our friends Dr Bethune,[42] Dr Bell and Pinney,[43] have either been left out or forced to resign, and new men thus constantly brought into the board, who not knowing the previous history of difficulties occasioned there, have lent the influence of their names to those whom they supposed with more experience than themselves, were [actuated] only by as pure and disinterested motives, until experience had taught them their mistake.

To <u>no member</u> of the board do I entertain any unkind feeling. I am not acquainted with many of the members of the present board personally, and have no doubt that they generally mean well, but this attempt to name the settlement at this point "Cresson" is no new thing, it was attempted when I was a member of the board and entirely discountenanced. it could no doubt greatly astonish most of the present members of the board of managers to know the various efforts that have been made as far back as the time of the

---

41. Elliot Cresson.

42. George Washington Bethune (1805–1862) was a Dutch Reformed clergyman from New York. He studied at Dickinson College and Princeton University and served as minister or pastor of various churches for most of his life. He was also involved in colonization efforts, most specifically with the New York Colonization Society, but he also served as a vice president of the ACS. As a young man, Thomas Buchanan considered becoming a minister, and Bethune served as his host and patron during this period. Abraham Rynier Van Nest, *Memoir of Rev. George W. Bethune, D.D.* (New York: Sheldon and Company, 1867).

43. John Brooke Pinney began his involvement with the ACS in the 1830s. After serving as a missionary in Liberia, he became temporary governor of the colony for several months in 1834. Upon his return to the United States, Pinney served on the executive boards of the ACS and the New York Colonization Society and as corresponding secretary for the latter. Pinney, who also edited the New York Colonization Journal, was an ally of the African Civilization Society. Staudenraus, *The African Colonization Movement*, 167, 240.

settlement of Bassa Cove by the slaves of Dr Hawes, to the present time to accomplish this object. two of the members of the board one of whom was my friend Govr. Buchanan stopped in one day to see a new map of Africa, when Mr Findly[44] showed them among other things the location of "Port Cresson," and ^ he was much surprised to learn from them that there was no such place, and that our Society had distinctly refused to acknowledge the name. it had fortunately not been engraved, and was of course omitted. Seeing the attempts again made of late to have the new settlement take this name and supposing that it was a matter that would rest entirely with the people of Bassa County themselves, without knowing the views entertained either by your Board or the Board of our State Society, I wrote to Stephen A Benson[45] saying that if it was named after any individual connected with the Col^n. Society that I thought it was due to the memory of our mutual friend Govr Buchanan to give it his name, it being near the spot of his first and last efforts in behalf of a cause and people for whom he had laboured long, had devoted the best energies of his life, and where he found his last resting place. I stated to Senator Benson that I did not believe there was more than one person in the United States interested in the Colonization Cause who would not be gratified with the name of Buchanan and prefer it to any other. And I feel well assured that had did the members of the board of our Socy known Thomas Buchanan as well as I know him, and also the history of the attempt by another prominent colonizationist to promote his own views in opposition to the known sentiments of his co-laborers, that this effort would be discountenanced now as it was fifteen years ago. And still believe that ninety nine hundreds of the Colonizationists of the United States would prefer the name of Buchanan, I do hope that your executive committee will use their power and influence to retain this name. I think that I am acquainted with the views of Colonizationists in this city and the interest of the cause here as well as any other person, for although not a member of the board, I have never lost a particle of my interest in the Cause, and I have therefore made free to speak my mind to yourself + to request you to make my views known to your committee not

44. Possibly Robert S. Finley, former agent for the New York Colonization Society. Staudenraus, *The African Colonization Movement*, 232.

45. Stephen Allen Benson (1816–65) was born free in Maryland. He emigrated to Liberia in 1822 and became active in politics there. He served as a secretary under Governor Thomas Buchanan and was a member of the Liberian legislature from 1842 to 1847. In 1853 he was elected vice president and two years later he assumed the position of president. Benson's presidency was noteworthy because, unlike many of the early Liberian presidents, he was a dark-skinned man and spoke several languages native to the area. *HDL*.

having the pleasure of a personal acquaintance with Mr Whittlesey[46] [page break] nor I believe with any of the other members except Mr Bradley and that not very recently.

Please excuse the length of this communication, hastily written, which is prompted from respect to the memory of my deceased friend, and by what I consider the interest of a cause we both have at heart and not from any personal objection to Mr C. + believe me very truly

yours.

Benjᵃ Coates

Philadelphia June 18ᵗʰ 1851[47]

Dr J.W. Lugenbeil[48]

Dear Sir

I duly received your favor in reply to my letter to Mr MᶜLain on the subject of the name of the new town in Bassa County on the scite of the present "Fishtown." I saw Mr MᶜLain for a few moments on his way to Boston and had some conversation with him on the subject and since then as suggested by him I have conversed with two members of the present board of Managers of our state Socy in —— to the subject. Revᵈ Howard Malcom D.D and Mr Davidson. Dr Malcom who is a new member was interested in the history of this business that I gave him, and views the action of Mr Cresson[49] as I do, as altogether irregular. I stated to him what Mr MᶜLain had said to me with regard to funds. he said the Socy had then $2000. in the hands of the Treasury. One thousand of which he intended sending on to Washington, + one thousand the board here were reserving to pay for some fifteen houses that they had directed Hon. Stephen A Benson[50] to erect at "Cresson." I suggested to him, that the whole of it should go through

46. Possibly Chauncey Whittlesey of Middletown, Connecticut, who organized the Middletown Juvenile Colonization Society and sent his former slave, Nugent Wicks, to Liberia. Staudenraus, *The African Colonization Movement*, 127.

47. ACS Papers 65:122:271.

48. Dr. J. W. Lugenbeel was an agent of the ACS and the author of *Sketches of Liberia: Comprising a Brief Account of the Geography, Climate, Productions, and Diseases of the Republic of Liberia* (Washington, D.C.: C. Alexander, 1850).

49. Elliot Cresson.

50. Stephen A. Benson was the second president of Liberia, from 1856–61.

your board, that the socy here was merely <u>auxiliary</u> which he acknowledged +
said he had not not thought of that before, that the parent soc'y only should
have made all [page break] the disbursements of this nature. the fact is the
board here had not more right to order those houses to be built at all, than to
name the town, both were entirely out of their province, this is the same difficulty we had with Mr Cresson when I was in the board and Dr M saw it so +
told me he had affronted him he supposed by opposing his long list of vice-
Presidents including Lord Palmerston + others calculated to make it appear
that this was a separate and independent socy. I understood him to say that
he would prefer that the new town should be called "Buchanan." I afterwards
saw Mr Davidson, Mr D. was a member of the board at the same time I was
and knew Gov[r] Buchanan personally, we were both among his most intimate
friends. Mr Davidson said he would decidedly prefer that the place should be
named "Buchanan" and he did not think that there was two persons in the
board who really cared a straw about it being called "Cresson," but that at the
time the last change was made in the board, when Dr Bethune,[51] Bell[52] +
others went out and some new men were brought in who knew nothing about
the position of the Socy and what had previously taken place, knowing Mr
Cresson as being very active in the cause were willing to gratify him ~~that~~ +
voted to call the town by his name. As to <u>any</u> member of the Board knowing
it or any other place in Liberia by the name of Cresson in 1834. it is a great
mistake. I was an active member of the Board at that time and know that the
name was entirely [page break] disclaimed, although one of two of the Hawes'
slaves who were sent out by the "Young Men's Colonization Socy of Penn[a]."[53]
then just organised, probably wrote back calling the place now Bassa Cove, or
very near it "Port Cresson" as they were instructed to do. Mr E Cresson +
Cha[s]. Naylor Esqr.[54] were the committee sent by the board here to see to their
embarkation.

But as you very properly say that it is a subject over
which the Executive Comm. has no control, the resolution asking the Liberians to name the new city "Buchanan" having been passed at annual meeting

51. George Bethune.

52. Possibly Philip Bell.

53. The Young Men's Colonization Society of Pennsylvania was organized by Elliot
Cresson in 1834 to supersede the older Pennsylvania Colonization Society when the latter chas-
tised Cresson for his behavior in England. This group became independent of the larger body and
with the New York Colonization Society founded the Bassa Cove community. Staudenraus, *The
African Colonization Movement*, 234.

54. Charles Naylor, a member of the Young Men's Colonization Society of
Pennsylvania.

of the Socy. So let us rest, until you should think proper in your individual capacity (being I presume well acquainted with Hon. S A Benson) should think proper to write to him + other influential citizens in Bassa County asking them to comply with the wishes of the Am. Col. Socy as expressed at their late annual meeting.

I have already written more than was necessary, but I thought it well to let you know the real state of the case and if all the members of the present board in this city were made acquainted with the history of this subject and the management of one of their members they would not think of him very differently from what I do. but I have no the least disposition to interfere with him further than that if I could prevent it, the name of "Buchanan" should not be given up for that of "Cresson."

Yours very truly
Benj^a. Coates

❖ 10 ❖

Philadelphia Octr. 11th. 1851.[55]

Rev^d. W^m. McLain.

My dear sir,

Your favor was duly rec^d. I shall be very glad if the Ex. Comm. approve of the suggestions of laying out the <u>City</u> of Buchanan on a large scale to include under the one corporation <u>all</u> the different settlements + villages from Fishtown to Bassa Cove, and make the place suitable for the requirements of a dense population, which it will probably have some forty or fifty years hence. this settled it will avoid any conflict of interest in settlements so close to each other in Bassa Cove + Buchanan. before receiving your letter I had learned from Davidson, Dr Malcolm and William Coppinger,[56] that the name of Buchanan had been retained by your committee and the matter thus finally settled, and both Davidson and Dr Malcolm were <u>quite satisfied</u> with the decision, altho' both members of the Colⁿ board here, but William who is in Cresson's interest was not so well pleased. he told me however that he should be just as much interested in the

---

55. ACS Papers 66:124:45.

56. William Coppinger is reported to have first worked for the Pennsylvania branch of the ACS as an office boy in 1838, at the age of ten. He later became secretary of the Pennsylvania Colonization Society and secretary/treasurer of the ACS. Staudenraus, *The African Colonization Movement*, 249.

welfare of the new settlement and labor as hard for it as if it had been called "Cresson" as he wished. I told him that nineteen twentieths of the colonizationists in the United States would decidedly prefer the name of Buchanan, he said he did not doubt it, but that Mr Cresson had been laboring for twenty years to have the place named after him, + would be exceedingly disappointed. William is a very worthy young man, brought [page break] up in the Colonization office, and known more about Colonization matters than all the board, but Mr C. has told him that he has remembered him in his will! and although he knows his character pretty well, yet it has had its influence. it is much better on many accounts that this matter should be settled as it is, for had it been called "Cresson," very little of the funds raised in this state would I apprehend go for any other purpose than in the building up of Cresson. By the last packet for New York I sent a memorial signed by most of the early + staunchest friends of the cause + by most of the editors of the daily press [here] the "North American" "Enquirer" "———" +c proposing to the legislature to lay out the City of Buchanan as I suggested to you. this was also adopted by the New York board who passed appropriate resolutions. Pinney[57] wrote to Roberts[58] + Hanson,[59] Dr. Bethune[60] wrote to the same effect, and I wrote to Roberts, Benson Teage + Warner + Geo. L S—— of [Bealy] so that a pretty strong influence has been brought to bear in favor of the proposition. if it receives the appropriation of the Executive Committee at Washington, which is the most proper body on this side the water to decide on it, I have no fear but that it will be adopted by the Liberian Legislature. however I will write again by this vessel and will be glad to have the names of Mr Gurley[61] + Dr Lugenbeil[62] + other friends of the cause in Washington not members of the Ex. Comm. to sign the memorial which I will forward to one of them, probably Mr Gurley

Please say to Dr Lugenbeil that I am much obliged to him for his letters and [page break] also for writing to Roberts and Benson on the subject I should have answered his letter but have been very much occupied with business.

57. John B. Pinney.

58. Joseph Jenkins Roberts.

59. John Hanson, of Philadelphia, was a member of the Pennsylvania Colonization Society and the owner of the ship *Liberia*, which took colonists to Africa. For a number of years Hanson engaged in trade with Liberia. Staudenraus, *The African Colonization Movement*, 135, 159, 161, 165.

60. George Bethune.

61. Ralph Randolph Gurley was an agent and controversial secretary of the ACS. He wrote *Life of Jehudi Ashmun, Late Colonial Agent in Liberia* (Washington, D.C.: J. C. Dunn, 1835).

62. J. W. Lugenbeel.

I had a letter
from Benson last week, requesting me to send him by the <u>very first opportu-
nity</u>. <u>six gold washers</u>. he also [mentioned] have purchased a tract in Bassa
County forty miles in the interior east of [Baxley] (40 <u>miles from [Baxley]</u>
toward the mountains) for the New Jersey settlement.

Will you please reserve me room in the vessel for Bensons' gold
washers, and also for <u>one</u> box of dry goods for him. the latter were ordered in
the summer but I have just received the samples which were then omitted.

Josiah Whites'[63] legacy I think will go to the Massachusetts College
Association. I have more confidence in New England management in matters
of education and particularly in Mr Tracy and have recommended my friends
who have the disposal of it to give that direction, altho' some of the members
of the col. board in this city wished it returned here to be applied to purposes
of education in Grand Bassa County, but I feared that it would not go into so
good hands. I however at their wish introduced certain members of the board
who were about organising an Educational Socy in this city + who had wished
me to meet them, to the parties having charge of the trust, + let them tell their
own story, but do not think they will get the money.

Yours very truly

Benjª. Coates

❖ II ❖

Philadelphia November 6th 1851[64]

Dr J.W. Lugenbeil

Dear Sir,

In looking over my letters, I find in one from
you, a small draft on me drawn by President Roberts in favor of Revᵈ. Wᵐ
MᶜLain[65] for Two Dollars. ($2.) which had been overlooked at the time I sup-
pose and presume therefore was not paid. enclosed please find the same.

I owe an apology for not earlier acknowl-
edging your letter, which came while I was much engaged during our busiest

---

63. Josiah White (1781–1850) was a Philadelphia entrepreneur who helped develop the
anthracite coal industry in Pennsylvania. At his death he bequeathed a large amount of money for
the education of African Americans and American Indians. *Dictionary of Quaker Biography*.

64. ACS Papers 66A:124:1:158.

65. Reverend William McLain.

season of the year. I am nevertheless exceedingly obliged to you for the interest you have taken in favor of our proposed new city of Buchanan[66] which I
trust will receive the unanimous sanction of the Liberia Legislature, and I am
convinced it will receive the hearty approval of nearly every friend of African
Colonization in the United States.

I sent to Mr Pinney[67] a blank memorial to the Legislature of Liberia,
a copy of that signed by Mr McLain + yourself. Mr P had it signed by Anson
G. Phelps, Dr Reese, Mr [D——way] and nearly all the prominent Colonizationists in New York and members of their board, but I fear that it did
not arrive in time for the vessel, as W^m. Coppinger[68] who went from here on
Friday Evening to see her off and by whom I sent my letter informed me on
his return that the vessel left early on Saturday morning + no letters arriving
that day by <u>mail</u> were received in time.

Yours very truly
Benj^a. Coates

❖ 12 ❖

Philadelphia Jany 10th 1852

Rev^d W^m McLain

My dear sir

As it is probable you have seen an article in
"Colonization Herald" written and inserted by our young friend W^m. Coppinger[69] who is entirely in Cresson's interest, entrusted with all his business,
and as Mr C informs him also <u>remembered in his will</u>!! I thought you would
be interested in what Pres^d Roberts[70] says on that subject in a letter I received
from him a few weeks since by the "Liberia Packet," and therefore have had
the extract copied for you which find annexed. by it you will perceive that
the question is in all probability <u>settled ere this</u> by the Liberia Legislature
naming the place "Buchanan" as of course they ought. Rev^d Dr [Stephens] of
St Andrews Church (Episcopalian) is the delegate appointed to represent this
state at the Annual Meeting. Cresson has got quite a number of Episcopalians
on the board and as they do <u>not yet know him</u>, are more inclined to think well

---

66. Liberian settlement of Buchanan.
67. John Brooke Pinney.
68. William Coppinger.
69. William Coppinger.
70. Joseph Jenkins Roberts.

of him than some of us who do know him. I had an interview with our Quaker Missionaries Eli + Sybil Jones ~~who~~ at that time since who returned in the "Liberia Packet" the were very favorably impressed with what they saw in Liberia, and I hope they may do some good in this country for their visit. they speak very highly of Roberts and seem very much interested in the [temporal] as well as Spiritual welfare of the people of the Young Republic. I [page break] think it probable that our friend will have to write to you in a day or two on a matter of business in relation to a draft of Bensons[71] on the "New Jersey Col^n Socy" for $754. For the purchase of territory for said socy. by the —— would it not be very appropriate for that socy or whosoever has the right to call the new town in the New Jersy settlement, "Alexander" after Dr Alexander of Princeton? A very pretty and well sounding as well as appropriate name. Will you not suggest it? Benson ways in his letter to me that this new purchase is the finest and most salubrious in Liberia. he thinks I may come out there and pay them a visit in perfect safety. Either Alexander or Alexandria would be pretty + appropriate names, altho' I would prefer the former.

Yours very truly
Benj^a Coates

❖ 13 ❖

Brooklyn, L. I. Jan.y 10/52

My dear Mr. Coates,

I heartily sympathize with all the sentiments expressed by you in your note of yesterday, but as my duties here, which, owing to the recent opening of my new church, are just now particularly keeping, will not allow me to go to Washington, I cannot assist Dr. Rule in forwarding your designs as you wish.

You are perfectly right in thinking that justice to the memory of our friend Buchanan's[72] faithfulness requires that a monument should be erected to his memory and I think that the Board[73] at Washington will order it to be done. I trust also that the new city[74] will by bearing his name be a monument more durable than any stone we could set up.

71. Stephen Allen Benson.
72. Thomas Buchanan.
73. Presumably, Bethune was referring to the board of the ACS, headquartered in Washington, D.C.
74. Buchanan, a Liberian settlement. Shortly before this letter was written (and before the news from Liberia could reach the United States), the nearby settlement of Fishtown suffered

One serious difficulty in the way is the difficulty and expense of transporting a pillar or obelisk of any size across the sea. The weight in proportion to a suitable height will be very great—it will occupy much room in the vessel and be hard to carry to and from it. To satisfy your mind on this subject enquire at any marble yard. If there be any stone at Bassa suitable and we can get the workmen there it would be better to build it on the spot; but if we send it from here it should be in blocks of no great size. It would be a pity if the monument should not be of commanding height. A thousand dollars expended on the spot might (I judge) to erect a tower of masonry a hundred feet high. An obelisk sent from this country (the expenses included) for that sum would not be twenty feet high.

Do they need a light house on the shore there? By combining the two objects (not inharmonious) we might accomplish something better than if we were to take them singly. Be these things as they may a monument and a handsome one too should be erected without delay.

I should be much mortified if E.C.[75] gains his egotistical wishes. His [offered will would] have little effect on me as in such case I should not be willing to take the <u>bill</u> [<u>will</u>?] for the <u>due</u> [<u>deed</u>?].

How sad it is that our noble cause should be so hampered by the selfish intrigues of a mean ambition!

My heart is strongly as ever enlisted for colonization, but like yourself for many reasons I have not of late been openly active as I once was. Should the time come when our help is needed I am sure that neither of us will be found absent or idle if alive. I made a speech at Newark the other day for the New Jersey movement, and quite enjoyed it but I am very, very busy in many more immediate duties and the <u>jangle</u> attending our Colonization affairs is very unpleasant to me.

I have been much gratified by hearing from you, and am as ever with great regard and respect.

very faithfully yours

Geo. W. Bethune[76]

Benjamin Coates, Esq.

---

an attack by area natives and was destroyed. Bassa Cove was also attacked twice, but it survived. The plan of the new settlement included both Bassa Cove and the former site of Fishtown under the name of "Buchanan." *African Repository*, vol. 27, 88, 247; vol. 28, 91, 139, 157, 167; Alexander, *A History of Colonization on the Western Coast of Africa*, 468–70; HDL 32; Staudenraus, *The African Colonization Movement*, 234–36.

75. Probably Elliot Cresson.

76. George Washington Bethune.

❧ 14 ❧

Philadelphia Feb 28th. 1852[77]

Rev[d]. W[m]. M[c]Lain,

Dear Sir

Your letter of Feby 26th. addressed to Coates +
Brown, with the Resolutions of the Ex. Comm. in relation to our claims on
the New Jersey Col[n]. Socy for $754. was received this morning, and we are very
much surprised to learn that the money has not been paid over by the New
Jersey Col. Socy., and also that ~~you~~ the Exec Committee has received no communication from the New Jersey Socy on the subject, as we addressed you at
their suggestion and gave an extract from the letter of their Secretary Dr.
J. G. Goble at the same time. We also have two letters from Chief Justice
Hornblower, President of said society, one of them dated in January stating
the money for this purpose, for the payment of this Territory ($754.) had been
raised by a special effort and the amount handed to the New Jersey delegates
to the late annual meeting to be paid over to the Treasurer of the Am[r] Col[n]
Socy +c +c. In a subsequent letter he referred to this money having been raised
for this purpose and paid over +c and lastly Dr Goble the Secretary states the
same thing in his letter, a verbatim extract from which we gave [page break]
you. You may judge therefore of our surprise to learn that the money has not
been paid and that the Exec. Committee has received no communication
from the New Jersey Socy on the subject. Of course we cannot expect the
Exec. Comm. to pay us Money that they have not received. This whole business seems indeed—as you state in a former letter—to be a "jumble of errors."
The New Jersey Socy as they state sent Messrs Moore + Benson[78] into the
interior to make an exploration with the view to purchase of a State Territory.
the purchase altho' not authorised at the time, they have since assumed and I
believe have name it "New Jersey." as Judge Hornblower says "they deem it
an advantageous purchase." Mr Finley wrote to us in the reception of ~~it~~ his
letter from Benson saying that the explo^ration was satisfactory, and that his
draft would no doubt be paid. Mr Meade the [present] agent also wrote to us
expressing the opinion that it would be paid. And the New Jersey Socy still
holds the order in our favor, as a voucher that they have paid us the amount
($754) under their circumstances. not doubting that we would soon receive
the money we went on + executed a further order from Mr Benson, which we

77. ACS Papers 67:125:280.
78. Stephen Allen Benson.

<u>would not</u> have done otherwise as he still owed us largely. and <u>after the</u> Packet <u>has sailed, and our goods have gone</u> we are informed [page break] that the New Jersy Socy are not authorised to purchase Territory but that they have raised the money, assuming the purchase to be a desirable one, and have paid it over to the Treasurer of the Am. Col. Socy. to whom they refer us for payment. You therefore see the position in which we are placed by the confused action [between] the Am + New Jersy Societies. I am fully aware of the irregularities of the case as explained by you, but we received a draft a few months since from Mr Benson in the <u>Pennsylvania Society</u> for houses built +c at <u>their direction</u> which was <u>promptly met</u> and Mr Benson would naturally suppose that the New Jersey Society had equal power and control over its funds with the Penn^a. Society, and as the latter society has continued a sort of independent action in their respect for some time, he did not know what latitude the parent society had tacitly allowed to its auxiliaries, and it does appear to me that the errors in this case belong quite as much to this side of the Atlantic as the other. As to the justice of our suffering for errors not of our own, or into which we may have been led by the actions of others, we must [lean] for their consideration. I must say however that in remark to which you took exception in a former letter, was made by me in a private note to yourself, of which I kept no copy but my impression was that I made no reference to the Executive Committee whatever, but the Ex. Board of the Am. Col. Socy at the annual meeting and certainly <u>no want</u> of respect for either the intelligence or business capacity of <u>any one was intended</u>. Yours very truly B Coates.

Philadelphia June 27th 1853[79]

Dr. J W Lugenbeil,[80]

Dear Sir,

An unusual piece of business has prevented an earlier acknowledgement of your favor [of] 16th inst —— $30. The [amt] of Mr. Gurley's[81] Dft in my favor forwarded to you for collection.

You will please accept my thanks for the trouble I have given, and can I at any time be of service to you, trust that you

79. ACS Papers 76:1:139:537.
80. J. W. Lugenbeel.
81. Probably Ralph Randolph Gurley.

will call on me as freely as I have on yourself. Mr. Gurley wished me to be paid, + [denied] that I should send it on, otherwise I would not have cared to do so. Whenever I can serve an old friend like Mr G. in so small a matter, I am very glad to do so. And would like to be able see him [more] prospering.

I regret that colonization is dragging. Had it not been for McLain[82] and Pinney,[83] it would have been dead long since. I have faith however that Liberia will grow, and eventually become of importance in the world, and one of the principal means for [page break] for the civilization of Western Africa.

I had thought once or twice of writing to you to ask [if] you ever had leisure! and if so to request [a] favor that when entirely disengaged you come look over the "African Repository" for a letter [of] Gerritt Smith's[84] in his correspondence with the Revᵈ Leonard Bacon D.D. in which he expresses in very strong terms his determination forever to stand by Colonization. "Let [others] forsake thee yet will not I in the spirit [afit]

I would like to have the exact words. A quotation of the whole paragraph if not too much trouble should you ever have a time of entire leisure, but do not give yourself any trouble about it. Mr. Gurley promised to send it to me, but has forgotten to do so. He recollected the passage to which I referred and could turn to it at once. It must have been I think about 1834, 1835, or 1836 as it was not many years afterwards that Gerritt became an anti-colonizationist. Alas for poor ——

"Is thy servant a dog that he —— to do —— great thing" is applicable to many in our day

82. William McLain.
83. John Brooke Pinney.
84. Gerrit Smith (March 6, 1797–December 28, 1874) lived in Petersboro, New York, most of his life. He attended Hamilton College and graduated in 1818. After inheriting his father's fortune, he became active in a number of religious benevolent organizations including the American Bible Society, the American Tract Society, and the American Sunday School Union. Smith also supported temperance, prison reform, and women's rights. Though he was an early supporter of the ACS, Smith eventually rejected the idea of emigration in favor of promoting the rights of black people in the United States. Smith was a member of the Liberty Party, which attempted to end slavery and discriminatory practices, in the 1840s. He ran for president as a member of the party in 1848, 1856, and 1860. In 1852 Smith was elected to Congress, but he resigned two years later in frustration over the Kansas-Nebraska Act and other anti-abolitionist sentiments in Congress. Deeply dedicated to serving black Americans, Smith donated his own land to those black people who wished to farm, and he assisted John Brown before the Harper's Ferry raid. The disastrous end to the raid prompted Smith to enter a mental hospital, where he stayed for eight weeks. From the beginning of the Civil War until his death, Smith continued his philanthropic activities. *ANB*, 20:187.

In haste I am dear sir very truly yours

Benj Coates

❖ 16 ❖

Government House[85]
Monrovia May 26th 1854

My dear sir

I have only a moment, by the U.S. Brig Perry, in which to drop you a line to say I am still here. In consequence of some derangement in the machinery of the Steamer Faith—which vessel, in course, ought to have sailed hence for England early in the present month—she could only make the passage to Sierra Leone, so I shall be a month behind the time I had expected to arrive in England.

I am glad to say that my health, within the last month or so, has considerably improved, still I feel the need of relaxation: and, besides, some little matters of a public nature seem to make it desirable that I should undertake another trip to Europe: not, however, as before to arrange matters of misunderstanding between the authorities here and foreign traders +c +c. I am happy to say, that since my visit to England in 1852 not the slightest difficulty has arisen between this Government and foreigners in consequence of our maritime regulations.[86]

I have no news of importance to communicate—everything is progressing with us as usual

I am, my dear sir
Yours truly
J. J. Roberts[87]

Benjm Coates Esqr

---

85. Roberts Collection, HCSC.

86. When Liberia was declared an independent nation in 1848, it was largely because of difficulties that had arisen between British traders and the colonial administration. After several British traders had had their goods confiscated for violations of the colony's trade laws, they complained to their government. Their claims were supported on the grounds that Liberia was neither a sovereign nation nor a colony of the United States, and it therefore had no right to impose duties on the coastal trade. Liberia responded by declaring its independence, with the blessing of the ACS.

87. Joseph Jenkins Roberts. See Letter 1, Roberts to Coates, July 8, 1848.

❖ 17 ❖

Philadelphia June 8th 1854[88]

Rev. Wm,. McLain[89]

        Dear Sir-

              I received this evening a letter from Pres^t Roberts[90] via England dated April 10th in which he says he will probably leave for <u>England</u> in the steamer for May from whence he will write to you. His principal object I believe is the benefit of his health, although he expects to benefit Liberia by his visit in "some degree." his daughter who is under Samuel Gurney's[91] care will return with him. He remarked that his homeward bound steamer by which he sent my letter arrived two days earlier than he expected and he was not able therefore to write even a line to you . He wished me to say to you that you will hear from him immediately on his arrival in England, if no opportunity occurs before. His letter contains nothing of particular interest or I would forward it to you. The price of palm oil he says is so high in England, and the demand has brought so many vessels to the coast and created such competition between traders that he fears they will quite over do the thing.

        Yours very truly   Benj^a Coates

❖ 18 ❖

Government House[92]

Monrovia August 26th. 1854

My Dear Sir

        On the receipt of this you will observe that I am still here, and likely to be for some time. By a succession of casualties to the English mail steamers, since May last, I have been disappointed of an opportunity to undertake the visit I contemplated to Europe—of which I advised you some months since, and which I presume accounts for my not having heard from you by any of the recent arrivals from the United States.

88. ACS Papers 73:1:134:371.
89. William McLain.
90. Joseph Jenkins Roberts.
91. Samuel Gurney.
92. The Government House, located in Monrovia, was the administrative center of the Liberian government. It was first named during the colonial period and housed the governor during that time. *BAP* 1:82.

The steamer Candace—homeward bound—is now ten days behind her time; and possibly she too has met with some accident. If so, I shall abandon, for the present year at least, my purpose of going abroad;—as before another month expires the season will have arrived when all Liberians—at—home should remain within the tropics.

In daily expectation of the arrival of the steamer I have delayed writing a line for any of my American friends till now—that is to go by the Shirley—thinking to write from England, whence my letters would reach the U.S. in advance of that vessel. The Shirley, however, sails the day after tomorrow, and in view of the possibility that some accident has happened to the Candace, and of consequence another disappointment to me, I must not allow her to depart without a line for you that you may know why I am still here. The weather, with us, has been unusually boisterous during the last two or three weeks, and maybe, has been so on the South Coast, which possibly has detained the steamer—in consequence of difficulty in landing, and receiving cargo. Should she arrive in a day or two—in good condition—you will probably hear from me before you will have received this.

With respect to public matters in Liberia I have nothing important to communicate. Our affairs, generally, I think are progressing in the right direction: nothing has occurred recently to disturb public harmony. A little political feeling is manifesting itself preparatory to the ensuing general election. Mr Roye[93] is trying to create some capital for the presidency—the public mind, however, seems not to tend in that way. He hopes by commencing

---

93. Edward James Roye was born in 1815 in Newark, Ohio. He attended Ohio University and in 1844 moved to Liberia, where he became successful in commerce. His political career began in 1849, when he was elected to the House of Representatives. He was later a senator and a member of the Supreme Court. In 1865 he became the chief justice of the Liberian Supreme Court, a position that he held until 1868. In 1854 Roye launched his presidential campaign when he started his own paper, *The Liberian Sentinel.* The paper had a limited impact and was discontinued in 1855. Roberts was correct in guessing that Roye's 1854 presidential bid would not have public support. In 1869, however, Roye was elected the fifth president of Liberia. He was the first Liberian president who was 100 percent black. Under his leadership, the Congoes of Liberia, those black people who had been recaptured from slave ships and "returned" to Liberia, gained equal status to Americo-Liberians. Despite this positive development, his term proved to be disastrous for him personally and for the nation. In 1871 Liberia received a loan from the British government that was intended to bolster the Liberian currency. The loan, the terms of which were not approved by the legislature, hurt the economy, and it led to corruption charges against Roye. A coup removed Roye from office in 1871, the result of the failed loan and his attempt to change the length of the president's term from two to four years. He was imprisoned with his son and several cabinet members. He died of unknown causes in an attempt to escape. J. Gus Liebenow, *Liberia: The Quest for Democracy* (Bloomington: Indiana University Press, 1987); *Historical Dictionary of Liberia.*

early to arrest, or turn the current. But no go, I think: nothing, however, is more uncertain than an election or the verdict of a jury.

Enclosed you will find the first of a set of Exchanges drawn by G.W.S. Hall[94]—8th. inst—on his father the Doctor[95] for Fifteen Hundred and Sixty two dollars, and fifty cents payable six months after date—which please collect at maturity for my account. By the way, I may mention here—what has just come to my knowledge—that a certain young man of this place imitates my hand writing so nearly that it requires close scrutiny to detect the fraud. I have no strong grounds for believing that he has practiced this with any wrong intention—though decidedly improper in him, or any one else. Yesterday, as soon as I heard of it I sent for and admonished him against such practices. He goes to the United States by the Shirley. In <u>confidence</u> a Mr. Chester is the person. I thought it well to give you a hint of this, as also to remind you that I never draw on you without advising you of the same in an unmistakable letter.

[Letter 18, Roberts to Coates, August 26, 1854, contains the following letter: Roberts to Coates, October 9, 1854.]

London Oct. 9th. 1854

Dear Sir:—The above you will observe was written to be forwarded from Monrovia. On the 27th., however, the Candace arrived, and in a few hours I was off—so I send it from here: And have only to add, as you will see from the dates, that we have had a long, very long passage. The Candace is very slow, and with all just as we reached the anchorage of Madeira[96] off jumped the screw[97]—which detained us there nine days refitting another. Fortunate for the passengers that it happened just where it did—except one poor fellow of our number who was thrown from a horse and killed. Th'o tedious, the passage in other respects was pleasant; weather delightful; and fellow

94. George Hall.
95. Dr. James Hall was George Hall's father. Originally from New England, he graduated from the Medical School of Maine in 1822. In 1831 he went to Liberia as a doctor for the ACS. In 1833, when illness caused him to return to the United States, he worked for the Maryland State Colonization Society as the organizer for the new colony of Maryland, just south of Liberia. In the fall of 1833, Hall sailed to Africa with colonists, and after picking up several families already living in Liberia, founded the colony of Maryland, around Cape Palmas. Hall was governor of the new colony until 1836, when he returned to the United States, again due to ill heath. He remained active with the Maryland State Colonization Society throughout his life. Penelope Campbell, *Maryland in Africa: The Maryland State Colonization Society, 1831–1857* (Urbana: University of Illinois Press, 1971); *Historical Dictionary of Liberia*.
96. The Madeira Islands belong to Portugal and are north of the Canary Islands and west of Morocco. *The Times Atlas of the World*, 10th ed. (New York: Times Books Group Co. 1999), plate 91.
97. "off jumped the screw": the connection holding the sails broke off.

passengers agreeable. And I am happy to say my health is greatly improved. We arrived at Plymouth[98] on the evening of the 4th. inst, but various circumstances have conspired to delay my sending this forward till now.

I am greatly obliged for your favor of July last, to the care of S. Gurney Esqr.[99] I have not yet seen the Rev. Mr Ward;[100] I hope to have that pleasure, and to meet him cordially. I am happy to say that I find my old friends here as deeply as ever, perhaps more so, interested in the welfare of Liberia. Mr G—seems to have discovered some of the bad traits in Hanson's[101] character and is quite satisfied he attempted to injure Liberia and myself without just cause. The secretary of the Anti Slavery Society, Mr. Chamerovzow,[102] and myself are on very good terms.

I am glad to say I found my daughter quite well, and much improved. I propose to return to Liberia by the November boat, and may hope to hear from you again before my departure. Next week I think of making a short trip to the Continent—shall be absent ten or twelve days, and will write to you on my return.

I have the prospect of obtaining a recognition of the Independence of Liberia[103] from several of the smaler German powers[104]—more anon. Upon

98. Plymouth is a port city in southwestern England, in Devon. It is on the southern coast of England, on the English Channel. *The Times Atlas of the World*, plate 52.

99. Samuel Gurney.

100. Samuel Ringgold Ward.

101. Augustus Hanson was born in 1815 in Accra, where his father was a government official. He was educated in England and then traveled to New York City, where he worked for the New York Committee of Vigilance and Mirror of Liberty. A minister, he was somewhat supportive of colonization. In 1850 he was made the British consul in Liberia. After reporting on corruption within the government, tension between him and J. J. Roberts grew. In 1852 Hanson was reassigned to Sherbo Island. *BAP* 3:287 n.

102. Louis Alexis Chamerovzow was an English novelist. He was an editor of the *Anti-Slavery Reporter* and became the secretary of the British and Foreign Anti-Slavery Society in 1852. In 1861 he defended an American fugitive slave, John Anderson. He was involved in creating the Treaty of Washington of 1862, which limited the international slave trade. *BAP* vol. 1.

103. Liberia became independent in 1847. Britain recognized the new nation as independent the next year, but the United States did not have diplomatic relations with Liberia until 1862. One of the reasons for the delayed recognition of Liberia by the United States was that many politicians, especially those from the South, feared that recognition of Liberia would lead to the presence of a black ambassador in Washington. When Roberts wrote this letter, only Great Britain and France had diplomatic relations with Liberia. The following countries also recognized Liberia before 1900: Belgium (1858), Denmark (1860), Italy (1862), the Netherlands (1862), and, by the 1890s, Portugal, Austria, Sweden, Norway, Brazil, and Haiti. Liebenow, *Liberia*; Harold D. Nelson, ed., *Liberia: A Country Study*, 3rd ed. (Washington, D.C.: Department of the Army, 1985), 247; and *HDL* 74.

104. In 1856 Liberia was recognized by Lubeck, Bremen, and Hamburg. *HDL* 74.

the whole I think I should be able to turn my visit to good account for the interest of Liberia.

> With kindest regards to self and family
> I have the honor to be, your
> obt[105] servant
> J.J. Roberts

Benjm. Coates Esqr
Philadelphia Pa.

U.S.

4 Hollis St. Cavendish Square
London October 16th. 1854

My dear Sir

It is very annoying that in consequence of the carlesness of the servant, which I have just discovered—the enclosed has not been posted. It is not so important, to be sure, but I feel that you would like to be early informed of my safe arrival. Well, it only brings you an additional line earlier than I had expected.

So far, I have had a very pleasant time here—have made a great many new friends—and have been able to interest some in Liberia. Night before last, in company with Mr. Ralston,[106] I had the pleasure of meeting, by invitation, General Webb,[107] of the N.Y.C. and E.,[108] Hon. R. Johnson,[109]

---

105. "obt." was used as an abbreviation for obedient.

106. It is not clear if Roberts is referring to Gerald Ralston or Gerard Ralston, or if the two Ralstons are in fact the same person. According to some sources, Gerald was the Liberian consul in London. He assisted Crummell, Blyden, and Garnet and helped the fugitive slave John Anderson settle in Liberia. Gerard, according to other sources, was from Philadelphia and a founding member of the Colonization Society of the State of Pennsylvania. Floyd J. Miller's *The Search for a Black Nationality* describes Gerard as being a former member of the Pennsylvania Colonization Society and the Liberian consul in Liberia. This, however, is the only source that indicated that Gerald and Gerard were the same person. Miller, *The Search for A Black Nationality*, 206; Staudenraus, *The African Colonization Movement*, 125, 182; *BAP*, vol. 1, 508; Hollis R. Lynch, *Selected Letters of Edward Wilmot Blyden* (Millwood, N.Y.: KTO Press, 1978), 59.

107. James Watson Webb (February 2, 1802–June 7, 1884) was born in Claverack, New York. He moved to his aunt's house in Salem, New York, after the death of his parents and later resided with an older, married sister. At the age of seventeen, Webb joined the army and had reached the position of lieutenant when he resigned in 1827. He was later given the title of general. Webb relocated to New York City and became the editor of *Morning Courier* with the help of his father-in-law. In 1829 Webb merged his paper with the *New York Enquirer* and ran the

late Attorney Gen. US., General Campbell, the new U.S. consul, Captain
Adams U.S.A. in route for Japan with the ratified Treaty,[110] and a gentleman
from California, whose name I misremember. Of course, we had a long conversation with respect to Colonization and Liberia; in which all seemed to
be greatly interested. I learned from Gen. Webb that he rather opposed the
Ebony steam ship scheme because he thought the principal parties were actu-
ated more by pecuniary interests—personal—than any desire to benefit Liberia.
He advocates steam communication between the U.S. and Liberia, and will

paper as the *Morning Courier and New York Enquirer* until he sold it to the editor of the *World*
in 1861. Webb was a relatively successful editor and was one of the six founding members of
the Associated Press. In 1853 and 1854 Webb made three trips to England to learn more about the
situation in Europe just before the outbreak of the Crimean War. Webb and Roberts probably
met in the third of Webb's trips. Though Webb joined the Republican Party by the mid-1850s,
he was by no means an abolitionist. Instead, he believed that the Republican Party was the true
conservative party and only supported emancipation when coupled with colonization. In 1861
Webb became the minister to Brazil and held that position for eight years. He then traveled
throughout Europe for two years before returning to New York. Garraty and Carnes, *ANB* vols.
19 and 22; James L. Crouthamel, *James Watson Webb: A Biography* (Middletown: Wesleyan University Press, 1969).

108. "C. & E." was an abbreviation for the *Morning Courier and New York Enquirer.*

109. Reverdy Johnson (May 21, 1796–February 10, 1876) was born in Maryland. He
graduated from St. John's College and served in the War of 1812. He passed the bar in 1816 and
began sixty years of legal practice in Baltimore the following year. Johnson became a state senator in 1821 and served in the legislature until 1828. Johnson became well known as a constitutional
lawyer in 1827 when he argued the case of *Brown v. Maryland* before the Supreme Court. A
wealthy man, Johnson was not always sympathetic towards those who were less fortunate. In 1834
a mob destroyed his house in response to his involvement in a bank failure. In 1845 Johnson was
elected to the Senate as a Whig who wished to retain the status quo with regard to slavery. Four
years later, in 1849, Johnson became Zachary Taylor's attorney general but resigned within a
year because of a personal scandal. Johnson resumed his law practice and served as a defense attorney in the *Dred Scott* case. Despite Johnson's negative feelings toward black people, he supported
the Union and became a member of the Maryland state legislature in 1861 and a Senator the following year. Johnson opposed the Emancipation Proclamation, but he came to support many
Republican ideas during Reconstruction. Johnson served as the U.S. minister to Britain in 1868.
His most famous Supreme Court case, *United States v. Cruikshank* (1875), came near the end of his
career; he argued that the fourteenth amendment only applied to states, not individuals. *ANB* vol. 1.

110. The "Treaty" was probably the Treaty of Peace and Amity (or the Treaty of Kanagawa as it was popularly known) between the United States and the Empire of Japan. This treaty
opened two Japanese ports to American ships, provided provisions for ships there, promised good
treatment for shipwrecked sailors, and a set up an American consulate in Japan. It is not clear why
Roberts would have been introduced to Captain Adams, a participant in the mission that created
the treaty. Commodore Matthew C. Perry, the American who lead the mission, was also active in
opening West Africa to American commerce. In 1843 Perry attacked several African tribes and
then signed agreements of "friendship and protection" with them. Roberts may have been familiar with Perry as a result of his West African activities. Thomas Brown, ed., *American Eras: Civil
War and Reconstruction* (Detroit: Gale, 1997), 51; "Treaty of Kanagawa," *The Kondansha Encyclopedia
of Japan*, vol. 4 (Tokyo: Kodansha, 1983), 135; Harral E. Landry, "Slavery and the Slave Trade in
Atlantic Diplomacy, 1850–1861," *Journal of Southern History* 27, no. 2 (May 1961): 184–207.

give his support to honorable enterprise in that way. He proposes to embody in a letter, for his paper, something upon this subject—in connection with Colonization—which he says will be read, and may be turned to good account.

He urged, as indeed did all the party, that I return to Liberia via United States; and thinks, at this juncture, were I to do so the chances of a recognition are decidedly favorable. I confess my difference of opinion. He says that General Pierce[111] would no doubt avail himself of the circumstance—in the hope of conciliating the North on the Subject of Slavery, and thereby make a little capital for himself—to recommend the measure in his next annual message to Congress. In the event of my taking that route, the Gen.—though opposed to the present Administration—assures me that he could and would render me important assistance. But I cannot adopt his suggestion: And further I am not at all so sanguine as he appears to be. He says Liberia would, long ago have been acknowledged by the U.S. Government but for Hayti[112] which they will not recognize. But with great deference to the opinions of the Gen. I think I understand the policy of his Gov^t. with regard to this question quite as well as he. We have yet to wait, I apprehend, some years to come before the Gov^t. of the U.S. will extend to us that civility.

111. Franklin Pierce (November 23, 1804–October 3, 1869), a native of New Hampshire, became the fourteenth president. He graduated from Bowdoin and became a lawyer in 1827. He served in the New Hampshire General Court in 1829 before becoming a U.S. Congressman in 1833 and a Senator in 1836. Pierce fought in the Mexican War, but an early injury cut short his participation. He was elected president in 1852 and broke with tradition when he delivered his inaugural address from memory. Pierce was often called a doughface as a result of his pro-South views, such as his support of the pro-slavery government in Kansas. When he lost his own bid for reelection, he was pleased with the election of James Buchanan, but unhappy when Lincoln, who he believed stood for everything he opposed, was elected in 1860. *ANB* vol. 17.

112. Throughout the middle of the nineteenth century, Haiti was a popular destination for those who advocated emigration of American black people. Many preferred Haiti to Africa because of the milder Haitian climate and the already established black government. Modern Haitian history began when the island became a French colony in 1697. During the French Revolution, the National Assembly promised to end slavery in Haiti, but this promise was never kept. Slavery there ended in 1804 with Haitian independence, the result of a slave rebellion lead by Toussaint (Breda) L'Ouverture. In 1824 there was a wave of emigration to Haiti by American black people, though the popularity of Haiti then waned until the crises of the 1850s, when Haiti again became popular among those who supported emigration. Despite the intellectual interest in Haitian emigration, there was never a large American black settlement in Haiti because many emigrants eventually returned to the United States. In addition, the government of Haiti was never stable: between 1843 and 1915, only one ruler completed his term. The problem of Liberia's diplomatic recognition by the United States probably had less to do with Haiti in politics than with southern Congressmen's reluctance to have a black diplomat in Washington. Staudenraus, *The African Colonization Movement*; Kwando M. Kinshasa, *Emigration vs. Assimilation: The Debate in the African American Press, 1827–1861* (Jefferson, N.C.: McFarland and Company, 1988), 138; Richard Haggerty, ed., *Dominican Republic and Haiti: Country Studies* (Washington, D.C.: Federal Research Division, Library of Congress, 1991).

I beg that you will send to me, Liberia, by the first vessel chancing to sail for the Coast, a couple bbls[113] flour, a bbl no 1 mackerell, and hundred pounds Hams, and do. [dozen] bacon sides, a keg of butter, and one of lard. Provisions are high here.

I am, my dear Sir,

Yours truly

J.J. Roberts

Benjm Coates Esqr
    Philadelphia Pa.

❖ 20 ❖

Philad^a May 3rd 1855[114]

Dr Jm Lugenbeil[115]

Dear Sir,

Will you do me the favor to present the enclosed draft of Rev^d.RR Gurley[116] for $30. to Mr. McLain[117] for payment and request him to send me a check for the same. And if he declines paying it please return it to me quickly if he is in Washington. if not, please return it to me. I sent it over once through an agency, when it was returned, without any reason for it, non-payment. Your attention to this will much oblige, Yours very truly

Benj^a Coates

❖ 21 ❖

Philadelphia May 22nd 55[118].

Rev^d. W^m McLain,[119]

Dear Sir,

I have this morning a few lines from President Roberts[120] dated April 4th in which he says that as consequence of over exertion in preparing to accompany the settlers to Cape Mount he has been prostrated

---

113. "bbls" was an abbreviation for barrels.
114. ACS Papers 76:139:270.
115. J. W. Lugenbeel.
116. Ralph Randolph Gurley.
117. William McLain.
118. ACS Papers 76:1:139:364.
119. William McLain.
120. Joseph Jenkins Roberts.

with fever, and has thus been prevented from writing to you by the "Shirley" as he had intended, and desires me to make the explanation to you.

He communicates nothing of interest except that Benson's[121] prospects of being elected to the presidency are brightening, and he (Roberts) feels pretty sanguine that he will succeed. he says "Augustus Washington[122] who some months ago seemed to favor the Whig party is now a strong Benson advocate." "Sam¹ Williams has all the time been on the [right] side."

Our friends are to have a meeting here this evening.

Yours very truly

Benjᵃ Coates

 22

Philadelphia June 15ᵗʰ 1855[123]

Revᵈ R. R. Gurley[124]

My dear Sir

A black man calling himself Charles Green who professes to have lived in Liberia six years called on me this morning. But he cannot tell me the name of the vessel he went out in, nor the name of the captain, nor any of the passengers. He says he returned to New York last November, in a vessel belonging to Messr Potter + Yates of New York, but cannot recollect the name of the vessel he returned in, nor the name of the captain, nor the name of any of the passengers. He can give me the names of President Benson[125] + Ex President Roberts[126] + Dr Snowden[127] but cannot

121. Stephen Allen Benson.

122. Augustus Washington (1820–?) was born in Trenton, New Jersey, and lived there until he was sixteen. He taught school at an early age and later attended Dartmouth for two years starting in 1842. He then became a daguerrotypist in Hartford, Connecticut. In 1853, he and his family emigrated to Liberia. In Liberia, Washington taught Greek and Latin at Alexander High School for over a year. He then became a sugar cane farmer and river merchant. He was also a member of the Liberian legislator and a judge. He wrote many letters for the *African Repository*, the journal of the ACS, and at least one of his letters, "Liberia As It Is," appeared in *Frederick Douglass's Paper* (December 15, 1854). Wilson Jeremiah Moses, *Liberian Dreams: Back-to-Africa Narratives from the 1850s* (University Park: Pennsylvania State University Press, 1998), 181–202.

123. ACS Papers 86:1:155:336.

124. Ralph Randolph Gurley.

125. Stephen Allen Benson.

126. Joseph Jenkins Roberts.

127. Isaac H. Snowden was admitted to Harvard medical school in 1850 along with Martin Delany and Daniel Laing. The ACS had provided assistance to Laing and Snowden and both promised to practice in Liberia upon the completion of their medical training. Students and professors did not welcome the three black men, and when Elizabeth Blackwell attempted to matriculate, the three men were expelled, because it seemed that their presence offered a precedent

recollect the names of any merchants in Monrovia except the McGill Brothers, nor of any other person whatever. Neither can he tell me the name of any
town or village in Liberia. He cannot even tell me the name of his next neighbors. He says he lives up the St. Pauls' River + that a gentleman died who lived
on the [page break] St. Pauls' river who was a large farmer but he cannot tell
his name. He cannot give me the name of a single person on the St. Pauls'
River. His only document is a letter in three pieces written by a Mr. Henry
Smith whom he says lives at 72 Benson St. New York who states that he has
letters from Revd R. R. Gurley that he emigrated to Liberia from Virginia in
1852 after buying the freedom of his father + mother whose expenses he paid,
but that he has children yet living in Fredericksburg Va. for whom he is
collecting money. This man Charles Green says he is from Fredericksburg but
that he was also a servant of Hon. Dixon H Lewis[128] of Alab. formerly U.S.
Senator. It is <u>possible</u> that he may be honest + his statement in the main
correct but I am <u>very much</u> inclined to <u>doubt it</u>. He says he saw Mr. Pinney[129]
in Liberia. I then asked him why he did not call on him in New York + get a
certificate from him. This he could not explain except by saying that he has
a letter from Mr. Gurley to Mr. Smith which he thought sufficient. Again
he says that [page break] he returned from Liberia last November while
this letter of Mr. Smiths is dated N. York <u>Aug.</u> 7. 1856. here is a discrepancy.
Altogether it appears to me the man is an imposter. I have sent him to the
Colonization, + as Mr. Coppinger[130] is not in, I have taken charge of his collection book + letter from Mr. Smith until I can hear from you.

Please answer by return mail either to
Mr. Coppinger or myself. As I may possibly be out of the city perhaps you had
better address Mr. Wm Coppinger at Colonization offices

Yours very truly

Benj^a Coates

---

that would open admissions to other "undesirable" or inappropriate students. Laing eventually
earned his M.D. from Dartmouth in 1854, and Delany apprenticed and practiced medicine in the
Pittsburgh area, but there is no evidence that Snowden ever continued with his medical education. Wilbur H. Watson, *Against the Odds: Blacks in the Profession of Medicine in the United States*
(New Brunswick, N.J.: Transaction Publishers, 1999).

128. Dixon Hall Lewis (August 10, 1802–?) was born in Virginia. He moved with
his family to Georgia in 1806 and then to Alabama after graduating college in 1820. Lewis was
admitted to the bar three years later. Beginning in 1826, Lewis served in the Alabama state legislature. Lewis was then elected to the House of Representatives and served from 1829 until 1844
when he became a member of the Senate. *Biographical Directory of the American Congress, 1774–
1996* (Alexandria, Va.: CQ Staff Directories, 1997), 1390.

129. John Brooke Pinney.

130. William Coppinger.

❖ 23 ❖

Philad^a Oct 27 1855[131]

Dr JM Lugenbeil[132]

Dear Sir,

Shall I again trouble you to collect the above small order on Mr McLain[133] for $25. that I advanced to Mr Gurley some two or three months time for his travelling expenses to New England. I do not know how my acct stands [fro.] the "Repository" but I know that I have not paid [page break] any bill for it directly from Washington altho' I have occasionally made contributions here to the general cause. If you have any charge against me please settle it out of the proceeds of this draft. If you have none, + have charged my paper to the Pennsylvanian Socy very good. I will settle with them In that case you may still deduct five dollars as a contribution towards the "Repository", and send me $20.

—— Yours very truly

Benj^a Coates

I sent you Nesbit's truthful! pamphlet a few days since but do not think it is worth replying to.

B.C.

❖ 24 ❖

Philadelphia Nov. 17th 1855[134]

Dr JM Lugenbeil[135]

My Dear Sir,

Please accept my thanks for your favor of yesterday with check for $20 + rect for $5. on acct of the Repository being together the amt of the Gurley[136] dft [draft] in my favor on Mr McLain[137] for money advanced him for his travelling expenses.

131. ACS Papers 77:1:141:141.
132. J. W. Lugenbeel.
133. William McLain.
134. ACS Papers 78:1:141:2:219.
135. J. W. Lugenbeel.
136. Ralph Randolph Gurley.
137. William McLain.

Colonization is uphill work I know, or rather raising money to carry out its operations, especially in these tight times. Money is exceedingly scarce here, as all here engaged in mercantile business have reason to know.

Yours very truly

Benj Coates

❖ 25 ❖

London May 15th. 1856

My dear Sir

You will have heard perhaps, ere this reaches you, of my arrival again in old England. We reached Plymouth on the 4th. inst and London on the 6th: All of us somewhat benefited by the voyage; though Mrs Roberts, as usual, suffered much of sea sickness. I am glad to say that my own health has very much improved.

I have no Liberian news of importance to communicate. At the time of leaving home our public affairs, I believe, were progressing satisfactorily. The difficulties at Sinou had been so far overcome as to give good ground for hope that the settlers there will experience no further interruption from the natives; still it is feared there will be much suffering among the people, for several months, in consequence of so many of them being driven from their farms, and their entire crops destroyed. I hope, however, that our fears, in this respect, are much greater than the actual condition of things warants.

I have some little matters of business to attend to in England, and in a couple of weeks will probably visit Paris to arrange some public matters connected with our government: After which, when I shall have heard from Mr. Tracy,[138] I think it somewhat likely that I may make a short visit to the States. In which case I shall hope and rejoice to see you once again.

---

138. Joseph Tracy (November 3, 1794–March 24, 1874) attended Dartmouth College and graduated in 1814. Tracy actively participated in the Liberia movement. He became the secretary of the Massachusetts Colonization Society in 1842 and held that position until his death. In 1858 he became an officer of the ACS. He also wrote about missionary activity in Liberia and played a role in the founding of Liberia College through his involvement with the Trustees of Donation for Education in Liberia. In addition, he was both a congregational minister and an editor. He worked on the *Vermont Chronicle* starting in 1829. In 1834 he began working for the Boston *Recorder* and in 1835 the New York *Observer*. He was married twice and had eight children. *BAP* 3:230 n.; *ANB* 18:623; "Joseph Tracy," *Appleton's* 6:152.

Enclosed I send the first of three bills of Exchange viz D.A. Wilson's[139] on Wm Rankin N.Y. $150. J B. [McLute] on Rev. Thomas Carllin N.Y. $50. John Day[140] and B.P. Yates[141] on Archibald Thomas Richmond Va $100. Total $300—which please collect at maturity, and place to my credit on your books.

I shall be glad to hear from you if you can find time to drop me a line. Address me to the care of G. Ralston[142] Esqr 21 [Token] House Yard, London. I have been so much engaged since I have been here, that as yet I have not fixed upon a permanent address. Should I visit the U.S. I think of leaving Mrs Roberts[143] and my daughter[144] in England, and must therefore, be somewhat particular in my arrangement, for a temporary home for them.

Mrs R. desires to be kindly remembered to you and the family: And believe me, my dear Sir

> Very truly
> > Your obt. Servant
> > > J.J. Roberts

Benjm Coates Esquire
> Philadelphia
> > United States

139. Reverend David Agnew Wilson, a Princeton University graduate, traveled to Liberia and became principal of Alexander High School in Monrovia from 1851 to 1858. While he was there, Edward Blyden attended the school, and Blyden succeeded Wilson as principal. When Blyden was later president of Liberia College, Wilson received an honorary degree from the institution. *BAP* 3:531 n.; Lynch, *Selected Letters of Edward Wilmot Blyden*, 20; Hollis R. Lynch, *Edward Wilmot Blyden: Pan-Negro Patriot, 1832–1912* (New York: Oxford University Press, 1967), 13, 150.

140. Reverend John Day (1797–1861) was born free in North Carolina and became a merchant. In 1830 he emigrated to Liberia, where he was a missionary and a teacher. He was involved in Liberian politics as a member of the constitutional convention in 1847 and as the chief justice of the Supreme Court from 1851 to 1861. *HDL* 40; Lynch, *Edward Wilmot Blyden*, 20.

141. Beverley Page Yates was Stephen A. Benson's vice president of Liberia from 1856 to 1860. He was the uncle of Blyden's wife and a wealthy merchant. *HDL* 26, 183; Lynch, *Edward Wilmot Blyden*, 38.)

142. For information on G. Ralston, see Letter 19, Roberts to Coates, October 16, 1854.

143. Jane Waring Roberts.

144. Mary Roberts was educated in England. When she returned to Liberia she worked with the Methodist Church there and later married a member of the Johnson family. Henries, *The Life of Joseph Jenkins Roberts*, 10.

❋ 26 ❋

Philad[a]. Sept 29th 1856[145]

Dr J.W. Lugenbiel[146]

My Dear Sir,

May I again take the liberty of troubling you to present this enclosed drafts to Mr M[c]Lain[147] for acceptance and return them to me. They were intended as you will perceive for Jn[o]. [Wistar] the Steward of the "Penn[a] Hospital for the Insane," but as the managers were tired of waiting for their money, I advanced it for Mr Gurley[148] and will hold these drafts myself.

Yours very truly

Benj[a]. Coates

❋ 27 ❋

Philad[a] Oct[o] 6. 1856[149]

Dr [smudged] JW Lugenbeil,[150]

Dear Sir

If it would not be troubling you too much I would like to avail myself of your kind offer to furnish me with a check for one hundred + fifty dollars for the first acceptance of Mr Gurley's[151] dfts to Mr M[c]Lain,[152] which I now enclose, endorsed for that purpose. I regret very much to hear of your continued poor health but trust you may be invigorated by this fine October weather.

I received a day or two since a pamphlet from Liberia by Mr Blyden[153] entitled a "Plea for [page break] bleeding Africa." I presume that you have

145. ACS Papers 80:144:343.
146. J. W. Lugenbeel.
147. William McLain.
148. Ralph Randolph Gurley.
149. ACS Papers 80:145:139.
150. J. W. Lugenbeel. Letter 9, Coates to Lugenbeel, June 18, 1851.
151. Ralph Randolph Gurley. Letter 10, Coates to McLain, October 11, 1851.
152. William McLain. Letter 1, Roberts to Coates, July 8, 1848.
153. Edward Wilmot Blyden (1832–1912) was a Liberian immigrant who played a major role in the nation's intellectual development. He was born on the Caribbean island of St. Thomas in the Virgin Islands, to free parents. When he was ten he and his parents moved to Venezuela, where he showed an early aptitude for languages by becoming fluent in Spanish. During 1844 the family returned to St. Thomas and Blyden met John P. Knox, a Presbyterian minister from the

read it and I would like to know your opinion of it, also what McLain and Gurley, + others of our friends in Washington think of it. I like it; it meets my views ~~very~~ but I fear it ^expresses^ ~~in~~ too strong an abolition sentiment to ~~most~~ suit all our friends in the South. It will no doubt have a very happy effect among our —— colored population in the North in making them friendly to Liberia, and I can hardly suppose it can do much harm among the <u>true</u> colonizationists in the South. They cannot but admire the manhood of those who assert for their race, full + complete equality with any, and every other people, although [page break] they may not, as <u>I am not</u> yet quite ^ ready to become a convert to the expediency of <u>immediate emancipation</u> preferring as I should a system that should <u>educate</u> and <u>prepare</u> the slaves for freedom so that they could appreciate the blessings of liberty which I would be glad to see universally established —— —— the world

Hoping to hear of your improved health.

I am very truly

Yours

Benj^a Coates

United States. Impressed with Blyden's intelligence, Knox mentored him and encouraged him to become a clergyman. Following Knox's urging, Blyden went to the United States in May 1850 to enter Rutgers Theological Seminary, but he was denied entrance because of his race. Other institutions followed suit. During his stay, Blyden met up with John Pinney, William Coppinger, and others involved in the ACS who succeeded in convincing him to emigrate to Liberia, which he did, arriving in Monrovia in January 1851. He continued his education at Alexander High School, where he advanced rapidly, soon becoming a lay preacher, then a tutor, then a full-fledged minister and the principal of Alexander. During the 1860s, while a professor at Liberia College, he traveled to the United States as Liberia's educational commissioner, to raise funds and to encourage new immigrants to Liberia. He held various other posts including that of the secretary of state (1862–64), minister of the interior (1880–82), president of Liberia College (1880–84), and ambassador to Britain and France (1886–90). His status was repeatedly threatened by Liberia's race politics, which pitted mulatto immigrants, who held most of the wealth and power, against full-blooded immigrants and the native Africans. He became estranged from many of Liberia's leading citizens, including J. J. Roberts, then president of Liberia College, who eventually became so aggressive that Blyden was forced to give up his professorship. As a result of these personal conflicts and a scandal involving Liberian President Roye's wife, Blyden fled to Sierra Leone after the deposition of Roye in 1871. "Blyden, Edward Wilmot," in *ANB* 3:79–80; Thomas W. Livingston, *Education and Race: A Biography of Edward Wilmot Blyden* (San Francisco: Glendessary Press, 1975).

❖ 28 ❖

Rev^d. R. R. Gurley.[155]

Philadelphia May 2nd 1857[154]

My Dear Sir,

I wish to subscribe for the "African Repository" for Rev^d. "Alexander Crummell."[156] for <u>one</u> year <u>commencing January 1st 1857</u>. Will you do me the favor to have all the numbers forwarded to him by the "M.C. Stevens" from Balt. from the first of the year to the present time. Enclosed is one dollar to pay for the same. I presume that you have read his admirable oration delivered at the anniversary of Liberian Independence at Monrovia in 1855.

Yours very truly   Benj^a. Coates

154. ACS Papers 147:1:167.

155. Ralph Randolph Gurley. Letter 10, Coates to McLain, October 11, 1851.

156. Alexander Crummell (1819–1898), a clergyman, scholar, and activist, was heavily involved in both the struggle for black rights and the development of Liberia. Born to a free black family in New York, he had parents who encouraged his education, but he met with repeated aggravation. His early education was in free schools in New York, and as a teenager he enrolled in Noyes Academy in Canaan, New Hampshire, along with Henry Highland Garnet. The townspeople disapproved of the biracial character of the school, however, and dragged its building (a log cabin) into a nearby swamp. Crummel spent three years at Oneida Institute during which he decided to enter the ministry. Again, however, he ran afoul of racial discrimination when he was denied entrance to the General Theological Seminary. He studied instead at Yale Theological Seminary under certain restrictions. Following a few lean years leading various churches in New Haven, Philadelphia, and New York, he traveled to England to raise funds for a new church. Impressed with the opportunities and freedom he discovered in England, he attended Cambridge University. After graduating in 1853, he and his family moved to Liberia under the auspices of the Protestant Episcopal Church. Crummell experienced successive disappointments in both his religious and intellectual endeavors during the two decades he spent there. In 1872 his political involvements forced him to leave the country, so he returned to the United States. After his return he spent his years in various ecclesiastical and intellectual pursuits, including the founding of St. Luke's, an independent black Episcopal church, and the American Negro Academy. Created in opposition to schools that sought to provide their black students with technical instruction, the purpose of the American Negro Academy was to give impetus to the creation of a class of black intellectuals. Crummell's ideological focus was on "Pan-Africanism," which stressed black racial solidarity and the necessity of creating a black civilization equal to, if not more exalted than, that of the white people. For more information on the "matter" McKim mentions, see notes to McKim letter from June 4, 1867. "Crummell, Alexander," in *ANB* 5:820–22; Wilson Jeremiah Moses, *Alexander Crummell: A Study of Civilization and Discontent* (New York: Oxford University Press, 1989); J. R. Oldfield, *Alexander Crummell (1819–1898) and the Creation of an African-American Church in Liberia* (New York: Edwin Mellen Press, 1990); Rigsby, *Alexander Crummell*.

�֍ 29 ✦

Philad. Oct. 3rd 1857[157]

Rev. A Crummell,[158]
   My Dear Sir,
        I have time to acknowledge the rect [receipt] of your interesting letter via England I fully agree with yourself & Mr Blyden[159] that the Colledge[160] should <u>not</u> be located in Monrovia. My friend Pinney[161] is also of the same opinion + I do not believe that there is any difference of opinion on that subject here. I would have written to my esteemed friend ExPresident Roberts[162] on this subject but learn that he is now in England— however I [page break] I have written a few lines to our excellent friend President —— requesting him to urge by all means that it should be placed in the Country & in some fair <u>healthy</u> location—either Clay Ashland or some other equally ——. My Dear Sir I am completely absorbed just now in my own affairs as hardly to be able to give even a thought to anything else. Still I do feel a great —— in the success of Liberia and of the College—I wrote to Mr Tracy[163] on the subject—and I cannot but hope that the decision which be re-considered and that it will not be placed in Monrovia.
       In great haste
      I am your assured friend,
       Benj Coates
The times here are perfectly <u>terrific</u>. Nothing like this ever seen before—our best oldest & strongest mercantile houses have nearly all had to succumb to the storm and thousands are now starving—with a long winter before them

---

157. This letter is reproduced, courtesy of HSP.
158. Alexander Crummell. Letter 28, Coates to Gurley, May 2, 1857.
159. Edward Wilmot Blyden. Letter 27, Coates to Lugenbeel, October 6, 1856.
160. Liberia College. Letter 60, Pinney to Coates, September 28, 1859.
161. John Brooke Pinney. Letter 8, Coates to McLain, May 16, 1851.
162. Joseph Jenkins Roberts. Letter 1, Roberts to Coates, July 8, 1848.
163. Joseph Tracy. Letter 25, Roberts to Coates, May 15, 1856.

✤ 30 ✤

Philad. Dec^b. 19th 1857[164]

Rev^d. W^m McLain[165]
    Treas^r Am Col Socy
    Washington City

Dear Sir,

    We rec^d a letter from Dr H [I] Roberts about two months since dated Augt. 20. 1857 in which he says he had written to you to pay us, two hundred and twenty dollars, $220.^30 a bal. due us of many years standing. As we have not heard from you on the subject, we wish to say that it will be quite a convenience to us to receive the amount if you are in funds.

    Yours very truly

        Coates + Brown [the letter is in Coates's handwriting]

✤ 31 ✤

Philadelphia Mch [March] 2nd 1858.[166]

Rev^d W^m McLain[167]
Secy + Treas^r Am. Col Socy[168]
    Washington City

Dear Sir

    Some five of six months since we rec^d a letter from Dr Henry I Roberts[169] dated Augt 20th 1857 saying that he had written by same vessel to you requesting you to pay us an old bal. of some $220.^30 with Int.

    We wrote to you after receiving his letter, + understood from you in reply, that at that time "The Am^er. Colonization Socy" was not in debt to Dr Roberts, but intimating that [page break] it might be soon. Supposing that by this time, there must be owing to him from the "Am Col Socy" enough to pay what he owes us we write to make the enquiry and if so, will be glad if you

164. ACS Papers 83:1:149:340.
165. William McLain. Letter 1, Roberts to Coates, July 8, 1848.
166. ACS Papers 83:1:150:204.
167. William McLain. Letter 1, Roberts to Coates, July 8, 1848.
168. The ACS. See Letter 8, Coates to McLain, May 16, 1851.
169. See Letter 30, Coates to McLain, December 19, 1857.

will remit to us as authorised to do, by him in his letter of August last say $220.[30] with Int from that date.

As we are very desirous of having this acct closed which has stood on our books for some six or eight years, your early attention to it will much oblige.

Yours very truly

Coates + Brown[170] [the letter is in Coates's handwriting]

❊ 32 ❊

Philad May 28th 1858[171]
Revd R. R Gurley[172]
        My dear Sir,
                    Some days since I had an interview with Revd M Browne[173] a minister of the Dutch Reformed Church who came in here at the suggestion of Mr Pinney[174] to obtain the agency for this state from the "Penna Colonization Socy"[175] but as the way did not seem to open here, I suggested to him to go to Washington + see if there was not an opening there, either in the office at Washington to fill the post lately occupied by by our excellent + lamented friend Dr. Lugenbeil,[176] or as a travelling agent or agent for some of the Southern states for which I suppose the Executive Committee have the power of appointment. From what I have seen of Mr Bourne I

170. See Letter 14, Coates to McLain, February 28, 1852.
171. ACS Papers 84:1:151:256.
172. Ralph Randolph Gurley. Letter 10, Coates to McLain, October 11, 1851.
173. Theodore Bourne, the son of abolitionist and anticolonizationist George Bourne, was a Dutch Reformed minister and a member of the New York Colonization Society. He believed that immigrants were taking jobs from American black people and that the situation for black people would not improve in the near future. Therefore, he advocated that black people emigrate to Yoruba. He supported the African Colonization Society and became one of its agents. While in England in 1859, raising money for the organization and defending the emigration movement, he announced that Martin Delany and his Niger Valley Exploring Party were part of the African Civilization Society, though this was not true. Bourne's attempt to unite the causes of the society and Delany was not enough to maintain his effectiveness, and by 1860 the society dismissed him as their agent. Following his termination as the society's foreign agent, conflict erupted between Bourne and Garnet. Bourne eventually lost interest in Liberian emigration, but he continued to support emigration to Jamaica and the Niger Valley. Miller, *The Search for a Black Nationality*, 183–92, 217–26; BAP 1:507.
174. John Brooke Pinney. Letter 7, Coates to McLain, May 16, 1851.
175. See Letter 7, Coates to McLain, May 16, 1851.
176. J. W. Lugenbeel. Coates to Lugenbeel, June 18, 1851.

should think he would make an [page break] agent. he made quite a favorable impression on me, + appears very zealous in the cause + disposed to go into it with him <u>whole heart</u> + <u>work hard</u>. He wished me to write to you to enquire what prospect there might be of his getting an appointment. Pinney can no doubt tell you more about him. It seemed to me that he might be very useful, either in the office, or, that he could advance the cause in many of the Southern states.

I would like to see his zeal and his talents applied to a good purpose and the South I am satisfied is the best field for him.

Some of our northern colored men are disposed to emigrate to Africa, on their own acct. independent of the Am. Colon. [page break] Socy. The travels + labors of Rev^d Mr Bowen[177] in Yoruba, and of Rev^d Dr Livingstone in Southern Africa, are opening their eyes, and enlighten them as to what Africa really is. of this they have had no knowledge heretofore. The two books of Livingstone + Bowen will I think do a great deal of good in this way.

I am not in liberty to state yet what is contemplated by some of the colored folks, <u>north</u> or this, but if it results as I think it will you will hear soon.

Yours very truly B. Coates

✾ 33 ✾

Philad. Octr 21st 1858[178]
Rev^d. R. R Gurley[179]
My Dear Sir,
I am so entirely out of the Liberia trade that I regret I cannot do anything to forward the views of Mr [Barbour] for I

177. Thomas Jefferson Bowen was a Baptist missionary, first sent to Africa in 1849 by the Southern Baptist Convention. His field of operations was the area referred to as "Yoruba country," and he remained there from 1850 until 1856, with a year's absence in 1852–53. From his experiences there he wrote *Grammar and Dictionary of the Yoruba Language, With an Introductory Description of the Country and People of Yoruba* (Washington, D.C.: Smithsonian Institution, 1858) and *Central Africa: Adventures and Missionary Labors in Several Countries in the Interior of Africa, from 1849 to 1856* (Charleston: Southern Baptist Publication Society, 1857; reprint, New York: Negro Universities Press, 1969). C. P. Groves, *The Planting of Christianity in Africa*, vol. 2 (London: Lutterworth Press, 1954), 70–73.
178. ACS Papers 85:1:153:70.
179. Ralph Randolph Gurley. Letter 10, Coates to McLain, October 11, 1851.

do not know of any one who would be likely to furnish the articles he wants, all of which would have to be purchased for cash.

By the last arrival of the Stevens I rec^d the enclosed letter from Ex President Roberts,[180] but as I have no acquaintance in Washington N.C. do not know how to obtain the information desired. I thought it probably however that you might know some one in Washington North Carolina or in that section, who would interest themselves to obtain the desired information. If so you will greatly oblige me, as well as Mr Roberts + Mr Anderson by communicating with them on the subject.

In case you cannot do anything, or know of no one to apply to please return the letter of Mr Roberts to me.

Yours very truly

Benj^a Coates

❖ 34 ❖

Provincial Freeman[181] Office

Chatham C.W[182]

Nov 20th /58

Benjamin Coates Esq: -

Dear sir, -

I beg to acknowledge the receipt from you of a pamphlet and "Gazette"[183] containing important matter relative to the Civilization of Africa.

---

180. Joseph Jenkins Roberts. Letter 1, Roberts to Coates, July 8, 1848.

181. The *Provincial Freeman* was first published in 1853 by Samuel Ringgold Ward, who was followed by a series of editors. The paper began regular weekly publication a year later, in March 1854. In 1856 Ward relocated from Toronto to Chatham, Canada West. The *Provincial Freeman* was a proponent of black self-help, opposing segregated settlements and institutions as well as major fund-raising efforts ("begging," as they termed it) on the behalf of black people. The paper encouraged escaped slaves to flee to Canada, and many of the people involved with the paper were active in aiding fugitive slaves. The paper initially opposed emigration, but by 1856, under the editorship of Mary Ann Shadd Cary, it served as the official organ of the National Emigration Convention in Cleveland. After surviving at least one interruption in publication, it ceased to publish sometime after 1860. *BAP* 2:217–18 n.

182. Chatham, Canada West. Located in present-day Ontario on the peninsula that approaches Detroit. Chatham was "the fugitive slave capital of Canada," with some 2,400 fugitive slaves within the city limits by 1856, and many more in the surrounding area. There were an estimated 50–60,000 black people in Canada West (essentially what is now the province of Ontario) by 1860. Victor Ullman, *Martin R. Delany: The Beginnings of Black Nationalism* (Boston: Beacon Press, 185).

183. Because Coates frequently enclosed copies of colonizationist newspapers, it is likely that this "Gazette" was a copy of the *African Repository*, which was published by the ACS.

Upon a careful examination of both the book and the letter in the paper we feel that the matter cannot be too forcibly urged upon the attention of the colored people of Canada as well as the United States.

We of the Freeman Office[184] have put the views express by you before some of our best informed and most reliable colored men among whom I may mention Abraham D. Shadd[185] J.H. Harris[186] G.W. Brodie[187] + H. Jackson[188] and they approve of it and of the suggestion made upon the same matter made through myself to them by Dr. Delany[189] that an organization be formed at no distant day

184. As of early 1856, the primary figures in the *Freeman* office were Mary Ann Shadd Cary, Isaac Shadd, and H. Ford Douglas. For financial reasons, the paper ceased publication briefly in 1858, when Isaac Shadd was arrested for taking part in the rescue of Sylvanus Demarest, a free black man who had been kidnapped, apparently to be sold into slavery. By the middle of the following year, Shadd had revived the paper as the *Provincial Freeman and Semi-Monthly Advertiser. BAP* 2:218 n.

185. Abraham D. Shadd (1801–1882), a free black born in Pennsylvania, moved to Wilmington, Delaware, where he used his house to hide fugitive slaves as they fled north. After moving to West Chester, he used his farm there for the same purpose. Shadd originally opposed colonization but came to support emigration to Canadian. He served on the governing board of the National Emigration Convention. In 1859 he was elected to a seat on the Raleigh Town Council, becoming the first black to win an elected office in the British North American Provinces. Mary Ann Shadd Cary was his daughter. *BAP* 2:165–66 n.

186. James Henry Harris, who moved to Chatham, Canada West, in the 1850s, where he was one of several men by this name, became involved in the antislavery and emigration movements. He was a member of the Chatham Vigilance Committee, an agent for the National Emigration Convention, and supporter of Delany's Niger Valley Exploring Party. *BAP* 2:398 n.

187. G. W. Brodie. Born in Kentucky, he moved to Chatham, Canada West, by the early 1850s. There he supported the *Provincial Freeman* through his business advertisements. He was a member of the Chatham Vigilance Committee and served as secretary for both the General Board of Commissioners of the National Emigration Convention and the Dawn Committee. *BAP* 2:333 n.

188. Harvey C. Jackson. A stage driver in Canada during the 1850s, Jackson moved to Chatham, Canada West, by 1855. He was a member of the Provincial Union Association, which promoted black self-help, and the Vigilance Committee, and he worked with W. H. Day and Harriet Tubman to aid fugitive slaves. Jackson may have collaborated with John Brown when the latter was in Chatham in 1858 to plan the raid on Harpers Ferry. *BAP* 2:395 n.

189. Martin R. Delany (May 6, 1812–January 24, 1885) was born in Charles Town, Virginia (now West Virginia). His mother was free but his father was a slave. The family escaped to Pennsylvania and eventually Delany moved to Pittsburgh, where he became a "cupper and bleeder" (a medical practitioner who treated patients by drawing blood). While in Pittsburgh he edited *The Mystery* and later worked on *The North Star* with Frederick Douglass. He attended Harvard Medical School from 1850 to 1851, but the Harvard administration did not allow him to continue. As a result of his difficulties as a black man in America, including his inability to gain a medical education, Delany came to believe that black people in America could never have equality unless they constituted a majority of the population. He thus came to support emigration to Central and South America and called for a National Emigration Convention. In 1856 he and his family moved to Chatham, Canada West, where he met John Brown, who was developing

From the number and enterprising habits of our people of Canada I think it probable that many will emigrate to the Youruba Country provided the subject can be put properly before them. Mr. Cary[190] I.D. Shadd[191] and myself have been agitating the matter pretty extensively for past few days and we see encouragement enough to confirm the opinion expressed above.

I have taken the liberty to to say this much to you through letter as pecuniary difficulties will prevent us from issuing a paper for a few weeks unless more fortunate than I think;[192] in the meantime however; we shall issue a circular or extra with notice of the subject. If we are enable to resume our regular issue, a full notice of the book and of the new organization shall not only be made but I am at liberty to say we shall advocate the emigration of our people and commercial advantages of the scheme heartily.

When Dr Delany brought the expedition matter before the Board[193]

---

plans to start a black nation within the Southern states. This plan foundered, and soon Brown began planning his raid on Harpers Ferry. Meanwhile, Delany decided to explore the Niger Valley in West Africa and with Robert Campbell spent a year in Africa. While in Africa, Delany came to support Liberia, a country he had disregarded in early years because he believed it was under the control of racist white people. After his trip to Africa, Delany stopped in England to raise money. While in England, Bourne, who was also there, told the English that Delany was part of the African Civilization Society. Eventually Delany allowed himself to accept Bourne's support as it gave him greater access to wealthy Englishmen. In 1860 Delany returned to the United States with the hope of eventually emigrating to Africa. In part because of the Civil War, Delany remained in the United States. He became a Union officer and during Reconstruction he worked for the government in South Carolina. He joined his family in Ohio in 1884 and died the following year. Dorothy Sterling, *The Making of an Afro-American: Martin Robison Delany, 1812–1885* (New York: Da Capo Press, 1996).

190. Probably Thomas F. Cary (?–1860). Married Mary Ann Shadd Cary in 1856. Helped found the Provincial Union Association, a black self-help organization, in 1854. Aided John Brown, but was unable to participate in the raid at Harpers Ferry due to his health. *BAP* 2:396–97 n.

191. Isaac D. Shadd (1829–1896). Shadd was Mary Ann Shadd Cary's brother, and he served, at various times, as a subscription agent, editor, and publisher for the *Provincial Freeman*. He hosted John Brown in 1858, when Brown visited Chatham, Canada West, to plan his raid on Harpers Ferry. Shadd also lead the Chatham Vigilance Committee's rescue of Sylvanus Demarest. *BAP* 2:369 n.

192. Seven members of the Chatham Vigilance Committee, including Isaac D. Shadd, were arrested for participating in the rescue of Sylvanus Demarest. Though the case was dismissed when it was learned that Demarest was free, not an escaped slave, the cost of defending the group was sufficient to prevent Mary Ann Shadd Cary from publishing the *Provincial Freeman* for a period. "Circular by Mary Ann Shadd Cary," *BAP* 2:392–93.

193. Possibly the General Board of Commissioners of the National Emigration Convention, also known as the National Board of Commissioners. It had nine members who formed committees on domestic, financial, and foreign relations, and there was also a foreign secretary. Martin Delany was the board's first head. The board explored various emigration options, with Delany studying Africa, J. T. Holly looking at Haiti, and James M. Whitfield examining Central

appointed at our Convention[194] we were not prepared to go beyon the appointment of a commission: in truth the old prejudice against the name "Coloniza-
[page break, word not continued] among colored people made a seeming
endorsement of it a matter of great caution, as they would not hesitate to
sacrifice those seeming to favor it. But for ourselves, we see in the new plan
a measure calculated not only to promote the civilization of Africa and the
destruction of slavery but to remove whatever feature of American Colonization was known to be objectionable to colored people.

You may depend upon us for an organization as besides Dr. Delany's
influence we are extensively known to the colored people through the paper
and a school now in their interest and which may be made an instrumentality.
I shall visit Philadelphia + other parts of the United States before long to create if possible an interest in our Paper + school[195] and shall be pleased if agreeable to you to receive any suggestions you may make for our guidance in this
advocacy of this matter. Our people only need proper information scattered
among them by means of the press and schools The young should be trained
Youruba-ward—those at least of enterprising minds, and cheap periodicals
will do the rest. A monthly or semi-monthly in Canada will no doubt help
the matter. It has been our intention to acquaint the pupils of our school with
Livingstone's work[196] and we are more than confirmed in the course by the
facts connected with this movement. In conclusion of this I trust not forward
letter from an entire stranger, we will advocate this matter if helped to do
so by friends of the movement through the instrumentalities I have named
and if not helped will do so any how by means of lectures before our people.
I am in the habit of talking before them and shall multiply occasions in this
behalf.[197] in future any how. In the mean time we stand prepared for and anxious to receive advice and instruction from gentlemen like yourself who have
large reputation among the philanthropic in both Europe and America. I trust
you will permit me to say just here that had we not thought it might be
considered presumptuous Mr. Shadd or myself would have asked for your

---

America. They condemned the ACS. The board's official organ was the *Afro-American Repository*.
Ullman, *Martin R. Delany*, 165–66, 174.

194. National Emigration Convention, Chatham, Canada West, possibly in 1858 (the
1856 convention met in Cleveland, Ohio).

195. Mary Ann Shadd Cary was an educator. In the fall of 1851, she started a school in
Windsor, but it closed in March of 1853. From 1860 to 1863, she ran a black school in Chatham. It
is unclear whether that is the same school to which she refers in this letter. *BAP* 2:185–86 n., 192 n.

196. Probably David Livingstone's explorations into the interior of Africa.

197. Cary was familiar with the abolitionist lecture circuit, having toured Michigan,
Illinois, and Wisconsin with H. Ford Douglas in 1856 to raise support for the *Provincial Freeman*.

counsel ~~three~~ two years ago at least, as I will explain to you if permitted so to do. Yours very respectfully

Mary A.S. Cary.[198]

❖ 35 ❖

Chicago, Jan 8th 1859.

Benj. Coates, Esq.,

My Dr friend:

I am now two letters in your debt. Your favor of the 29th ult.,[199] and 4th inst., have both been duly received, and, I trust, properly appreciated -

I am proud to be able to inform you that your kind wishes in regard to the favorable progress of Mrs Wagoner's health, is now being realized, as she has nearly got back to her usual health.

You have spoken of the Rev H.H. Garnett,[200] and Wm Whipper,[201] in connection with the exploring party[202]—of your wish that they would, or

---

198. Mary Ann Shadd Cary (1823–1893) first attended a school for free black people in Wilmington, Delaware, and later attended a private Quaker school in Pennsylvania. She became a teacher at black schools in the Mid-Atlantic region and New York City. In 1849 she published *Hints for the Colored People of the North*, an examination of economics and racism. She moved to Canada West in 1851 to help fugitive slaves. By 1854, working on the *Provincial Freeman*, she became the first woman newspaper editor in North America. *BAP* 2:192 n.

199. "ultimo," or the month preceding the present one.

200. Henry Highland Garnet. Letter 3, Coates to Douglass, June 27, 1850.

201. William Whipper (1804?–1876) was born in Lancaster, Pennsylvania, to a white father and a slave mother. In the 1820s he moved to Philadelphia and became a grocer. He moved to Columbia in 1835 and began a business partnership with Stephen Smith. The two men went on to become the wealthiest American black people in the years before the Civil War. Their assets included a lumberyard, a ship on Lake Erie, railroads, and land in Pennsylvania and Canada West. Whipper was involved with the Underground Railroad and help lead slaves to freedom in Canada West. He was also a leader of the black convention movement, an annual gathering of free African Americans to consider remedies to American slavery, and he supported moral reform. He helped found the American Moral Reform Society in 1835 and worked on its journal, the *National Reformer*. In the 1840s he supported racial segregation and the African Civilization Movement though he came to denounce both causes by the 1850s. After the Civil War he was vice president of the Pennsylvania State Equal Rights League. *BAP* 3:129–30.

202. Wagoner is probably referring to the Niger Valley Exploring Party organized by Martin Delany in 1858. Originally the party consisted of five members: Delany, Robert Douglass Jr., Robert Campbell, Amos Aray, and James W. Purnell. In October 1858 Campbell disassociated himself from the group. Meanwhile, in the summer of 1858, Garnet came to support emigration. It was perhaps Coates's wish to replace Campbell with Garnet or a similarly respected black leader. This did not happen; Campbell rejoined the Exploring Party in December and Garnet became the leader of the African Civilization Society. In 1859 Delany and Campbell were the

could, accompany said party. I believe that were such men to accompany that party, it would give great confidence to those who are silently looking on and waiting for further developments. The former of these gentlemen, Mr Garnett, I am not personally acquainted with, but the latter, Wm Whipper, of Columbia, Pa., I had the pleasure of becoming acquainted with at the colored National Convention, held at Rochester N.Y. in '52.[203] On being introduced to him, I became at once so pleased and interested in him, that I deliberated and counselled with him, more than with any other man, on the occasion referred to. I found him to be a man of liberal sentiments, comprehensive and practical views, consequently I should think him to be just the man to go on such a Mission as the one to which you have referred

Now, friend Coates, I have talked this enterprise over among my brethren here, and, I must be frank to tell you, that so averse have they been to the Colonization Society, that, though they cannot urge any potent reasons against your enterprise, still, they are disposed to wait until they get further and fuller expressions of future developments. I too, have always been opposed to, and acted against—by resolutions, and otherwise, the Colization Society, and, therefore, I am constantly asked by colored men here, if I have changed my views on that subject. I answer I have not; and, that I do not look upon your enterprise in the same light as I do upon the Colonization Society. I tell them, as I have told you, that I favr it as an enterprise which does not contemplate the removal of the entire free people of color from the United States, as does, the Colonization Society. I am frequently told that as precept and example should go together, whether I contemplate going to Africa with my large family. I answer, that under the peculiar circumstances of my individual case—at my time of life, etc etc., I may not go. The fact is, my friend, the colored people have so long been the subjects of so many conflicting views and opinions, both by the Government and people, that it affords just grounds why colored men should be apprehensive, and, therefor, slow to move in this direction—and especially since the almost universal sentiment, expression and action have been averse to the colonization movement. Thus, you need not be surprised to find that auxiliary Societies will be slow in forming -

---

sole remaining members of the Party and traveled to Africa. After the trip, Delany spent several months in England and eventually joined the African Civilization Society. Miller, *The Search for a Black Nationality*.

203. Wagoner misidentified the year. The Rochester convention was held in 1853 and was the first such convention in five years. Attacks on the ACS served to stifle more productive discussions concerning emigration, even though many delegates were beginning to look towards this as the best option. Miller, *The Search for a Black Nationality*, 134–38.

It strikes me that if a line of steamers could be established by colored capital, or a union of capital—nonproscriptive, or otherwise, to run between this country and Africa, thus opening up facilities for visiting that country, that it would be a powerful agent in promoting your enterprise. And it might be made a paying concern.

There is an important branch of knowlege which I could wish were more generally possessed by we colored men—the want of which, prevents us, in great measure, from entering important enterprises. I allude to a business education. I am inclined to think, that with the knowledge would come the disposition. It might be, however, that the necessity would call up the knowledge. This train of thought, leads to a contemplation of a commercial college for colored men. But enough for the present.

I must not omit to acknowledge the receipt of the pamphlet you sent me containing Alexander Crummell's[204] oration. I will read it, God willing, with care and attention.

With great respect,

I am, Dr sir

Your obt humbl srvt.

H.O. Wagoner[205]

❈ 36 ❈

Philadelphia Jany 13th 1859[206]

Revd R. R Gurley[207]

My dear Sir

I have been intending for some time writing to you to thank you for your kindness in attending to my request in regard to the matter of [our] —— Anderson at Washington N.C. + our mutual friend Ex President Roberts[208] + Mr A will also feel under obligation

---

204. Alexander Crummell. Letter 28, Coates to Gurley, May 2, 1857.

205. Henry O. Wagoner was a Chicago barber and abolitionist. Like many well-off African Americans, Wagoner opposed emigration. Wagoner, along with other Chicago black people, attempted to win voting rights in Illinois in 1855 but was unsuccessful. In the years just before the start of the Civil War, Wagoner came to reevaluate his position and wrote a letter, published in *Douglass' Monthly*, in favor of emigration. Wagoner and Douglass met at a Chicago convention and remained friends throughout their lives. Wagoner was one of the original black subscribers of Douglass's *North Star. BAP*; Kinshasa, *Emigration vs. Assimilation*.

206. ACS Papers 85:1:1554:36.

207. Ralph Randolph Gurley. Letter 10, Coates to McLain, October 11, 1851.

208. Joseph Jenkins Roberts. Letter 1, Roberts to Coates, July 8, 1848.

to you. I have been reminded of my [remissness] by receiving the "African Repository"[209] yesterday, + hasten to do what has been so long neglected.

Africa is at present attracting considerable attention from our colored people. It is very difficult for them to get over their old + deep prejudice against the "Colonization Society" so that the very word "Colonizaton" gives umbrage [page break] but they are gradually getting over it. The civilization movement based on anti slavery principles has taken so well, that there are numbers now wishing to go to Youraba at once. But as this cannot be I have advised them to go to Liberia and I am inclined to think that a great many in the spring will conclude to do so. If at the next annual meeting the Society would take strong ground against the extension of slavery + the re-opening of the foreign slave trade + should have no pro slavery speeches —— it would work a great change in the minds of our intelligent colored population whose minds have lately been awakened to the great inducements of emigration to Africa + have become interested in all that pertains to it. Livingstone's travels have done much, and also Mr Bowen's book and lectures, with other efforts made by [page break] the friends of Africa. I fancy if your friends have had any doubts in regard to the good results of this new civilization movement you may assure them that it has already created more interest in Liberia as well as in Youraba than has ever been entertained before. The cause of African colonization will thus receive an accession of strength which it has long needed, + if matters are prudently managed + the Society should take the true Christian ground against the increase + extension of slavery, either from Africa or elsewhere, it will stand in the estimation on our colored people as it never stood before. A great many of them are watching it closely. Many consider the African Civilization Socy[210] only African Colonization under another name which it really is, except that it professes to be anti slavery.

209. *The African Repository*. Letter 23, Coates to Lugenbeel, October 27, 1855.
210. The African Civilization Society was founded in New York in September 1858. One of its sponsors was the British Free Produce Movement, which promoted products made by free labor. The Society sought to establish a colony in Yoruba (West Africa) where the three Cs— commerce, civilization, and Christianity—could be pursued. It is unclear, however, who deserves credit for the creation of the Society. According to some sources, Benjamin Coates claimed that he formulated the idea for the Society, while others credit Henry Highland Garnet. Garnet seems to have been the highest-ranking officer of the Society, while Coates was only one of several vice presidents. However, soon after the creation of the Society, most elected positions were held by white people. As a result of the lack of black leadership and the position played by Coates, who was tied to the much-hated ACS, many black people, including Douglass, did not trust the organization. Distrust of the Society was not pervasive and many black people were active allies, such as Henry M. Wilson, the pastor of New York City's Seventh Avenue Presbyterian Church. In the first years of its existence, the Society was financially very weak and sent Theodore Bourne, a

Father + sisters are all pretty well + desire to be remembered to yourself + family.

yours very truly Benj. Coates

❖ 37 ❖

Chicago, Jan 31ˢᵗ 1859.

Benj. Coates, Esq,
   Philadelphia,
      My dear friend:
         I received your kind favor of the 27th inst., on Saturday evening,
and on Sunday Morning, yesterday, as we were going to church,[211] or rather
where we go every Sabbath to hear discourses on the "Harmonial Philosophy",
we met a friend of ours bringing those books from the P.office [post office].
The children, on seeing them, were quite delighted; and so, when we returned,
a distribution took place. And in order to extend to them the larges liberty, I
allowed the eldest to divide them. She, Marcellina Melissa,[212] gave to the sister next her in age, Lucilla Eveline, "Africa's Mountain Valley,"[213] and to Henry
Oscar, the next but one, Jⁿᵒ [Jonathan] Henry having died, "The New Republic"[214]—retaining for herself "Abbeokuta."[215] They have already commenced
to read them. Marcellina has a great desire to become a teacher. They all

---

white abolitionist, to England to raise money. There he met Delany, who was not associated with
the Society; Bourne and eventually pressured Delany into an alliance. The goal of a West African
colony declined in importance with the Civil War, and from 1863 to 1867 the Society concentrated
on educating new freed black people. By 1864, Garnet was no longer part of the African Civilization Society. BAP 5:9; Philip S. Foner, *History of Black Americans: From the Compromise of 1850
to the End of the Civil War* (Westport, Conn.: Greenwood Press, 1983), 173–87; Miller, *The Search
for a Black Nationality*, 192, 260–62; Ullman, *Martin R. Delany*, 213–19; Richard MacMaster,
"Henry Highland Garnet and the African Civilization Society," *Journal of Presbyterian History* 48,
no. 2 (Summer 1970): 95–112.

211. The A.M.E. Church on Jackson St. in Chicago is mentioned in Robert L.
Harris, "H. Ford Douglas: Afro-American Antislavery Emigrationist," *Journal of Negro History*
62, no. 3 (July 1977): 223. It is possible that this is the same church.

212. Marcellina M. Wagoner was Martin R. Delany's secretary from 1863 to 1864 as
he worked to recruit black troops for the Union Army. BAP 2:522 n. 3.

213. William Augustine Bernard Johnson (?–1823), *Africa's Mountain Valley, or, the
Church of Regent's Town, West Africa* (London: Seeley, Jackson, and Halliday, 1856). Same title is
also listed as being written by Maria Louisa Charlesworth (1819–1880) and published in 1857.
Coates purchased this book in bulk from Robert Carter and Brothers; the receipt from this purchase is in the Benjamin Coates letters. See Letter 130, Carter to Coates, October 21, 1868.

214. Possibly Helen Cross Knight (1814–1906), *The New Republic*, 2nd ed. (Boston:
Sabbath School Society, 1851).

215. *Abbeokuta; or, sunrise within the tropics: an outline of the origin and progress of the
Yoruba Mission* (New York: R. Carter and Brothers, 1859), was first published by J. Nisbet in

desire me to express to you many thanks for the books. Permit me also to thank you for the kind and flattering expressions which you have been pleased to express for myself. Above all, do I thank you for the deep and abiding interest which you take in the general welfare of that unfortunate people with whom I am identified; and most earnestly and sincerely do I wish you may live to realize and enjoy the fruits of your labor of love towards the African and colored people.- I regret to see expressions, likes those referred to, of my brother, George T. Downing.[216] I have lived long enough to understand how I can differ with my fellow men, and still believe them sincere, honest, earnest friends and brothers. I feel that a greater liberality, charity and brotherly love should characterize all the reformers and and Anti=Slavery men, as theirs are professedly labors of love and good will towards man-

In a previous letter, I hinted something about a commercial college, but upon this subject, I will not now stop to dwell upon, but will speak more upon it hereafter. I can look abroad a discover quite a number of classical scholars and Literary men among us, but of business scholars, which is equally important, I think I see a sad want. If either is to be lacking, a nation or people can get along better without Literary men than without business men. It is an old but true saying, "business before pleasure." But I must close. By the way, we met with rather a sad accident to = day. Late in the afternoon the sparks from the engine set fire to our clothes on the line, which my wife and children had washed early in the morning, being dry at the time, and in a close yard, burned nearly all of them up. No other damage was done. But enough for the present.

Yours truly

H.O Wagoner[217]

London and Robert Carter and Brothers in the United States. By 1858 the sixth edition was in print. Sarah Tucker is listed as the author of some editions.

216. George T. Downing (1819–1903) was born in New York City and attended Hamilton College. From the catering business he established in the 1850s, he became one of the wealthiest black men in America. Like many other black leaders, Downing was suspicious of the ACS and believed that the plan to grow cotton in Africa was an excuse to rid the United States of free black people. Downing's distaste for emigration extended to the African Civilization Society, which he viewed as an outgrowth of the ACS. Downing had little respect for Henry Highland Garnet and wished that he "will not long be entwined in this spool of spurious Coates' cotton." Downing was one of the few black leaders whose opposition to colonization was unwavering. Committed to struggle to improve life for black people in America, between 1856 and 1860 Downing attempted to end segregation in Rhode Island schools. After the Civil War, Downing fought for Reconstruction acts that would advance black equality. Foner, *History of Black Americans*; BAP, vol. 4, 317–18; Richard Blackett, "Martin R. Delany and Robert Campbell: Black Americans in Search of an African Colony," *Journal of Negro History* 62, no. 1 (1977): 1–25.

217. Henry O. Wagoner. Letter 35, Wagoner to Coates, January 8, 1859.

❖ 38 ❖

[Col. Office] N.Y. Feby 9th/59

Friend Benjamin

I am happy to say [Ella]²¹⁸ has been convalescent for a week. She did not recognize me nor speak a word until Agnes²¹⁹ had been home a week. We receive her as if from the dead + gratefully acknowledge the divine mercy in her recovery. It was not of human skill.

Your sister²²⁰ must consider Agnes fatigue as an excuse for not writing to announce the joyful result. Besides constant attendance by day she has sat up two whole nights + has the care of her now all the time.

I have seen the "Anglo African"²²¹ but have been so pressed for time as scarcely to have looked into the [members]. I intended to notice it in this Months Journal but could not.

I will send the Journal to Meyers,²²² but am sorry he allowed Bourne to draw out from [him] an attack upon Delaney.²²³ I fear the idea of himself or his Brother going to Yoruba,²²⁴ has had an influence on his mind.

218. Ella was Pinney's wife. She was sick with rheumatism much of her life. See Letter 153, Pinney to Coates, March 26, 1869.

219. Agnes was one of Pinney's daughters.

220. Coates had three sisters: Beulah, Mary, and Sarah. It is not clear to which sister Pinney refers.

221. The *Anglo-African Magazine* was started by Thomas Hamilton in January 1859 and, although it ran for only fifteen issues, was considered to be the best black periodical. It was published monthly in New York until March 1860, when Hamilton was forced to stop publication due to financial difficulties. While the magazine existed, frequent writers included Martin Delany, J. T. Holly, Frances Ellen Watkins (Harper), J. C. Pennington, and J. M. Smith. While Hamilton initially intended to pay those who wrote for the magazine, he was unable to do this. He also published the *Anglo-African* weekly news sheet from July 23, 1859, to March 1861. Bullock, *The Afro-American Periodical Press*, 57–66; Armistead S. Pride and Clint C. Wilson II, *A History of the Black Press* (Washington, D.C.: Howard University Press, 1997), 46–47.

222. Jonathan J. Myers was a Wisconsin businessman who was part of a group of black people from the area who expressed interest in returning to Africa. In 1858 he met with Delany, and later Myers's group and a group of black people in Chatham, Canada, commissioned Delany and his Niger Valley Exploring Party. In 1859, when Delany and Bourne were in England, Myers was there with his son, but he was not there for the purpose of abolition or emigration. Myers never emigrated to Africa, but he might have gone to Haiti. Miller, *The Search for A Black Nationality*, 171–82, 218, 231.

223. Martin R. Delany.

224. Yoruba was mainly used as a geographical term defined by a language group of West African tribes. Generally, the area was defined to be east and south of the Niger River and slightly east of Lagos. Most of what was then considered Yoruba is now Nigeria. The Yoruba area consisted of three zones. The coastal area was twelve miles wide and was swampland. The plains area was forty miles wide and contained rain forest. The interior plateau had trees and grasslands, depending on the location. The major crops of the area included yams, maize, bananas, cassava,

I have not seen Ruffin[225] attack. Where does he live? I should like to see it. I think he will be ready to say "quits" + acknowledge he caught a "Tartar"[226] Agnes + my wife desire kind remembrance to yourself + sisters. Agnes threatens to finish her visit in Phil[a] "next spring". I doubt. This morning we have news of Dr Goble[227] death! How sudden! He was in fine health with us at Washington + now summond to judgment. We are but shadows + have no [abiding city here]. With much love I am truly yr obliged friend
J.B. Pinney.[228]

---

coco-yams, beans, pumpkins, and peppers. Prior to European and American settlement, this was one of the most urban parts of Africa. Eva Krapf-Askari, *Yoruba Towns and Cities* (Oxford, England: Clarendon Press, 1969), 1–6, 177 map; Daryll Forde, *The Yoruba-Speaking Peoples of South-Western Nigeria* (London: International African Institute, 1969), 1–15.

225. Edmund Ruffin (January 5, 1794–1865) was a Southern plantation owner, best known early in his lifetime for his work on restoring the agricultural potential of Virginia soil with a marl-fertilizer combination. Later he was known as one of the South's greatest advocates for secession. When only one Southern state threatened to leave the Union during the crisis in 1850, Ruffin was disappointed. He firmly believed that black people were inferior to white people and that their natural state was slavery, though he did not use the Bible to justify this belief. He believed that Liberia was poorly run and opposed the spending of federal and state money on the ACS and Liberia. In 1858, he published a pamphlet, "African Colonization Unveiled," which was one of the few pamphlets maligning the ACS. Ruffin knew of Coates, but the two probably never met. In his diary, which he kept from 1856 until his death, Ruffin mentions receiving two pamphlets from Coates on February 1, 1859. One of the pamphlets was Coates's *Cotton Cultivation in Africa* and the other was probably written by Alexander Crummell. On February 18 Coates is mentioned again; this time Ruffin has received two pamphlets from Coates, both written by black people. Ruffin writes that he will send Coates pamphlets from the other side. As to be expected, these pamphlets had little effect on Ruffin. Though he was nearly seventy when the Civil War began, Ruffin fired the first shot at Fort Sumter. When the South lost the Civil War in 1865, Ruffin committed suicide. William Scarborough, ed., *The Diary of Edmund Ruffin*, vol. 1 (Baton Rouge: Louisiana State University Press, 1972), xvii–xlii, 266–307.

226. "A person who on being attacked proved to be too strong for his assailant; especially in the phrase 'to catch a tartar.'" *Webster's New International Dictionary*, 2nd ed., ed. William Allan Neilson (Springfield, Mass.: G. and C. Merriam Company, 1934).

227. Coates refers to Dr. Goble in a letter written to McLain. Goble appears to have been the secretary of the ACS.

228. John Brooke Pinney. Letter 22, Coates to Gurley, June 15, 1855.

❖ 39 ❖

Columbia Feby 24/59

Benjamin Coates Eq
    Philad^d.
      Dear Sir
          Your very interesting letter of the 22^d inst is rec^d. and for the approval you have given of my letter to Miss Griffiths[229] you will please accept my thanks.
          I ought ere this have acknowledged the receipt of your very interesting pamphlet on the subject of "Cotton,"[230] and if there is any merit in my letter it wholly belongs to you, for without it the letter would not have been written. I have ever been anxious that my race should be [redeemed] from the influence of prejudice & Slavery, both physically + mentally, and my object in writing that letter was to dispel as far as in my power some of the mental prejudices of our people against Africa, and every thing Afr relating to the future improvement of our race, through the agency of African instrumentalities.
          I did contemplate following up the subject with one or two more letters, but perhaps it is best to defer for the present,
          I will however not [withhold] from you the fact, that your <u>practical</u> consistency as a man,—a phlanthopist + Christian on the whole subject of the

229. Whipper is probably referring to Martha Griffith (Browne), but it is unclear how the two knew of each other. Griffith was born somewhere in Kentucky to a slave-holding family. She came to oppose slavery, freed the family's six slaves, and helped them settle in Ohio. She wrote *Autobiography of a Female Slave* (New York: Redfield, 1856) and another abolitionist work. Partly because of her publications, Griffith was forced to leave Kentucky in the mid-1850s; she settled in Philadelphia. She was a member of the Garrisonian movement and toured Great Britain in 1860 to raise money for the cause before relocating again to Boston. In 1867 she married Albert Gallatin Brown. Griffith Browne died in 1906. *BAP* 1:480.

230. In 1858 Coates published his pamphlet, *Cotton Cultivation in Africa*. Coates's argument extends for twenty-one pages and is followed by thirty pages of testimony. Coates contends that Southern slavery will end when it ceases to be profitable. He notes that cotton plant is more productive in Africa and that free labor there is cheaper than American slave labor. Therefore, cotton can be produced less expensively in Africa and could flood the English market. In addition to cotton, Coates suggests that coffee and rice can be grown in Africa at a lower cost to the consumer. Coates mentions in his pamphlet that though American black people are needed in Africa for the success of the project of cotton cultivation, no more than one-tenth of the black population in the United States would be encouraged to emigrate. Finally, Coates cites Liberia as an example of what a nation in Africa could accomplish. The testimony in the pamphlet includes a letter from a Mr. Clegg describing his experience growing cotton in Abeokuta, Nigeria; an address by Mr. Campbell, the British consul at Lagos; Dr. Livingstone's testimony; a letter from Reverend Alexander Crummell; and a description of the efforts made by President Benson.

future welfare of the Colored race, has commanded my regard and esteem for a number of years,

I am familiar with all your public efforts as well as the munificence of your private patrony of the various objects in operation for our improvement. As a people we have been cradled in dishonor & cannot soon be raised to glory.

If we could become more tolerant in disposition, we might possibly sooner be able to see eye to eye, and be as one man united in a single cause for the overthrow of those evils from which we suffer.

I have not time at present to branch of on these subjects, but I expect to be in the city in a few days, when I shall avail myself of the privilege of visiting you.

With the hope that you may live to see your long cherished hopes blossom like the rose I remain yours truly

Wm Whipper[231]

❖ ❖ ❖

State Agricultural Rooms
Wisconsin Farmer
————o————
published Monthly by
Powers & Hoyt
Madison, Wisconsin
————o————
$1,00 per anuum
D. J. Powers J. W. Hoyt[232]

❖ 40 ❖

Madison, Wis.,[233] March 2 1859.

My dear sir:

I am in receipt of your very polite letter and essay on the "[growing] of Cotton in Africa"[234]—for both of which I thank you. I have also recived

231. William Whipper. Letter 35, Wagoner to Coates, January 8, 1859.
232. This letter is written on *Wisconsin Farmer* letterhead.
233. Address is printed on paper as part of the letterhead.
234. *Cultivation of Cotton in Africa.* Letter 39, Whipper to Coates, February 24, 1859.

through Washington (hence the day) the report of Dr. Hodgkin.[235] The Doctor was formerly if I do not mistake—a lecturer at Guy's Hospital London—where I recived my proffessional education. Therefore his name, character and status are all familiar to me. How strangely linked do we at times—find our efforts to do good—and the pupil after the labre of more than a quarter of a century—following the lessons of humanity as one end of the world—which were taught him as the other. My proffession I have already told you—by birth and education I am an Englishman—by practice—I have sought to do good to humanity of every grade and color—simply because in this only and in the quiet worship of God do I find any real pleasure. In my native town in England—it was my happiness to do a great amount of good—in building —— —— works—or rather in originating them—schools, churches and chapels followed. The Friends—Misses Lloyd + Houstin connections of the Gurneys—well always my aids. Here—I have sought to build up a Medical School—we have none in the state.[236] We are only waiting funds. Our organization is complete. I am also trying to get a Hospital for the poor built—and have succeeding in obtaining a grant of two valuable lots from the city—and may when the times are better—be able to build. I have been for several years president of a charitable society—for the English poor.—and the poor and the rich have just returned me a third term—as their alderman for the ward in which I live—and this without a single opposing voice—from party

235. Thomas Hodgkin (1798–1866) was a London physician and a Quaker. He became a reformer in 1830 and was a member of the British African Colonization Society and the Aborigine's Protection Society. In 1833 he wrote a pamphlet defending the ACS. The report to which Hobbins refers is probably Hodgkin's response on behalf of the Royal Geographical Society. In 1858 J. S. Myers and Ambrose Dudley wrote a letter to Hobbins. They wanted to know what location in Africa was best for settling freed slaves. Martin Delany attached his name to the letter shortly before it was sent. Hobbins received the letter and forwarded it to the Royal Geographical Society in London. Hodgkin answered the letter, and his response was also sent to the President of Liberia, Benson, and Thomas Clegg. Hodgkin suggested the Niger Valley area in West Africa and within the year Delany and Robert Campbell set off on the Niger Valley Exploring Party. (Louis Rosenfeld, *Thomas Hodgkini* (Lanham, Md.: Madison Books, 1993); Richard Blackett, "Martin R. Delany and Robert Campbell: Black Americans in Search of an African Colony," *Journal of Negro History* 62, no. 1 (January 1977): 1–25.

236. Though the Wisconsin state legislature passed a bill in 1848 that would have allowed a medical school, the state had no formal medical training until the 1890s. Judith Walzer Leavitt, "A Note on Medical Education in Wisconsin," in *Wisconsin Medicine: Historical Perspectives*, ed. Ronald L. Numbers and Judith Walzer Leavitt, 186–87 (Madison: University of Wisconsin Press, 1981).

or person. Such is my course—and I write this—that you may at all times—depend upon my cooperation in any good work.

Yours very truly

Joseph Hobbins[237]

❖ 41 ❖

New York

April 27. 1859

Benjamin Coates Esqr

I thank you for your last kind letter and also for "Life at three Score"[238] an excellent book—interesting to all, and especially to a man at the age of two score, and four.

Mr Bourne[239] has never at <u>anytime</u> shown me a letter from you relating to the subject which has of late been so much in our minds—and of course I feel a delicacy in asking him to do so. The Board[240] have anonimously acceded to his wishes regarding the change, and the mission to England, only one thing remaining to be done, that is the selection of a presiding officers. I now look upon the turn of things as being beyond our control, and we can do, is to let them go, and endevour to regulate them. As Mr Bourne will go to England I think your advice as to his best course there will be useful.

237. Joseph Hobbins (January 24, 1816–December 26, 1894) was a pioneering Madison surgeon born and educated in England. Hobbins moved to Massachusetts in 1841 and returned to England three years later. In 1854 he relocated to Madison, Wisconsin, with his family, where he remained until his death. In addition to his medical practice, Hobbins was active as a member of the Madison Horticultural Society, the Madison Society for the Prevention of Cruelty to Animals, and the Madison Literary Club. Hobbins supported the Union during the Civil War, but he was not notably active as an abolitionist. Guenter B. Risse, "From Horse and Buggy to Automobile and Telephone: Medical Practice in Wisconsin, 1848–1894," in *Wisconsin Medicine: Historical Perspectives*, ed. Ronald L. Numbers and Judith Walzer Leavitt (Madison: University of Wisconsin Press, 1981); Reuben Gold Thwaites, *Joseph Hobbins, MD* (Madison, Wis.: Madison Literary Club, 1894).

238. *Life at Three Score* was originally a sermon by Albert Barnes delivered in the First Presbyterian Church in Philadelphia on November 28, 1858. It was later published and went through at least three editions. Among other things, it emphasized the value of temperance.

239. Reverend Theodore Bourne. See Letter 38, Pinney to Coates, February 9, 1859, and other Garnet letters.

240. Garnet is probably referring to the board of the African Civilization Society. In February 1859, the board was made up of eighteen members. Ten of the board members were black, including Garnet, Henry M. Wilson, and Robert Hamilton. The eight white members included Theodore and Francis Bourne and Isaac T. Smith. At least three of the white members were also members of the New York State Colonization Society. *BAP* 5:10.

Also D Smith DD[241] is selected by the Board as a suitable person to take the chair—He is a man of great influence—and what may be called a judicious abolitionist. We are making arrangments for our anniversary—Theo. L Cuyler[242]—J.S Martin[243]—Dr J.B Smith.[244] Also D Smith DD—and another person are engaged to speak, and we confidently expect to have the assistance of Henry Ward Beecher.[245] We shall take the Church of the Puritans[246] or the Cooper Institution. Will you come on, and be with us. We hope to take our stand at once, among the first class institutions of the land. Every day our cause moves onward. The anniversary will take place on the 11th of May. I believe God is with us, and he will overule all for our good, and his own glory.

I am yours truly

Henry Highland Garnet

241. "DD" was the abbreviation for Doctor of Divinity.

242. Theodore Ledyard Cuyler (January 10, 1822–February 26, 1909) was involved in the abolitionist movement. His father, who died when Cuyler was four years old, was Gerrit Smith's roommate at Hamilton College. Cuyler came to support temperance at a young age and founded the National Temperance Society much later, in 1865. He worked as a minister in New York City for much of his life, and he was close friends with Henry Ward Beecher, preaching at his church on at least one occasion. Theodore Ledyard Cuyler, *Recollections of a Long Life* (New York: Baker and Taylor, 1902); and *ANB* 5:143.

243. John Sella Martin (1832–1876) was born a slave and, despite being sold eight times between 1838 and 1856, he learned to read and write at an early age. Around 1856 he settled in Chicago and met Henry Ford Douglass and Mary Ann Shadd Cary. He soon moved to Detroit and became a Baptist minister. In 1859 he moved to Boston where he came to support slave revolts and the African Civilization Society. In 1861 he made the first of several trips to Great Britain, where he encouraged British support for the Union. He worked as a minister in London for two years and then returned to the United States, where he worked as the minister for the First Colored Presbyterian Church in New York City. He returned to England as a member of the AMA soon after. In 1868 Martin settled in Washington, D.C., as pastor of the 15th Street Presbyterian Church. For the next several years he struggled with financial difficulties and an addiction to opium and laudanum. He committed suicide in 1876. *BAP* 5:68–69; *ANB* vol. 14.

244. Joshua B. Smith (1813–1879) was born in Coatesville, Pennsylvania. He attended school with the help of a local Quaker woman. He moved to Boston in 1836 and started a restaurant there thirteen years later. Allying himself with William Lloyd Garrison, he became the vice president of the New England Freedom Association. He fought to desegregate Boston public schools, became the first black Freemason in St. Andrew's Lodge, and was elected to the state senate in 1873. When Smith died, he was still in debt as a result of the Civil War. *BAP*.

245. Henry Ward Beecher (June 24, 1813–March 8, 1887) was the son of Lyman Beecher and the brother of Harriet Beecher Stowe. He graduated from Amherst College in 1834 and became a minister. He protested the Fugitive Slave Law and was involved with sending guns to Kansas. He became an active supporter of the Republican Party, and during the Civil War he spoke in England to prevent English support for the South. In 1872 he was accused of adultery and the civil trial resulted in a hung jury. The event split the family apart. In addition to his activity as an abolitionist, Beecher believed in the compatibility between religion and science. *BAP* 1:486; *ANB* 2:467.

246. The Church of the Puritans was located in New York City.

❖ 42 ❖

Rochester. May 2ᵈ 1859

Benjamin Coates Esqr:

My dear Sir: [It would] give me great pleasure to be present at the
sixth annual examination of the classes of the Institute for Colored Youth[247]
on Wednesday and if it were a week later I should certainly endeavor to be
there—but as matters now stand the thing is impossible. I have been quite
busy for the past two weeks in the preparation of a eulogy upon the late Hon.
William Jay[248]—which, I am to deliver in New York on the 12ᵗʰ in Mr Garnets
Church,[249] this, with other engagements—which could not be postponed, has
prevented my looking into the large volumes you—were good enough to send

247. While public schools for white students were founded as early as 1818, there were
no similar schools for black students until 1820. In 1832 Richard Humphreys, a Quaker, left
$10,000 for a school for black children. With these funds, the ICY, a co-ed school, was estab-
lished in Philadelphia in 1837. Alfred Cope was treasurer of the corporation that ran the school
and Ebenezer Bassett was one of its early principals. Under Bassett, black leaders such as Henry
Highland Garnet, Alexander Crummell, and Frederick Douglass were invited to speak to the students. In 1863 the school became a center for recruiting black soldiers, and many of the Institute's
students enlisted. During Reconstruction many graduates moved South to teach newly freed
black people. In 1903 the ICY moved and became Cheyney State University. *BAP* 4:353–54; Eliza
Cope Harrison, *For Emancipation and Education: Some Black and Quaker Efforts, 1680–1900* (Philadelphia: Awbury Arboretum Association, 1997); Charlene Conyers, *A Living Legend: The History
of Cheyney University, 1837–1951* (Cheyney: Cheyney University Press, 1990).

248. William Jay (June 16, 1789–October 14, 1858) was the son of John Jay. William Jay
studied law, though he never practiced. In 1818 he became a Westchester, New York, County
Judge, a position he held until 1843, when pro-slavery democrats had him removed. He supported
the abolition of the slave trade in Washington, D.C., and helped fund the New York City Anti-
Slavery Society. A pamphlet he wrote in 1835 rejected colonization and supported immediate
emancipation. *ANB* 10:11–12; Staudenraus, *The African Colonization Movement*, 228.

249. Henry Highland Garnet became the pastor of New York's Shiloh Presbyterian
Church (originally called First Colored Presbyterian Church) in September 1856, following the
tenure of Samuel Cornish and Theodore Wright. Garnet used the church to support various abolitionist activities, including the underground railroad. In October 1858 Garnet organized black
speakers to promote a reading room, which lasted until June 1860. In 1861 Garnet had trouble with
the trustees of the church, and when he went to England to raise money they closed the church
and removed him from his position. Eventually it was agreed that Garnet would retain his job
and that Reverend John Gloucester would be pastor in Garnet's absence. During the Civil War,
the church was used to recruit soldiers and to raise money for black people who had been freed
during the war. Garnet also reopened the Religious and Literary Reading room. Although the
board of trustees, who disapproved of Garnet's activities, then resigned in protest, Garnet continued his activities until the church was destroyed in 1863 during the New York City draft
riots. Schor, *Henry Highland Garnet*; "Garnet, Henry Highland," in *African-American Culture and
History*, vol. 2, ed. Jack Salzman, David Lionel Smith, and Cornell West, 1087–89 (New York:
Macmillan Library Reference, 1996); Miller, *The Search for A Black Nationality*, 82, 191.

me last week. The discourse of Dr. Barnes[250] I read at once—and with sincere satisfaction—A real good and Cheerful old man—just such an one as we all may wish to be when we reach, if we ever reach, his advanced age.

You are right in attributing to me the favorable notice of Doctor Barth's Travels[251]—I stand where I have stood for several years on the subject of Africa—deprecating any public and general movements of the free colored people of this country towards Africa—and yet glad to see [individual] efforts— whether commercial—argicultural or Missionary for the development of the resources of the country.

I have laid aside your letters to read on my return from New York— as also the volumes you have kindly sent me. I am much obliged by your continued favors in this line—but if you give me these Books with any other purpose than to place in my way the means of an intelligent understanding of Africa and the various enterprises having reference to it—I fear that you will loose your patience with me. I am no nearer to the African Civilization Society[252] than several months ago—I have not time to go into the reasons why—nor indeed, is it necessary. My reasons wise or foolish have been repeatedly stated—and I am willing to let them stand.

Very glad I should be to see—you, & should it be in my power— I may run down to Philadelphia from the meeting in New York, and call upon you.

250. Albert Barnes (December 1, 1798–December 24, 1870), was a Presbyterian pastor. He wrote several pamphlets about the relationship between slavery and Christianity, including "An Inquiry into the Scriptural Views of Slavery" in 1846 and "The Church and Slavery" in 1857. Though he was an early supporter of the ACS, he never became a member and came to believe that the Fugitive Slave Law was in direct conflict with the Bible. He was troubled by ill health after 1852 and died in Philadelphia. *ANB* 2:128.

251. *Travels and Discoveries in North and Central Africa* (New York: Harper and Row, 1857) was written by Heinrich Barth (1821–1865). Barth was born in Hamburg, Germany, and attended the University of Berlin. In 1848 he joined a British-sponsored exploration of Africa lead by James Richardson, a member of the British and Foreign Anti-Slavery Society. Adolf Overweg, who was also German, was the third member of the expedition. The goal of the mission was to suppress the slave trade and to encourage other trades. The three arrived in Africa in 1850 and stayed for five years. Barth, who traveled more than 10,000 miles, was the only member of the team to survive. In 1855 he returned in England and spent three years writing his five-volume work, which was published in both German and English. He then returned to Germany, where he was a professor of geography at the University of Berlin until 1863. Helen Delpar, *The Discoverers: An Encyclopedia of Explorers and Exploration* (New York: McGraw-Hill Book Company, 1980), 75.

252. African Civilization Society. Letter 36, Coates to Gurley, January 13, 1859.

I have no one associated with me ~~kn~~ now in my paper—and have the work to do myself so that I cannot so easily leave as when Watkins[253] was with me.

Very Truly Yours

With Respect and Esteem

Frederick Douglass

❖ 43 ❖

Chicago, May 27/59

Benj. Coates Esq

    My dear friend:

       I only snatch as much of my pressed time from business matters as will serve to apologize + acknowledge the receipt of the package of valuable books and papers which you have been so kind as to send me; to take this opportunity of thanking you for the same.

       The package directed to H.F. Douglass,[254] I delivered to his family, as he was not at home at the time, nor has he been home since.

       Be assured, my dear friend, that I will give as much attention to the perusal of those books and papers, from time to time, as are correspondent with a proper digestion of the same. I say this, because I think I feel the force

---

253. William Watkins (1801–1858) was born free in Baltimore. In 1820, he established his own school for black children. He was an opponent of colonization as early as 1826 and a founding member of the American Moral Reform Society, though he left the organization two years later. He wrote several articles in black newspapers using the pseudonym "A Colored Baltimorean." He was also an associate editor for the *Frederick Douglass' Paper* for several years until he left for Toronto in the late 1840s. As a result of the increasing hardship for American black people in the years preceding the Civil War, Watkins began to alter his anti-emigration stance and became an agent for the Haitian emigration movement. From Canada he occasionally wrote articles under the name "A Colored Canadian" until his death. BAP 3:96–97; Miller, *The Search for a Black Nationality*, 243.

254. Hezekiah Ford Douglas (1831–1865) was born into slavery in Virginia, but he escaped in 1846. Douglas was a self-educated man who mastered many fields of study, particularly the Bible, and became a talented orator. He was an influential figure in the convention movement and was appointed to the National Board of Commissioners at the 1856 National Convention. Douglas believed that the Constitution was a pro-slavery document and that he, and other African Americans, owed no allegiance to the United States. In the mid-1850s he moved to Chicago, where he became co-proprietor of the *Provincial Freeman*, Mary Ann Shadd Cary's newspaper. He fulfilled some editorial duties but served primarily as a lecturer. He moved to Canada for about two years, and heralded it as the place from which slavery could be attacked, but by late 1858 he had returned to Chicago and became an agent for the Central American Land Company. This is what he was likely doing at the time of the writing of this letter to Coates. BAP 2:18, 337–38 n.; Foner, *History of Black Americans*, 144, 157, 160; Harris, "H. Ford Douglas," 94–95.

of the truth, that "Many read, but few understand." Granting this to be so, then may the spirit of Him who promulgated this <u>truth</u>, or thought, help me, and humble individual, to understand, and therefore, read to acceptance, and a proper appreciation of what <u>is</u> <u>truth</u>, calling us to <u>action</u>

Your friend + Bro

H O Wagoner[255]

❖ 44 ❖

[256]Cleaveland June 7/59

Mr Benjamin Coates
        Philanthropist
     Respected Sir
        Having made your accuaintance by the letter published in Douglas' Paper[257] and still more thoroughly by the pamphlet on "Cotton in Africa"[258] sent to C H. [Targoton] of this Office.[259] We are very desirous to know if you simpathise with us and approve the movement in which we have enlisted your views, should we be so fortunate as to receive them. will have their due influence on the minds of our friends

I am Sir

Your appreciative an obt servant

J D Harris[260]

255. Henry O. Wagoner. Letter 35, Wagoner to Coates, January 8, 1859.

256. Enclosed with Harris's letter is a document from the Central America Land Company detailing the establishment of a colony for black Americans in Central America. The flier includes quotes from Blair, Doolittle, King, Gerrit Smith, Horace Greeley, and Rev. J. Theodore Holly. The list of officers of the organization includes President Joseph Wilson, Secretary Justin Holland, Treasurer F. H. Morris, and Agents and Commissioners J. Denis Harris, H. Ford Douglass, and R. A. Harper. Also included is a blank share for the Central America Land Company with a face value of $50.

257. *The North Star.* Letter 3, Coates to Douglass, June 27, 1850.

258. *Cultivation of Cotton in Africa.* Letter 39, Whipper to Coates, February 24, 1859.

259. The Central American Land Company is considered by many to be the brainchild of Francis Blair Jr. and his family. Blair, a congressman from Missouri, believed that sending black people to Central America would solve the race problem in America and end slavery, and he presented his idea to Congress in 1858. It is not clear if Blair or Harris is responsible for the foundation of the organization, but it was established in the summer of 1859. Various supporters of the company included J. Theodore Holly, James M. Whitfield, Alfred V. Thompson, and H. Ford Douglass. Harris and Douglass were also agents of the group. The plan failed when the government of Guatemala, the preferred location for the settlement, declared that only white emigrants were welcome. Foner, *History of Black Americans*; Miller, *The Search for a Black Nationality*.

260. J. Denis Harris was a black plasterer from Cleveland. Harris supported the emigration movement and made his debut as a black leader in 1858 at the Ohio convention, where he

❖ 45 ❖

Windsor[261] June 14/59

Mr Coats

Please inform me from what source I can obtain correct information [relating] to Africa I know two or three enterprising colored persons who are desirous of going there as teach and business men They are capable and upright and ~~while~~ yet they do not feel willing to accept the offering presented by the American Colonization Society,[262] any information which you will give will be most gratefully rewd [reward] by myself and husband[263] together with many others

Yours respectfully M E Bibb Cary[264]

---

argued against Day's anti-emigration resolution. The following year Harris became a lecturer for the Ohio State Anti-Slavery Society. In conjunction with Congressman Francis Blair Jr., Harris formed the Central American Land Company in an effort to start a black nation in Central America. When the organization failed, Harris came to support Jamaican emigration. In 1860 he went to the Dominican Republic; his book *Summer on the Borders of the Caribbean Sea* (New York: A. B. Burdick, 1860) describes his experiences on Hispaniola and the history of the island. Miller, *The Search for a Black Nationality.*

261. Windsor, Canada West, is located in what is now the province of Ontario, directly across the Detroit River from Detroit, Michigan.

262. The ACS provided transportation for free black people to Liberia. Many black people, however, did not support the ACS, believing that the organization's white membership was merely attempting to protect slavery by deporting free black people, who could be seen as a threat to the institution of slavery. Exactly what is meant here by "the offering presented by" the ACS is unclear; it may simply refer to an offer for transportation to Liberia.

263. Isaac N. Cary (?–1874) was Bibb Cary's second husband (Henry Bibb having been the first). Isaac Cary supported Haitian emigration. He was Mary Ann Shadd Cary's brother-in-law, and he worked for a time on her paper, the *Provincial Freeman. BAP* 2: 380 n.

264. Mary Elizabeth Miles Bibb Cary (1820–1877) was born in Rhode Island to Quaker parents. She married abolitionist Henry Bibb in 1848, and the two moved to Canada West in 1850 after the Fugitive Slave Law was passed. There the couple worked for the Refugee Home Society and from 1851 to 1853 published the *Voice of the Fugitive.* They fought bitterly with Mary Ann Shadd Cary and her paper the *Provincial Freeman.* Shadd Cary opposed plans for black self-isolation, such as those of the Refugee Home Society (which provided land for fugitive slaves, thus forming separate black communities). Shadd Cary also opposed seeking support from white people (or "begging" as it was termed). Bibb Cary was a founding member of the Anti-Slavery Society of Windsor, served as the corresponding secretary of the Refugee Home Society, was an officer at the 1854 National Emigration Convention held in Cleveland, and ran a private school in Windsor. *BAP* 2:110–11 n.; Robin W. Winks, *Blacks in Canada* (New Haven: Yale University Press, 1971), 205–6, 261.

❖ 46 ❖

Address Detroit Michigan
New York June 16th. 1859

Benj[n] Coates Esqr
  My Dear Sir,
      I am this morning in my office just returned from Geneva,[265] where on Tuesday evening I attended the wedding of of friend H.M. Schiffelin.[266]
      I will try today to have the order for Blackledge filled up.
      Do impress upon him and others in Liberia the folly of invoicing articles sent to our market so high. I doubles their duties + does no good.
      As to Green[267] I have heard of him for two years past as an arrant importer and presume rumor does not —— him In great haste
your truly
      J.B. Pinney[268]

[Written along left side of page:]
I shall by less than $40.

265. Geneva, New York, is located near the finger lakes in the western part of the state. It was incorporated in 1806 and is the site of Geneva College, where Elizabeth Blackwell became the first woman to attend medical school in 1849. A number of citizens of Geneva were also active in the abolitionist movement. James Duffin organized the Geneva Anti-Slavery Society and the Geneva Moral and Mental Improvement Society. He later emigrated to Haiti with his family and other Geneva black people, but he soon returned to New York. http://www.geneva.ny.us/community/historty.html; BAP 4:400.

266. Henry Maunsell Schieffelin made his fortune as part of the pharmaceutical firm W. H. Schieffelin and Fowler. He was a member, and sometime president, of the New York Colonization Society. When Edward Blyden asked him to finance a mission to explore the interior of Liberia, Schieffelin agreed, supporting Benjamin Anderson for more than a year. Schieffelin later encouraged Blyden to come to the United States to recruit students for Liberia College and to encourage emigration. Lynch, 48; Livingston, *Education and Race*, 129; *The Pharmaceutical Era*, vol. 1 (New York: D. O. Haynes and Company, 1887), 26.

267. Green may have been Augustus Green or Beriah Green.

268. John Brooke Pinney. Letter 8, Coates to McLain, May 16, 1851.

❖ 47 ❖

Freetown, Sierra Leone,[269]
July 14. 1859.

Benj. Coates, Esqr.
        Respected Friend,
                I take this opportunity of informing you that we[270]
have arrived [thus] far on our journey. This evening we depart hence, and after
stopping at Cape Palmas,[271] Cape Coast Castle[272] + Acra[273] we ~~will~~ expect to
be at Lagos[274] about the 22nd instant. We have had a very pleasant voyage.[275]

269. Freetown, the capital of Sierra Leone, was founded in 1792 as a colony for "freed slaves, Nova Scotians, Maroons and liberated Africans." At the time of his writing this letter, Campbell was traveling on the *Ethiope*, which had sailed from England and reached Freetown on July 12. Cyril P. Foray, ed., *Historical Dictionary of Sierra Leone* (Metuchen, N.J.: Scarecrow Press, 1985), 75; Miller, *The Search for a Black Nationality*, 207.

270. It is unclear as to whom this refers, because he would not yet have met up with Martin Delany.

271. Located on the southern tip of Liberia. Cape Palmas was a repatriation settlement sponsored by the Maryland Colonization Society. When he reached Cape Palmas, Campbell met with Alexander Crummell. *Historical Dictionary of Liberia*; Miller, *The Search for a Black Nationality*, 207.

272. Cape Coast was the British headquarters on the Gold Coast from 1664 to 1877. The Cape Coast Castle was a fort first built in 1652 by the Swedes, then in 1664 the British continued the project, building most of the structure that Campbell refers to. Daniel Miles McFarland, ed., *Historical Dictionary of Ghana* (Metuchen, N.J.: Scarecrow Press, 1985), 59–60.

273. Accra, an "important trade center during the Atlantic Slave trade era," located in the Gold Coast Colony, ninety miles east of Cape Coast. McFarland, *Historical Dictionary of Ghana*, 15.

274. A Yoruba town that was ceded to the British in 1861 by King Dosumu. A. Oyewole, ed., *Historical Dictionary of Nigeria* (Metuchen, N.J.: Scarecrow Press, 1987), 185.

275. Campbell was traveling to Yoruba to meet Martin Delany for the latter's Niger Valley Exploring Party. One group that supported the trip was made up of the Chatham, Canada West–based William Day, Isaac Shadd, and George Brodie. In their words, the purpose of the expedition "is to make a Topographical, Geological and Geographical Examination of the Valley of the River Niger . . . and an inquiry into the state of Africa . . . without any reference to any Emigration there as such. Provided, however, that nothing in this instrument be so construed as to interfere with the right of the Commissioners to negotiate in their own behalf." Despite these words, there was little doubt that the interests of Delany and Campbell lay primarily in examining the possibilities for emigration to the region. Delany, who had earlier opposed emigration to Africa, still opposed Liberia in 1859 due to its association with the white-run ACS. Historian Richard Blackett suggests that the works of Thomas Bowen and David Livingstone, with which Benjamin Coates was very familiar, may have had a strong influence on Delany's opinions of Africa. Ullman, *Martin R. Delany*, 217; Blackett, "Martin R. Delany and Robert Campbell," 3–4.

Bathurst on the Gambia[276] is the only other African port at which we have stopped since our departure It is a far better place than this. The American consul told me that he has not known of a case of fever for over six months. The white settlers are few, and the others are all natives. The Gambia is navigable for 600 miles for very large vessels. The steamer Dover, a vessel large enough to have crossed the Atlantic is now used by the Government for on the River which it assends to that distance. The exports are ground nuts, + hides. Ten or a dozen enterprising intelligent colored Americans settling at Bathurst, and at McCarthy's Island[277] a little further up the River would do well if engaged only in the cultivation of produce for supplying the foreigners and the garrison, (soldiers natives) besides contributing largely to the civilization of the people. I have am taking a few notes of the places at which we stop which I shall sent to the N [American] for publication as soon as possible after arriving at Lagos. I informed you in my last I think that the British Government has furnished us its direct protection, and also gave me free passage to Lagos. I have now in my possession a dispatch from Lord Malmesbury[278] to Lieut. Lodder the Acting Consul[279] in place of Consul Campbell, deceased, with instructions respecting us [A] copy of this and also some details respecting our work since I left America I shall also forward in my letter to the N.A. That fearful pestilence the yellow fever has is mading dreadful havoc among the Europeans at this place. In little more than two months forty five out of 90 or 100 white inhabitants have died. Six Roman Catholic Clergymen from France who arrived here a short time since have —— one died with two or three days of each other. The natives too have been troubled with the small pox.
Your sincere friend Robt Campbell[280]

276. Bathurst, located on the Island of St. Mary's, at the head of the Gambia River, was founded in 1816. The capital of Gambia during British rule, Bathurst served to control access to the River. Harry A. Gailey, ed., *Historical Dictionary of the Gambia* (Metuchen, N.J.: Scarecrow Press, 1987), 37–38.
277. Known as Lemain Island in the eighteenth century, the British renamed the island when they claimed it in 1823. It became their primary "enclave in the interior." Georgetown was the primary settlement on the island. Gailey, *Historical Dictionary of the Gambia*, 99.
278. James Howard Harris (March 25, 1807–May 17, 1889) was the third earl of Malmesbury, became a member of the House of Lords in 1841, and became the English foreign secretary in 1852. While in England, Campbell obtained letters of introduction from influential Englishmen, such as Malmesbury. Upon his arrival in Lagos, Campbell presented Malmesbury's request that the British consul offer him "your advice and assistance in the selection of such a situation as shall by its fertility be calculated to meet their [the exploration party's] wishes." Miller, *The Search for a Black Nationality*, 208; *ANB* vol. 9.
279. Edward F. Lodder.
280. Robert Campbell, born in Jamaica, was teaching at the ICY in Philadelphia at the time he was enlisted for Martin Delany's Niger Valley Exploring Party. Because Benjamin

❖ 48 ❖

23 Bible House
New York
July 17.1859

Benj.ⁿ Coates Esqr
 My dear friend.
 This day I enter upon my temporary duties of probis secrty [secretary] and the first scratch of my pen is in answer to your last kind note. I thank you for the purusal of Mr Campbell's letter[281] which I would return at this time had I not left it at home. I will send it in my next. I deeply regret that the management at this office was such as to drive from us these men who I think were —— improperly, if not badly used. But the thing is done, and we must make the best of it—it may be they —— maybe won back with fair and candid usage.
 Mr. Bourne[282] is actually on his way to England he sailed in the city of Baltimore on Saturday. The result of his mission is you to be [harmed] and

---

Coates was a member of the Board of the ICY, and board members were required to frequently visit the school and to oversee classes, this is likely how Coates and Campbell came to know each other. Campbell shared Coates's belief in the production of free-labor cotton in Africa, and an 1859 ICY report stated that Campbell had "determined to embark on an exploring expedition to Africa, for the purpose of ascertaining the best localities for the growth of cotton." Exactly how Campbell ended up in Delany's party is unclear, but it appears as though the two had never met before Campbell joined the expedition. Delany enlisted Robert Douglass Jr. of Philadelphia for the trip, and Douglass appears to have then recruited Campbell. Campbell and Delany had a number of conflicts before leaving America, with Campbell even announcing his resignation from the party in *Frederick Douglass' Paper*, only to rejoin shortly after. The major point of contention concerned funding for the trip. As money proved scarce, Delany found it difficult to maintain the ideal of keeping his expedition free from white influence. Campbell, much to Delany's chagrin, was seeking aid from the African Civilization Society and the ACS. In Africa their trip was a success, as they accomplished their goal of signing a treaty with the Egba that allowed for emigrants from the United States to settle on Egba land. On April 10, 1860, Delany and Campbell left Africa and set sail for England, where they would report on their findings. Both Delany and Campbell would soon publish reports of their trip, the former the *Official Report of the Niger Valley Exploring Party* and the latter *A Pilgrimage to My Motherland*. Campbell eventually returned to Africa, where he settled in 1862. Linda Marie Perkins, "Fanny Jackson Coppin and the Institute for Colored Youth: A Model of Nineteenth Century Black Female Educational and Community Leadership, 1837–1932" (Ph.D. diss., University of Illinois, 1978), 83–84; ICY, *Reports, Etc., 1859–1884*, May 16, 1858; Blackett, "Martin R. Delany and Robert Campbell," 9; Miller, *The Search for a Black Nationality*, 174, 193, 195–96, 216, 265.
 281. Robert Campbell. Letter 47, Campbell to Coates, July 14, 1859.
 282. Theodore Bourne. Letter 38, Pinney to Coates, February 9, 1859. Bourne was sent to England by the African Civilization Society in the summer of 1859. His position as the organization's foreign agent was terminated the following year. According to Garnet, Bourne sent him

I hope it may be profitable to our good cause. As he is only [secrtry pro tem] it is likely we shall provide a few [man] one before long Mr Constantine,[283] of Vermont a returned African Missionary a good man and [trust] I believe is talked of. He is an efficient speaker a prudent person, and Baptist Minister— he is also a good agent, and is up to the times. Mr Bourne I am sorry to say has lost the confidence of the coloured people, and until another one is selected the fate of the society is sealed. What think you of it? Please let me know.

I find we are behind in the rent of the office, and, we are needing money to pay for some printing.[284] We propose a national fair of the works of art, and skill and industry of the couloured people some time in next year, and we wish to get out our circulars for that purpose that they may circulate in the ——— of larger meetings through the country. The idea is well, and unniversaly reused by the people and if carried out, I believe it will do much good for the society. Without pressing you, may I ask if you will send us a subscription—and perhaps some other friends in your city may do the same.

Is it true as Dr. J. [dicune] Smith says that Stephen Smith[285] is not with us? It is news to me.

"libelous letters" and attempted to tarnish his reputation among English abolitionists. Although the conflict between Garnet and Bourne was obvious by 1860, there are few indications other than this letter that Garnet considered dismissing Bourne in 1859. *BAP* 5:507 n.

283. Alfred A. Constantine (May 5, 1812–July 9, 1902) was born in Massachusetts, though he lived in Vermont for much of his youth. In 1840 he was ordained a Baptist missionary and married Mary Fales, a missionary among the Marshpee Indians. Beginning that year, Constantine served as a missionary in Liberia until 1842, when poor health forced him to return to the United States. Upon his return, Constantine resumed his activities as a minister in Vermont. In October 1859 he became the corresponding secretary of the African Civilization Society. He died in Summit, New Jersey. Miller, *The Search for a Black Nationality*, 258; American Baptist Missionary Union, *The Missionary Jubilee: An Account of the Fiftieth Anniversary of the American Baptist Missionary Union* (New York: Sheldon and Company, 1871); Crocker, *History of the Baptists in Vermont.*

284. The African Civilization Society was never economically successful. As Peter Ripley notes in the *BAP*, "The African Civilization Society found it easier to gain endorsements than to achieve its financial goal" (5:9). Bourne, in fact, was sent to England to raise money for the organization.

285. Stephen Smith (1797–1873) was born to a slave woman in Pennsylvania. In 1816 he bought his freedom and established a lumber business in Columbia, Pennsylvania. In the 1830s he and William Whipper became business partners. Martin Delany once said Smith is "decidedly the most wealthy colored man in the United States" (*BAP* 4:316 n.). In addition to his financial success, Smith was actively involved in the black community. He was ordained in 1831 and became the pastor of New York City's African Methodist Episcopal Church. He was instrumental in organizing the American Moral Reform Society, a conductor on the Underground Railroad, and involved in the black convention movement. During the Civil War, Smith helped recruit black men for the Union army. Like many free black people, Smith was skeptical of African colonization

Are you not astounded at the fearful intelligence of the actual re-opening of the African slave trade?[286] What can we, what ought we to do?
I am yours truly
Henry Highland Garnet[287]

 49 ❖

Mr Coates   Burlington, NJ Aug 8/59
dear frn:
Some months ago you sent me a pamphlet in relation to the African Civilization Society,[288] which has proved extremely servicable and interesting.
I write to know if you have any other printed matter on the same subject. I am greatly interested in the subject, and would gladly pay for any thing of the kind, and will call on you and get whatever there may be of later date than that contained in the pamphlet referred to.
Very respectfully Yours
Edmund Morris[289]

---

and firmly opposed to the ACS. It is not as clear, however, how he felt about emigration and the African Civilization Society. *BAP* 3:316 n.; Louis R. Merlinger, "The Attitude of the Free Negro Toward African Colonization," *Journal of Negro History* 1, no. 3 (June 1916).

286. Officially, the African slave trade in the United States ended in 1808, long before Garnet wrote to Coates. It remained illegal throughout the country until slavery itself was banned. Even the confederate constitution officially banned the African slave trade and attempted to make provisions to enforce that prohibition. However, in the late 1850s, many Southern journals and politicians, such as South Carolina's L. W. Spratt and James D. B. De Bow, talked about reopening the slave trade. Garnet's "fearful intelligence" may have come from one of these sources. In addition, international attempts to stop the slave trade slowed considerably in the years before the Civil War. The Webster-Ashburton Treaty of 1842 included a provision that both the United States and Great Britain would patrol the African coast and prevent the transportation of slaves. The United States never enforced this article very strenuously, but England, because it stood to gain economically by limiting slavery in other parts of the world, began patrolling the coast in the early 1850s. By 1858, however, the British recognized that suppression of the slave trade was expensive and that societies with newly freed black people, such as Haiti, faced economic hardship. Thus, by the time Garnet wrote to Coates, the slave trade was resurrected de facto. Ludwell H. Johnson, *Division and Reunion: America 1848–1877* (New York: John Wiley and Sons, 1978); MacMaster, "Henry Highland Garnet and the African Civilization Society"; Landry, "Slavery and the Slave Trade in Atlantic Diplomacy"; Harvey Wish, "The Revival of the African Slave Trade in the United States, 1856–1860," *Mississippi Valley Historical Review* 28, no. 4 (March 1941): 569–88.

287. Henry Highland Garnet. Letter 3, Coates to Douglass, June 27, 1850.

288. African Civilization Society. Letter 36, Coates to Gurley, January 13, 1859.

289. Edmund Morris (August 28, 1804–May 4, 1874) was born a Quaker in New Jersey. At the age of twenty, Morris began working for the *Bucks County Intelligencer*. During the next

Saratoga Spa[290]
New York
Aug 17.1859

Benj. Coates Esqr.

My much esteemed friend. I am greatly in your your debt for several unanswered letters, but if you know the amount of my publick, and private engagements just now together with bodily afirmaties, I am sure you would excuse me. Most of the time I last wrote I have been on the wing. I arrival in Philadelphia on Saturday night, and left 12 Sunday night and was poorly[291] during that time. I could not therefore enjoy the satisfaction of calling upon you. Even in this retreat there is no rest for me. Both in private, and in public our course is the great topic of discussion. On Monday night I spoke in the St Nicholas' Hall to a very large audience, on the "Re-opening of the African slave trade, and the duty of the American people in relation to the great crime." This was by a com an invitation of a committee of 30 young coloured men, resident at Saratoga, representing almost every state in the union. On Friday by another invitation I am to speak on the "Destiny of the coloured race in this country" This after noon I am to speak in the palace of the Water cure establishment by invitation of the proprietors.

The Board of Directors have unanimously elected Rev. A A Constantine[292] to the office of corrsponding secty of our society. An excellent spirit is in the man. He is a returned African missionary of the Baptist persuasion, of childlike spirit gentleness—for earnest, and intirely devoted to his work. He is to enter upon his duties nominally on the 1st of Sept—and actually on the 1st of Oct. He is evidentaly, an honest Christian man. Moderate and easy in his manners, but a throughogh out spoken anti slavery man of the "Green Mountain" stamp.

---

several years, Morris worked for several newspapers, including the *Ariel*, Pennsylvania's *Saturday Evening Bulletin*, and New Jersey's *Gazette*. During and after the Civil War, Morris was part of the New York *Tribune* and Philadelphia's *The Press*. Morris's work as a journalist included articles about farming and the first example of the use of multiple colors. R. C. Moon, *The Morris Family of Philadelphia: Descendants of Anthony Morris, born 1654–1721 died* (Philadelphia: Author, 1898–1909); *Appleton's* 4:412.

290. Saratoga Springs, a resort area known for its mineral springs, is located about twenty miles northeast of Albany.

291. Somewhat ill.

292. Alfred Constantine. Letter 48, Garnet to Coates, July 17, 1859.

It is agreed by our friends to let Downing[293] and —— through the news papers. I intend to go to Boston, and New Bedford[294] in a few days. I thank you for the letters you sent, me, which I now return. The good work seems to go on. Please excuse this scrawl. I am surrounded by several ladies, and children whose tongues seem to be hung on springs. It is therefore hard to think or to write.

I am yours truly

Henry Highland Garnet[295]

✤ 51 ✤

Liberia Government Schooner Quail

off Bassa Augt 22^d 1859[296]

Benjamin Coates Esqr

Dear Sir

I am in receipt of your two interesting favors of the 10 & 11th of May for which please accept my thanks. They came to hand on the morning of the 14th ult^o when I was about leaving the Capitol on an official visit to the leeward Counties and Settlements + as you will perceive by my letter, I have made a lengthy trip of it, but indulge the hope of reaching home this evening and that I may find the Stevens[297] still in port by which it is my purpose to send this + other letters. My visit to the leeward has been very agreeable to me, after an absence from those settlements for so long a time owing to our having no vessel for nearly 13 months, until the arrival of the Quail, a fine vessel 13 tons

293. George T. Downing. Letter 37, Wagoner to Coates, January 31, 1859.

294. New Bedford, Massachusetts, with its thriving maritime and whaling activity, had a large and active black population throughout the nineteenth century. According to the 1860 census, there was one black person for every 13.5 white people in the town. The large black population allowed black people to influence elections and to mount public protests. In 1834 an anti-slavery society was founded there. Seven years later, the citizens of New Bedford helped a fugitive slave. New Bedford black people came together to protest the ACS in 1852. Six years later they protested the *Dred Scott* decision. Among New Bedford's famous residents was Frederick Douglass, who moved there after escaping slavery. *BAP* 3:44, 302, 362, 421, and 4:113, 391; B. P. Hunt, *Why Colored People in Philadelphia are Excluded from the Street Cars* (Philadelphia: Merrihew, 1866).

295. Henry Highland Garnet. Letter 3, Coates to Douglass, June 27, 1850.

296. Roberts Collection, HCSC.

297. The ship *Mary Caroline Stevens*, owned by the ACS. See Letter 28, Coates to Gurley, May 2, 1857.

larger than the Lark, + admirably adapted as a guarda Coasta; a present from
H. B M. Government to our Government. Much praise + gratitude are due
to Mr Consul General Ralston[298] of London + Mr Consul F. W. Foy Jn[r] Esqr
for the zeal + attention with which they supervised her outfit +c +c

Our settlers in the leeward Counties, are of opinion, that my visit to
the leeward will prove of incalculable benefit, especially to the natives at the
different points, large + numerous tribes of whom I met in council, + had more
interesting interviews; and I am rejoiced to be able to say, that today I feel
more encouraged and hopeful (amounting to assurance) of their becoming
civilized + fully identified with us in every respect, in a shorter time, than I
have ever felt before.

I have read with lively interest, the Constitution +Circular of the
organization of my Colored brethren in the U.S. entitled the African
~~Colonizaton~~ Civilization Society.[299] Our Heavenly Father seems to be inclin-
ing their hearts toward their father land + their duty. The Mendi + Stevens
brought out some apparently valuable men. I have made Dr. DeLaney's[300]
acquaintance; he is inexpressably delighted with Liberia + considers it a
country good enough for anyone to live in. Should his despatches reach the
U.S. they will speak for themselves. Liberians of all classes, af if forgetting
all his past opposition to us, magnanimously threw open their arms + gave
him a cordial welcome: Thank God Liberia is moveing onward most encour-
ageingly, + large majority of our citizens have imbibed a spirit of industry to
an extend I have never before witnessed in Liberia, + I assure you it rejoices
my heart. I thank you for the advice you gave respecting the encouragement
of such industrial pursuit as will lead to national wealth & independence.

I have to close for want of time without saying as much to you as I
wish on various points.

By the Mendi, I have arranged to make a remittance to Messrs
Coates + Brown.[301] The papers kindly sent by you came safely to hand, please

298. Gerard Ralston. See Letter 19, Roberts to Coates, October 16, 1854.

299. African Civilization Society. See Letter 36, Coates to Gurley, January 13, 1859.

300. Martin Delany (see Letter 34, Cary to Coates, November 20, 1858), en route to
Yoruba to begin his Niger Valley Exploring Party, arrived in Monrovia on the *Mendi* on July 12
and remained in Liberia until mid-September. Although he had opposed colonization or emigration to Africa, he was impressed with Liberia, much to the satisfaction of Benson and other
Liberians, who hoped that Delany's new interest in Africa might benefit Liberia. Benson met
with Delany briefly and then embarked on the voyage up the coast that he discusses in this letter. Miller, *The Search for a Black Nationality*, 201–5.

301. Coates & Brown. See Letter 14, Coates to McLain, February 28, 1852.

accept my thanks. When I reach Monrovia, should I find the Stevens there, and can spare a few moments, I will try and add a few more lines.

with sentiments of

profound respect

I subscribe myself

yr obt servant

Stephen "A" Benson[302]

❖ 52 ❖

Boston August 27 1859

Benj Coates Esq
    Dear Sir

        Your very acceptable favor of the 24 has just been received and is now before me. I can assure you that nothing could have given me more pleasure than the intelligence it contains of the arrival of Mr. Campbell[303] at Africa and the very pleasing success thus far of his glorious mission. God grant that the entire commission may prove a complete triumph. My great interest in and anxiety for its success has made me quite impatient to hear from them. You have evidence therefore how much relief your very opportune letters affords me. I am asked daily by those to whom I apply for aid whether we have any reliable official information from the Yoruba district.[304] &c &c. I have wished a thousand times that I had been there, it would be more gratifying to me than it would to be able to say that I had been in every other country on the globe. I am happy to inform you that the 3 vol arrived—2 Elli's visits[305] & 1 Bowen's travels to Africa[306]—just on the eve of my returning here I was just finishing also my critical review of the late convention held in this city by Geo. T. Downing[307] & clique which I am now prepared and will deliver as a lecture to the public. At the moment of theirs spasmodic excitement they were quite jubilant, but having since settled down to sober reflection they have

302. Stephen Allen Benson. See Letter 8, Coates to McLain, May 16, 1851.

303. Robert Campbell. See Letter 47, Campbell to Coates, July 14, 1859.

304. Yoruba, Africa. See Letter 34, Cary to Coates, November 20, 1858.

305. William Ellis (1794–1872) wrote *Three Visits to Madagascar During the Years 1853–1854–1856, Including a Journey to the Capital: With Notices of the Natural History of the Country and the Present Civilization of the People*. The book was published in 1858 and a slightly longer edition was released the following year.

306. In 1857 Thomas Jefferson Bowen (1814–1875) published *Central Africa*.

307. George Downing. See Letter 37, Wagoner to Coates, January 31, 1859.

become somewhat alarmed at their own doings and are manifesting considerable uneasiness respecting my review. Mr Garnett is to be here early next week Mr Martin[308] is here boarding at the same house that I do (Oriental House 83 [Southers] Street) so that we are anticipating a good time for African Civilization next week. The arrangements for the meeting are made for here and New Bedford. But all the facts taken into account I am happy to assure you that we will lose nothing to our cause from that convention or what a thousand such men as Downing have or may do. They have very greatly aided in giving us prominence and importance.

Edward Atkinson Esq[309] is a very excellent man I took the liberty to give him your address. He has manifested considerable interest in me and our cause generally. He is a person of great business talents I have depended on his influence to some extent to aid me here.

Mr Martin has not those books and will be happy to receive them. My very dear sir:—you will please accept the deep gratitude of my heart for the valuable and generous donation of those 3 vol on Africa prompted by that kindness and benevolence which has so long distinguished you as the true and invincible friend of my suffering race.

with great respect

J.B. Smith[310]

P.S. It occurs to me that two of the books were the same by Elli's visits &c I thought you probably made a mistake intending to give me some other work in the place of one of them If so the exchange be made when you send Mr Martins as I can give him one of mine

J.B. Smith

308. John Sella Martin. See Letter 41, Garner to Coates, April 27, 1859.

309. Edward Atkinson (February 10, 1827–December 11, 1905), born in Massachusetts, entered the dry goods business at the age of fifteen during a period of his family's financial difficulty. First a Free Soiler, and then a Republican, he became a member of the New England Emigrant Aid Company, an organization that attempted to establish free labor settlements in Kansas. After the Civil War, Atkinson supported equal rights for black people. Atkinson is most famous for the Boston Manufacturers' Mutual Fire Insurance Company, which he began in 1878. During his lifetime, he penned several pamphlets, including *Cheap Cotton by Free Labor* in 1861, *On Cotton* in 1866, and *Addresses upon the Labor Question* in 1886. *ANB* vol. 1.

310. John B. Smith. See Letter 41, Garnet to Coates, April 27, 1859.

❖ 53 ❖

Allegheny City Aug. 29ᵗʰ. 1859

Benj. Coates Esq.

Dear Sir: On my return from Canada last Friday I
found myself the recipient of your kind favor in the shape of 3 volumes of
"Travels" in Africa:[311] for which accept my thanks, also for your former favor,
a pamphlet on the "Cultivation of Cotton in Africa" which though unac-
knowledged till now, has not been unapreciated or forgotten. You were rightly
informed in regard to my interest in "African Civilization", but you give me
credit for too much of disinterested benevolence, if you suppose, as your letter seems to indicate, that I am interested in it only as a means of good to the
native African, I am selfish enough to regard Africa, and its civilization, as a
means to my own advancement and elevation as a land of refuge, if not for
myself, for my children: for though I manage to live in this Slavery-cursed
country, and even enjoy life to some degree, yet I cannot but hope and believe
that my children, (should I be <u>blessed</u>! with any,) will require a freer field
and a <u>fairer</u> <u>fight</u>, than this country can be expected, from present indications,
to afford them. Could I live over the past of my pilgrimage, my own free feet
should press the soil of the Father-land.

Believe me grateful for your gift, and anxious to render it beneficial
to myself and my race

Very Respectfully Yours
M H Freeman[312]

311. Coates sent books on Africa to several people during 1859.
312. Martin H. Freeman (1826?–1889) took part in Martin Delany's colonization
efforts. He graduated from Middlebury College and was, for a time, the principal of Avery College in Pittsburgh. In 1954 he was appointed special foreign secretary of the National Board of
Commissioners, which was created by the National Emigration Convention held by Delany in
that year. He emigrated to Liberia in 1863 and became a professor of Mathematics and Natural
Philosophy at Liberia College in 1864. He died in Liberia in 1889. Lynch, *Edward Wilmot Blyden*,
40; Miller, *The Search for a Black Nationality*, 153, 173, 265.

❖ 54 ❖

Augusta[313] Sept 6th 1859

Mr Benj Coates
           Dear Sir
Yours of 23[d] ult. rec[d] also the books for express. Many thanks for your kindness, Bowen[314] I've read—you seem to have reather proscriptive ideas of the
South.- if the North had minded its own business—there would by this time
been schooles for us, all over the south.—the proscriptive laws enacted North
and South, would never been thought of Negro inferiority has been sung so
often that like a well told Ghost story—people begin to believe it.—it will
have its run but we continue to advance in numbers and knowledge.—preparing for hunting the dark skinned of this continent in a strong body.—we'll
meet in the tropic.—Brazili moves north the w.s.[315] planter moves south.—
each from pressure of free white labour.—we meet in Central America, a
Chieftain, and the few sickly whites will soon be swallowed up we are far from
being in dispair,—we are getting schooled.—we will unite with the Indian,
you wont.—mutial suffering will make us firm brothers.—in that country we
will end in being conquerors even if whiped in every pitched battle.—disease
will thin your ranks if nothing else will.—the year nineteen hundred is looked
forward to with hope.—during the past 30 days over 500 slaves has passed
through this city on the way to our promis land from Virginia &c—and the
mass dont pass this way.—force put us North, destiny is bringing us back,—
we are patient.—here we [are] steal into the ranks of the white, by cross-
breeding we all wish we were white.—there the wish ceases to exist.—white
will condecend to be made Yellow Bellies—[greasary]—the same nature, if in
this as that Country is their home thy wish to be like the people thy live with,
even the Proud English and French find it hard to make their sons in this
country be proud of the Father land, time washes out the feeling to be of
this people we <u>must</u> be like them—your labours in the cause of mankind, God
will reward you.—the regeneration of Africa her march is steadily onward.—
Europe will see to it—I have no fears of it w.s. had better colonize us here.
She will want us—we are her hope for the full development of the American
tropic, being her neighbour, Africa's commerce will go to the North of her side

313. Probably Augusta, Georgia, the county seat (Richmond County) and the second
largest city in Georgia.
     314. For information about Bowen's *Travels*, see Letter 52, Smith to Coates, August
27, 1859.
     315. Perhaps an abbreviation for "white southerner."

the water.—if w.s. could wipe her eyes clear. get rid of the ghost she would see it and act upon it.—we wait—your servt

RAH[316]

❖ 55 ❖

Burlington, Sept. 8/59

Benj. Coates, Esq.

dear Sir On returning home last night I find your letter + book, and am greatly obliged to you. The Liberia article comes in capital time; + will do more good than in the N. Am[317], which has no position or influence of value to the great cause. I will use it as suggested—its coming <u>in advance</u> of all previous publication is especially desirable, as they in N.Y.[318] don't want second hand news.

I did call as you supposed, and will repeat it in hopes of better luck next time.

Very truly Yours
E Morris[319]

❖ 56 ❖

52 Laurens Street
New York
Sept.9.1859

Benj Coates Esqr

My Esteemed friend. In consequence of absence from this city it has not been in my power to acknowledge your favours until now. I did not

316. "RAH" is probably Robert A. Harper. A number of Harper's letters can be found in the microfilm of the ACS and the handwriting is virtually identical.

317. The *North American* (Philadelphia) was founded in 1839 and advocated tariffs, industry and federal regulation of business, and other political stances. It merged with the *Daily Advertiser* in 1839 and the *Commercial Herald* the following year. The *North American* supported "ultra-Protestantism" in the early 1840s and received financial support from the Harrison administration. The paper allied itself with the Whig party and merged with its only rival, the *United States Gazette*, in 1847. It was then published under the name the *North American and United States Gazette* for the next thirty years. Robert Louis Bloom, *The Philadelphia North American: A History, 1839–1925* (New York: n.p., 1952), 23.

318. Morris is mostly likely referring to the New York *Tribune*, the newspaper for which he worked.

319. Edmund Morris. Letter 49, Morris to Coates, August 8, 1859.

receive the package of books until yesterday and I am truly thankful for them. Had you sent me their weight in gold, the first use I would made of the treasure would have been to purchased the [very] volumes you sent me. I shall read them, and think.

From the "London Morning Star" I learn that Mr. Bourne[320] has actually started under the most flattering auspices. A meeting was held for him in London attended by such men as Dr. Hodgkin[321] and Gerrard Ralston[322]— the former I know and he is a [host] in himself. If he is wise he will have fair sailing, and under God, sure success. After all our fears, he may yet do well. Let us hope so. I have sent a copy of the account of his meeting to the "Journal of Commerce"[323]—and will try the "Evening Post"[324]

Mr. Fred Douglass[325] is our bitter unrelenting enemy, and I fear will endeavour to injure our cause in England as he has [done] here at home. My dear friend Benjamin Coates is deceived in the man if he expects anything else from him. What think you of Robt Campbell?[326] He is not to be relied upon in our cause. He is selfish—selfish! He uses us just so far as it suits his purpose, and then drops us. Such was his course in England, now he writes

320. Theodore Bourne (Letter 38, Pinney to Coates, February 9, 1859) arrived in England in the summer of 1859. Soon after commencing his work there, Bourne informed Garnet that English abolitionists supported the African Civilization Society because they believed it would end American slavery. Bourne convinced Thomas Hodgkin to support the Society. Despite the fact that Bourne eventually brought Delany into the fold of the organization, he did not remain the Society's agent in England and relations between Garnet and Bourne soured. Miller, *The Search for a Black Nationality*, 218–21.

321. Thomas Hodgkin. Letter 40, Hobbins to Coates, March 2, 1859.

322. Gerard Ralston. Letter 19, Roberts to Coates, October 16, 1854.

323. The New York *Journal of Commerce* was published daily from September 1, 1827, until June 1893, when it became the New York *Journal of Commerce and Commercial Bulletin*.

324. The *Evening Post* was founded by Alexander Hamilton in 1801 as a Federalist paper. By the 1850s at least two contributors to the paper were Free Soilers and founders of the Republican Party. The newspaper attacked the 1850 fugitive slave law and became "as firmly as 'black Republican' organ as the [New York] Tribune." Allan Nevins, *The Evening Post: A Century of Journalism* (New York: Boni and Liveright, 1922).

325. Frederick Douglass was, according to many, the most respected voice in the black community in the 1840s and 1850s. Douglass's insistence, through the *North Star*, that emigration was not the way to end slavery, drew support away from Garnet's African Civilization Society. In the summer of 1859 Douglass planned his second trip to England. In the aftermath of John Brown's raid of Harpers Ferry in October of that year, Douglass followed through on his earlier design to avoid being arrested. Schor, *Henry Highland Garnet*.

326. Robert Campbell sailed to England in April 1859 and raised money there for the Niger Valley Exploring Party. While in England, he received a letter of introduction from Lord Malmesbury, which referred only to the desire of British black people, not African Americans, to settle in West Africa. The English government then paid for his travel to Africa through cotton interests.

you, he is under the protection of the British government. What then is to become of the Africo American type of our new Empire? He lacks decission and steady purpose. But we will not [hedge] up his way—yet <u>I will say he has had eneough</u> <u>for one man.</u> I trust our friends will contribute directly to the society—and then we shall do something that shall be seen.

What shall we do to lay the foundation of the grand theatre of our society's operation in Africa? That is the important question. As yet the first stone is not laid—and will not be on the basis of the thousands already given. We must change our course. good men, and true can be obtained, who will work for us. The very moment we make a right beginning, and <u>actually</u> take the field, ample funds will be forth coming. Think not that this is a complaining letter—My soul is full of hope—the sky is brightening—and there is nothing to discourage.

Mr Constantine[327] will take the office about the 1st of Oct. I am yours truly

Henry Highland Garnet[328]

❖ 57 ❖

Benj. Coates Esq
    Philadelphia; Pa.
    Permit me to make a general acknowledgment for various books, papers and documents that I have received from your hands in relation to Africa for several years past. More particularly, would I acknowledge with gratefulness the Recent Receipt of these very interesting works on Africa. God is certainly bringing about a great crisis in the affairs of that dark continent. He is now preparing the way for the fulfillment of the prophecy which predicts that "Princes shall come out of Egypt; and Ethiopia shall soon stretch forth her hands unto God."[329] And I thank Him that He has put it in your heart to be a cooperator with Him in this grand design. Respectfully Yours &c
New Haven Sept. 13th 1859   J.T. Holly[330]

327. Alfred A. Constantine. Letter 48, Garnet to Coates, July 17, 1859.
328. Henry Highland Garnet. Letter 3, Coates to Douglass, June 27, 1850.
329. Psalms 68:31.
330. James Theodore Holly (October 3, 1829–March 3, 1911) was born free in Washington, D.C., where he was raised Roman Catholic and attended Dr. John Fleet's school until his family moved to New York City in 1844. Beginning in 1848, Holly worked as a clerk for the American Missionary Society. After the passage of the Fugitive Slave Law, the Holly family moved to Burlington, Vermont, where Holly became interested in the emigration movement. He

Burlington, Sept. 15/59

Benjamin Coates, Esq.

dear Sir. Your favor of yesterday rec'd. I had sent to N.Y. an article on Washington some days ago, but they preferred others then on hand, + so deferred "Liberia not a Failure," until after the Commercial Adv.[331] This is extremely unlucky, as early and exclusive matter is the great desideratum. Still, so much was added in my article that the Com. knew nothing about, that I hope it may not be thrown aside. I think Mr. Coppinger[332] deficient in judgment, + Mr. Pinney[333] even more so to select any other channel than the Tribune. Common courtesy requires that we should serve our <u>friends</u>. Besides, the Com. is half dough face. However, let this pass, and hope to do better next time.

Truly Your obliged
E Morris[334]

That article "Bantering with Bankruptcy,"[335] would have kept a week longer, + so made room for "Liberia not a Failure."[336]

---

corresponded with the ACS and eventually moved to Windsor, Canada West, to assist Henry Bibb with the publication of the *Voice of the Fugitive*. Holly supported Bibb's Refugee Home Society, which, despite the criticisms of Mary Ann Shadd (Cary), bought land and then sold it to black immigrants. As a result of the racism and criticism Holly faced in Canada, he returned in 1854 to the United States, where he served as a school principal for several months before becoming an Episcopal minister in 1855. He dreamed of becoming a Haitian missionary, but funds were not available; he took the position of the rector of St. Luke's Episcopal Church in New Haven. While in New Haven, Holly acted as the principal of a local school from 1857 to 1859 and founded the Select School for Young Colored Ladies and Gentlemen. When James Redpath became the Haitian Commissioner of Emigration in the United States in 1860, he appointed Holly as an agent of the society. Holly emigrated to Haiti in May 1861 along with a number of New Haven black people. The emigrants faced poor conditions there, and Holly's mother, his wife, and two of his children died. But Holly remained dedicated to Haiti, and he made several trips in the next few years to raise funds. When Ebenezer Bassett became the U.S. minister to Haiti, Holly served as his secretary. Holly also assisted Frederick Douglass when the latter served as U.S. minister from 1889 to 1891. In November 1874 Holly became the first bishop of Haiti. Despite his new position, he never fully recovered from his personal financial difficulties. Dean, *Defender of the Race*.

331. Morris is probably referring to the New York *Commercial Advertiser*, which was published daily between October 2, 1797, and January 30, 1904.

332. William Coppinger. Letter 10, Coates to McLain, October 11, 1851.

333. John Brooke Pinney. Letter 8, Coates to McLain, May 16, 1851.

334. Edmund Morris. Letter 49, Morris to Coates, August 8, 1859.

335. The article "Bantering with Bankruptcy" did not appear in the *Weekly Tribune* in September or October 1859.

336. The article "Liberia not a Failure" did not appear in the *Weekly Tribune* in September or October 1859.

❖ 59 ❖

Off of *Anglo African*[337]
New York Sept.19.59

Benj. Coates Esq.

Dear Sir

Your of the 17th containing Five Dollars ($5) for subcriptions to the "Weekly Anglo African"[338] is rec[d]. I will forward the back nos. thro our mutual friend Mr. Pinney.[339]

You will please accept my thanks for your kind offer to be e one of 10 or 20 to give $10 each toward making up a Libary fund.[340] I am happy to say that I have already rec.[d] the pledge + cash of two others.

I would gladly have published Mr. Washington's letter,[341] but when it reached me I had sufficient matter ahead for two papers + finding it in Fredrick Douglass Paper[342] for last week I concluded to give Dr Delany's[343] letter the preference.

337. The office of the *Anglo-African* was 48 Beekman Street in New York City. The *National Anti-Slavery Standard* was published from the same address.

338. Hamilton began publishing the *Anglo-African* July 23, 1859, and continued until March 1861. In the spring of that year the newspaper was sold to Lawrence and Redpath, two Haitian emigrationists. They changed the newspaper's name to *The Pine and Palm* and used it to promote Haitian emigration. The venture was not successful, and the Hamiltons bought the paper back in August of the same year. They published it under the name the *Weekly Anglo-African* until 1865. Bullock, *The Afro-American Periodical Press*, 57–59.

339. John Pinney. Letter 8, Coates to McLain, May 16, 1851. It is unclear how Hamilton would have known Pinney. Hamilton's father William and brother Robert were opponents of emigration and therefore would have disliked Pinney, who was associated with the New York Colonization Society and the ACS. Hamilton, however, was not as firmly anti-emigration and may have known been familiar with Pinney through his emigration work. The last paragraph of this letter suggests that Hamilton was much more open to emigration than other members of his family and therefore Pinney might have used his position in the black community to promote emigrationist views. *BAP* 5:27.

340. Although it is not clear how it started, there was a movement to raise enough money to buy subscriptions of the *Anglo-African Magazine* to place in all the public libraries in the United States. In the November issue of the magazine, there is a list of contributors to the fund. Both Benjamin Coates and Gerrit Smith are listed as having donated ten dollars. Another unnamed person also gave ten dollars to the fund. All other contributors gave less than five dollars each. Bullock, *The Afro-American Periodical Press*, 59; William L. Katz, *The Anglo-African Magazine*, vol. 1, 368.

341. Augustus Washington. Coates to McLain, May 22, 1855.

342. *The North Star.* Letter 3, Coates to Douglass, June 27, 1850.

343. It is not clear to which letter Hamilton refers. Delany had several pieces in the *Anglo-African Magazine*, but none of them was a letter. The January issue carried his article, "The Attraction of Planets," and chapters twenty-eight through thirty of his novel *Blake: or the Huts of America*. The February issue published his article, "Comets," and the first five chapters of *Blake*.

So far from being "fearful of publishing" Liberian intelligence were I able I would secure the services of a good correspondent as that kind who should keep our readers posted up in regard to everything of moment occuring there. I am aware that much [sensitive] has been manifested by many of our people in regard to Africa, but I am happy to say that it is fast wearing away— and, my idea of a good newspaper is a journal that will furnish intelligence coming from whatsoever quarter it may, whether it offend the few or many

Again thanking you for the interest taken in the enterprize

I am

Yours with respect

Tho⁵. Hamilton³⁴⁴

 ❖ 60 ❖

N.Y Sep 28. 1859

Benjamin Coates Esqr

My Dear friend

Your very welcome letter of 23ᵈ was duly received but found me in such a hurry by reason of many letters & some purchases to go per Ocean Eagle³⁴⁵ &c & that not until she was off could I get a moment to reply. Yesterday she sailed see Com. Adv. of yesterday.

Today besides many office duties I have been writing to several parties to secure $22,000 for the College in Liberia.³⁴⁶ If this additional sum

Each issue through July contained several chapters of Delany's novel, but none of the issues for the rest of the year contained any material by Delany. It is possible, however, that Delany had material in the *Weekly Anglo-African*. Katz, *The Anglo-African Magazine*, vol. 1.

344. Thomas Hamilton (April 20, 1823–May 29, 1865) was born in New York City. His father, William Hamilton, was already known throughout the abolitionist community as an advocate for free black people. Thomas Hamilton was one of three sons and became involved with black periodicals at a young age, when he worked for the *Colored American* in 1837. In 1841 he started his own paper, the *People's Press*, which lasted several months. Before starting another newspaper, Hamilton worked for the *Evangelist* and the *National Anti-Slavery Standard*. In 1859 he began the *Anglo-African Magazine* and the *Weekly Anglo-African*. The *Anglo-African Magazine* lasted for fifteen issues. The *Weekly Anglo-African* survived until 1861, when it was sold. Within the year the Hamilton family bought the paper back and resumed publication. When Hamilton died, his brother Robert continued publishing the paper. Hamilton also published several books. Frankie Hutton, *The Early Black Press in America, 1827 to 1860* (Westport, Conn.: Greenwood Press, 1993), 37, 51, 161; Bullock, *The Afro-American Periodical Press*, 55–58.

345. A ship.

346. The Liberian legislature passed a bill in 1851 that established Liberia College. The New York Colonization Society, of which Pinney was a member, provided much of the money

could be secured i.e. subscribed before the decision at Albany in Mr Phelps will case,[347] I think we should be sure of having his $50,000 legacy. Cannot more be done in Philadelphia? Time flies.

The book (I suppose) at all events two boxes directed to Washington[348] came the day you wrote by express. But for your letter I should have had no idea whence they came or of their contents. I forwarded them to the care of D.B. Warner[349] + wrote to Washington to pay the expenses $2.

Thank you for the enquiry. We are all well. Agnes is seriously disposed to go South to teach this winter + so try and get me out of debt! Is not that heroic?

Give our love to all at your very pleasant home. We think and talk of our little Angel. Benny said yesterday that "after two years I will go up & kiss [Maudia] We love to listen "to his child faith" prattle.

I am truly yours [ever]

J.B. Pinney.[350]

P.S. George Hall,[351] has just come in & sends plenty of respect.

---

needed to found the institution. A group in Boston agreed to pay the salary of one professor and raise money for scholarships. J. J. Roberts became the first president of the college when it opened in 1862 and traveled frequently to raise funds. Liberia's most well-known scholars, such as Alexander Crummell and Edward Blyden, were teachers at the college. Soon after the death of Roberts, Pinney was appointed president of the college and assumed his duties in 1878. He attempted to move the college from Monrovia to a more central location in the country. When his plan failed six months later, he resigned from his position and returned to the United States. Blyden became president of Liberia College one year after Pinney left. It was under his leadership that the first indigenous students were accepted in 1881. Despite steps taken by Blyden, the college remained a primarily Americo-Liberian institution until the 1950s. Liberia College became the University of Liberia in 1952. *BAP* 3:231 n., 472 n., and 5:260 n.; Liebenow, *Liberia*; Amos Sawyer, *Emergence of Autocracy in Liberia: Tragedy and Challenge* (San Francisco: ICS Press, 1992); Lynch, *Edward Wilmot Blyden*.

347. Anson Green Phelps. Letter 1, Roberts to Coates, July 8, 1848.

348. Pinney may be referring to Augustus Washington, a Liberian merchant and politician. For more information, see Letter 59, Hamilton to Coates, September 19, 1859.

349. Daniel Bashiel Warner (1815–1880) was the third president of Liberia. He was born free in Baltimore, Maryland, and, with his parents, emigrated to Liberia in 1823. Before he became president he served in the Liberian House of Representatives and twice as secretary of state and vice president. *HDL* 26, 147, 183–85.

350. John Brooke Pinney. Letter 8, Coates to McLain, May 16, 1851.

351. George Hall. Letter 18, Roberts to Coates, August 26, 1854.

❖ 61 ❖

Oberlin, Ohio; October 12th 1859

M[r] Coates,

Dear Sir

You must excuse me for writing to you, being an entire stranger to you. I shall without any great ceremony relate my object in writing to you. I am a native of Africa and came to this country in the Fall of 1856 with Rev Geo. Thompson[352] then returning as a missionary from the Mendi Mission I came over for the purpose of getting an education and then to return and do good in my native land. I have been from the time I arrived (1856) up to the present time living in the family of Mr Thompson he all the while giving me my board and tuition and I assisting myself by manual labor; next Spring however he is to remove from Oberlin and consequently I must be obliged to go home this Fall unless I am aided in some way. I need to study four years more and then I shall have gone through a course of study. I am willing to help myself in any way if I can have any person or persons to help me. I have written to the Hon Gerrit Smith[353] and he has helped me in some measure. To you also Sir I appeal for aid. Do not turn a deaf ear to my entreaty. I know you are interested in the welfare of Africa and have always given largely towards the evangelization of that country. If you would wish to know any farther concerning me please write to my address or to Rev George Thompson, Oberlin Ohio. Hoping that my letter may receive favor in thy sight.

I remain yours sincerely

Thomas

Tucker[354]

352. This may have been British abolitionist George Thompson (1804–1878).
353. Gerrit Smith. Letter 15, Coates to Lugenbeel, June 27, 1853.
354. Thomas DeSaliere Tucker lived in Sherbro, Africa, before coming to the United States for his education. He entered Oberlin's preparatory program in 1858 and the college itself two years later, earning his A.B. in 1865. He then attended Straight University, where he obtained an LL.B. Oberlin College, *General Catalogue of Oberlin College, 1833–1908: Including an Account of the Principal Events in the History of the College, with Illustrations of the College Buildings* (Oberlin, Ohio: Author, 1909).

❧ 62 ❧

New York Dec 27/59

Benj Coates Esq
    Dear Sir
        I am now spending a few days in this city. I am intending to visit Phila as early as the 30th inst. Can any arrangement be made to render my visit advantageous to our cause? If there could be a meeting secured for me at Bethel Church[355] or some other convenient place I should like it. I thought you would know the very man to direct to the work of getting up such a meeting. And I might through you probably succeed in getting up some meetings among the whites—churches and otherwise especially as there has been no agent in the city. Mr. Constantine[356] has just informed me that he has written in relation to the same matter.
    Dear sir I shall be happy to hear from you at your earliest convenience.
        Yours Truly
        J.B. Smith.[357]

❧ 63 ❧

Brooklyn Sept 6 1860
Benjamin Coates Esqr
    Dear Sir
        Please excuse my boldness in addressing you. My object is to assertain Dear Sir whether you have on hand any more of your valuable Pamphlets, Cotton Cultivation in Africa[358] Published 1858. I am the Agent of the African Civilization Society[359] in New York I have been West and I need some to send to some of the friends —— West If you have any on hand and will send me a few copies you will greatly oblige your unworthy servant.
        A. Prince Agent A.C.S.

355. Bethel Church. Letter 62, Smith to Coates, December 27, 1859.
356. Alfred A. Constantine. Letter 48, Garnet to Coates, July 17, 1859.
357. John B. Smith. Letter 52, Smith to Coates, August 27, 1859.
358. *Cultivation of Cotton in Africa*. Letter 39, Whipper to Coates, February 24, 1859.
359. African Civilization Society. Letter 36, Coates to Gurley, January 13, 1859.

"'Am. Coln. Socy' . . . a very obnoxious organization": Civil War Years, 1862–1865

Even before the 1863 Emancipation Proclamation, which directed the Civil War toward ending slavery, many abolitionists had new hope that African Americans' lives would be changed by the federal government's retreat from protecting slave holders and their property. Reformers like Benjamin Coates now divided their attention between Washington, Liberia, Europe, and the South, diverting some of their resources to assisting ad hoc schools for freed people springing up across the South.

But the debate about the merits of emigration did not subside, and although Coates supported programs for black Americans—presumably to prepare them to succeed in Africa—many African Americans continued to view emigration as a venomous plot to rob them of their stake in the nation they had helped to build.

The fewest number of letters in the two collections of our volume (only seventeen) are from the Civil War years. Perhaps Coates was biding his time await-ing the resolution of the conflict, or perhaps his correspondence from this time has perished. From what survives here, however, it is clear that Coates pinned his hopes on promoting and disseminating the pro-Liberian writing of Alexander Crummell. Focusing on the fact that Crummell was not of mixed blood (as was Roberts), Coates and his friends touted the intellectual possibilities of pure-bred Africans. Still, Coates counseled Crummell against actually speaking before gatherings of the American Colonization Society, lest Crummell alienate "colored friends" who regarded the society as "a very obnoxious organization."

❖ 64 ❖

Philadelphia Jany 13th 1862.[1]

Rev^d. Alexander Crummell,[2]

My dear Sir -

I was glad to hear from you through Mr Coppinger[3] a few days since, who showed me your letter—and it then occurred to me to make a suggestion to you in regard to the publication of your book.[4] If you are not already aware of this fact, you will probably soon learn it, that the publishers generally receive much the larger portion of the profit from any successful work, leaving but a small portion for the author— Now as you have already obtained a large number of subscribers you should have the entire profit to that extent—and I think you can bargain so as to get the number you require at the cheapest rate if you put the matter in the right shape—I would therefore suggest that you should call on one or two good respectable publishing houses—such as Harper & Bros. and Carter & Bros. New York and see what the cost will be for an edition of say four thousand copies as you are aware that a large edition can be got up much more cheaply per vol. than a small edition—and I presume that an edition of three or four thousand vol. can be got up to cost not over 20 or 25 [cts] per vol. Then see if the publisher will furnish you with one thousand copies ~~to supply it~~ at the average cost of the entire edition of say 4.000 copies—with which to supply your friends who have subscribed to you for the book—and then publish the other three thousand copies on joint acct. Giving you one third or one half the profits of what they may sell as your share—Otherwise if you do not make the bargain in this way they will probably propose to publish an edition for you of one thousand copies + put all the expenses of publishing—setting up

1. Courtesy HSP.
2. Alexander Crummell (see Letter 28, Coates to Gurley, May 2, 1857) was, at the time, in the United States lecturing on Africa and acquiring books and instruments for Liberia College. Dismissed from his previous job at Mount Vaughan High School in April 1861, he immediately departed for the United States, arriving in May 1861. In March 1862 Crummell, Edward Blyden, and J. D. Johnson were appointed by the Liberian government to travel to the United States and work to encourage emigration to Liberia. Crummell was still in the United States, and the other commissioners met him there in May. Despite the efforts of the commissioners, the coming of the Civil War changed black Americans' hopes for a future in the United States, and the emigration cause experienced decreasing support. Oldfield, *Alexander Crummell*; Rigsby, *Alexander Crummell*.
3. William Coppinger. See Letter 10, Coates to McLain, October 11, 1851.
4. Crummell, *The Future of Africa*. See Letter 65, Coates to Crummell, February 3; Letter 66, Coates to Crummell, February 20, 1862; and Letter 69, Coates to Crummell, April 14, 1862.

+c on the <u>first</u> edition of 1000. copies which will make the cost much more per vol to you, while the succeeding editions being already in type will cost very little to <u>them</u> besides the paper and binding.

I think if you can make an arrangement of this kind so as to get one thousand copies for yourself at the lowest rate—say at one fourth the cost of the entire edition of four thousand copies it would be better to do so, even if you did not get more than one fourth the profit on the remainder that may be sold by the publisher—but I think you ought to get at least 25 prct or 33 1/3 prct on all the sales made by the publishers over & above your own take— whatever they may be.

I merely give this suggestion as a general idea altho' I am not much acquainted with the business, and probably by this time you may know more about it than I do—I am glad to learn from your letter that your children[5] are recovering from the indisposition in which you found them.

Mr. Pinney[6] called to see me a few days since on his way to Washington—he stated among other things that he wanted Mr Johnson[7] & yourself to address the <u>board</u> of managers of the "Am. Coln. Socy."[8] This may do good & I do not see at present any particular objec- tion to it—but I think your views are correct in regard to the injury it might have on your influence with your colored friends in the North if you were to speak at the public meeting of the "Am. Coln. Socy." + thus identify yourself in their minds with what is regarded by <u>them</u> as a very obnoxious organization.

With my best wishes,

I am very truly Yours

Benj. Coates

P.S.

The very fact of your having already obtained so many subscribers for the book is evidence that it <u>will sell</u> & therefore not altogether a doubtful experiment for the publisher—and as they will not therefore view the risk of <u>loss</u> which they would do on an untried work they can afford to give you a larger share of the profit and if you can find a publisher inclined to be gener- ous he will perhaps allow you 40 or 50 prct of the profits <u>after</u> <u>furnishing</u> your 1000 copies

5. Crummell had six children, three of whom survived to adulthood.

6. John Brooke Pinney. See Letter 8, Coates to McLain, May 16, 1851.

7. Probably J. D. Johnson, a Liberian merchant who was one of the three com- missioners sent to the United States by the Liberian government in 1862. Lynch, *Edward Wilmot Blyden*, 27.

8. The ACS. See Letter 8, Coates to McLain, May 16, 1851.

❖ 65 ❖

Philadelphia Feby 3rd 1862[9]

Revd Alexr Crummell.[10]

My dear Sir,

I had hoped to have seen you ere this, as your last letter gave me to suppose that you would after visiting Hartford, return here via Princeton, + Burlington N.J.[11] I feel quite an interest that you have your book published to the best advantage to yourself and + the cause, and as I stated in my last I thought this could be accomplished better through one of the large publishing houses who have their agents, or connections in all the principle cities of the U. States, + in England, much better than your doing it yourself, provided that they could be induced to extend a little liberality especially as you could show from your own list of subscribers already obtained, that it was not altogether an experiment + could not prove a failure, or result in a loss to themselves. Both Mr Tracey,[12] + Mr Pinney[13] called to see me on their return from Washington + they both agreed with me in this view of the case, as I had already expressed to you. But I presume that ere this you have probably decided one way or the other, and I should be glad to hear from you on the subject to know how you are progressing [page break] If you have concluded to put the work into Mr Grey's hands + publish it altogether on your own account, I should think you ought to have at least 2000 copies, which he will probably give you for $600. and if I can be of service to you, should it be necessary to advance a part or the whole of the amount I shall be glad to do so, + trust you will not hesitate to call on me, altho' I have objections to giving my name, in these times to one I do not know + who does not know me, besides being established on principal in this matter. If however you have not yet done any thing in the matter and cannot make a satisfactory arrangement with any of the large publishing houses, would it not be better, if you instead visiting this city soon, to see what can be done here. I should be glad to go with you to one or two of our publishers here, + think it can be done at least on as good terms as were proposed to you in New York when you wrote to me last.

9. Courtesy HSP.

10. Alexander Crummell. See Letter 28, Coates to Gurley, May 2, 1857.

11. Crummell was in the United States to raise interest in emigration to Liberia (see Letter 64, Coates to Crummell, January 13, 1862).

12. Probably Joseph Tracy (see Letter 25, Roberts to Coates, May 15, 1856), despite the fact that Coates rarely misspelled a name.

13. John Brooke Pinney. See Letter 8, Coates to McLain, May 16, 1851.

I think that a least 2000 copies of the work could be sold without the aid of the large publishing houses, but if they were to take it in hand could probably effect a sale of 10,000 to 20,000 copies, + then benefit the cause of African civilization + enlightenment.

       Very truly Yours

            Benjª Coates

P.S.

      Several enquiries have been made of me lately in regard to you + your book; when it would be out + the prospect +c +c

❊ 66 ❊

                    Philadelphia Feby 20th 1862[14]

Revd Alex Crummell[15]

       My Dear Sir,

             I am glad to know that you have made an arrangement to have your book published by Scribner Co. that will relieve you of the trouble + vexation incident to a business you are unaccustomed to. alth° the terms are not quite so liberal as I had hoped they would offer. I presume however that of course you are to receive a percentage on the copies they dispose of through their different agents themselves, altho' you do not say so.

             You may draw on me <u>at sight</u> for one hundred dollars as proposed whenever you may need it, to be returned at your convenience when you have received payment for the copies sold.

             Do you read the Tribune? See Mr Price's report of the liberated slaves at Port Royal S.C.[16] to Mr Chase, in yesterdays

---

14. Courtesy HSP.

15. Alexander Crummell. See Letter 28, Coates to Gurley, May 2, 1857.

16. In 1861, in an effort to strengthen the naval blockade of the South, the Union army captured the Sea Islands, which lie along the coast of South Carolina. When it was evident that there was an imminent Federal attack, the islands' handful of wealthy white residents abandoned their plantations, leaving behind a population of nearly ten thousand slaves. The Federal Treasury Department saw the Union victory as a chance to collect some needed cash through the sale of the Sea Islands' high-quality cotton crop. Northern abolitionists saw it as an opportunity to demonstrate the capability of former slaves. Secretary of the Treasury Salmon P. Chase chose Edward Pierce, a lawyer from Boston, to go to the Sea Islands to investigate the situation there and attempt to organize the black population such that the cotton could be harvested and the workers could be educated and given the skills necessary for independent existence. In order to seize this opportunity, Northern abolitionists organized to supplement the government's efforts.

"Tribune" 19th inst[17] and the article from Fraziers' Magazine in today's paper ~~from~~ by John Stuart Mill,[18] both very interesting.

Yours very truly

Benj[a] Coates

❖ 67 ❖

Haverford College[19]

4 mo 8. 1862

Esteemed Friend

Benj Coates

Permit me to return my sincere thanks for the interesting volume received from thee yesterday, as also for a statistical pamphlet which thou sent me some time since. Both were very acceptable. Crummells book[20] is not only interesting but evidences a cultivated mind. If I recollect rightly the author is not of mixed blood, but of pure Negro descent. I have been very favorably disappointed, in my own acquaintance with Coloured people in finding, so large

---

The New England Education Commission, Port Royal Relief Commission, and New York National Freedmen's Relief Association all sprang up within months of the taking of the islands. These societies, which expanded their efforts as the war progressed, sent supplies and teachers in the name of elevating the freedmen. The project, which has since been referred to as the rehearsal for Reconstruction, experienced measured success despite several obstacles. One teacher noted that Union soldiers often held negative views of the slaves and acted violently toward the freemen. Furthermore, although much of the land in the area had been abandoned, it was not distributed to the freedmen, as many had hoped, but was instead sold to Northern investors. Nevertheless, the newly constructed schools were successful and several remain today. Willie Lee Rose, *Rehearsal for Reconstruction: The Port Royal Experiment* (Indianapolis: Bobbs-Merril Company, 1964); Foner, *History of Black Americans*, 410–18; Edith M. Dabbs, *Sea Island Diary: A History of St. Helena Island* (Spartanburg, S.C.: Reprint Company, 1983); Laura M. Towne, *Letters and Diary of Laura M. Towne*, ed. Rupert Sargent Holland (1912).

17. Coates refers to "Light on the Slavery Question: The Negroes in South Carolina: Report of the Government Agent," a lengthy report by Edward Pierce to Salmon P. Chase, published in the New York *Daily Tribune* on February 19, 1862, in which Pierce gives his impression of the condition of the plantations and slaves on the Sea Islands of South Carolina. Pierce arrived in mid-January and submitted his report—the same one that was published in the New York *Daily Tribune* and other papers—on February 3. Rose, *Rehearsal for Reconstruction*, 3–31.

18. Mill's article—originally published in the February issue of *Fraser's Magazine*, a British monthly journal, and republished in the New York *Daily Tribune* on February 20, 1862— presented an argument for the moral justification of the North's involvement in the Civil War.

19. Haverford College was founded in 1833 by the Orthodox faction of the Philadelphia and New York Quakers as a place to educate their sons.

20. Mitchell is most likely referring to *The Future of Africa* (see Letter 64, Coates to Crummell, January 13, 1862).

an amount of capacity and talent, in the pure African. It is now quite a question with me, whether there is not <u>more</u> stamina where the blood is unmixed. To thyself & Dr. Tyng[21] the appearance of this book must be especially grateful, as an evidence to you that your concern for the intellectual and religious advancement of this injured race has not been in vain. Once more thanking thee for this excellent work. I remain

Thine

Wm F. Mitchell[22]

❖ 68 ❖

My dear friend,

    Benjamin Coates

        Many thanks for thy gift of Crummell's very interesting volume on the "Future of Africa."[23] How significant the title! and fraught with what hopes for the philanthropist and the Christian!

        If a word of sympathy can be of any value, let me express my sense both of the nobleness and the fruitfulness of thy efforts in behalf of a despised and degraded race. I can wish thee no higher earthly reward than that thee may see them attended with continued and increasing success.

Believe me Ever

Very truly thy Friend

Thomas Chase.[24]

Haverford

4th mo. 10th. 1862

21. Stephen Higginson Tyng (March 1, 1800–September 3, 1885) was born in Rhode Island and graduated from Harvard in 1817. He became an Episcopal deacon in 1821 and entered the priesthood in 1824. During his career, he served at St. John's Church in Washington, D.C., Queen Anne's Parish in Maryland, St. Paul's Church and Church of the Epiphany in Philadelphia, and St. George's Church in New York. At the time of the Civil War, Tyng was active in the American Bible Society and the American Tract Society. He became the first president of the National Freedmen's Relief Association in 1862.

22. William Foster Mitchell (?–June 16, 1892) was born an Orthodox Quaker in Nantucket, Massachusetts, and he died a Friend even though he was not a member of the society during the middle of his lifetime. Mitchell was an active educator and served as an administrator at the Penn Charter School, the principal of Roberts Vaux Public School, the superintendent of Haverford College (1861–62), and a teacher at Howard University. He was also involved with the Bethany Mission for Colored People. *Friends Intelligencer* 49 (1892): 489.

23. Crummell, *The Future of Africa*. See Letter 64, Coates to Crummell, January 13, 1862.

24. Thomas Chase (June 16, 1827–October 5, 1892) was born in Worcester, Massachusetts, and graduated from Harvard in 1848. After working as a tutor at Harvard for three years,

69 ❖

Philadelphia April 14th 1862[25]

Rev[d] Alex[r] Crummell[26]

My Dear Sir,

I was disappointed in not seeing you when last in this city, as I had ~~expected~~ hoped to and as I may not see you again before leaving the country, it seemed to me that I should hardly be doing justice to you, to myself, or the cause without expressing more fully than I have done, my appreciation of the value of your book,[27] and the good results that must attend your visit to the United States at this time.[28]

As you are aware I am not much given to compliments, + have such a distaste to what may seem like flattery that I do not always commend, when perhaps I should, but often go to the other extreme, + take the liberty of a friend in criticising pretty freely where I think the occasion demands. But in your book I really do not find any thing to criticise, and to speak of it at all, as I should, may not be altogether in good taste, as in doing so I may assume that my opinions are of more value than they really are. But without affecting any modesty on the subject I may say, that having more than thirty years since labored earnestly in the Colonization cause, in its darkest day when only the untiring energy of youth saved it from collapse + having retained the same interest ever since, I ought to know what were the high inspiring motives that activated myself + my co-laborers that induced us to devote our time [page break] and our interests to this work, and I may say therefore that I have seen no-where, I know of no work that so fully + entirely expresses my views in all respects as the "Future of Africa." Your letter to Dr Dunbar[29] appealing to the

---

Chase became a classics professor and commenced a thirty-year teaching career at Haverford College in 1855. In 1875, he became the president of Haverford, a position he held until ill health forced him to resign in 1866. Chase earned his LL.D. from Harvard in 1878 and was active in the New Testament Company of the American Committee of the Revision of the Bible *Friends Intelligencer* 48 (1892): 665; *Friends Review* 46 (1892–93): 206.

25. Courtesy HSP.

26. Alexander Crummell. See Letter 28, Coates to Gurley, May 2, 1857.

27. *The Future of Africa.* See Letter 64, Coates to Crummell, January 13, 1862.

28. Crummell was in the United States to raise interest in emigration to Liberia. See Letter 64, Coates to Crummell, January 13, 1862.

29. Coates is referring to a chapter in Crummell's newly published book, *The Future of Africa*, entitled "The Relations and Duties of Free Colored Men in America to Africa: Addressed to Mr. Charles B. Dunbar, M.D., formerly of New Yok City, but now a citizen of Liberia." This letter was also published separately in 1861, when it met with widespread approval and paved the way for Crummell's visit to the United States later that year. Oldfield, *Alexander Crummell*, 67.

free colored population of the United States, while claiming for them their just + equal rights in America, points out very forcibly the advantages that enterprising men will have in emigrating to Africa + the blessings that civilization will confer on that continent + on the entire race. It is hardly necessary therefore for me to express the great satisfaction that I take in finding that your views + principles accord so <u>entirely</u> with my own, + coming from one of pure African blood exemplifying at the same time the capacity of the Negro race. the Future of Africa is just <u>the</u> book that I like to place in the hands of those who take an interest in the elevation of our oppressed + downtrodden people.[30] Your visit to the United States at this time I cannot but think is most opportune. The <u>true</u> philanthropist must desire the well being of the whole human family, wherever scattered, of every race + color, + in every clime, and a <u>true</u> abolitionist must desire to see slavery abolished <u>every where</u>, in Africa as well as in America + cannot but feel an interest in the Civilization + Christianization of Africa. Some of my friends were at first rather jealous of my proposed settlement at Abbeokuta, in Egba[31] + Youraba country,[32] + the organization of the "African Civilization Socy,"[33] [page break] fearing that it might conflict with the interest of Liberia, but such was not the <u>intention</u> + such was not the fact. Such was the deep seated prejudice in the minds of nearly the entire colored population against the colonization enterprise, that they would not listen with patience to any argument on the subject, and the very name of Liberia was obnoxious to them. It was almost labor lost to talk on the subject even to ~~such~~ men ~~as~~ like Delany + Robt Campbell, or Wm Whipper or Fred^k Douglass,[34] all of whom had a personal regard for me. But after Livingston[35] + Bowen[36] had shown the comparative healthfulness of the high table land of the interior of Africa in the Egba, + Youraba country, I thought it best to direct attention to that region, knowing full well,

30. Coates sent copies of Crummell's *The Future of Africa* to William Mitchell (see Letter 67, Mitchell to Coates, April 8, 1862); Thomas Chase (see Letter 68, Chase to Coates, April 10, 1862); and George Allen (see Letter 75, Allen to Coates, April 23, 1863).

31. The Egba are a subgroup of the Yoruba people. They split off from the Oyo empire during a civil war in the nineteenth century and settled Abeokuta, Nigeria, which became the site of the first Christian missionary activity in the area. *Historical Dictionary of Nigeria*, 188–89.

32. Yoruba, Africa. See Letter 34, Cary to Coates, November 20, 1858.

33. African Civilization Society. See Letter 36, Coates to Gurley, January 13, 1859.

34. Martin Delany (see Letter 34, Shadd Cary to Coates, November 20, 1858); Robert Campbell (see Letter 47, Campbell to Coates, July 14, 1859); William Whipper (see Letter 35, Wagoner to Coates, January 8, 1859); Frederick Douglass (see Letter 4, Coates to Douglass, June 27, 1850).

35. David Livingstone. See Letter 32, Coates to Gurley, May 28, 1858.

36. Thomas Jefferson Bowen. See Letter 32, Coates to Gurley, May 28, 1858.

that an interest once created in Africa must accrue to the interest of Liberia, even should a successful + prosperous settlement be made elsewhere. As a matter of <u>expediency</u> + <u>policy</u> therefore I suggested a new organization, avoiding the obnoxious term of Colonization, and the result has not disappointed my expectations, indeed my hopes were more than realized, for as Mr Garnet[37] very justly remarked before he left for England, that if not a single person went to Youraba, at this time, a strong ~~an~~ interest had been awakened in Africa, the results of which you have experienced in your intercourse with our colored population, while had your visit to America been two years earlier you could hardly have had a hearing in many places, where you [page break] have been now most favorably received. I merely mention this as a part of the history of this work, + from the remark in your book in reference to that proposed settlement it appeared to me that you rather misapprehended the true state of the case or rather did not appreciate it in <u>all its bearings</u>. My firm opinion is that the time is not very distant when Dahomey,[38] + Ashanti,[39] as well as large parts of the Egba + Youraba Countries, with the adjacent kingdoms, will be civilized + Christian states, forming probably <u>part</u> of the <u>Great Republic of Liberia</u>. I may not live to see this, but you may, or should you not see it yourself, probably your children will. This you may think a very sanguine anticipation scarcely warranted by any present indication of the rapid advance of civilization (of Christian civilization). But my dear sir, when I first undertook the colonization cause, surrounded as it was by every discouragement, everything was dark + gloomy. My friends thought I was spending my energies in a hopeless task. Colonization was then exceedingly unpopular, its earliest friends had nearly all become discouraged + left it, its receipts did not cover the expenses of agents +c in America. Yet we worked on. My friend Thomas Buchanan[40] went to Liberia, a first + a second time, + gave his life to the cause. He founded Bassa Cove, now Buchanan,[41] which I induced the Legislature of Liberia to name after my valued friend who went with my advice to Liberia. Thomas Buchanan, Topliff Johnson + myself then took an

37. Henry Highland Garnet. See Letter 3, Coates to Douglass, June 27, 1850.

38. Dahomey was an African kingdom that occupied what is now southern Benin. It came into existence after the conglomeration of several states in the 1720s. Its principle industry was the sale of slaves until the slave trade came to an end around 1840, at which point emphasis was shifted to the export of palm oil. "Dahomey," *Encyclopedia Britannica*, vol. 3, 848.

39. The Ashanti empire controlled what is now southern Ghana during the eighteenth and nineteenth centuries. The Ashanti people engaged in the slave trade until it came to an end. "Ashanti empire," *Encyclopedia Britannica*, vol. 1, 621.

40. Thomas Buchanan. See Letter 8, Coates to McLain, May 16, 1851.

41. Buchanan. See Letter 8, Coates to McLain, May 16, 1851.

active + leading part in infusing new life in the cause + now what do we see as the result, an Independent Republic which Roberts, Teage, Benson, Warner, + Benedict[42] + their co laborers have placed I trust on a solid foundation, + which you + Blyden[43] + others are laboring so zealously + successfully to carry forward. That you may be enabled to continue in this noble + glorious work, + that you

[Written vertically along the left margin of the last page:]
may live to see + enjoy the result of your labors, as I have been permitted to realize in my lifetime so far the result of my hopes + expectations, is the sincere desire of Your friend Benjᵃ Coates.

H Reps[44]
April 24th 1862

My dear sir

The tax bill will not become a law for a month or two, and its ultimate shape is quite uncertain. Meanwhile, applications for office under come in ——ful numbers.

It will if possible to do so afford me sincere pleasure to secure you a place under it. My hands will be very full but if your friend Judge —— will ask it—I know he can command it.

Yours very truly
Wm D Kelley[45]

42. Joseph Jenkins Roberts (see Letter 1, Roberts to Coates, July 8, 1848); Hilary Teage (see Letter 10, Coates to McLain, October 11, 1851); Stephen Allen Benson (see Letter 8, Coates to McLain, May 16, 1851); and Daniel Bashiell Warner (see Letter 10, Coates to McLain, October 11, 1851). Samuel Benedict (1792–1854) was born a slave in Georgia and immigrated to Liberia in 1835, after his owner freed him. He served as a judge prior to Liberia's independence and was president of the 1847 Constitutional Convention. He unsuccessfully challenged J. J. Roberts for the presidency but was appointed Chief Justice of the Supreme Court. *HDL* 25.

43. Edward Wilmot Blyden. See Letter 27, Coates to Lugenbeel, October 6, 1856.

44. This letter seems like it could be to Coates—the envelope is addressed to him—but it is not clear since his name is not on the letter itself.

45. William Darrah Kelley (April 12, 1814–January 9, 1890) was born in Philadelphia and moved to Boston after being apprenticed to a jeweler. He returned to Philadelphia in 1838 and studied law. In 1841 Kelley was admitted to the bar. Kelley served as a prosecutor starting in 1845 and became a judge six years later. Kelley was one of the founders of the Pennsylvania Republican Party and resigned his judgeship to run for Congress in 1856 as a Republican. He lost the

❖ 71 ❖

New York 6 Oct 1862
Benj[n]. Coates Esq.
        Philad[a]
            Dear Sir
                    Your paper of 1st. inst came duly to hand contents
noted. I have delayed answering it expecting to have heard from Mr Ross
in reply to your letters of 12 mo 6th. ult but have not as yet had any letter from
him. Meantime I learn from Mr Pooles attorney at Halifax that the legal
preliminaries to a foreclosure sale of the quarry under the mortgage will be
complete about the 1st November next unless something is done to prevent it.
I think you had better allow me to write the atty. that you will take up the —
— if he will send them on. they are made payable on the face of them at the
Park Bank in this city
                    on recpt of your letter I saw Mr. [Leary] and showed it to him. he
desired me to say that ~~owing to his absence from the city~~ he was absent from
the city when your letter to him of 25th. reached and it was laid aside for him
but escaped his notice and he was not aware you had written him until his
attention was called to it by the paragraph in you letter to me. If you will draft
such an amount as you wish him and Mr Ross to [sign] or other creditors I
will see that it is done by giving the matter my personal attention We have but
little time to loose in the matter and I will be glad to hear from you at your
earliest convenience
                    I remain
                        Yours truly
                            LRM [Say]
I have written Mr Ross enclosing him a copy of your letter of 1st inst.

1856 election but won in 1860. As a member of Congress, Kelley supported the Emancipation
Proclamation and many Republican Reconstruction acts. He submitted a bill that would have
allowed universal male suffrage for those who could read but his bill never passed. Kelley also
supported the effort to end streetcar segregation in Philadelphia and endorsed protective tariffs.
ANB vol. 12.

❖ 72 ❖

27. Bible House
New York, Oct. 9. 1862.[46]

Benjm Coates, Esq.

Dear Sir,

Knowing how deeply interested you are in everything that pertains to Liberian educational interests, I cannot, while appealing to others on the subject, pass by you without at least informing you of the movement.

We are trying to establish a "Book Concern" at Monrovia, from which, at a cheap rate, school books and other educational works may be furnished to the Liberian community.

We have great difficulty now in getting books of a suitable kind. We get from time to time, donations of books from this country; but they are generally scattered copies of different works—furnishing no convenience for a class. And if we order school books we are obliged to do so through the merchants, and before we can get them they cost so much that very few care or can afford to buy. Many who would buy books and read more do not on account of the troublesome and expensive manner in which they are now obtained.

Now the object of the "Book Concern" is to enable us to keep on hand in Monrovia (and we hope to grow by and by so as to have branches in other settlements) a regular supply of school books +c of various kinds to the amount of $300 and secure them at such prices here as to be able to furnish them to the people of Liberia at the price at which they are retailed in New York.—The proceeds to be used in purchasing fresh supplies—the fund being a permanent and sacred fund to be diverted to no other object.

I have already secured for this very desirable object $200. If I can raise the three hundred, we shall have a fair beginning: and it may in time become so important an institution as to furnish the literature of all West Africa. For a long time, we have felt the need of such a Book concern, but have not known how to supply it.

Messrs. Roe Lockwood + Son[47] of this city have expressed themselves favorably to the project, and have promised to lend us their assistance in carrying it out.

46. In 1862 Blyden left Liberia, bound for the United States, to encourage American black people to emigrate to Liberia. He returned late in 1862 to take up his new professorial position at Liberia College. Livingston, *Education and Race*, 46–55.

47. Roe Lockwood & Son was founded in 1798 in Bridgeport, Connecticut, by Lambert Lockwood, who moved to New York in 1816. Originally under another name, it became Roe

I have already engaged books from them to the amount of money collected, but they think—and so do I—that the collection does not embrace a sufficient variety to make a bookstore attractive for besides books, we need stationary +c + I think I shall be able to raise another hundred dollars, but it must be done within a few days, as I expect to sail for Liberia on the 20th inst. Can you interest any of your friends to this matter? Please let me hear from you as soon as possible

Respectfully Yrs.

Edwd. W. Blyden[48]

27, Bible House,
New York Oct 15/62

❧ 73 ❧

Benj. Coates, Esq

Dear Sir,

I have just received enclosed w a kind note from you twenty dollars towards our Book Concern.[49] Accept my sincere thanks.

I trust that your labour and benevolence on behalf of Liberia, will not be in vain—may God bless + prosper you—

Faithfully yrs.

Edwd. W. Blyden[50]

Lockwood & Son when Lambert's son, Roe, and his son, George, took over the business. In 1862 Roe passed the firm on to George, who ran it until his death in 1888, when the firm ceased business. Roe Lockwood & Son was primarily a bookselling concern, although it did publish books occasionally, including reprints of Audubon's *Birds of America* and *Viviparous Quadrupeds of North America*. John Tebbel, *A History of Book Publishing in the United States* (New York: R. R. Bowker, 1972), 354.

48. Edward Wilmot Blyden. See Letter 26, Coates to Lugenbeel, October 6, 1856.
49. The Liberian Book Concern. See Letter 72, Blyden to Coates, October 9, 1862.
50. Edward Wilmot Blyden. See Letter 27, Coates to Lugenbeel, October 6, 1856.

❖ 74 ❖

Philadelphia Feb. 10th 1863

Rev^d. R. R. Gurley[51]
    Colonization Rooms
        Washington City
           My dear sir.

As my two nephews Henry T Coates, & George M Coates Jr.[52] propose to visit Washington during the present College vacation, I have requested them to call + see my friend Mr. Gurley. They will wish to visit the Capital while Congress is in session, and any other object of interest, to which you can probably direct them.

Never having been in Washington myself I do not exactly ^ know what is to be seen, and cannot therefore direct them where to go. But do not give yourself the least trouble with them as they are abundantly able to find their way about the City, with some general directions from yourself.

George you knew when he was a small boy but I suppose you would not recognize him again.

I was very sorry to hear of the illness of our friend Mr Pinney[53]—is he still in Washington? + if so how is he?

Sincerely yours,
    Benj^a. Coates

❖ 75 ❖

Oberlin April 23rd 1863

Benj. Coates Esqr
    Philadelphia
        Penn^a
        Dear Sir

We have the pleasure of acknowledging the receipt of 2 valuable books from yourself as a donation to the Oberlin College Library; viz.

---

51. Ralph Randolph Gurley. See Letter 10, Coates to McLain, October 11, 1851.

52. Henry Troth Coates (1843–?) was the son of George Morrison Coates Jr. (Benjamin Coates's brother George, not the George Morrison Coates Jr. mentioned here), and George Morrison Coates Jr. was the son of Joseph Potts Hornor Coates. At the writing of this letter, George was a senior at Haverford College and Henry had graduated from the same institution the year before. *Catalogue of the Officers and Students of Haverford College*, 1863 and 1864.

53. John Brooke Pinney. See Letter 8, Coates to McLain, May 16, 1851.

"Liberia's Offering"[54] + "The Future of Africa"[55] by the Rev. Messrs. Blyden[56] + Crummell[57] respectively.

You will please accept our hearty thanks for the same in behalf of the College.

> Very Resply [Respectfully]
> Geo. N. Allen[58]
> Treas. Instion. [Institution]

❖ 76 ❖

BENJAMIN COATES[59]   GEO. MORRISON COATES

COATES, BROTHERS,   127 Market Street,

COMMISSION MERCHANTS,   PHILADELPHIA, April 7 1864

For the Purchase and Sale of

WOOL

Rev[d]. W[m] M[c]Lain[60]—Financial Secy Am Col[n] Socy[61]

Colonization Rooms

> Washington City

> Dear sir,

> I have just rec[d] protest of a draft drawn on you by W[m] H Lynch in favor of A J Johns Treas[r]. Approved by D B Warner[62] acting President of the Republic of Liberia dated Monrovia July 19th 1862

---

54. Edward W. Blyden, *Liberia's Offering: Being Addresses, Sermons, etc.* (New York: John A. Gray, 1862). Published at the end of Blyden's book is a twelve-page letter from Blyden to Coates discussing the Colonization movement. Blyden wrote the letter on June 7, 1862, and notes that Coates is a philanthropist above all and thanks him for the books he has sent. Blyden goes on to express the appreciation of the Liberian people towards the ACS for all that the society has done. He notes that few in Liberia are bitter towards anticolonization abolitionists as their opposition was based on their good will towards black people.

55. Crummell, *The Future of Africa*. See Letter 64, Coates to Crummell, January 13, 1862.

56. Edward Wilmot Blyden. See Letter 27, Coates to Lugenbeel, October 6, 1856.

57. Alexander Crummell. See Letter 28, Coates to Gurley, May 2, 1857.

58. George Nelson Allen (1838–1871) was a graduate of and professor at Oberlin College. He served as secretary and treasurer from 1863 to 1865. Oberlin College, *General Catalogue of Oberlin College*, int. 130.

59. The first five lines of this letter constitute the Coates brothers' printed letterhead, with the exception of the month, day, and last digit of the year.

60. William McLain. Letter 1, Roberts to Coates, July 8, 1848.

61. The ACS. See Letter 8, Coates to McLain, May 16, 1851.

62. Daniel Bashiell Warner. See Letter 10, Coates to McLain, October 11, 1851.

for One hundred & twenty five ^{06}/100 dollars—$125.^{06} no. 143 which was for-warded to me for collection by Ex-President Joseph J Roberts.[63]

As the notary states that "he went to your place of business + found the Office closed + no one there to pay it" as his reason for protesting, I have thought it best before returning it to Liberia, to write to you to enquire, whether it would have been paid if your office had been open, + to know whether it will be paid if I forward it again to Washington.

If not I will to write to ^{Ex} President Roberts as soon as practicable, + you will oblige by an early reply.

Yours very truly

Benj^a Coates

❊ 77 ❊

BENJAMIN COATES   GEO. MORRISON COATES[64]
COATES, BROTHERS,   127 Market Street,
COMMISSION MERCHANTS,   PHILADELPHIA, October 13th 1864
For the Purchase and Sale of
WOOL
Wm Coppinger Esq.[65]

Dear sir,

A short time since I received a letter from Rev^d. J. Theodore Holly,[66] infoming me that he had been appointed Consul for the Republic of Liberia it Port au Prince, Haiti[67] and making certain suggestions of what may needed in connexion therewith, which he no doubt supposes will interest the friends of Liberia in the United States, and as he states there is no salary connected with the offices, + he has no means of his own, it will devolve ~~I suppose~~ on the friends of Colonization to supply the necessities of the case. As one of those friends I am willing to do <u>something</u> if others should deem it advisable to furnish the articles required. But I have so many demands on my purse of late, which is getting <u>very light</u>, since the great decline in wool that I cannot afford to do a great deal. I would be willing

63. Joseph Jenkins Roberts. See Letter 1, Roberts to Coates, July 8, 1848.

64. The first five lines constitute the Coates brothers' printed letterhead, with the exception of the month, day, and last digit of the year.

65. William Coppinger. See Letter 10, Coates to McLain, October 11, 1851.

66. James Theodore Holly. See Letter 57, Holly to Coates, September 13, 1859.

67. Haiti. See Letter 19, Roberts to Coates, October 16, 1854.

however to contribute $10. (say Ten dollars) in a general contribution for the purpose, or if it is thought best to confine it to a few I will be one of <u>twenty</u> or one of <u>ten</u> persons to make up the requisite amount to be divided equally between the parties subscribing. I do not know what better to do with the letter than enclose it to you as I have not time to attend to it.

Yours truly,

B. Coates

❖ 78 ❖

BENJAMIN COATES   GEO. MORRISON COATES[68]
COATES, BROTHERS,   127 Market Street,
COMMISSION MERCHANTS,   PHILADELPHIA, Nov. 1ˢᵗ 1864
For the Purchase and Sale of
WOOL

Wᵐ Coppinger Esq.[69]
   Colonization Rooms
      Washington D.C.

Dear sir

A short time since I received a letter from Wᵐ H Johnson[70] of Canandaigua N.Y.—similar to the one he sent you, published in the last "Repository"[71]—by some oversight I did not read it until after the time he said he would leave for Vermont. After reading I enclosed it to Jo. P Crozer[72] who returned it to me with $5 for Mr Johnson + wishing to

---

68. The first five lines constitute the Coates brothers' printed letterhead, with the exception of the month, day, and last digit of the year.

69. William Coppinger. See Letter 10, Coates to McLain, October 11, 1851.

70. Henry W. Johnson was a barber from Canandaigua, New York. In 1864 the *African Repository* reported that the New York Supreme Court admitted him to the bar. Upon obtaining his law certification, Johnson attempted to persuade the ACS to send him and his family to Liberia, where he would practice law. An article in the *African Repository* states that Johnson's goals before leaving the United States were to raise money for his daughter's education and to acquire a small law library. Coates's money was probably for one of those two purposes. Another letter from Johnson, published in the African Repository in 1868, reports his satisfaction with Liberia. *African Repository* 40, no. 7 (July 1864); 40, no. 11 (November 1864); and 44, no. 10 (October 1868).

71. *African Repository*. See Letter 15, Coates to Lugenbeel, June 27, 1853.

72. John Price Crozer (January 13, 1793–March 11, 1866) was born in Springfield, Pennsylvania, and became a manufacturer of cotton goods. He then moved to Upland, Pennsylvania, where he was involved in a variety of charitable activities. Crozer donated $45,000 in 1858 for an educational building that later became a Baptist theological seminary. He was instrumental in the foundation of a normal school, which was used as a hospital during the Civil War. In 1861

contribute same and five dollars, I enclose herewith a $10. note for Mr J. from Mr Crozer + myself. I have so many demands on me that I cannot give to each as I would like to, but had supposed that Mr Crozer would have given at least $10. himself. + in that case I should have done likewise. But I do not think it becomes me to exceed Mr C. in matters of this kind. Please send it to Mr Johnson with what you may receive from others.

Yours very truly

John P Crozer $5   Benj Coates
Benj. Coates $5 | $10 Enclosed

❖ 79 ❖

Penn^a Lodge, Nashville, Jan.28.65

Mr. Benj. Coates:

I am one of the teachers in Mr. Mitchell's[73] mess at Nashville and he has told me that you took him into a bookstore when he was in Philada. and wanted him to buy anything he chose to have.

I am very sorry that I was not there to suggest what to purchase and I said so to Mr. Mitchell, and he replied "You may write to Mr Coates about it," so I take advantage of his permission to do so. The colored children all have a talent for drawing, and I am very fond of it too, so I would like to teach it in my school, and I would like to have some drawing cards to begin with. Coe's drawing cards will do very nicely, and as I should have a large class of beginners, I shall want a good many packages of the same number, say twenty packages of No. one and twenty packages of No. two.

I have blackboards and chalk crayons but I would like some drawing pencils and paper. I think Faber's pencils are the best Nos. 1, 2 and 3, and a few of No. 4. I am not very particular about the quality of the paper, but I would like it to be white. Then I shall want some rubbers to erase marks. This is all I shall want in this direction, tho. I think it would be nice to have some drawing books for the most proficient of my pupils by and by. In a school of

---

Crozer was a member of the Philadelphia Christian Commission. He also endowed a professorship at Bucknell College. Crozer and his family participated in the colonization movement. Crozer was a life director of the ACS. His brother died in Africa and was also involved with the ACS. When Crozer died, he left $50,000 for "Missions Among Colored People of this Country." *Appleton's* vol. 2; *ANB* vol. 4; *African Repository* 40, no. 7 (July 1864).

73. William F. Mitchell (see Letter 67, Mitchell to Coates, April 8, 1862), a Philadelphia Quaker, was superintendent of Nashville's freedmen's schools at this time. Robert C. Morris, *Reading, 'Riting, and Reconstruction* (Chicago: University of Chicago Press, 1976), 69.

125 children, like the one in which I am teaching, I think I should have a class of forty ready to do something quite creditable in drawing in the course of a few months.

Besides these things, I would be very much pleased to have some rewards of merit for my pupils. very high-colored fancy ones please them best. They are a great help in the government of the school.

Then I would like a set of maps from which to teach Geography. I think it an excellent plan to make the children familiar with the shapes of countries by means of them; but I should prefer 1 globe to even a set of maps, I mean a nice large globe.

I also want a numeral frame to teach my little ones to count but I think that what I have mentioned is rather too much for one person to contribute, and so I will mention here that I do not expect anything but the drawing cards, but I make a list of the others because I have no doubt there are many benevolent persons in your city, interested in the colored people who would gladly send something useful of this kind if they only knew what to send, and ~~some~~ any one of the articles I have named would make a very useful and acceptable gift.

Very respectfully,
Evelyn E. Plummer.[74]

 80

BENJAMIN COATES   GEO. MORRISON COATES[75]
    COATES, BROTHERS,   127 Market Street,
    COMMISSION MERCHANTS,   PHILADELPHIA, Feb. 6th 1865
    For the Purchase and Sale of
    WOOL
Mr Wm Coppinger[76]

Dear Sir,

I wrote to Mr J P. Crozer[77] a few days since enclosing your letter, + Mr Crummel's.[78] He returned them to day, with

74. Evelyn Plummer was probably a teacher in one of the freedmen's schools in Tennessee.
75. The first five lines constitute the Coates brothers' printed letterhead, with the exception of the month, day, and last digit of the year.
76. William Coppinger. See Letter 10, Coates to McLain, October 11, 1851.
77. John Price Crozer. See Letter 78, Coates to Coppinger, November 1, 1864.
78. Alexander Crummell. See Letter 28, Coates to Gurley, May 2, 1857.

the enclosed mem. [memorandum] saying he would forward $20 to you. Please find enclosed my check for $30. to go with it, making $50. together, hoping that you may find some others to add the other $50.

> as ever very truly yours   Benj. Coates.

❖ 81 ❖

Boston Feby 13. 1865

Benjamin Coates
> 127 Market St.
>> Phila

Dear Sir

Your letter of the 8th inst is before me. I am amused to see here a mans imagination sometimes runs away with him. it is more dangerous than a frightened horse. but lest you should continue under grave doubts as to the propriety of the circulars I issue, I will enlighten you and through you all the good people of Philadelphia whose "curiosity" may be similarly xcited, and you are at liberty to read this to all such persons as you meet them.

First My circular means what is expressed in it, no more, no less.[79]

Second I discussed in Oct. 1856 that John C. Fremont[80] was not fit to be President of these United States, and have not since that time advocated his claims to that office.

Third I was accidentally placed in communication with him last summer, and used the little influence with I possessed to induce him to withdraw from the contest for the Presidency. I have not as yet had occasion to regret it.

Fourth If you do not see the necessity for the course I am pursuing, I do, and shall continue my work untill I find the antislavery men of the country doubt its propriety.

---

79. In January 1865, Stearns, a very successful Massachusetts businessman, sent a letter to vice president–elect Andrew Johnson, enlisting his support for having Massachusetts' abolitionist governor John Andrew be appointed to President Lincoln's cabinet. Andrew's staunch anti-slavery position, argued Sterns, would strengthen the federal administration's position with northern radicals. Stearns sent the same letter to dozens of other antislavery leaders, including Gerrit Smith and perhaps to Coates himself. Nothing ever came of this lobbying effort. Charles E. Heller, *Portrait of an Abolitionist: A Biography of George Luther Stearns, 1809–1867* (Westport, Conn.: Greenwood Press, 1996), 187.

80. Frémont (1813–1890) entered the presidential race in 1856 on the Republican ticket on a platform opposed to the extension of slavery. He was defeated by Democrat James Buchanan. "Fremont, John Charles," *ANB* 8:459–62.

<u>Fifth</u> I never have been a leader and dont expect to be one, have held only one office in my life, that of Com. of Mr Stantons Majors,[81] and have made up my mind never to accept an other, therefore I am not influenced by the hope of political preferment.

<u>Sixth</u> Granting all you say in favor of Mr. Lincoln, he is mortal, and liable to all the conditions of mortality, as such he is in need of good advisers and believing Gov. Andrew[82] would be of service to him in that capacity, I am doing all I can to induce Mr Lincoln to accept him as a member of his cabinet.

<u>Seventh</u> I voted for Mr Lincoln in November last and also at his first election, + shall continue to support him as long as I believe he is worthy of the confidence of an abolitionist.

<u>Eighth</u> My authority for sending these circulars is that, Ninety five of the Hundred of antislavery men all through the country approve of them which is evident from the large number of letters I daily receive, very many of them from your state, and so long as I continue to receive such letters, not only from the <u>quiet</u> antislavery men of all the states, but also from many ~~persons~~ who stand high in public estimation, I shall continue to issue them.

<u>Ninth</u> I regret you spent money for the election of John C. Fremont in 1856. Had you then known as much as I did, you would have saved your cash for a better investment.

<u>Tenth</u> I trust you will appreciate the frankness of my answer to your long letter, and my goodwill towards you in striking your name from my list of many thousands of Antislavery men so that you will not in future be troubled with my circulars

    Truly Your friend
    George L. Stearns[83]

81. Stearns pursued the recruitment of black soldiers using private resources during part of the Civil War until 1863, when Secretary of War Edwin Stanton brought Stearns's organization under the auspices of the federal government, giving Stearns the rank of major. Stearns held this position until January 1864, when he resigned because of dissatisfaction with the government's treatment of black soldiers and with Stanton's policies. Heller, *Portrait of an Abolitionist*, 145–67.

82. John A. Andrew (1818–1867), governor of Massachusetts in the 1860s, was, like Stearns, an opponent of slavery. A lawyer, he gave Stearns legal advice after John Brown's attack on Harpers Ferry. In 1864 Stearns lobbied unsuccessfully for Andrew to be given a seat in Lincoln's cabinet. "Andrew, John A.," *ANB* 1:489–90; Heller, *Portrait of an Abolitionist*, 106, 187.

83. George Luther Stearns (1809–1867), a successful dealer in lead pipe, used his money to pursue the abolition of slavery. He played a key role in providing John Brown with weapons and financial support for his raid on Harpers Ferry, and after Brown's capture Stearns fled to Canada for a short while. During the Civil War he fought for emancipation, and, once that had been achieved, led an effort to recruit black people into the Union Army. As part of his

❈ 82 ❈

E W. Clark & Co.- Bankers[84]
　　Philadelphia July 15 1865
Benj. Coates, Esqr.
　　Dear sir
　　　　Your favor of is at hand enclosing ch [check] for $150. which has
been placed to the C. ^ as contribution of Dr Thos. Hodgkins[85] of London. I will
acknowledge the amt recd from him, in the next publication of contributors
　　　Yos truly
　　　　EW Clark Treas^r
　　　　Penn^a Freedmen's Rel As[86]

❈ 83 ❈

Philad^a. Oct. 31. 1865
Mr Wm Coppinger[87]
　　My dear Sir
　　　　　　I had fully intended replying to your letter,
asking me to present the wants of the emigrants for Liberia from Lynchburg

---

ongoing political activities he helped found and finance several publications, including the *Commonwealth*, the *Nation*, and the *Right Way*. Heller, *Portrait of an Abolitionist*; Frank Preston Stearns, *The Life and Public Services of George Luther Stearns* (Philadelphia: J. P. Lippincott Company, 1907); "Stearns, George Luther," *ANB* 20:591–92.

　　84. The first two lines constitute E. W. Clark and Company's printed letterhead, with the exception of the month, day, and last two digits of the year. E. W. Clark and Company was founded in 1837 by Enoch W. Clark in partnership with his two brothers and his brother-in-law. In 1857 Enoch Clark died and Edward W. Clark (the author of this letter) took over his position. John Thom Holdsworth, *Financing an Empire: History of Banking in Pennsylvania*, vol. 2 (Chicago: S. J. Clarke Publishing, 1928), 833–37.

　　85. Thomas Hodgkin. See Letter 40, Hobbins to Coates, March 2, 1859.

　　86. The Pennsylvania Freedmen's Relief Association. In 1862, after the Union army captured the Sea Islands, the Port Royal experiment began (see Letter 107, Schofield to Coates, March 12, 1868). The Port Royal Relief Commission was founded in Philadelphia to support the teaching project. In July 1862, the organization changed its name to Pennsylvania Freedmen's Relief Association. This new name linked the association with the National Freedmen's Relief Association, an organization founded in early 1862 in conjunction with the AMA. In 1866 the Pennsylvania Freedmen's Relief Association merged with the American Freedmen's and Union Commission (AFUC), a group that established schools for poor black people and white people until 1869. Morris, *Reading, 'Riting, and Reconstruction*.

　　87. William Coppinger. See Letter 10, Coates to McLain, October 11, 1851.

& vicinit, to the Freedmens Association with which I am connected, but the letter was mislaid & in the hurry of business was overlooked. However as respects the Penn.ᵃ Freedmens Assn[88] I can say that we are under great discouragement at the present time. our obligation for the salary of teachers that we have employed is upwards of five thousand dollars per month and not a dollar in the treasury! & worse than that we do not see how or where it is to come from. the interest seems very much to have died out, or [page break] turned into other channels, as we find it almost impossible to collect money, while the demand at present for clothing is greater than ever in addition to the large amt due to teachers which we have assigned to pay.

You can readily see therefore that it is impossible for us to do any thing for the emigrants—even if we could do so. But I do not think that either association could feel warranted in appropriating funds for one object that was contributed for another object even supposing that it was equally good or more deserving. Friends association[89] is nearly as poor as the other & greatly in need of funds—also to pay the salary of teachers—& could readily spend to great advantage at least a half million for clothing +c +c [page break] if it could be obtained. I have already given to both these, and to other similar objects of an interesting nature. I gave Mr Crummell[90] $25 for himself & about $70 or $75 in books for Liberia of his own selection for the Lyceum of Monrovia.[91] Still if there is yet very urgent need for clothing for any of the emigrants I should be willing to contribute my mite to the object say $20

If you think best you may draw on me for the amt (Twenty dollars) if it is really needed & the Society cannot furnish it.

88. Coates is probably referring to the Pennsylvania Freedmen's Relief Association (organizations dedicated to the relief of freedmen during and after the Civil War changed their names frequently). See Letter 82, Clark to Coppinger, July 15, 1865.

89. Presumably the Friends Freedmen's Association.

90. Alexander Crummell. See Letter 28, Coates to Gurley, May 2, 1857. Crummell was in the United States during 1865 to bring his daughters, attending Oberlin at the time, back to Liberia, because they had run out of money. While there, he attended the Episcopal General Convention in Philadelphia. Moses, *Alexander Crummell*, 156; Oldfield, *Alexander Crummell*, 86–87.

91. Coates is perhaps referring to the Athenaeum Club, an institution founded in 1864 by Crummell and Edward Blyden. It was meant to educate and reform Liberian youths by engaging them in debates, discussions, and lectures. In 1867 it was dissolved. Rigsby, *Alexander Crummell*, 122; Lynch, *Edward Wilmot Blyden*, 46–47.

Mr Crummell's address before the Penna Colonization Socy[92] at the Church of the Epiphany last Sunday ___ week, was an excellent production & Bishop McIlvain[93] followed him in a very eloquent address.

Yours very truly Benj. Coates

92. The Pennsylvania Colonization Society. See Letter 8, Coates to McLain, May 16, 1851.

93. Charles Pettit McIlvaine (1799–1873) was an Episcopal bishop who had crossed paths with Crummell, also an Episcopalian, before. After his theological studies, McIlvaine served as chaplain and professor at West Point and rector at a church in Brooklyn before he was elected bishop of Ohio in 1831, an office that he held for several decades. He often traveled to foreign countries, including England, where he made contacts within the Church of England. When Crummell first journeyed to England, he carried a letter of invitation from McIlvaine introducing him to members of the Anglican church. "McIlvaine, Charles Pettit," *ANB* 15:84; Oldfield, *Alexander Crummell*, 26.

3

"... not because they are <u>Negroes</u>, but because they are <u>Men</u>": Reconstruction Years, 1866–1880

Benjamin Coates's commitment to relieving the plight of black people did not end with emancipation. In the post–Civil War years, he supported a number of organizations—Quaker and non-Quaker—in projects to educate freed people and to prepare them to be competitive in modern society. In these years many reformers—black and white—recognized the common humanity of "the poor of all classes," and they dedicated their energies to ameliorating the impoverishment of white southerners.

The seventy letters that cover the last fifteen years or so of Coates's active life (although he lived until 1887, he appears to have been in ill health in his final years) reveal his concern that American philanthropists understand the main tragedy of American slavery. As Coates described it in his letter to William Coppinger (dated May 24, 1866), the tragedy was that black Americans were "Men, whose interests have been neglected, whose rights have been outraged, and whose manhood has been almost crushed out of them."

But these letters also reveal Coates's conviction that Africa, not America, was the best place for black people. Much of the focus of the schools he supported continued to be on preparing black Americans to be leaders or responsible citizens in Liberia. He never directly addressed the question of how the return to Africa would be financed, and he never gave up on the idea that, if it could be arranged, black people would choose to "return" to Africa and that they could flourish there.

❖ 84 ❖

Philadelphia May 24th 1866

W[m]. Coppinger Esq
     My dear sir,
         Your favor of yesterday is just received.
While thanking you for the compliment of placing my name among some of
the prominent + distinguished men of the century I am not at all surprised
that your data touching myself is quite meager, for the very obvious reason
that there is not much to be had. The only merit I may have or for which I
am known out of the usual + private walks of life, is the interest I have taken,
in, and the effort I have made on behalf of the sadly neglected African race.
But as I have expressed it in the Third Resolution of a series I offered on the
2nd. of April 1866 ∧ (+ which were adopted,) at our Penn[a] Freedmen's Association[1] when we united with the Union Commission,[2] to include ∧ the poor
whites of the South as well as the blacks in our labors. My sympathy for them
is not because they are black, not because they are Negroes, but because they
are Men, whose interests have been neglected, whose rights have been outraged, and whose manhood has been almost crushed out of them. (You will
see the resolution in the Penn[a] Freedmen's Bulletin[3] for April of this year.) As
to this feeling, while my efforts while my efforts in the cause of humanity have
been chiefly on behalf of the African race, as peoples most needing assistance,
yet by no means exclusively so. I was one of the early members [page break]
of the "Union Benevolent Association"[4] of this city whose aim has been to

---

     1. Coates is probably referring to the Pennsylvania Freedmen's Relief Association. See
Letter 82, Clark to Coates, July 15, 1865.
     2. The AFUC was a coalition of secular freedmen's relief organizations that joined
together in 1866 in an attempt to coordinate their efforts. While this coalition made significant
contributions to black education in the South, its feuds with other relief organizations decreased
its effectiveness. During the 1860s there was an ongoing ideological debate over the religious
content of black education, with the AFUC advocating nondenominational common schools, and
organizations such as the AMA seeking to provide an evangelical and frequently denominational
education. The AMA eventually fomented such dissent within the ranks of the AFUC that its
funding and support dried up and the group was dissolved in 1869. Ronald E. Butchart, *Northern
Schools, Southern Black People, and Reconstruction: Freedmens' Education, 1862–1875* (Westport, Conn.:
Greenwood Press, 1980), 77–95; *American Freedman* 1, no. 1 (April 1866): 3.
     3. The *Pennsylvania Freedmen's Bulletin* was the publication of the Pennsylvania
Freedmen's Relief Association. The *Bulletin* was first published in February 1865 and was issued
sporadically until March 1868, when it merged with the *American Freedman*, the journal of the
AFUC.
     4. The Union Benevolent Association was founded in 1831 as a private charity to dis-
tribute money, clothes, and fuel to the poor. Distribution was based on the opinions of the Lady's

relieve the immediate wants, to elevate + improve the character of the poor of this city of all classes, to teach them how to live, + to become self-supporting + good useful members of society. It is as its title designates it a Union of Christian men of all religious denominations unsectarian in character. I am now the oldest member member of the board (not in years, but in membership). You are aware of my connections with the Colonization Socy. Having aided to form "The Young Men's Colo. Socy of Penn[a]."[5] some thirty five or thirty six years since at a time when the Coln cause was ~~at its~~ in a very depressed state ∧ when some of the earlier + earnest friends of this cause had become discouraged + lost heart, this young life blood then thrown into the enterprise ~~cause~~, the great energy + spirit of this heir association of which Rev[d]. Jn[o] Breckenridge[6] was President seemed to infuse new life into the cause, the city of Buchanan[7] was built, + Liberia now lives, a grand success, acknowledged as an Independent Republic, showing the ability of the Negro race in the conducting of affairs of state + nationality as well as in the humbler pursuit of picking cotton. You refer to my age. I was born on the 16th day February 1808. (am therefore about one year older than Pres[d]. JJ Roberts,[8] + Pres[d] Lincoln.) As a member of the 'Socy of Friends" my education was necessarily antislavery. When quite young having read Clarkson's history of the slave trade[9] [page break] I resolved then when I became a man I would do what I could toward the abolition of slavery + the slave trade. hence I became an abolitionist + am now vice president of the "Penn[a]. Abolition

Board and Visiting Committee, which visited the poor in their homes and determined what they needed. The association, which became a trust in 1837, is still active. Jean Barth Toll and Mildred S. Gillam, eds., *Invisible Philadelphia: Community Through Voluntary Organizations* (Philadelphia: Atwater Kent Museum, 1995).

    5. The Young Men's Colonization Society of Pennsylvania. See Letter 9, Coates to Lugenbeel, June 18, 1851.

    6. John Breckinridge (July 4, 1797–August 4, 1841) was born in Kentucky. The spelling of the family's last name probably changed (from Breckinridge to Breckenridge) two generations before John's birth, hence the name is spelled differently in various sources. Breckinridge entered the College of New Jersey in 1815 and became licensed by the Presbyterian church in 1822, then served as the chaplain for Congress until 1823, when he was ordained and became a pastor in Lexington. During the 1830s, he lived and worked in Baltimore as a professor at Princeton Seminary in New Jersey and as secretary and general agent for the Board of Foreign Missions. He is best remembered for his debates with Archbishop John Hughes of New York over the differences between Presbyterianism and Catholicism. *ANB* vol. 3; *Appleton's* vol. 1.

    7. Buchanan, Liberia. See Letter 8, Coates to McLain, May 16, 1851.

    8. Joseph Jenkins Roberts. See Letter 1, Roberts to Coates, July 8, 1848.

    9. Probably Thomas Clarkson (1760–1846), *The History of the Rise, Progress, and Accomplishment of the Abolition of the African Slave Trade by the British Parliament* (New York: John S. Taylor, 1836).

Socy."[10] (a position I have long held) instituted by the first citizens of Penn[a].
a large proportion of whom were members of the "Society of Friends," Dr
Benjamin Franklin[11] being one of the first Presidents. In my reading, I was
also much interested when a boy with Mungo Park's[12] ~~narrative of his~~ travels
in Africa, also Dehman[13] + Clapperton's[14] narratives, + others of the same
character all of which led me to take a deep interest in the Africans in their
native home. (~~Africa.~~) ~~Therefore~~ when therefore the organization of the Y M
Colo[n]. Socy of Penn[a]. was named to me, my sympathies it accorded entirely
with its grand design + ^ I have ever since been both an abolitionist + colonizationist, holding that a true colonizationist is the highest type of an abolitionist, in other words as I once said to distinguished colored man who was
decided ~~violent~~ opposed of the Colonization Socy. ~~that the difference~~ + yet professed to be a thorough abolitionist, that the difference between us was this—

10. The Pennsylvania Abolition Society (PAS), the short title for the Pennsylvania
Society for Promoting the Abolition of Slavery; the Relief of Negroes Unlawfully Held in
Bondage; and for Improving the Condition of the African Race, was founded in April 1775. During the antebellum years, the PAS repeatedly appealed to the legislature for the gradual abolition
of slavery. Beginning in 1797, the society also supported several short-lived schools. Coates was
vice president of the society for many years. Bacon, *The History of the Pennsylvania Society for Promoting the Abolition of Slavery*.
11. Benjamin Franklin (January 6, 1706–April 17, 1790), printer, scientist, and statesman, was born in Boston and moved to Philadelphia in 1723. In 1787, he became the sixth president of the PAS. *ANB* vol. 8; Bacon, *The History of the Pennsylvania Society for Promoting the Abolition of Slavery*.
12. Mungo Park (September 10, 1771–January 1806) was born in Great Britain and
educated as a surgeon at Edinburgh University. After several years as a medical officer on an East
India Company ship, Park was invited to accompany Joseph Banks on an exploration in Africa
in 1795. Park discovered the direction the Niger Valley flowed on this trip and after various difficulties, including imprisonment by Arabs, returned to England in 1797. Park published his
book *Travels in the Interior Districts of Africa* (London: n.p., 1799) and worked for some years as a
physician before returning to Africa in 1805 to learn more about the course of the Niger River.
Many members of the group died of illness. Park himself disappeared in 1806. *World Explorers and
Discoverers*, 332–34.
13. Dixon Dehman (January 1, 1786–May 8, 1828), born in London, joined the British
army at the age of fifteen. He then attended the Royal Military College before joining an African
expedition with Walter Oudney and Hugh Clapperton (see following footnote) in 1821. Conflict
broke out between Oudney and Dehman as each believed himself to be the leader of the trip.
Nevertheless, the group became the first European party to find Lake Chad. Dehman returned
to England in 1825 and published *Narrative of Travels and Discoveries in Northern and Central
Africa* in 1826. Dehman then went back to Africa, where he served as the Superintendent of Liberated Africans in Sierra Leone until his death. Bohlander, *World Explorers and Discoverers*, 150–51.
14. Hugh Clapperton (May 18, 1788–April 13, 1827) was working on a ship by the age
of thirteen. He, like Dehman, joined the army before joining Oudney's African mission. When
he returned to England in 1825, he published his journal. He then made a second trip to Nigeria,
where he died. Bohlander, *World Explorers and Discoverers*, 113.

that <u>my</u> abolitionism was <u>world wide</u> while his was <u>United States wide</u>—that while <u>he</u> was laboring earnestly for the abolition of slavery in America I was <u>also</u>, but that my sympathies were not bounded by geographical limits—that the man born on the banks of the Congo of Niger was as much my brother as the man born on the Mississippi or Delaware—that if slavery was an evil + a crime in America [page break] to four millions of the African race, ~~in America~~ ~~how~~ it was equally ~~desirable~~ a crime + evil in Africa and that if Christianity + civilization was desirable for the four millions here this blessing should be extended to the untold millions there, and also that therefore I hold that a man cannot be a true + thorough abolitionist without being a colonizationist. these were my views then, these are my views now. And while I have been laboring the larger part of my life in the cause of education and am now connected with two of the largest associations in the country for imparting education to the free men of the southern states, viz the "Penn². Freemen's Asso" (<u>unsectarian</u>) + "Friends Asso.[15]" (orhodox Friends) as well as increased efforts through schools of a higher order, such as "The Institute for Colored Youth,"[16] where the classics + higher branches of mathematics are taught to qualify the pupils to become teachers either in America or Africa yet my interest has never lessened in the same great work that is being carried on in Africa, especially in field of our early efforts—Liberia—If you can cull anything from the foregoing to make a paragraph out of to suit your purpose, you will ∧ show ~~possess~~ more skill in that way than I possess. As there is not much to be said, it should of course be short. My idea in writing the foregoing was that as I have always been both a consistent abolitionist, + an earnest colonizationist through life, even through all the conflicts of party feeling, recognized as such by abolitionists of all shades of color, + all shades of opinion, by black men in America as well as black men in Africa, that some statement of this fact—of my being probably the only man in America who has held this position in the same degree would probably be the more suitable notice to attach to my name. Perhaps however you might extract a short paragraph from EW Blydens[17] letter to me, which was published in a part of this edition of his book ("Liberia's Offering"[18]) that would answer your purpose as well.

15. The Friends' Association of Philadelphia and Its Vicinity for the Relief of Colored Freedmen, founded in November 1836, hired men and women to teach freedmen in the South, primarily in Virginia and North Carolina. Richard L. Morton, "'Contraband' and Quakers in the Virginia Peninsula, 1862–1869," *Virginia Magazine of History and Biography* 61, no. 4 (October 1953): 419–29.

16. The ICY. See Letter 42, Douglass to Coates, May 2, 1859.

17. Edward Wilmot Blyden. See Letter 27, Coates to Lugenbeel, October 6, 1856.

18. Blyden, *Liberia's Offering*. See Letter 75, Allen to Coates, April 23, 1863.

[Written vertically on the left-hand side of the fourth page:]
If you have not a copy in Washington, I can lend you one. I would like you
to send the 'African Repository" to W. B. Scott,[19] editor of the "Colored Tennessean"[20] at Nashville. Mr. Scott is a very intelligent man, —— by President
Johnson,[21] also by Seward,[22] Sumner[23] + Kelly!![24]

19. William B. Scott worked for a newspaper in Knoxville as a young man. In April
1865, with the help of his son, he began the *Colored Tennessean* in Nashville. The next year they
moved to Maryville, Tennessee, where they edited either the *Blount County Democrat* or the
Blount County Republican. Pride and Wilson, *A History of the Black Press*.
20. The *Colored Tennessean*, also known as the *Tennessean*, was published daily from
April 1865 until March 1866. In 1866 the paper became a weekly and was owned by Scott, Waring & Co. James P. Danky, ed., *African-American Newspapers and Periodicals: A National Bibliography* (Cambridge: Harvard University Press, 1998).
21. Andrew Johnson (December 29, 1808–July 31, 1875), born in Raleigh, North Carolina, began his political career as mayor of Greenville, Tennessee, in 1834 and served in a variety
of local offices before being elected to the U.S. House of Representatives in 1843 and elected governor of Tennessee in 1853. Though Johnson himself owned slaves, other supporters of slavery,
such as Jefferson Davis, did not trust his commitment to the institution. In 1857 Johnson won a
seat in the U.S. Senate. In the months before the outbreak of the Civil War, Johnson remained a
Unionist, supporting Breckinridge during the 1860 campaign. When the Civil War erupted, he
fled to the North and became the only Senator from a southern state to remain loyal to the Union.
As a result of his political position, Johnson was appointed military governor in 1862 and was
selected as Lincoln's vice president in 1864. Johnson's attitude toward the South was mixed; he
supported the Emancipation Proclamation, but believed that the South had never really left the
Union and therefore did not believe southerners had to become citizens after the war. His Reconstruction policies did not require suffrage for freedmen, and he vetoed a number of bills passed
by Republicans, such as the Freedmen's Bureau. Johnson succeeded Lincoln as president after the
latter was assassinated in 1865. The election of 1866 brought many radical Republicans into Congress, and his clash with them led to his impeachment in 1868; he was acquitted by one vote.
Although Johnson's presidency was filled with strife, it was not the end of his political career. He
was reelected to the Senate in 1876. *ANB* vol. 12.
22. William Henry Seward (May 16, 1801–October 10, 1872) was born in New York,
graduated from Union College in 1820, admitted to the bar in 1832, and elected governor of New
York in 1838 (he remained governor until 1843). As governor, Seward was active in the political
antislavery movement. He allowed jury trials for fugitive slave cases and attempted to repeal racial
barriers at the polls. In 1856, he joined the newly formed Republican Party. Although Seward was
one of the nation's most famous Republicans, he did not seek the presidency; instead, he served
both Lincoln and Johnson as Secretary of State. Seward was a political abolitionist, but he did
not support emancipation as a goal of the Civil War, because he thought Southerners should
free their slaves voluntarily. He did, however, eventually support the Thirteenth Amendment.
Biographical Directory of the American Congress, 1774–1996; ANB vol. 19.
23. Charles Sumner (January 6, 1811–March 11, 1874) was one of the North's most
famous political abolitionists. Raised as a Unitarian, he championed the causes of the underprivileged. Sumner attended Harvard and Harvard Law School, passing the bar in 1834. In the 1840s,
he worked for education and prison reform and was a founder of the Free Soil Party, which sent
him to the Senate in 1851. Six years later he was reelected as a Republican, but he was absent from
the Senate until 1859 because of a beating he received from Brooks of South Carolina in response
to an antislavery speech he gave in 1856. After the Civil War, Sumner advocated the rights of black
people and played a crucial role in convincing the Senate to recognize Liberia and Haiti. He

[Written vertically on the left-hand side of the second page:]
Mr. Scotts' paper has a large circulation. I have given him a copy of "The Future of Africa[25]" by A Crummell[26] + other colonization documents which he was very glad to get, the whole subject being new to him. Yours truly.
B. Coates

 85

Philadelphia May 26th 1866
W[m]. Coppinger Esq.[27]
My dear Sir,
After mailing my letter to you yesterday, it occurred to me that I had misconceived the object of your enquiry, + that you wished to know <u>who</u> I am, rather than <u>what</u> I am. <u>What I am</u>, or what my efforts <u>have been</u> for the African race you probably know as well as I do. I am therefore quite mortified that from the impulse of the moment I should have penned so much to you on that subject. The letter you will please to destroy.

My family is one of the oldest Quaker families in this state, both my paternal + maternal ancestors having come over with William Penn, or about that time, Henry + Elizabeth Coates, with their son Henry from whom we are descended emigrated to this country from England in 1684, + Jn°. + Mary Horner came about the same time. the latter purchased + settled at White Hill near Bordentown,[28] (near the residence of Commodore Stuart)[29] in preference

---

opposed the annexation of Hawaii, however, for fear that the islands' ethnically diverse population would never receive equal treatment from American white people. *Biographical Directory of the American Congress, 1774–1996*; Frederick J. Blue, *Charles Sumner and the Conscience of the North* (Arlington Heights, Ill.: Harlan Davidson, 1994); *ANB* vol. 21.

24. William Darrah Kelley. See Letter 70, Kelley to [Coates?], April 24, 1862.

25. Crummell, *The Future of Africa*. See Letter 64, Coates to Crummell, January 13, 1862.

26. Alexander Crummell. See Letter 28, Coates to Gurley, May 2, 1857.

27. William Coppinger. See Letter 10, Coates to McLain, October 11, 1851.

28. Bordentown, New Jersey, is located south of Trenton in Burlington County. It was first settled in 1681 by Thomas Farnsworth, a Quaker, and his family. The town was later named for Joseph Borden. In 1740, a Quaker meetinghouse was built there. *Inventory of the Church Archives of New Jersey*.

29. Coates may be referring to Joseph Steward, who arrived in the colonies in 1682 at the age of 14 with James Harrison, an agent for William Penn. Harrison and his companions settled across the Delaware River from the present-day location of Bordentown. At the time of his marriage in 1695, Steward bought land in New Hanover Township in Burlington County. E. S. Stewart, *The Steward Family of New Jersey* (Philadelphia: Allen, Lane and Scott, 1907).

to settling in Philad. where he was offered by Wm Penn, a whole square, or block in the central part of the city, if he would locate here. his son John purchased where Princeton N.J. now is, ~~stands~~ + owned the lands where the college now stands which [page break] he donated to that Institution. My father George M Coates was born in 1779 + is now living, aged 87. My mother Rebecca H Coates died in 1852. But still all this you do not want, neither do suppose that my own age is important. as I stated yesterday, I was born Feb 16. 1808.

    The only portion of my letter of yesterday worthy of attention is the suggestion in the latter part, that you should send "The African Repository"[30] + the Colonization ^ documents to W.B. Scott[31] editor of "The Colored Tennessean" of Nashville, Tenn^{ee}. Mr Scott is a very intelligent light colored man, formerly residing at Knoxville Tenn^{ee} ~~where~~ having removed there some years since from Charlotte N.C. he was a delegate for Knoxville to the Colored Convention[32] at Nashville last year, + while there it was suggested by some of his White + Colored friends that they ought to have a newspaper of their own to advocate their own interests, which would do them more good than any other measure. He had no money but he started with his son, with only <u>four dollars</u> + a half capital! ($4.^{50}). They went in debt for about $1200. which they still owe + the object of his visit North at this time was to obtain this sum from the Northern friends of the cause, he came [page break] strongly recommended by President Johnson[33] who had known him in Knoxville, + who also contributed $25. towards his paper. W^m H Seward[34] contributed $20. He also brought a strong letter from Hon. W^m D Kelly.[35] I had a good deal of conversation with him, he had never been North before + was aware he has much to learn + is desirous of obtaining information on all subjects pertaining to the interest of his race, or rather of the African race, altho he seems to have but a small portion of African blood in him. His paper has now existed <u>one year</u> + has fully supported itself. it has a large, +

---

    30. *The African Repository.* See Letter 15, Coates to Lugenbeel, June 27, 1853.

    31. William B. Scott. See Letter 85, Coates to Coppinger, May 26, 1866.

    32. The State Convention of the Colored Men of Tennessee was held in Nashville from August 7 to 10, 1866. The convention met to discuss the present and future of black Tennesseans and passed resolutions calling for the state and national government to guarantee full legal equality, including the rights to vote and to serve on a jury. Philip Foner and George E. Walker, eds., *Proceedings of the Black National and State Conventions, 1865–1900* (Philadelphia: Temple University Press, 1986), 1:112–14.

    33. Andrew Johnson. See Letter 84, Coates to Coppinger, May 24, 1866.

    34. William H. Seward. See Letter 84, Coates to Coppinger, May 24, 1866.

    35. William Darrah Kelley. See Letter 70, Kelley to [Coates?], April 24, 1862.

increasing circulation, with a good advertising patronage. but he has not made enough to pay off his indebtedness. I think any document sent to him will be well placed. He was quite interested in Crummell's book "The Future of Africa,"[36] which I gave him + was very glad to receive various documents + pamphlets. ~~that I gave him~~

Please <u>destroy</u> the letter I sent you yesterday, as I am not satisfied to have any in existence speaking thus of myself. I have been + am connected with various Benevolent Institutions in this city such as "The Prison Discipline Socy,"[37] Provident Socy[38] +c +c. But this is not to the purpose. Yours very truly Benj[a] Coates

❖ 86 ❖

BENJAMIN COATES   GEO. MORRISON COATES[39]
    COATES, BROTHERS,   127 Market Street,
    COMMISSION MERCHANTS,   PHILADELPHIA, June 1st 1866
For the Purchase and Sale of
WOOL
W[m] Coppinger Esqr.[40]

My dear Sir

Nearly all our schools for the Freedmen[41] are suspended for the summer vacation for the teachers. Most of the old, + probably several new schools will be opened in September. If you will be pleased to remind me to do so I will with pleasure send you a complete list of

36. Crummell, *The Future of Africa*. See Letter 64, Coates to Crummell, January 13, 1862.

37. The Philadelphia Society for the Alleviation of Miseries of Public Prisons was founded in 1787 and became the Pennsylvania Prison Society in 1887. Roughly one-third of the early members of the society were Quakers. Members included Benjamin Rush, Benjamin Franklin, and Roberts Vaux. Early efforts of the society included lobbying for solitary confinement to keep prisoners from corrupting each other, lobbying for reform through labor, visiting prisoners, and giving assistance to men freed from incarceration. It is still active today. Toll and Gillam, *Invisible Philadelphia*, 630–31.

38. The first five lines constitute the Coates brothers' printed letterhead, with the exception of the month, day, and last digit of the year.

39. The Provident Society for the Employment of the Poor was founded in 1824 during a period of backlash against societies that encouraged idleness among the poor. Toll and Gillam, *Invisible Philadelphia*, 142, 278.

40. William Coppinger. See Letter 10, Coates to McLain, October 11, 1851.

41. Coates probably means the schools of the Pennsylvania Freedmen's Relief Association.

the names + location of all the teachers, of both associations having schools for the <u>blacks</u>. The Penn^a Association[42] has united with the "Am. Freedmen's + Union Commission"[43] which will make no distinction of race or color, + considers the whites as good as the black ~~so long~~ <u>when they behave themselves properly</u> + therefore will not exclude them from their schools. As <u>most</u> of the scholars however in all the schools will be of the African race, + "The Freedmens + Union Comm." will exclude <u>none</u>, (whether white or black) I had better send you a list of all the teachers + all the schools. Please remind me to do so if I should forget it. The June no of the "African Repository"[44] came to hand today. I will mail a copy to W.B. Scott,[45] as it will probably not come [soon] even if you have already sent it to him.

Yours very truly

Benj^a Coates

❖ 87 ❖

BENJAMIN COATES   GEO. MORRISON COATES[46]
    COATES, BROTHERS,   127 Market Street,
    COMMISSION MERCHANTS,   PHILADELPHIA, June. 6th 1866
    For the Purchase and Sale of
    WOOL

Wm Coppinger Esq.[47]

Dear Sir,

Your favor of yesterday is just to hand— in reply I have only to say that if my letter answers your purpose, keep it, + make use of it as may seem to you best. Always having a particular dislike to egotism in others, I could not feel satisfied to speak of myself in such a way as I might speak of others in similar circumstances, and I feared that my letter falling into the hands of others who did not know the circumstances under which it was written would appear very egotistical. The chief point I wished to make was that I was both an abolitionist + colonizationist and all

42. The Pennsylvania Freedmen's Relief Association. See Letter 82, Clark to Coates, July 15, 1865.

43. The afuc. See Letter 84, Coates to Coppinger, May 24, 1866.

44. *The African Repository*. See Letter 23, Coates to Lugenbeel, October 27, 1855.

45. William B. Scott. See Letter 84, Coates to Coppinger, May 24, 1866.

46. The first five lines constitute the Coates brothers' printed letterhead, with the exception of the month, day, and last digit of the year.

47. William Coppinger. See Letter 10, Coates to McLain, October 11, 1851.

true philanthropists like Dr Hodgkin[48] should combine both as he did. They are both necessary portions of the same great work of humanity. I have not only lived to see the success of the colonization enterprise in the recognition of the Independence of Liberia by all the enlightened nations of the world including our own, but also the success of the efforts for the abolition of slavery, and I have <u>lived down</u> the the bitterest opposition of some of our anti-slavery colored men who could not believe in any good in Colonization + could have no patience with any one who engaged in it. Robert Purvis[49] was one of the very few who was then bitter, + now considers me one of the best friends of his race. A year ago the most enterprising + intelligent of our colored people framed an association styled, "The Social, Civil, + Statistical Association," + got up a course of popular lectures [page break] having engaged some of our most prominent men both white + black as lecturers. They sent me a complimentary ticket for the platform—which I accepted—+ in going into the room below where the Comm. + lecturers were. Robert Purvis introduced me to the lecturer for the evening, Jnᵒ. M Langston,[50] a colored

48. Thomas Hodgkin. See Letter 40, Hobbins to Coates, March 2, 1859.

49. Robert Purvis (1810–1898) was born free in Charleston, South Carolina, to a white cotton broker and a free mulatto mother. The Purvis family moved to Philadelphia, and when Purvis's father died seven years later he left his fortune to his family, enabling Purvis to attend private schools in Massachusetts. Becoming interested in the antislavery movement at an early age, Purvis began his career in abolitionism by standing with James Forten in opposition to African colonization. He became a charter member of the AAS in 1833 and soon after traveled to Britain to promote the antislavery cause. In Philadelphia he was active in the Underground Railroad and was involved in other organizations that aided fugitive slaves. In 1842, following a race riot during which his house was attacked, Purvis moved his family to a farm in Byberry, Pennsylvania, fifteen miles from Philadelphia. He believed in radical Garrisonian principles and endorsed the use of violence in resisting the Fugitive Slave Act. After Frederick Douglass remarked about Purvis's father's involvement in the cotton industry, the two broke publicly and were not wholly reconciled until thirty years later. Purvis was an energetic orator who was actively opposed to slavery and African colonization all his life. "Robert Purvis," *ANB* 17:948–50.

50. John Mercer Langston's (1829–1897) father was Ralph Quarles, a white slave-owning Virginian, and his mother was a part Native American, part black former slave who had been emancipated by Quarles. Langston and his brothers were the beneficiaries of their father's will in 1834 and they moved to Ohio, where they lived with friends of the family to avoid discriminatory laws in Virginia. After receiving a scattered primary education, Langston enrolled at Oberlin College's preparatory department in 1844, graduated with an A.B. in 1849, and intended to study law. Refused admission by several law schools, he returned to Oberlin, entered its theological school, and graduated in 1853, but he never became a minister. In pursuit of a political career, he found a mentor and legal tutor in Philemon E. Bliss, passed the Ohio bar exam in 1854, and was elected township clerk in 1855. Some suggested in 1868 and 1872 that he run for vice president on the Republican ticket. In 1869 he founded the law department at Howard College and was associated with the college until 1875 as a professor, dean, vice president, and acting president. In 1877 he was appointed U.S. minister and consul general to Haiti, a position he held until 1885.

lawyer from Oberlin, Ohio. Mr. Langston asked is this Mr Coates the Colonizationist that was? Yes I replied + the Coates the colonizationist that is. He
remarked why Mr Coates do you say the Colonizationist that is. I stated th to
him that I was a thorough abolitionist, + could not be such without being a
Colonizationist, that I could not limit my sympathies by geographical bound-
aries +c giving him the same lesson that I had [some] [smudged] years before
given to C. L. Remond[51] of Salem Mass. in the Antislavery office here. Both
Langston + Mr Purvis felt the force of my remarks + the strength of my position, Mr Purvis remarking that it was only of late years that he had really
known + understood Mr. Coates. Mr Purvis had formerly made ^ me a subject of his public as well as private denunciation, as one most to be feared
for my antislavery character + position, and in a communication to Fredk
Douglass' Papers[52] had gone so far as to style me the most Jesuitical of all the
Colonizationists in the United States. As Mr Douglass published my reply
which was very caustic, + endorsed me, it aided much if it did not create a very
bitter feeling between Douglass + Mr Purvis, who had before been warm
personal friends, + I am glad to say I believe of late have become reconciled +
are friends again. I only mention this in showing the great change the time +
circumstances have brought about. Yours very truly

Benj^a Coates

The pinnacle of his political career came in 1890 when he was elected to the U.S. House of Representatives. After his term he remained in Washington, D.C., where he practiced law and continued his crusade for black rights. "John Mercer Langston," *ANB* 13:164–66.

51. Charles Lenox Remond (1810–1873), a prominent black orator, was the son of
prominent members of the Salem, Massachusetts, black community. He attended Salem's black
school and became involved in antislavery activity, traveling through New England in the 1830s,
lecturing and seeking subscribers to William Lloyd Garrison's *Liberator*. The AAS hired him as a
lecturing agent in 1838, and in 1840 the society sent him as a delegate to the World's Anti-Slavery
Convention in London. In the 1840s, when Frederick Douglass entered the lecturing circuit the
two sometimes joined forces and toured together. For Remond, as for many black people, the Fugitive Slave Act was the catalyst for him to reconsider his support of moral persuasion and opposition to violent resistance and slave rebellions. During the Civil War he traveled the North and
helped to recruit black soldiers. When poor health forced him to drastically reduce his lecturing in
1867, he retired to his home in Wakefield, Massachusetts. "Charles Lenox Remond," *ANB* 18:335–37.

52. *The North Star*. See Letter 3, Coates to Douglass, June 27, 1850.

❖ 88 ❖

Charlotte, N.C. July 25 1866[53]

Mr B. Coates,

My Dear Sir—The commission of one error after often leads us into others.—Since writing you the other day I am tempted to repeat the error, if it be one, in order to give you the inclosed and accompanying newspaper evidence of the —— feeling of the people of my state towards the U.S. and for your information in other matters in which you may feel an interest.—I ask your attention specially to the communications from Gov. Worth[54] + Genl Robinson.[55]—I was not aware when I wrote you last that Genl Robinson had succeeded Genl Ruger.-

Scarcely a day passes in any county in the state in which there is not some outrage—of murder, theft, burglary or something of that nature committed, not always by Negroes, but in their simplicity they are often made the tools of worse white men, and all suffer by law together, hence the necessity of unusual vigilance, and thus much material can be gathered for misleading the public mind north,—and I give you my word it is thus used -. Two weeks ago was court in Charlotte, and Twelve Negro men were whiped at the whiping post, for larceny,—every one of them convicted in court by a jury the evidence in every case but one being Negro testimony.—One of them a man who had been long known in Charlotte, and had established sufficient character to induce one of our business men to entrust him as Drayman + and while this extraordinary conviction and punishment was going on he was caught in the act of stealing his employers goods—On the Monday after Court a Negro man employed as fireman in our mill, receiving $20.00 per month—paid every Saturday evening, and had no family, was caught stealing flour from our sizing

53. The letterhead is that of the Rock Island Manufacturing Company and bears the names of "J.A. Young, John Wilkes, M.L. Wriston, and Jas. Earnshaw." The company was formed in 1848 by a group of Charlotte businessmen that included Young. It produced cotton and wool yarn and was one of the few local mills that survived the Civil War, although it went bankrupt in 1870. Janette Thomas Greenwood, *Bittersweet Legacy: The Black and White "Better Classes" in Charlotte, 1850–1910* (Chapel Hill: University of North Carolina Press, 1994), 115–17.

54. Jonathan Worth (1802–1869), a native North Carolinean and the son of Quaker parents, started his career by apprenticing as a lawyer. He soon became involved in politics, serving several terms in the state legislature. He opposed secession, but he served loyally as state treasurer during the Civil War. After the war he was elected governor twice, in 1865 and 1866. Despite his previous resistance to secession, his essential conservatism caused his critics to brand him an opponent of reunification. "Worth, Jonathan," *ANB* 23:883–84.

55. Young was referring to John C. Robinson, who succeeded Thomas Ruger as Assistant Commissioner to North Carolina for the Freedman's Bureau on June 20, 1866, and held the position until November 31 of that year. George R. Bentley, *A History of the Freedmen's Bureau* (Philadelphia: University of Philadelphia, 1955), 216.

Room. He confessed it to me, and the only regret he expressed about it was, that he had stolen from his employers.—Now how easy it would be for a paragraph like that sent you in my last to be written, conveying the idea that our courts were dealing harshly with freedmen, and yet the writer could refer to a colour of truth to sustain him.—The Dr Webb murder I cut from a northern paper this morning.—It might be said that I had selected these instances of outrage because they were committed by the Negro. Such is not the fact. I give these as the chapter of crime now being written in my own community.—I have never had a word of difference with a Negro since their emancipation—my sympathies are with them—I have eleven of them amongst my dependants, and my desire and effort is to educate instruct and elevate them. I believe the greatest danger they have to apprehend is from the good intentions but misdirected efforts of their friends north and from such ignorant or wicked misrepresentations as are published to mislead public opinion north in regard to the south.—Again I ask the pardon for intruding these matters upon you. I know no other man north to whom I would send them.

I remain, dear sir,

very respectfully

Yours John A Young[56]

[Attached to Letter 88, Young to Coates, July 25, 1866, was the following article from the Charlotte, North Carolina *Daily Carolinian*, n.d.:]

To the People of North Carolina.

EXECUTIVE DEPARTMENT OF N.C.

Raleigh, July 23, 1866

I publish the following letter and order from Brevet Major General Robinson, for the information of the judicial officers, and other citizens of the State:

BUREAU REF'S., FREEDEEN, ABAN'D

LANDS, HEADQ'RS ASS'T COM.

STATE OF NORTH CAROLINA,

Raleigh, N.C., July 13, 1866

His excellency Jonathan Worth, Governor, &c., Raleigh, N.C.

Governor:—I have the honor to acknowledge the receipt of your letter of the 11th, inst., calling my attention to an act of the General Assembly,

---

56. John A. Young was a Charlotte, North Carolina, businessman and politician. He held several political offices in North Carolina, including delegate to the state convention in 1861 and mayor of Charlotte in 1871. A Whig, Know-Nothing, and proponent of secession in the years before the Civil War, he held to his views after the war as a member of the Democratic-Conservative party that opposed the Republicans. Greenwood, *Bittersweet Legacy*, passim.

passed in 1865, and to the ordinances of the State Convention repealing the provisos of the 9th section of said act, and so modifying the 11th section that "there now exists under the laws of this State, no discrimination in the distribution of justice to the prejudice of free persons of color," and desiring to be officially informed how, in my opinion, the question of jurisdiction now stands in matters relating to freedmen.

In reply I have the pleasure to inform your Excellency that I have this day issued an order (a copy of which is enclosed) directing the officers and agents of the Freedmen's Bureau to refer all cases to which freedmen are parties, to the proper County and State Courts, with the single exception of claims for wages due under contracts approved or witnessed by officers of the Bureau.

I have made this exception for the reason that the condition of the freedmen is believed to be such that they cannot be subjected to the delay sometimes incident to proceedings in civil Courts.

Trusting that my action may prove satisfactory to the civil authorities, and that there may be no obstacles to the fair administration of justice to all persons, I have the honor to be,

> Very Respectfully,
> your ob't serv't
> JNO. C. ROBINSON,
> Brevet Maj. Gen'l._____

> BUREAU REF'S., FREEM'N AND AB'D}
> LANDS, HDQR'S ASS'T COM.
> OF N. CAROLINA.

GENERAL ORDERS}

No.3.

His Excellency the Governor of North Carolina, having officially notified the Assistant Commissioner that "there now exists, under the laws of this State, no discrimination in the administration of justice to the prejudice of free persons of color," all officers and agents of the Bureau will hereafter refer all cases to which freedmen are parties, to the proper County of State authorities, according to the nature of the case, with the single exception of claims for wages due under contracts approved or witnessed by officers or agents of the Bureau, which, not admitting of delay, will be adjudicated as heretofore.

In case of any failure, neglect or inability of the civil authorities to arrest and bring to trial persons who have been or may hereafter be charged with the commission of crimes and offences against officers, agents, citizens, and inhabitants of the United States, irrespective of color, officers in charge of districts are hereby directed to arrest and detain such persons in military confinement, until such time as a proper judicial tribunal may be ready and willing to try them.

By Command of Brev't Maj. Gen. Robinson,

CLINTON A. CILLEY, A.A.G .

It is known that there are persons in the State, and out of it, who have sought to make the impression that our judicial officers and juries are so inimical to persons of color, and persons among us who were soldiers in the United States army during, the late civil war, or who refused to serve in the Southern armies, that such persons cannot expect justice in our courts. Citizens of this State, who had served in the army of the United States, have filed petitions, addressed to the President of the United States, charging that they were persecuted by our courts, and praying for protection. Upon a reference of the petitioners to me, by the President, I have made such investigation as satisfied me, beyond a doubt, that there was no ground for the filing of such petitions. And these investigations, after having been submitted, in detail, for examination, have in each case drawn forth a response of like satisfaction from the national authorities.

Inquisitions have been made, and *ex parte* statements taken from persons who claim to have been aggrieved by the action or non-action of our courts and juries. None of these, as yet, so far as I know, even if taken as true, prove anything to the prejudice of any judicial officer of the State. The ability and purity and impartiality with which justice has always been administered in this State, even where a negro appealed to our Courts to assert his freedom, have never been questioned at home or abroad. Our present judicial corps will not suffer by comparison with their predecessors at any period of our history. I have referred to these things only to justify me in asking at this time for peculiar diligence and circumspection on the part of all Justices of the Peace, Sheriffs and other judicial and executive officers, in the discharge of these official duties. One of the unhappy sequents of the late civil war is an increase of crime—particularly larceny and burglary, and the too frequent failure to apprehend and punish the criminal. Every good citizen should co-operate with the officers of justice in bringing every violator of the criminal law to justice. We can, in no other way, expect a return of the quiet and security which distinguished our State before the war.

It ought to be, and I hope it is, the wish, not only of the judiciary, but of every intelligent white man in the State, to protect the lately emancipated negro in all the rights of person and of property, to which he is entitled under the laws, and thus induce him to confide in our justice, and encourage him to be honest and industrious and to acquire property and take care of it.

JONATHAN WORTH,
Governor of North Carolina

July 25-1t

[Also attached to Letter 88, Young to Coates, July 25, 1866, was this article from an unidentified periodical in Statesville, North Carolina, July 24, 1866.]

SPEECH BY HON. J. G. RAMSAY.

At Olin Academy, Iredell co., N. C., June 7th, 1866—concluding remarks.

FELLOW-CITIZENS:—We have just emerged from a long, cruel and most desolating war. But yesterday, we beheld the rugged and horrid field of battle.

> "And there lay the steed with his nostrils all wide,
> But through them there rolled not the breath of his pride,
> And the foam of his gasping lay white on the turf,
> And cold as the spray of the rock beating serf."

> "And there lay the rider distorted and pale,
> With the dew on his brows and the gore on his mail;
> And the tents were all pillaged, the banners all gone,
> The lances unlifted, and the trumpets unblown.

But yesterday we beheld the lurid planes and smoking embers of our towns and cities. Our cattle, from more than a thousand hills and homesteads, were driven away or destroyed—our barns and granaries pillaged—our houses rifled and burned—our persons, and those of our loved ones, often insulted and sometimes outraged, while tens of thousands of the good, and the brave fell upon the field of strife, to rise no more, and sleep the sleep which knows no waking, except that of the trumpet of the resurrection. To-day we behold the physical, intellectual and moral wrecks of the conflict scattered around us. Our private enterprises and public works political, educational, agricultural, professional or otherwise, are paralyzed, and in many instances vitally injured. Our finances including our school funds, completely wrecked.—Thousands of those who have survived unnatural conflict are maimed and helpless for life, while our social fabric has sustained the tremendous shock of having four millions of slaves, occupying a most subordinate and menial position suddenly emancipated and thrown upon society, upon terms of freedom and equality.

In many respects we are poor indeed. We had many of us, to begin life anew—to divest ourselves of old notions, prejudices and habits, and build up our private fortunes, and our disorganized social fabric, under new, untried, and discourageing circumstances. Private enterprise and energy must now assume much, that has heretofore been accomplished by incorporated associations and State munificence. This may, perhaps in the end result in much good. The thoughts of our people will be turned to a proper appreciation of the blessings of education, from beholding the desolations which ignorance—with her concomitants of vice, superstition and crime—must engender, in the absence of educational facilities, and society may emerge from the desolations of these times, to a brighter and more endearing future.

I do not presume to divine what Providence has yet in store for us; nor do I believe it to be the duty of a christian people either to be greatly solicitous on this point, or unduly anxious to exculpate themselves from all blame, in regard to the causes which have resulted in their defeat. The Almighty, who doeth his will among the armies of heaven and the children of men is everywhere. His ways, although often mysterious and inscrutable, are not always so. He purifies the elements by the storm and the nations by the sword, and overturns and overrules all for the general, universal ultimate good. Who can say that we cannot safely rest in His hands; and at the same time accept the issue of the late conflict as a vindication of the ways of God to man? Although in trouble on every side, and perplexed, let us by no means despair—'though cast down, let us not feel that we are destroyed. But our future depends so much, in my opinion, upon the manner in which we accept our situation, with its consequences, that I hope to be pardoned for saying, we will never be a happy and a prosperous people until we lay aside many of our preconceived opinions and prejudices and go forth to the interpretation of the ways of Providence in His late dealings with us, with the minds of men purified and chastened by the fires of the conflict, and firmly resolved to receive the *truth, whatever it may be, and to follow and abide by it, wherever it may lead.*

The work before us is no less than the reorganization of society, out of heterogeneous and discordant elements and the re-building of liberty itself. The present and future *status* of the freedman cannot be ignored in this work. Let us continue to treat him kindly. He needs food and raiment; let us employ him. He is ignorant; why should we not instruct him? He is vicious and depraved; let us apply the balm in Gilead and point him to the Physician there.—But even after this is done let us strive, even against principalities and power, to colonize him. I advise this because I fear that nothing short of it will prevent the ultimate miscegenation of the races, or the banishment of our own race from the land of our birth and the graves of our sires.

But let me not be misunderstood. We must take care of ourselves before we can take care of others. But if the freedman can save anything by honest industry to enable him to educate his children, in schools separate and distinct to themselves, I see no good reason why we should transfer to the people of the North the office of imparting that instruction which we are so much better entitled to give.—But, I repeat it, we must first look to ourselves. Our own children must be cared for, and the poor orphan children of the war. Let physical desolation reign around us; it can be endured and may ultimately be repaired. Let social troubles environ us; these too can be tolerated for a time and may give way to prudence and perseverence. But we cannot, we must not permit our children to grow up in ignorance and vice. The blight and the mildew, the avalanche and the storm pass away with the changing seasons and may not return; but ignorance and vice grow stronger and more more violent as time waxes old, and respond to no medication but the surgery of extirpation itself. The march of armies has ceased; let the march of intellect go on. If necessary, let our bodies be less sumptuously fed, and gaily attired, that our children may be fed with intellectual and spiritual food. If our common schools cannot be resuscitated, let teachers be employed in every neighborhood by voluntary associations. Let the halls of our Academies and Colleges be open and stand open; but above all, let the Church, in these days of demoralization and spiritual declension, stand firm and we may look with confidence for our regeneration and disenthralment.

History—our own history—furnishes us with examples for our encouragement and emulation. Bancroft tells us "when New England was poor, and they were but few in number, there was a spirit to encourage learning." The University of Harvard arose and flourished by the exertions of an indigent people, for, says the same historian, "once at least, every family, in each of the colonies gave to the college at Cambridge twelve pence, or a peck of corn, or its value in unadulterated wampumeag."

Wheeler cites Martin as authority for saying that at the end of the royal government in North Carolina in 1775, "literature was hardly known, and that there were in the whole province, but two schools, those at Edenton and Newbern.["] This however, must be a mistake, because we read, on the next page of Wheeler's history, that "the Rev. David Caldwell, about the year 1767, opened a school in Guilford county, and his *log cabin* served for many years to North Carolina, as an Academy, a College and a Theological Seminary." But there were men of education and intelligence—intellectual giants—in those days.—Even the masses, perhaps, were better educated, considering their opportunities, than they are at present.—The explanation is easy; children were taught at home; parents and guardians followed the custom which became a law in New England, and would 'not suffer so much barbarism, in the families, as not to teach their children and apprentices so much learning as might enable them perfectly to read the English tongue.'

At the close of the revolution the people had no money; in this respect our present situation very much resembles theirs. But in the year 1793, the corner-stone of the University was laid; and before the war not only was a school fund of millions of dollars accumulated, and a common schools affording extraordinary advantages, brought to the door of almost every child in the State, in its length and breadth, was studded over with the beautiful adornments of High Schools, Academies and Colleges. The obstacles in our way, in the accomplishment of like achievements, are not greater than they were with our fathers. The blighting effects of the late conflict, and the veneration our people feel for its heroes, cannot be greater than our fathers endured and felt, but they acted upon the principle that

"The warrior's name
Tho' pealed and chimed by every tongue of fame,
Sounds less Harmonious to the grateful mind,
Than he who fashions and improves mankind."

If we would achieve like results, we must follow like counsels, and put forth corresponding exertions.

But let us not despair of the Republic. "Sometimes it is said that man cannot be trusted with the government of himself. Can he then be trusted with the government of others? Or have we found angels in the form of Kings to govern him? Let history answer this question." Let us exercise patience, forbearance, forgiveness, and "charity, which is the bond of perfectness," and all may yet be well. The passions and prejudices which impelled to strife, and protracted the bloody scene, have not yet subsided. The smoke of battle, and the tumult of conflicting hosts have scarcely, as yet, cleared and died away. As participators in these scenes, we ought not, perhaps, to sit in judgment upon our own acts. But while we should not be too anxious to press into history our judgment upon the late conflict and while to *exparte* decisions should be rendered, it is our duty and our privilege to submit facts, to a candid world, and there leave them, for the present at least, that posterity may profit by them.

History, I repeat, forbids us to despair. Other nations have grown strong and great through civil wars, rebellions and revolutions, and why may not ours? The eventful history of the English people furnishes the most instruction, as well as the most truthful illustration of this assertion. Before the coming of Christ, Julius Caesar led his victorious cohorts into Britain and conquered those sturdy islanders, who remained for the most part subject to the Romans for nearly four centuries. Then came the Saxon, who after a contest of a century and a half, firmly established himself upon British soil, and forever stamped the name of Anglo-Saxon upon a people united by coercion. Next came the Dane, who cemented this union by the imposition of a like yoke, and the perpetration upon the Anglo-Saxon of atrocities far more cruel than the Saxon had imposed upon the English. This union was intensified by the advent of the Norman, who after another conflict of a hundred and fifty years, during which the English suffered the most intolerable oppression, completed his conquest and seated himself upon the English throne. After the lapse of nearly five centuries more, during which the Saxon superceded the Norman line, and the kingdom was torn and destructed between the rival houses of York and Lancaster, the head of the first Charles was brought to the block, and the commonwealth established under Cromwell.—Finally in 1688, the great revolution occurred which placed a Dutch prince upon the English throne, and consummated the fifth conquest of the English people.

Thus, we see that England, good old England, whose people at this moment perhaps, enjoy more freedom than any other upon the face of the globe—renowned not less for the arts of peace, than the triumphs of war—for the renown of her bards, historians and statesmen, than for the love and affection of her sons—England, upon whose empire the sun never sets, has for more than eighteen hundred years grown in greatness, in strength and in freedom, notwithstanding her conflicts and vicissitudes. And every true Englishman to-day, is proud of Hampden, Pym, and Cromwell, and points to *magna charta*, which her study barons at Runnymede wrested from imbecile tyranny, as at once the evidence and the source of her true greatness.

And may we not hope that when the noise and tumult of our unhappy conflict shall have subsided; when the passions, prejudices and resentments of the hour, shall have passed away and reason shall have fully resumed her calm and peaceful sway, some great hearted historian—some American McCauley—will arise who will deal out impartial justice, alike to Davis and to Lincoln, to Lee and to Grant, and above all who will rescue the memory of the great and the good Jackson, from any unhallowed aspersions?

> "His spirit was simple, grand and pure;
> Great to conceive, to do or to endure;
> Yet the rough warrior was, in heart a child,

Rich in love's affluence, merciful and mild.
His sterner traits majestic and antique
Rivalled the stoic Roman or the Greek;
Excelling both, he adds the Christian name,
And Christian virtues make him more than Fame."

The past is gone and it comes not back again; but we can, and we should walk by the light of its experience. The present is ours; it is an hour for discretion and judgment, for forbearance and charity. The future is before us, and hope yet remains in the box of Pandora; let it beckon and enspirit us on, although is should be as deceptive as the mirage in the desert. In the pathway of nations over the sands of time, as in the pilgrimage of the solitary traveler, there are caravansary stations—oasises, with their cooling shades, green swards and limpid, gushing fountains to allure, to inspire and to refresh.

"Let us then be up and doing,
    With a heart for any fate;
Still achieving, still pursuing,
    Learn to labor and to wait."

Charlotte, N.C. July 31 1866[57]

Mr B. Coates,
    My Dear Sir—Your kind letter and your slip from the Oxford Miss paper are both recᵈ I thank you for them. I love to receive and read your letters, and hope an occasional exchange of views and facts may be mutually beneficial.-
    Every good man in the South favours the education of the negro, as much as the white race. The difficulty with us is the want of means to do eather. The effort of the Northern philanthropists is for the Negro alone, and is directed thus because the White race south is considered unfriendly towards the black,—and acting under that impression, their teachers and agents who came amongst us are biased in their feelings towards the whites, and, as a

57. The letterhead is that of the Rock Island Manufacturing Company and bears the names of "J.A. Young, John Wilkes, M.L. Wriston, and Jas. Earnshaw." See Letter 88, Young to Coates, July 25, 1866.

class, are regarded by southern whites, as wanting in that spirit of liberality and elivation of sentiment which are necessary to secure confidence and coop- eration.—We learn that it is not unusual for the negro to be prejudiced against us by those having charge of their education, and with these impressions we cannot look upon them as friends. These impressions may not be fully correct, but they exist, and I know there were some grounds for them, and hope they may have been, or will be removed.—Until they are, there can be but little useful cooperation between the efforts of the sections.—The evidence of its existence is shown in the address of the citizens of Oxford Miss.- We are doing much in many ways to promote the education of the race, + it is the disposition of our people to continue it. We cannot do it with success while we are compelled to regard the ruling powers of the North, as unfriendly to us as a people, in the South, and as intending to use the Negro race to strengthen their powers for the purpose of degrading and dispoiling us.—Such is now our feeling, and we are resolved to do our duty in endeavoring to releave ourselves and the ruling powers of the U.S. from such misdirected and distructive pol- icy.—I should not have written this, but I desire to introduce to you by letters, in a few days, an intimate friend of mine who will be a delegate to the Phil[a] Convention of the 14 prox.—who you will find to be a gentlemen of temper- ate and liberal views.

The enclosed slip is from our morning paper.—The Lady abused is the wife of Mr Elam Query, one of our most respectable Citizens, and one of the most indulgent of owners to slaves. I am personally acquainted with him. The negro was once his slave, and has remained with him since his freedom, and Mr Query says always before deported himself well. If I were to keep up this matter of sending accounts of such outrages you would begin to under- stand our condition here with this treacherous race amongst us unrestrained, but I promise you I will not. You may conclude I am unfriendly to him.

I remain sincerely + truly yours <u>John A Young</u>[58]

[Attached to Letter 89, Young to Coates, July 31, 1866, was the following arti- cle from an unknown periodical, dated "30th July":]

Horrible Outrage.

To-day, in the absence of her husband, who was in the city on business, a horrible outrage was committed upon a highly re-spectable lady, at her home about twelve miles distant from the city. She was ra-vished by a negro, who succeeded in accomplishing his hellish purpose.

We refrain from giving names.

58. John A. Young. See Letter 88, Young to Coates, July 25, 1866.

The Mayor and Police are on the the the track of this fiend, with every prospect of cap-turing him. We hope he will meet his just desserts.

❧ 90 ❧

Charleston S. C.
Mch 29th 1867

Benj Coates
    Dear friend
        I write in haste to say that your letter enclosing check for $100. came safely to hand yesterday. I will write you further on the subject another time.
        I acknowledged the receipt of the "garden seeds" at the time I received them, and will only say now that they were distributed to good purpose. Some went with a party of Colonists to Florida; some to John's, Edisto, and Wadmelaw I[ds59] and the rest, I sent into the interior. I have no doubt that they will be the means of putting food into the mouths of many otherwise destitute persons.
        Excuse this hasty note, and return my thanks to Dillwyn Parrish[60] and the other friends for the expression of confidence in me, which Caleb Clothiers[61] "check" implies.

Sincerely Yours
Reuben Tomlinson[62]

59. Johns, Edisto, and Walmalaw Islands are part of the Sea Islands off the coast of South Carolina. Johns Island is the most northeastern island of the three, with Walmalaw slightly west. Edisto is southwest of Walmalaw Island.

60. Dillwyn Parrish (September 8, 1809–September 17, 1886) was a Quaker (Race Street Meeting) who lived Philadelphia most of his life. After graduating from the College of Pharmacy at the age of twenty-one, he established a pharmaceutical business. Involved in a variety of medical aspects throughout his life, he was president of the College of Pharmacy, a founder of the Orthopaedic Hospital, and a corporator of the Women's Medical College of Pennsylvania. An active abolitionist, he was president of the Pennsylvania Society for Promoting the Abolition of Slavery and Improving the Condition of the African Race, a position formerly held by his grandfather. *Friends Intelligencer* 43 (1886): 609.

61. Caleb Clothier (?–January 13, 1881) was a Hicksite Quaker, actively involved in the abolitionist movement. *Friends Intelliegencer* 37 (1881): 778; Alfred Lief, *Family Business: A Century in the Life and Business of Strawbridge and Clothier* (New York: McGraw-Hill Book Company, 1968).

62. Reuben Tomlinson was a Philadelphia Quaker (Race Street Meeting) and a bank clerk. In 1862 he began teaching on St. Helena Island, S.C., remaining there as teacher and superintendent until 1865. Tomlinson, who assisted General Rufus Saxon in settling forty thousand

P. S. The Political pot is boiling here, and I hope you will not be misled by the newspaper statements respecting the course of the "Rebels" and the Colored people The latter are all right I think; and I am surprised that the Tribune should be fooled into thinking that Wade Hampton[63] & Co. mean anything else but mischief.

R. T.

❖ 91 ❖

Philad April 1/67

My dear Sir

It is late but I before I retire acknowledge your note of this morning. I am glad to have the letters you have sent me. I will lay them before the Com.[64] Their time is much the same with very many others wh. have reached

---

freedmen on the South Carolina coast, became a member of the South Carolina House of Representatives in 1868. Four years later Tomlinson lost his bid for governor. He served on the board of the Greenville and Columbia Railroad before returning to the North in 1877. Benjamin, *The Philadelphia Quakers in the Industrial Age*; Rose, *Rehearsal for Reconstruction*; Morris, *Reading, 'Riting, and Reconstruction*.

63. Wade Hampton (March 28, 1818–April 11, 1902), the son of a wealthy South Carolina planter, became a member of the South Carolina state legislature in 1852. Reelected twice, he then went on to the state senate. Although he believed that it was in the best interest of the Southern states to remain in the Union, he fought for the South during the Civil War, despite his lack of military experience, as a successful leader of an elite Southern regiment. After the war, Hampton supported limited black suffrage. He chaired the state Democratic Executive Committee during the 1868 presidential election, but then withdrew from politics until 1876, when he was elected governor under the banner of home rule and the expulsion of Northern Republicans from the state. In spite of the rhetoric of Hampton's campaign, he did not attempt to strip black people of their newly won rights. Martin Delany's support for Hampton during the gubernatorial race is evidence of Hampton's political moderation. Soon after commencing his second term as governor in 1878, Hampton was elected to the Senate, a position he held until 1891. *ANB*, vol. 9; Edmund L. Drago, *Hurrah for Hampton: Black Red Shirts in South Carolina During Reconstruction* (Fayetteville: University of Arkansas Press, 1998).

64. Welsh is probably referring to the United States Sanitary Commission, of which he was a member. Soon after the outbreak of the Civil War, many women answered the government's request for nurses. Dorothea Dix and Dr. Elizabeth Blackwell founded the Woman's Central Association of Relief (WCAF), loosely based on the work done by Florence Nightingale and the British Sanitary Commission during the Crimean War. The WCAF, which was based in New York City, provided much needed improvements for soldiers, raising hygienic standards in camps, improving soldiers' diets, caring for wounded troops, compiling a directory of hospital occupants, and building houses near railroad stations to shelter soldiers while they awaited transport. The WCAF developed into the Sanitary Commission, which was signed into law by Lincoln in June of 1861. Most of the volunteers and agents of the commission were women, but the majority of leaders were men. Henry Bellows, Alexander Dallas Bache, Frederick Law Olmstead, and

us. A great many individual appeals are flowing in but it is impossible to take them up. We will do the best we can towards the relief of communities with the means placed at our disposal which I find will be small compared to the destitution. There is much suffering both from the failures of the crops + the effects of the war. When did a people more effectually place the poisonus chalice to their own lips? They are in want + we must do what we can both to feed the hungry + teach the ignorant. Very truly

Jno Welsh[65]

M[r] Benj Coates no 127 Mkt St

We have put 3000 bus.[66] corn in each No Carolina So Carolina bus. + ordered 4000 bus. brt[67] today for No Alabama where they are very badly off.

❖ 92 ❖

Philadelphia April 6th 1867[68]

W[m] Coppinger Esq.[69]

My dear sir

As the slavery Question is now settled, and the complete enfranchisement of the blacks so well assured, I have time to devote a little more attention, (not more interest) towards Africa. You know [thy] my interest in the Negro is not confined either to that portion of the

---

George Templeton Strong were all officers of the Sanitary Commission. Despite criticism, the commission provided a much-needed service. After the war, two organizations, the American Public Heath Association and the American Red Cross, replaced the commission. *American Eras: Civil War and Reconstruction, 1850–1877*, Judith Ann Giesberg, *Civil War Sisterhood* (Boston: Northeastern University Press, 2000); *The Civil War Dictionary*, ed. Mark Mayo Boatner III (New York: David McKay Company, 1987).

65. John Welsh (November 9, 1805–April 10, 1886) was born in Philadelphia and entered the dry goods business as a teenager. Following his father's death, Welsh joined his brothers' sugar importing business. Welsh's other activities included a brief tenure as the president of the North Pennsylvania Railroad, which he held for one year, resigning when thirty-nine children were killed in an accident. During the Civil War Welsh was an active member of and raised funds for the Sanitary Commission. He also helped plan Philadelphia's Fairmont Park, served on the Centennial Board of Finance in 1876, and became the U.S. minister to Great Britain in 1877. Welsh returned to Pennsylvania two years later due to ill health. He was actively involved with the University of Pennsylvania throughout his lifetime and supported the foundation of a women's college there. *ANB* 23:34–35.

66. "bus." is an abbreviation for bushels.

67. "brt" is an abbreviation for brought.

68. ACS Papers 100:187:42.

69. William Coppinger. See Letter 10, Coates to McLain, October 11, 1851.

race in America, or the greater body of people still in Africa, and while I am desirous of securing to this much abused, + neglected people, all their rights under the law in America (complete <u>political</u> + <u>social</u> <u>rights</u> + <u>elevation here</u>) yet I do not want to see it <u>confined</u> to them here, but that these blessings shall <u>through</u> <u>them</u> redound to the glory of God our common Father, + to the Good of the <u>whole race</u>. While therefore I cannot sympathise with those who profess to be Colonizationists <u>to get rid of the Negro</u>, under the plea (as anti Christian as it is anti Republican) that this is a "<u>White</u> <u>Man's</u> <u>Government</u>" I cannot but recognize the fact, that they were originally the children of the Tropics, and altho' <u>in a measure</u>, acclimated here, yet not entirely so, and that their inclinations, + the laws of their nature which are the laws of God will <u>gradually</u> <u>attract</u> <u>them</u> [page break] to warmer, and more congenial climes. Hence I believe that <u>in time</u>, after they have been thoroughly educated and enlightened here, it is probable that the mass of the black + colored population will gradually gravitate towards Mexico, the West Indies, + South America, some drawn thitherward by self interest, + some from a sense of duty. While a larger portion will no doubt seek their fatherland, either as Missionaries, or as emigrants in the pursuit of wealth taking with them to all these countries, the English language, our Protestant Christianity, and the principles of enlightened republican government, thus becoming the regenerators of a great part of the continent. This emigration, <u>gradual</u> altho' it may, + should be, will no doubt be accelerated ~~by~~ by a rapid of increase of immigration from Europe to those shores, of Germans, Irish, Norwegians +c, accustomed to our colder clime. who will continually press the Negro southward. ~~as this population —— they will~~ In addition to this impelling force we must bear in mind that in a very few years there is every probability of the completion of the great Pacific Rail Road across the continent to California which will open the way for a large portion of the overcrowded population of China. For several years past there has been a constantly increasing influx of Chinese into California + Oregon, and from the great need of laborers in the southern states, is there [page break] not every reason to believe that we shall soon have millions of this people seeking work among us? A people accustomed to live + thrive where a white or black man will starve, living on the merest pitance, or on the offal rejected by white + black alike. Here there is a new problem, + extended field for labor + usefulness to the true philanthropist. A new people to educate, to civilize, to <u>Christianize</u>, to prepare them for the great missionary work, which an over-ruling Providence may need to carry on this work in their own native land, among the dense populations of Asia, where the civilized Caucassian has so far made but little impression, + scarcely perceptible progress.

This is not an imaginary theory, but judging from the experience of the past ten years, what we may pretty surely calculate upon. In the mean time the black population among us <u>must be educated</u> + I am glad to say are being rapidly educated, in literature, in politics, or the art of self government, in true religion, + in the arts + sciences belonging to a high civilization, so as to fit them to become intelligent + valuable citizens of our common country, or to qualify them as missionaries to heathen lands. You are aware that I have taken great interest in this field of labor, ~~work~~ almost ever since the commencement of the war, + the taking of Beaufort + Port Royal So. Ca.,[70] and is it not extremely gratifying to ^ see the unanimity with the southern people themselves our now coming into the work, or at least giving it their approval, so that with the numerous Northern Associations engaged in this enterprise, soon to receive an [page break] additional aid + stimulation in the Peabody Fund,[71] ^ the benefit of which will, I believe be extended to the poor of the southern states without any distinction of color or race, recognizing only the broad Christian charity that seeks the most needy, "The American Freedman's Union Commission"[72] (which includes many of our northern Freedman's Associations) occupying very much the same ground of excluding <u>none</u> from their schools on account of color or race, who are really deserving, + need an education. We may soon calculate on having the southern states completely regenerated, + reorganized, (or reconstructed) with an educated + intelligent population and each working together for the good of all, we shall have not only a united government but a united people, a union of [smudged] hearts, a union of hands, of interests + purposes. While the black man is thus assured of ^ his equal rights + duties here, as a citizen of our common country, he will

---

70. Beaufort and Port Royal are part of the Sea Islands in South Carolina. See Letter 66, Coates to Crummell, February 20, 1862.

71. The Peabody Fund was named for its founder, George Peabody (1795–1869). Peabody was born to working-class parents and started work at an early age in his brother's dry goods store. In 1815 he became a partner with his uncle, a dry goods wholesaler, and after his uncle retired he became the senior partner. In the 1830s he expanded his business to London, where he experienced enormous success. He devoted his wealth to philanthropic causes, donating millions of dollars to establish institutes in Peabody, Massachusetts, Salem, and Baltimore. Yale and Harvard also received sizeable contributions. The Peabody Fund (known officially as the Southern Education Fund) was created after Peabody visited the United States in 1866 and was informed of the desperate situation of education in the postbellum South. He believed that a working school system was essential to the reconstruction of the South, and he donated some $3.5 million to Southern education to encourage free public schools for black and white children, support black colleges, and establishing normal schools throughout the South. "Peabody, George," *ANB* 17:184–86; Franklin Parker, *George Peabody: A Biography*, rev. ed. (Nashville: Vanderbilt University Press, 1995), 160–67.

72. The AFUC. See Letter 86, Coates to Coppinger, June 1, 1866.

be fitted as he has never been before, to any great extent, to carry the blessings of Christianity, + civilization to other lands. I believe therefore that in a <u>year or two</u> from this time that ~~the~~ a considerable portion of our black population will be thus qualified, and <u>then</u> having learned for themselves the great attractions that Africa possesses to the man of enterprise, to the farmer, the mechanic, the merchant, + the missionary, it will require I apprehend strong inducement to keep many ~~here~~ from seeking a wider field for usefulness, + greater avenues to wealth + prosperity, when they shall become fully satisfied of the vast treasures, as yet undeveloped in their father land. To aid to some extent in extending this information, I have it in contemplation to furnish to a number of Sunday School Libraries connected with the schools under the care of the different associations with which I am connected, copies of the most useful + interesting books from which the most reliable information can be obtained such as "Abbeokuta,"[73] "Africa's 'Mountain Valley," "The New Republic" +c and it is in this regard that I have now written to ask any suggestions that you may have to give. From the breaking out of the rebellion till now I have felt that my main work was at <u>home</u>, to secure, the emancipation, the <u>enfranchisement</u> + the education of

[The remainder of this letter is written vertically on the left sides of the fourth and first pages:]

our colored people in our midst. these objects attained, + secured, I wish to see all these blessings extended to other lands, where the African race have so far developed in the greatest measures their full stature, their ability without the aid of the white man of conducting successfully [page break] an independent nationality. Yours very truly Benj[a] Coates

Philad[a] Apr 7 1867[74]

My dear sir

   I have just written a very long letter to you, much longer than I had intended when I commenced, + yet I find I have not said what I wished ——. A day or two since, I had a letter from Rev[d] A Crummell,[75] he informs me that he has resigned his position in the College,[76] having had some difficulty

73. Sarah Tucker, *Abbeokuta*; Johnson, *Africa's Mountain Valley*; Helen Cross Knight, *The New Republic*. See Letter 37, Wagoner to Coates, January 31, 1859.

74. ACS Papers 100:187:43.

75. Alexander Crummell. See Letter 28, Coates to Gurley, May 2, 1857.

76. Liberia College. See Letter 29, Coates to Crummell, October 3, 1857.

with the directors, or trustees, and I infer is doing nothing + is very poor. On thinking over the matter, I feel pretty well satisfied that Mr Crummell can at this time do much more good to his people, to the cause of education + enlightenment among the black population of the United States than he can do now in Liberia, and at the same time, he may be the means of diffusing reliable information in regard to Liberia + Africa generally ∧ better than he could do if he were especially engaged in the colonization cause. Such a man as Mr Crummell would command attention + respect from all in the southern states, black + white, alike as a representation [page break] of the black race a full blooded negro + a Christian gentleman, it strikes me he is the very man to be engaged in the cause of education among his own people + for his long residence in Africa + the great interest he takes ∧ in Liberia, no one I think could aid so much the interest of his adopted country, while at the same time educating the blacks + whites of the south in their duties towards each other. I had thought of writing to Genl Howard[77] on the subject in case he knew of any opening for such a man. If he could get the position of a principal in some large educational establishment say in Richmond, or Charleston S.C in Savannah or New Orleans, or Nashville, + could occasionally travel through the states for a year or two, there is no calculating how much good he could accomplish. I should prefer that he should come [page break] here to travel through the South ∧ not as a colonization agent, as it might arouse a prejudice against him at the outset that would injure his usefulness, but would I prefer to see him occupy some prominent + important position either under the Freedmans Beureau,[78]

---

77. This most likely refers to General Oliver Otis Howard, but it could also refer to General Charles Howard, his brother. O. O. Howard (1830–1909), a career soldier who also involved himself in charitable causes, graduated from West Point in 1854 and rose to the rank of brigadier general by 1865. At the end of the Civil War he was appointed commissioner of the Freedman's Bureau, a position that he held until 1872 and gave him influence over the shape of freedman's aid during the Reconstruction. He was one of the founders, a trustee, and the namesake of Howard University; he served as its president from 1869 to 1873. After the closing of the Freedman's Bureau, he commanded armies in the West as part of the effort to control the American Indians. He retired from the army in 1894 and spent the rest of his life in politics and in founding the Lincoln Memorial University in Tennessee. Charles Howard was also a founder of the university and was on its board of trustees for many years. "Howard, Oliver Otis," ANB 11:311–13; Rayford W. Logan, Howard University: The First Hundred Years, 1867–1967 (New York: New York University Press, 1969).

78. The Bureau of Refugees, Freedmen, and Abandoned Lands—also known as the Freedmen's Bureau—was created on March 3, 1865, was under the jurisdiction of the War Department, and was charged with managing abandoned lands and providing freed slaves with rations and land. Headed by Oliver O. Howard, the bureau's major contribution was to education. In concert with private organizations, it established more than a thousand schools and paid for teachers to staff them, built hospitals, and distributed food to needy southerners. On May 29, 1865, President Johnson issued a pardon that restored much of the abandoned land to its original

under the Peabody Comm.[79] or some state institution, where his talents would be appreciated, his education, + scholarship made widely known, + where his extensive information in regard to Africa + all that pertains to the welfare of his race can be most usefully applied. The Lincoln Institute at Oxford Chester Co Pa, originated by Rev[d] J.M. Dickey,[80] is I believe a Presbyterian Institution, if so, it would not do. He might perhaps get a professorship in the Avery College at Allegheny Pa., but I do not think that is the place for him. Please think this matter over, + write to me on the subject. Yours very truly Benj[a] Coates

❖ 94 ❖

Germantown 5 mo. 17, 1867

My dear friend,

Thy kind letter was duly received, and I have tried to give it due consideration. The great duty the white race owe to the coloured one in this country, and the grave importance to the latter of aid from the former to enable them to advance in civilization, and maintain advancements already made, were never more apparent to me than now. Hence I cannot but feel a deep interest in the Institute for Coloured Youth,[81] which is, perhaps, the most effective and well designed agenciesy of its extent, in our country, to secure the advancement of the coloured people. But as I am a member of two, or three Boards already which I have not deemed it safe for me to attend for several months, and which I wish to attend as soon as able to do so, it seems to me that it would be unwise and unfair to accept a position in the management of the Institute under these circumstances. No association would be more agreeable to me than with the members of the Boards as proposed but this pleasure must be forgone for the present.

Affectionately thy friend
James Rhoads[82]

Benjamin Coates,

owners, much to the disappointment of the Radical Republicans. The bureau was dissolved by Congress at the end of June 1872. Bentley, *A History of the Freedmen's Bureau.*

79. Peabody Fund. See Letter 92, Coates to Coppinger, April 6, 1867.

80. John McElroy Dickey (1789–1849) was born in South Carolina. He became a minister in 1814 and moved to the Indiana Territory to preach. While there he organized many Presbyterian churches and published *A History of the Presbyterian Church in Indiana. Appleton's* 2:171.

81. The ICY. See Letter 42, Douglass to Coates, May 2, 1859.

82. James Rhoads (1828–1895) was a Philadelphia area doctor involved in many charitable endeavors. He pursued medicine at the University of Pennsylvania and established his

❖ 95 ❖

~~United States Sanitary Commission~~
American Freedmans Union Commission[83]
    No 76 Johns Street—P. O. Box 5,733
    Lyman Abbott,[84] Gen. Sec   J. M. McKim,[85] Cor Sec
                                        New York, May 24.1867

B. Coates Esq
        Phila
        My dear sir
        What you say about Crummell[86] interests me very much. I know him well + esteem him highly. I will consider the matter + in due time let you hear from me.

                                J M McKim

---

practice in Germantown, Pennsylvania. Eventually, because he was forced to give up his medical work due to health problems, he involved himself in freedman's aid efforts in the South and, later, in activism on behalf of Native Americans. He was president of the Indian Rights Association for a few years, and then he served as the first president of Bryn Mawr College from the 1880s until his retirement in 1894. *Memorial Minute respecting our late friend, James E. Rhoads* . . . ; Cornelia Meigs, *What Makes a College? A History of Bryn Mawr* (New York: Macmillan Company, 1956), 34–37.

83. The AFUC. This letter was written on letterhead. See Letter 84, Coates to Coppinger, May 24, 1866.

84. Lyman Abbott (1835–1922) was a figure of significant stature in the late nineteenth and early twentieth centuries. His first profession was law, but he soon abandoned it to become a Congregationalist preacher in Indiana, after which he was offered the position of general secretary of the newly formed AFUC. In 1869 the AFUC disbanded because it felt there was no longer a need for a national organization dedicated to bringing education to the south. The efforts of the AMA to gain control over the AFUC's schools and sources of funding probably played some part in the demise of the commission. After 1869 Abbott began to write and edit for *Harper's Magazine* and the *Illustrated Christian Weekly*. In 1876 he became the associate editor of Henry Ward Beecher's *Christian Union*, and in 1881 he became the sole editor of the magazine (later renamed the *Outlook*). Brown, *Lyman Abbott*; "Abbot, Lyman," *ANB* 1:29–30.

85. James Miller McKim (1810–1874), after graduating from Dickinson College and entering the Presbyterian ministry in 1835, read some of William Lloyd Garrison's writings and became dedicated to the abolition movement. He was a delegate to the founding of the AAS, and he served the Pennsylvania Anti-Slavery Society in various administrative capacities from 1840 to 1862, when he founded the Port Royal Relief Committee (which became the Pennsylvania Freedman's Relief Association). He helped organize the American Freedmen's Aid Commission, and when it merged with the American Union Commission in 1866 he was named corresponding secretary of the resulting AFUC. "McKim, James Miller," *ANB* 15:115–17.

86. Alexander Crummell (see Letter 28, Coates to Gurley, May 2, 1857). For more information on the "matter" McKim mentions, see Letter 96, McKim to Coates, June 4, 1867.

❖ 96 ❖

American Freedman's Union Commission[87]
No 30 Vesey Street—P. O. Box 5,733.
Lyman Abbott, Gen Sec[88]   J. M. McKim[89] Cor Sec

New York, June 4, 1867

Benj Coates Esq
Phil[a]
Dear friend

I saw Gen Howard[90] the other day and endeavored to interest him in McCrummell.[91] He says if Mr McCrummells friends will raise a sum sufficient to endow a professorship in Howard University[92] McC shall be the professor. This is the most I get him to say on the subject.

Yours truly
J M McKim[93]

87. The AFUC. This letter was written on letterhead. See Letter 84, Coates to Coppinger, May 24, 1866.

88. Lyman Abbott. See Letter 95, McKim to Coates, May 24, 1867.

89. James Miller McKim. See Letter 95, McKim to Coates, May 24, 1867.

90. Probably General Oliver Otis Howard. See Letter 93, Coates to [Coppinger], April 7, 1867.

91. This is a reference to Alexander Crummell (see Letter 28, Coates to Gurley, May 2, 1857), although in this letter McKim seems to have misremembered his name. When this letter was written Crummell was living in Liberia but became increasingly unhappy there. In 1866 he had resigned from his professorship at Liberia College due to an ongoing conflict with the trustees and administration of the college. His relationship with the Episcopal establishment in Liberia was also tense. As a result, it seems possible that he was seeking a position outside Liberia. Acquainted with Coates and other colonizationists, Crummell welcomed their support. In a letter to William Coppinger on April 7, 1867, Coates informed Coppinger of Crummel's resignation from Liberia College and mentioned the possibility that Crummell might return to the United States. He also wrote that he "had thought of writing to Gen¹ Howard on the subject." From Coates's letter and McKim's correspondence to Coates (this letter and the one of May 24, 1867), it appears that Coates may have attempted to arrange for Crummell to be a professor at the newly formed Howard University. Evidently, the efforts of Coates and McKim were unsuccessful, because Crummell remained in Liberia for several more years. He returned to the United States in 1872 and was a religion instructor at Howard University from 1895 to 1897. "Crummell, Alexander," ANB 5:820–22; Walter Dyson, *Howard University: The Capstone of Negro Education: A History: 1867–1940* (Washington, D.C.: Graduate School, Howard University, 1941), 459; Logan, *Howard University*; Moses, *Alexander Crummell*; Oldfield, *Alexander Crummell*; Rigsby, *Alexander Crummell*.

92. Howard University, located in Washington, D.C., was created in March 1867 with the purpose of providing black youth with the opportunity for a higher education. The university was not open exclusively to black people; there were some white students in its early classes as well. Logan, *Howard University*.

93. James Miller McKim. See Letter 95, McKim to Coates, May 24, 1867.

Germantown 6 mo. 28. 1867.

Benjamin Coates,

My Dear Friend,

Thy interesting letter reached me yesterday, and its subject takes such hold upon my mind that I desire at least that a meeting of the friends mentioned should be held —— and we seriously consider what may be our duty in this matter.—Being about to leave home for a few days it will probably be as late as next 6th. day before I can see these parties + report to thee their conclusion.

    Affectionately thy friend,

        James E Rhoads[94]

        1701 Filbert Dr

        7.18.67.

My Dear Friend -

    I want to call thy attention to an article of Yardley Warner's[95] in the Friend, 7[mo] 13th—under the head of "The Poor in Our Midst."[96] I do not subscribe to the Friend, or I would show it to thee.

    Y. W. ought, I should think, to be added to the list of founders of the coming "Friends' Free First-Day School Association."[97]

        Thine Truly,

        H Hartshorne[98],

Benjamin Coates

94. James E. Rhoads. See Letter 94, Rhoads to Coates, May 17, 1867.

95. Yardley Warner (?–January 7, 1885), an Orthodox Quaker from Germantown, Pennsylvania, taught freed black people in the South. In 1869 he moved to Tennessee where he founded a school. Warner died at the age of seventy in South Carolina. Benjamin, *Philadelphia Quakers; The Friend* 58 (1885): 192.

96. Warner's article, "The Poor in Our Mist," suggests that help is needed not only for the poor in the South, but also for the underprivileged in Philadelphia. Warner cites the ICY as a good start but not enough. *The Friend* 41 (July 1867): 367.

97. English Quakers first opened first day schools in the middle of the nineteenth century to teach working-class adults. The schools produced many converts. In the 1860s Quakers in Philadelphia opened similar schools with less success. Black First Day Schools founded by Quakers produced few converts. It is not clear exactly what Hartshorne means by "Friends' Free First-Day School Association." Benjamin, *The Philadelphia Quakers in the Industrial Age*; Linda B. Selleck, *Gentle Invaders: Quaker Women Educators and Racial Issues During the Civil War and Reconstruction* (Richmond, Ind.: Friends United Press, 1995).

98. Henry Hartshorne (March 16, 1823–February 10, 1892), an Orthodox Quaker who attended Haverford College, obtained his M.D. from the University of Pennsylvania in 1845 and

❖ 99 ❖

Wilmington 8.15 1867

My dear friend
   Bnj. Coates

I paid a visit at New Bedford a short time ago, and while there attended their (Friends') First-day school, which is conducted in a way quite different from those that are held in Phil[adelphia], and in this region,— Remembering the pleasant eve'g we had at Dr. Hartshorne's[99] in the spring and the discussion of this subject, and thinking the changes they have introduced in the manner of carrying on their school at N. B. will interest thee, I have wished for an opp'ty of telling thee of them. As we may not meet very soon I feel tempted to put into writing what I saw. The aft. mtg. commences at 4 O.C. and is held in the usual manner of a Friends mtg. for about 20 minutes, giving time to any minister who may wish to speak to the children and teachers, to do so. The whole ~~mtg~~ congregation present then [resolved] itself into a First day school, and Bible classes: the teachers separating with their children to different parts of the house and the adults who were not occupied in teaching, falling into classes of 6 or 8 and occupying themselves in the joint study of the Bible, searching the Scriptures. Chas. Taber[100] acted as Supt. and took some minutes at the beginning or end of the school in a general exercise, reading and commenting on a chapter, calling for texts &c.—The whole was done with great simplicity—not wanting in earnestness—and it was a pleasant thing to see the differnt adult "classes" seated together to examine and compare views on passages of Scripture, familiar indeed to us all, but always yielding some new idea or interest to a conversational examination by 2 or more jointly. The "first class" consisted of W.C. Taber,[101] the head of the mtg.

---

then taught at Haverford, the Women's Medical College of Pennsylvania, and Girard College. From 1873 to 1878 Hartshorne was the editor of *Friends Review*. He traveled to Japan late in life and died in Tokyo. *Dictionary of Quaker Biography*.

   99. Probably Dr. Henry Hartshorne. See Letter 98, Hartshorne to Coates, July 18, 1867.

   100. Charles Taber (1822–1887) seems to have been a publisher. *Friends' Review* 39 (1887): 319.

   101. William C. Taber (?–1886) was a member and elder of New Bedford Monthly Meeting. *Friends' Review* 39 (1886): 617.

with Geo Howland,[102] Jos. Grinnell,[103] Saml Rodman[104] and some other middle aged and old men: the second of Matthew Howland[105] and 6 or 8 others, some of them apparently —— men.

The day I was there the no. present was smaller than usual, but the interest is increasing, and the no. often large, many coming who would desert the aft. mtg. as dull and lifeless. All the members of the congregation may take part, as teachers or scholars: all are at liberty to do so of course, and many persons come to see and hear who would not come to silent mtg. M Howland writes me that there were present lately 160—85 children and 75 adults: "Before we made the change about 6 or 8 months since we used to have about 30 persons present at our First-day afternoon mtgs. and they used to be dull and stupid seasons, now they are always interesting, and our experience so far is that it works well."

I hope thy concern for the introduction of First day schools as a means of building up and holding together the languishing mtgs. of the Society of F. will not die away. The influence of such a movement as then proposed could not fail of being for good I think: and perhaps the result of the experiment at N. B. may encourage thee to persevere in bringing the subject to the notice of the officials, without whose sanction it will be uphill work. My father, whose name was mentioned, is I think quite ready to lend his aid. -

Excuse my long letter—longer than I intended,
   and believe me
      Thy friend sincerely
        W. S. Hilles[106]

102. George Howland Jr. (1806–1892) was a prominent individual in New Bedford's active whaling industry. He also held many civic positions, including mayor of New Bedford and in the Massachusetts legislature, where he argued for the abolition of slavery. William Logan Rodman Gifford, *George Howland, Junior* (New Bedford, Mass.: privately published, 1892).

103. Joseph Grinnell (1789–1885) was a New Bedford merchant who made a quick fortune serving as a New York agent for New Bedford whale-oil merchants. He was elected a representative of Massachusetts in the U.S. Congress for four terms from 1843 to 1851 and he played a key role in bringing the cotton processing industry to New Bedford. "Joseph Grinnell," *Appleton's* 3:1; "Joseph Grinnell," *ANB* 8:3–4.

104. Samuel Rodman (1792–1876). Born in Nantucket, Rodman moved to New Bedford later in life. Zephaniah W. Pease, *The Diary of Samuel Rodman: A New Bedford Chronicle of Thirty-Seven Years, 1821–1859* (New Bedford, Mass.: Reynolds Printing, 1927), 6–9; *Friends' Review* 30 (1876): 141.

105. Matthew Howland (?–1884) was the half brother of George Howland Jr. and joined him in the whaling business that they inherited from their father. *Friends' Review* 38 (1884): 218; Gifford, *George Howland, Junior*.

106. William S. Hilles (1825–1876), a Quaker, graduated from Haverford College in 1842, taught there from 1844 to 1845, and then engaged in "various civic causes at home" in

❖ 100 ❖

613 Market St. Phil.

8 mo 27.1867

My kind friend

　B. Coates

　　Thy note of the 23rd has lain unanswered for several days but its contents have been meanwhile revolving in my mind—I enter into thy feeling and hope when the time comes to participate to some extent in the work.— For several reasons however I believe I shall not be able to take the initiatory step which thou kindly proposes.—

　　I am like the guests who when invited had each his excuse. Let me state mine, which is an occupancy of time too full to admit of adding <u>anything</u> at present. My duties to my intended wife, the oversight of building at our future home, the settling up of my father's estate, and the necessity of close watching of my business, in a dull and unprofitable season, render it I believe impossible ~~I believe~~ for me to do aught than to meet with the others when they come together, without taking it upon me to lead in the matter.

　　This excuse does not mean apathy towards the work for I do not doubt that there may be very excellent service for the Lord in the path thou art desirous of leading Friends into.

With much respect + esteem,

I am thy friend

Wm Evans.[107]

Wilmington, Delaware. From his later letter (see Letter 106, Hilles to Coates, February 25, 1868) it is clear that he remained involved in charitable activities, but no mention is made of these in Samuel Hilles's *Memorials of the Hilles Family*. . . . The book does, however, list William S. Hilles's many business endeavors. Samuel Eli Hilles, *Memorials of the Hilles Family* . . . (Cincinnati: Samuel E. Hilles, 1928), 43–49.

　　107. Probably the son of William Evans (d. 1867), a Philadelphia Quaker. See *Friend* 40 (1867): 328. See also Letter 123, Whipple to Coates, August 27, 1868, for a W. Evans Jr. and Sr.

❖ 101 ❖

Fairfield 11/10 mo '67

Dear Friend

Writing is so difficult for me that I have to study brevity + so run the risk sometimes of seeming to be rude or dogmatic But thou writes on a subject upon which to make myself clear, I sh^d. have to write the bulk of a medium pamphlet I can [section completely crossed out] therefore only give thee a few headings + trust to thee to fill up the chapters. The Castle of Sin is mighty. The children of men are pygmies—their weapons straws. With a good stiff straw one may pick a little mortar out of the joints of the huge edifice If the Ruler of the Pygmies says:—Pick—as obedient subjects they must pick. They may even raise a little dust, now + then, if a considerable company pick together, + if their range of vision is in proportion to their pygmy bulk, they may perchance fancy the castle is coming down. But some will perceive that this is not likely to be. Yet, at the word of command, they pick too. It is for them a good discipline. They know their Ruler has in his armory artillery with which he could at once destroy this castle. Why he does not, they do not know. They do not dare even to ask; but they believe that one day he will. They pick then, not because they anticipate the destruction or material diminution of evil, but simply in the spirit of obedience. They are being trained—drilled. If they obey orders, they do well. They act when they are bid to act, + when the command is withheld, they refrain. They refrain although they see a deal of mischief being done by the garrison that mans the castle. None of the disciplined make battle with their weapons of straw or reproach their fellows that they dont join in conflict—command or no command. They dont cry out: It's enough to see the castle. that's your authority for making the attack. They dont raise such an outcry + in such a tone, against the existence of this stronghold of Sin, as seems to rebuke their Ruler that he suffers it still to exist. They call not in question his hidden counsels. They know him to be wiser than they are. They trust him + they obey him They know that he will in the fulness of time, slowly or more quickly, as seemeth him meet, exercise his sovereignty over sin- + in the meantime their function is simple obedience to his commands. They are not too much trouble if, at times, he allows to sin a wide range + does not call upon them, at every juncture, to do open battle with the enemy. They believe that he does all things well—whether in acting or in suffering. And they feel that their own knowledge + ability is so small, that they can of themselves accomplish nothing. They do not doubt that if he wants them, he will call upon them, for every particular service he may have for them, + that

if they give good heed, they will always know his voice. Dost thou understand
my parable + its application? J. Evans (whose services I fear are nearly done)
can explain + amplify with more ability than thy decrepid friend
     A Cope[108]
[There is another piece of paper with this letter. It is unclear whether it was
originally sent with this letter or with another.]
6th day—Please excuse my forgetfulness—I now return Crummells[109] letter
+c—for the perusal of w[h] I am obliged. I subscribe for a periodical in Eng[d]
which I believe was for the athenaeum.[110] Had I better stop it? Into whose
hands will it go? If into a public Library, I will not stop it—but if in to the
hands of somebody who may only value it as waste paper, I had rather spend
the money in some other way—It is the Intellectual Observer—devoted to
popular science.

       ❖ 102 ❖

Dear Friend-[111]
     Thy letter of 10th mo 10th. was rec[d]. yesterday—the parable I believe
I understand. Yet probably thou would fill up the chapters, differently from
what I would -with an abiding faith in their Ruler, and in His Commands.
May not the children of men Pygmies tho' they are, work for the overthrow
of evil, even the Castle of Sin, with such weapons as may be placed in their
hands? The faith that will remove mountains.—mountains even—of prejudice, + doubt, will not hesitate or falter on account of what may seem to
Pygmy eyes the insufficiency of the materials wherewith it is to work. But
should the children of men, neglect the plain and emphatic commands of
their Ruler, to work with the weapons He has given them, thinking the slow
process of picking will never reduce the Castle of Sin—and await for Him to
come with his heavy artillery? May they not again experience His coming, +

---

108. Alfred Cope (1806–75), a Philadelphia Quaker. In partnership with his brother,
Henry Cope, he took over his father's shipping business, and in 1842 moved to Fairfield, his home
in Germantown. He contributed to an array of organizations and institutions including the Institute for Colored Youth. *Dictionary of Quaker Biography*.
    109. Alexander Crummell. See Letter 28, Coates to Gurley, May 2, 1857.
    110. The Athenaeum Club. See Letter 103, Coates to Crummell, October 14, 1867.
    111. This letter has no signature or date and seems unfinished, but it is clear from the
handwriting and content that it is Coates's response to a letter written to him by Alfred Cope.
See Letter 101, Cope to Coates, October 11, 1867.

with garments rolled in blood—destroying not only the Castle of Sin but punishing at the same time his faithless children who were not found in the path of duty?

Surely my dear friend, the one experience of this kind ~~should be suff~~ that we have just had should be sufficient for us or for this generation at least so it seems to me. Perhaps however I may have misapprehended thy parable—or do not see its applicability to the case before us. Can there be any difference among "Friends" as to the commands of our Master? or what our duty may be? "Therefore to him that knoweth to do good, and doeth it not, to him it is Sin."—"Work while it is called to day, for the night cometh when no man can work." +c +c. these commands seem to me so explicit that they cannot be disregarded. I feel well assured that thou would not wish, <u>even to seem</u> to lessen this weight. Yet I would ask, whether in thy opinion, the fear that many good and valued "Friends" [~~here~~] have entertained ~~of~~ "Creaturely activity"—"unsactified zeal" in "their own willings + ———nnings" +c +c may not be carried too far? and that the too frequent repetition of a wise caution in such phrases as I have quoted above, may not tend to repress, + discourage many young and tender minds from entering into what they regard as the path of duty? Those who ~~may be~~ naturally diffident of their own abilities for the work before them, may thus find an excuse for relapsing into indifference, slothfulness ease + quiet—thus burying the talent that was committed to their care for the Master's use. Our natural tendencies, if I mistake not, are rather to self indulgence, ~~rather~~ than to disinterested efforts for the good of others. Do I presume too much therefore in asking one who has shown his faith by his works.—who by his life and conversation—by acts that speak louder than words—to lend his influence and encouragement to those who may be benefited by his advice, + stimulated, by his example to labor for the elevation and improvement of the neglected little ones, + for the depressed and lowly of whatever race, color, or condition? Is this not a generall call extended to all of the Pygmy race, even to the weakest of them by their Ruler. Has He not created them for a good + wise purpose—to do His work as He has commanded even for His own glory?—and are any warranted in holding back from the work, on account of their own weakness—when they remember "That not many wise men after the flesh, not many mighty, not many noble, <u>are called</u>:" "But God hath chosen the foolish things of the World to confound the wise; and God hath chosen the weak things of the world to confound the things that mighty; and base things of the world and things which are despised hath God chosen, yea, and things which are not to bring to nought things that are; that no flesh should glory in his presence."

❖ 103 ❖

Philad^a Octr 14th 1867[112]

Revd Alex^r Crummell[113]

My Dear Sir,

I rec^d your favor of June 14th about a
month or six weeks since and regret to learn from it that the "Athenaeum"[114]
is dead and that black men in Liberia are not so much superior in religion +
morals than their white brethren in America as we could wish. "Rum + lust"
are alas the great evils here, + have increased so much as to be truly appaling.
We are getting over the slavery question pretty well but I cannot see how we
are to eradicate these other evils except by some similar convulsion by the
mighty hand of Him who rules the universe, and purifies us through suffering. Well may it be for us if a part of the punishment for our crimes, the crimes
alike of omission + commission, may be inflicted on us here. I send you occasionally some newspapers that will perhaps keep you posted in regard to our
political affairs. You will see that we are losing the elections, or at least losing our majorities in most of the states where elections have been held within
the past few months, and the amendment[115] proposed for the Constitution of
Ohio to give [page break] the blacks the right to vote is lost by some 30.000!
when we had an overwhelming majority last year. This is a sad reverse. Still it
does not entirely discourage us. On the next morning after election I went to
Mr [Froony] of the Penn^a Freedmans Aid Assn[116] to stir them up to redoubled
efforts before the revolution shall bring the Democrats into power. We have
certainly gained a great deal and it cannot all go back. Slavery cannot I think
ever be re-established, + the freedmen have learned much that cannot be
taken from them. Had I known of this opportunity in time I believe I should
have forwarded to you the books you need for your Sunday Schools.[117] But

---

112. Courtesy HSP.

113. Alexander Crummell. See Letter 28, Coates to Gurley, May 2, 1857.

114. The Athenaeum Club. See Letter 83, Coates to Coppinger, October 31, 1865.

115. On April 6, 1867, the Ohio General Assembly proposed an amendment to the
State constitution that would allow all males to vote in elections. The population voted on the
measure in October, defeating it by 38,353 votes. When the Fifteenth Amendment was presented
for ratification in 1869, the Ohio legislature initially refused to ratify it but later did so under pressure. Frank U. Quillin, *The Color Line in Ohio: A History of Race Prejudice in a Typical Northern
State* (Ann Arbor, Mich.: George Wahr, 1913), 97–102.

116. The Pennsylvania Freedmen's Aid Association. See Letter 82, Clark to Coates,
July 15, 1865.

117. Crummell administered churches and schools at several settlements in Liberia.
His daughter Fannie and son Sidney were teachers in them, as was Crummell himself. He was

both our Freedmens Associations[118] <u>are very poor</u>, with <u>empty treasuries</u> and the public interest has very much died out it is very <u>difficult</u> to collect money, especially as business of all kinds is in a very depressed state. Very few are making money.

You did right in putting my name down for a copy of the new paper "The African Republic." [page break] I shall be glad to aid its circulation if possible. Alfred Cope[119] to whom I showed your letter asked me what would become of the "Intellectual Observer" now that the "Athenaeum" is dead? I told him that I thought there was a <u>Library</u> + reading room attached to the College[120] and that I supposed you would have it transferred to that, unless in your opinion it could do more good in some other way. I was much interested in knowing what you are doing + especially in the increase of Churches and Sabbath Schools. Perhaps I may be able to aid you with books for the latter after a while, as I do not propose to abate my interest in Africa while laboring to inspire the downtrodden in America.

With my best wishes for your success and your own individual welfare, I am as ever

Sincerely Yours,

Benj. Coates

Please remember me to Pres.t Warner, Ex Pres.t J J Roberts, Mr Blyden, Aug. Washington[121] + other friends

---

perpetually without the support necessary to realize his ambitions for these schools, however, hence the request for books to which Coates alludes. Moses, *Alexander Crummell*, 170–73.

118. Coates probably means the Friends Association of Philadelphia and Its Vicinity for the Relief of Colored Freedmen and the Friends' Association of Philadelphia for the Aid and Elevation of the Freedmen, the respective aid societies of Philadelphia's Orthodox and Hicksite Quakers. Youra Qualls, "'Successors of Woolman and Benezet': The Beginnings of the Philadelphia Friends Freedmen's Association," *Bulletin of Friends Historical Association* 45, no. 2 (Autumn 1956): 82–104; Henrietta Stratton Jaquette, "Friends' Association of Philadelphia for the Aid and Elevation of the Freedmen," *Bulletin of Friends Historical Association* 46, no. 2 (Autumn 1957): 67–83.

119. Alfred Cope. See Letter 101, Cope to Coates, October 11, 1867.

120. Liberia College. See Letter 29, Coates to Crummell, October 3, 1857.

121. Daniel Bashiell Warner (see Letter 10, Coates to McLain, October 11, 1851); Joseph Jenkins Roberts (see Letter 1, Roberts to Coates, July 8, 1848); Edward Wilmot Blyden (see Letter 27, Coates to Lugenbeel, October 6, 1856); and Augustus Washington (see Letter 21, Coates to McLain, May 22, 1855).

❖ 104 ❖

Monrovia, January 11, 1868

Benjamin Coates, Esq
    Dear Sir,
        Your very interesting and complimentary letter of November last was duly received—for which please accept my thanks.

I am just now too feeble, just recovering from a severe attack of bilious fever to refer to the various points you touched upon. I shall reserve this for some future day. You are at perfect liberty to republish any portion of my writings you see proper—and I only feel thankful that, God has so honored me as to enable me to put forth words that men who have been laboring in the cause so near my heart before I was born think it worth while to reproduce. I should like to ask the favor however of having prefixed to the work the enclosed dedication.—and having the corrections made which I also enclose.

I am now deeply interested in direct and energetic mission work and among the aborigines. My intercourse with the Mussulmans of the interior by means of the Arabic with which I am now sufficiently acquainted to make it available, has convinced me that a highly intelligent people exist in our interior neighborhood—and the sooner we undertake to evangelize and incorporate them among us the better for us.

I am ready to go out to Boporah[122] and establish a mission among the Mandingoes[123] there. They have recently made the most earnest application for schools.

Corrections to be made in the Address in the Repository Nov. 1867[124]
On page 326 line fifteenth for "their interior" read the interior.
page 327 line 6th for teacher read traveler.
"329 line 4th for the hoe read his hoe
"330—line 23rd after Liberia insert period

---

122. Boporo was a native town seventy-five miles from the Liberian coast. Blyden made several journeys there to determine the extent to which Islam had spread into the area, and he hoped at various times to establish a school in Boporo. Blyden believed that Islam was a more "natural" religion for Africans in general, because it did not force them to live like Europeans or Americans. He was also excited by the Islamic tradition of scholarship and study. Livingston, *Education and Race*, 76, 107, 109; Lynch, *Selected Letters of Edward Wilmot Blyden*.
123. The Manding, a tribe of native Africans who lived mainly in western Liberia. *HDL* 121.
124. Edward W. Blyden, "Liberia as a Means, not an End," *African Repository* 43 (November 1867): 321.

"332 line 20th for <u>principle</u> read <u>principal</u>

"   " After freedom in line 25th insert a dash and colon after U. States.

In the later line for <u>rega</u> read <u>regia</u>.

Page 334 line 3rd insert a comma after <u>all</u> and remove it after <u>that</u>.

Page 334 line 6th read civilization for cultivation

Page 335—line 28—for <u>These</u> read <u>There</u>

"340 line 22 (exclusive of poetry) for <u>would</u> read <u>should</u>

On page 341 line 7th (exclusive of poetry) for <u>with</u> Africa read <u>to</u> Africa—put a period after <u>night</u>: begin the following word <u>the</u> with a capital T. and insert <u>is</u> after night in the following line.

Corrections to be made in The Mountains Lebanon Address in the Repository, Dec. 66.

On page 361. Line 28. for <u>Dneitry</u> read <u>Dmitry</u>

One page 367 line 33 for <u>colonization</u> read <u>civilization</u>

On page 369 line 3 for <u>on</u> read <u>in</u>.

　　　Dedication-

Henry M Schieffelin Esq.[125]

　　　of Yonkers, New York.

who by his unwearied and munificent benefactions has done so much to forward the educational, agricultural and commercial interests of Liberia, the following pages are respectfully dedicated by their Author.

　　　　　Very respectfully Yrs.

　　　　　Edwd. <u>W Blyden</u>[126]

❖ 105 ❖

　　　　　Monrovia Jan. 23. 1868

Benjm Coates, Esq

　　　Dear Sir,

　　　Your very kind and flattering letter dated on November last has been duly received.

　　　I beg to assure you that I heartily appreciate the generous feelings which prompt you to take such kind notice of my writings[127] and I feel

---

125. Henry M. Scheiffelin. See Letter 46, Pinney to Coates, June 16, 1859.

126. Edward Wilmot Blyden. See Letter 27, Coates to Lugenbeel, October 6, 1856.

127. Blyden's recently published book was *Liberia's Offerings* (1862). It is likely that his correspondence, speeches, and essays were published much more frequently. For example, the

thankful ~~that~~ if anything I have been enabled to say is thought worthy of reproduction by one who has been so long and faithful a laborer in this great cause. I shall certainly feel honored if you think proper to republish any portion of my writing.

I am now deeply interested in the interior work[128] and I am doing all I can night and day to promote it. Excuse brevity as I am pressed for time and Believe me, dear sir, Yours gratefully

Edwd W Blyden[129]

 106

Wilmington 2.25/68

My dear Friend
    Benj. Coates
    I should not have been so long in answering thy letter in regard to the Colored institute,[130] had I not understood that there was no <u>immediate</u> necessity for an answer.—After turning it over in my mind for some time, with my inclination strongly in favor of accepting thy proposal, I feel obliged to give a reply in the negative: Reason, I have not time nor energy to spare to devote to the work.

    This I think thee must allow to be a sufficient reason.—I may say however, that it is very likely I should not have come to this conclusion were I not conscious that I have sometimes allowed myself to overstate my ability, by undertaking more than I ought: and have done both myself and the cause injustice therby. We have an anniversary mtg. of our Freedman's education asso.[131] on 6th day evening of this week, and it w^d give us pleasure if thou could attend it. -

January 1869 issue of the *African Repository* contains an excerpt from Letter 129, Blyden to Coates, October 10, 1868. *African Repository* 45 (January 1869): 28.

128. In the 1860s Blyden became interested in the inhabitants of the interior of Africa as a result of encounters he had with traveling Muslims, who often, in contrast to the neighboring tribes on the coast, could read and write in Arabic. He saw them as a confirmation of his belief that it was possible for Africans to develop their own form of civilization, appropriate to their background, without the unnatural imposition of American and British practices. To further this end, he taught himself Arabic and convinced the president of Liberia College, J. J. Roberts, to allow the introduction of Arabic into the curriculum. Livingston, *Education and Race*, 74–80.

129. Edward Wilmot Blyden. See Letter 27, Coates to Lugenbeel, October 6, 1856.

130. Probably the ICY. See Letter 42, Douglass to Coates, May 2, 1859.

131. Probably the Friends Freedmen's Association, but possibly the Pennsylvania branch of the AFUC.

We have raised and spent about $10,000. during the year, besides the amt. contributed by the Bureau[132] in Lumber +c, and by the Blacks in tuition money, and Board of teachers. -

Thy sincere friend
W. S. Hilles[133]

Benj Coates

❖ 107 ❖

St. Helena I.[134] March 12.th/68

Esteemed Friend.

The last mail brought me a package of seeds and as "B.C.". was written in the corner I suppose I may thank thee for them, which I do most sincerely. I shall plant some of the flower seeds immediately and in this warm climate they will soon cheer us with their bright cheerful faces—faces that always open upward, teaching us to open our hearts and lives to light and strength that comes from above.

Miss Towne[135] gave us some seeds which were gratefully received by our children. Many of the larger ones are often away at work, especially the orphans who have to raise their own crops, or those whose parents are too old to work. Several begin to hoe by daylight, do their allotted task and then walk 5 or 6 miles.

I have three girls that come in a boat, across the creek, when they can get one, or the tide is not too low, or the wind too high—otherwise they have to "walk round"—nine miles.

132. Most likely the Freedmen's Bureau. See Letter 93, Coates to [Coppinger], April 7, 1867.

133. William S. Hilles. See Letter 99, Hilles to Coates, August 15, 1867.

134. Saint Helena Island is one of the largest of the Sea Islands off the coast of South Carolina (see Letter 66, Coates to Crummell, February 20, 1862). It is located approximately fifty-five miles south of Charleston and thirty-five miles north of Savannah. Neighboring islands include Port Royal, Ladies Island, Edisto Island, and Paris Island.

135. Laura Matilda Towne (May 3, 1852–1901) was born in Pittsburgh, Pennsylvania. Her family moved to Boston after her mother's death and then to Philadelphia later. Towne, who may have been born a Quaker, attended the Women's Medical College of Pennsylvania. In 1862, after the Sea Islands had been captured by the Union army, Towne applied to the Port Royal Relief Committee and was sent as a federal agent for contraband relief. She opened the William Penn School on Port Royal with Ellen Murray that year, remaining on the island, as both a teacher and a doctor, for the rest of her life. Today the Penn School is a black culture center. Selleck, *Gentle Invaders*; Towne, *Letters and Diary of Laura M. Towne.*

Excuse the digression from a strictly business note, but these facts and gratifying to the workers in the cause.

All our thanks for the seeds.

Respectfully thy friend

M. Schofield[136]

Box. 3.

Beaufort[137]

<u>S.C.</u>

❖ 108 ❖

Appomattox Va

March 17th/68

B. Coates Esqr

Dear Sir:-

Those who formerly questioned the capacity of the freedmen for mental improvement, and opposed the introduction of Education among them, have only to look at the surprising progress they have made, in this Dist since the close of the war, to be convinced of their mistake. We remember the incredulous smile—which —— greeted the "primer brigades" at every corner, in 1865, as they marched in solid columns to the school-house. They told us that they sincerely wished that Providence had endowed them with mental capacity but contended it was impossible that their hopes of acquiring a knowledge of books could ever be realized. They gave them credit for studious habits, orderly deportment, and neatness in their attire; but even these things they attributed to the novelty of their position and their proverbial fondness for imitating the whites. They predicted that the school-room would soon loose its attractions and the unlearned primer moulder amid the dust and cobwebs in the garret. They thought the herculean labors of the teachers would

136. Martha Schofield (February 1, 1839–February 1, 1916) was born in Pennsylvania. Her family was Orthodox Quaker, but Schofield was educated by Hicksites. By 1863 she had already taught black students in Philadelphia for over a year. In 1865 she traveled to the South and taught on Wadmelaw Island, Edisto Island, and St. Helena Island. In 1868 Schofield moved inland to Aiken, South Carolina, where she began her own school and taught until 1882. One of Schofield's students, Matilda Evans, was the first black woman physician in the United States. Selleck, *Gentle Invaders*; Katherine Smedley, *Martha Schofield and the Re-education of the South, 1839–1916* (Lewiston, N.Y.: Edwin Mellen Press, 1987).

137. Beaufort, South Carolina, is the largest city on Port Royal. Foner, *History of Black Americans*.

produce no other results than the overwhelming conviction that they had undertaken an impossibility. They pointed to the stupendous efforts of missionaries in Africa, and demanded to be shown the results of their labors. But they were mistaken. The primer has been mastered and transferred to some younger aspirant for scholastic honors, and reading, writing, arithmetic, geography and history are following each other in astonishing rapid succession. The "primer brigades" are now seen with books and slates, copy books and pens. They are very proud of their schools. His interest and ours are identical. We must obey the same laws, till the same soil, (plant the same seeds) and practice the same economy and self denial, if we would recover from the political and social revolution through which we have passed.- The seeds reached me duly. The Bill reached me after I had distributed the ~~seed~~ them. They were very much needed and are appreciated. I will enclose a bill for more, and will pay the price, by return mial after receiving them. The freedmen are very busy ploughing "corn-ground" and making Garden. Have a flourishing schools, and am very busy. Hope our good friends up North, will keep the ball rolling.

Very Respectfully

Alvin Varner

❖ 109 ❖

Washington

April 7.th 1868

Benjamin Coates Esq

My dear Sir

I herewith enclose draft for $30 in part payment for the sum you so kindly loaned us. I regret very much my inability to send a larger amount owing to the suspension of my pay during a great portion of my absence. I hope to send the balance in a month or two.

Please present my respectful regards to your Father + Sisters + believe me yrs most respectfully

I M^{c}D. Gurley[138]

[On the next page begins another letter, from E. M. Gurley.]

My dear Sir,

138. Presumably one of the sons of Ralph and Eliza Gurley, most likely the "Mackie" referred to by Eliza Gurley.

I have often thought I would write and explain to you the occasion of the long delay in refunding the loan with which you so kindly accommodated us. But I have had an anxious winter.

On our return from the north in the autumn it was very evident that Mackie had not improved by his land travel and our Physician recommended a sea voyage.

Mr Gurley[139] having for a longtime expressed an earnest desire to visit Africa once more and the comm' kindly offering to him and to our son a passage in the Soc' Ship to sail in a few days for Liberia, the way seemed providentially opened for the gratification of this long cherished wish as also a good opportunity for Mackie to try the effect of the sea.[140] We made hurried preparations for their voyage; their journey to Charelston and other contingencies involved considerable expense, and, as Mac could not recieve pay during his absence, my means were restricted. The debt to you, was among the last matters mentioned by him, (since he, as well as myself felt deeply your kindness in our misfortunes) just before he left, and the first on his return home. He has been benefitted by the trip, but how he will bear confinement to the desk of his office (where he was kindly recieved on his return) remains to be seen. A Physician here has always insisted that Macs constitution required active employment.

Mr Gurley enjoyed his visit on some accounts but is not improved by the voyage—sometimes I fear was injured by it. But he was feeble when he left, and the desire I mentioned, a with my anxiety about Mackie, alone reconciled him to the great undertaking. A brief report will soon be published[141] a copy of which will be sent you.

Husband writes with me in kindest remembrances to your venerable father, your sisters and yourself.

Very truly

Yrs.

E M Gurley[142]

---

139. Ralph Randolph Gurley. See Letter 10, Coates to McLain, October 11, 1851.

140. Gurley had been to Liberia twice before. The first time, in 1824, he was sent by the ACS to investigate and resolve a dispute between the settlers and their governor, Jehudi Ashmun. On his second voyage, in 1849, he represented the U.S. government, which sent him to produce a report on Liberia. This third voyage does not seem to have had any official purpose.

141. Nothing seems to been published under Ralph Randolph Gurley's name during this time period. The report may have come out in an issue of the *African Repository* (in which case it is unlikely that Coates would have needed a copy of the report, since he was almost certainly a subscriber).

142. Eliza McLellan Gurley (1810?–1872), the wife of Ralph Randolph Gurley.

Sharpsburg, Washington Co. Md. Apr. 20th, 1868
        Benjamin Coates Esq.
My Dear Friend And Benefactor:
I was truly glad to hear from you by your thrice welcome letter which I received Saturday evening last, bearing date Philad'a April 17th inst., which was accompanied by the box of books you were so kind as to favor us with and which we so much deeded. I regret that I was obliged to disturb you with the question of salary +c in my last letter, but as it was a matter of so great weight with me, I could not refrain from mentioning it. I fully understood the matter myself Mr. Coates until I saw Mr Kimball,[143] who gave me to think that other arrangements had been made. And as I had not been directly informed to that effect I of course was placed in a doubting position. I have made a full statement of the necessary facts to the coloured people here, and they are willing to do all they possibly can to keep the school in progress. They are extremely well pleased with my plans of instruction, an evidence of which is, that one of the families has sent after their grandchildren nearly a hundred miles up the canal, to come here to attend the school. They are calling in all the children who can well come from all directions and distances who can possibly come to take advantage of the opportunity now offered, and, which they have so long felt the need of, to acquire something of a knowledge of books. I am extremely well pleased with the selection made in the assortment [of] books sent. I have been very much annoyed with the inappropriate and illg-gotten-up ones I have been obliged to use here thus far. As soon as I get my scholars broken in to the use of the new books, I shall have a very interesting [page break, possibly a page missing here] I am only sorry that it will not be as large as I wish it to be; The coloured population of Sharpsburg is very small indeed as compared with that of other Southern towns of its size. I should say that Sharpsburg has a population of about sixteen hundred people, not more than 150 of which are colored including all ages. I was very much surprised at this fact when I discovered it, for I expected to find at least 400 or 500. I shall have a much larger school in winter than I have now; for all the young men and women who are now at work abroad will be here to attend school in winter. I shall be obliged to place my chief dependence on my night-school for salary; for there are too few families here to afford much more than

143. John Kimball, the Superintendent of Freedmen's Bureau schools in the Washington, D.C., district. Johnson's school was probably under Kimball's jurisdiction. Bentley, *A History of the Freedmen's Bureau*, 204.

a bare living for the teachers services in summer. I could not probably obtain more than ten or twelve dollars per month over and above my board for anything more than about three month services in the year. I very much fear Mr. Coates, that I shall be compelled to rely upon the avails of the books for salary through the Summer. However if other arrangements can provided I shall be most happy to avoid drawing anything from that source. I shall certainly do all I possibly can to get through without distressing those farther whom I have already received more from than I could have asked for in reason. If I am obliged to appropriate the books' money to uses of my own, through absolute necessity, until I can do otherwise, and afterward can so arrange, I shall not fail to make it good, ~~in~~ when I am able by means of increased funds in after time. I cannot express my gratitude to you for the generous offer in relation to the money which shall be received for the books. I am very well pleased with the appearance of the country about here; and may providing I can make suitable arrangements, establish a nice little home for myself here and bring my family here. The coloured people have already become very much attached to me and would do all they possibly could to render my residence among them permanent, and pleasant. I could get real estate at very reasonable rates here, and. Town lots of 1/4 acre are selling at $40. each, and an abundance of good limestone can be had for the mere quarrying to build with. I will write you as often, Mr. Coates, as I think your patience will allow, giving statement of progress, success +c. I will also report to you on the relative appreciation of the books forwarded as I become more acquainted with them by use in school.—Thoug I have not the least doubt that I shall be more and more pleased with them judging from present brief examinations of them. Please write to me as often Mr. Coates as convenience will permit you. Also please remember me in gratitude to all my sincere friends of the Comm. Excuse leangthy letter. I am, in gratitude and respect, your obedient servt.

     Ezra A. Johnson.[144]

❖ III ❖

Washington May 8th '68

My dear Sir,

     I recieved through my son the cancelled note for $40 unpaid, and I know not how to express to you my thanks for this unexpected kindness. I felt

---

144. It seems likely that Johnson was a teacher in the Freedmen's Bureau school in Sharpsburg, Maryland.

greatly mortified at the delay of our payments My husband[145] said he was not much suprised since it was in accordance with with your well known character.

I enclose a copy of the address of the people of Liberia to him on his arrival there written by Dr Smith[146] the soc'ys Physician.

You have doubtless seen Dr. Tracy's[147] Memorial[148] which explains their extravagance of expression. That the blessing that scattereth yet increaseth may continue to be yours in the prayer

of yrs most truly

+ respectfully

E M Gurley[149]

[Letter III, Gurley to Coates, May 8, 1868, contains a copy of the following address:]

Address of Dr Jas S Smith for the people of Grand Bassa and the Republic of Liberia

Esteemed friend,

For the people of Grand Bassa and of the Republic of Liberia we greet you—we extend to you the hand of friendship and in the sincerity of our hearts we exclaim welcome, welcome, thrice welcome, Ralph Randolph Gurley[150] the tried, steadfast and untiring friend of Liberia. We embrace you in our arms, we press you to our hearts, we recognize in you a father of Liberia We rejoice to meet you and thank Almighty God that your life has been precious in his sight.

You have crossed the ocean to see us and we have assemble here to greet you and thank you for you kind regard and ~~apprie~~ remembrances for us, and to express our high appriciation of the inestimable services you have rendered us in the erection of this African nationality.

We love our country, and we regard the establishment of the Republic of Liberia as one of the great events of this glorious nineteenth century, the morning star of its glory; and, as we love our country, so do we love the friends

145. Ralph Randolph Gurley.

146. James Skivring Smith (c. 1825–?), born in Charleston, South Carolina, immigrated to Liberia in 1833. He trained under Dr. James W. Lugenbeel, completing his medical education at Pittsfield Medical Institute in Massachusetts. He was active in Liberian politics, holding the offices of secretary of state, senator, vice president, and president. *HDL* 161.

147. Probably Joseph Tracy. See Letter 10, Coates to McLain, October 11, 1851.

148. *Memorial of the semi-centennial anniversary of the American Colonization Society, celebrated at Washington, January 15, 1867. With documents concerning Liberia* (Washington, D.C.: American Colonization Society, 1867).

149. Eliza McLellan Gurley. See Letter 109, Gurley and Gurley to Coates, April 7, 1868.

150. See Letter 10, Coates to McLain, October 11, 1851.

of our country, and especially those who planned the bark[151] of state, built, and launched her, and committed her to our care. It is a gift that we trust under God, to transmit unimpaired to our latest posterity. This gift, some of our benefactors have sealed with their lives, and to them our gratitude is unbounded.

Among the early and tried friends of Liberia, the name of Ralph R Gurley stands prominent, and we venerable and Rev Sir, say in the fullness of our hearts we thank you—The palms that have sprung up ~~and~~ in every direction and yield rivers of oil, that invite the merchant fleet of legitimate trades that you see in our harbors, thank you—no longer do the hell hounds of the devil slave traders, infest our coasts and strip Africa of her sons + daughters—no more do the tribes on this coast shudder to see a white man—their smiling faces thank you. Slave barracoons[152] are no more to be seen. They are numbered with the things that have passed. But churches of the living God, with steeples pointing heavenward, houses of respectable dimensions and architectural by construction that would not disgrace any city of christendom rise up and thank you— ~~Halls of justice~~ Schools and Colleges Halls of justice and Executive mansions and departments, swell the number, and cry aloud we thank you—the influx of emigrants who hail this as the promised land, and the Ethiopians in the far interior as they catch the sound from us and our children, will continue to cry we thank you. Thus we have glanced at the changes which have taken place in this land that you so much love since you visited it nearly half a century ago with the immortal Ashmun—May his ashes rest in peace, and may her ever live in the hearts of a grateful people!

To be less figurative, we know that you must rejoice with exceding great joy when you witness the changes, moral, physical and intellectual that have taken place in this country since your first visit in Aug'st 1824, and remember that you have acted an important part to bring about these changes.

The presentation on your part of a free constitution to the people of Liberia in 1824, and the adoption of that constitution by the people, laid sure and steadfast the corner stone of this African nationality, the Republic of Liberia, which holds a respectable position among the ~~nations~~ of the nations of the earth for she is the hope of Africa. Pardon us for passing over a subsequent visit of your labors of love for Africa for pure philanthropic principles with strong faith and able statesmanship but we fear that we may weary you borne down by the weight of years—a long life spent for us. So we must bring these delightful excercices to a close.

151. Small sailing ship.
152. Barracks or prisons.

We pray that you will be returned in peace and safety to the bosom of your family, and that the reminisences of Liberia will cheer your declining years and that the God whom you have served will be with you to the end of life and crown you with glory for your labor of love.

❧ 112 ❧

BENJAMIN COATES.[153]   GEO. MORRISON COATES.[154]
GEO. M. COATES JR.[155]   WILLIAM M. COATES.[156]
   COATES, BROTHERS,   127 Market Street,
   COMMISSION MERCHANTS,   PHILADELPHIA, May 20th 1868
For the Purchase and Sale of
WOOL
William Coppinger Esq.[157]
       My Dear Sir
          I have engaged through my friend J. J Roberts,[158] Revd E W Blyden[159] to write or compile a history of Liberia up to the present time. I wish it to be under the supervision of Hon J.J Roberts + Hon D.B. Warner,[160] two of the oldest + most capable citizens of Liberia, who are acquainted with much of the history of the Republic in which they took a very prominent part + did much to build up.

          I have a letter to day from Mr Blyden dated April 10th saying that he will undertake the work, (I suppose in the terms I have proposed) and requesting me to send him any recent work on Liberia, + West Africa, also Livingstons[161] + Barker's last works. He also

153. ACS Papers 102:191:1:276. The first six lines are incorporated into the Coates brothers' letterhead, with the exception of the month, day, and last digit of the year.

154. George Morrison Coates Sr. (1779–1868) was Benjamin Coates's father.

155. George Morrison Coates Jr. (1817–1893), Benjamin Coates's brother, joined him in his wool business in 1857, after George Jr.'s own business, selling "cloths and cassimeres," failed. John W. Jordan, *Colonial Families of Philadelphia* (Chicago: Lewis Publishing, 1911), 658.

156. William Morrison Coates (1845–1869) was Benjamin Coates's nephew and the son of George Morrison Coates Jr.

157. William Coppinger. See Letter 10, Coates to McLain, October 11, 1851.

158. Joseph Jenkins Roberts. See Letter 1, Roberts to Coates, July 8, 1848.

159. Edward Wilmot Blyden. See Letter 27, Coates to Lugenbeel, October 6, 1856.

160. Daniel Bashiell Warner. See Letter 10, Coates to McLain, October 11, 1851.

161. Presumably Coates is referring to David Livingstone, who had published two books by the time this letter was written, and who was still in Africa on his last expedition. See Letter 32, Coates to Gurley, May 28, 1858.

wants the "The New Englander"[162] for July 1867, + wishes the Penn^a Colonization Socy[163] to present to "Liberia College"[164] a full set of "The Colonization Herald"[165] from the commencement to the present time.

Now my object in writing is to enquire how far you can aid me?
either by suggesting the names of the books I want, + inform me where they
are to be procured, or [get] [smudged] them for me at my expense. I [page
break] also wish to publish a pamphlet or small volume containing two of the
best addresses from President two from President Benson[166] + two from President Warner, two from Crummell,[167] two from Hilary Teage[168] two from EW
Blyden, (of the two for the latter I wish one to be his address of "Mount
Lebanon" in celebration of Liberias Independence,[169] of those from Crummell, I think, The English Language in Liberia, + his address at Epiphany
Church Philadelphia,[170] I should prefer. Would not this make an interesting
book showing the talents of the Negro? + at the same time showing what
Liberia is, + what Liberia has accomplished for the Negro race. Any aid you
may be able to give me in getting up these two interesting works will greatly
oblige me, + greatly advance the interest of Liberia + the Negro race.[171] I have
a nephew[172] in the publishing business who knows how to get up a book in

162. A religious journal.
163. The Pennsylvania Colonization Society. See Letter 8, Coates to McLain, May
16, 1851.
164. Liberia College. See Letter 29, Coates to Crummell, October 3, 1857.
165. The *Colonization Herald*. See Letter 7, Coates to Douglass, January 16, 1851.
166. Stephen Allen Benson. See Letter 8, Coates to McLain, May 16, 1851.
167. Alexander Crummell. See Letter 28, Coates to Gurley, May 2, 1857.
168. Hilary Teage. See Letter 10, Coates to McLain, October 11, 1851.
169. Coates is referring to "Liberia: Past, Present, and Future," an address Blyden gave
in 1866 on Mount Lebanon in Syria. Edward Wilmot Blyden, *Liberia: Past, Present, and Future*
(Washington, D.C.: M'Gill and Witherow, 1869).
170. The first is "The English Language in Liberia," delivered in Liberia in 1860. The
second is probably "The Progress of Civilization Along the West Coast of Africa," delivered in
1861 at many locales in the United States, including the "Church of the Epiphany, Philadelphia."
Crummell, *The Future of Africa*, 9, 105.
171. This book, as Coates envisioned it, does not seem to have been published. The
addresses of Blyden and Crummell were published, either before or after the writing of this
letter. In the case of Blyden's address, it was published in 1869 along with another of Blyden's
addresses, "The Negro in Ancient History," both by the same publisher. Preceding each address
is a brief note, written in Philadelphia in July 1869, containing information about Blyden. There
is no author given for the note preceding "Liberia: Past, Present, and Future," but the author
of the note for "The Negro in Ancient History" was Coates, and the content of the two notes is
similar enough that it does not seem unreasonable to assume that both were written by him.
Many addresses of this type also appeared in the *African Repository*.
172. Henry Troth Coates (see Letter 74, Coates to Gurley, February 10, 1863) was head
of the publishing firm of Henry T. Coates & Co. Originally Davis & Porter (managed by Charles

the best style. Has Dr. Joseph Tracy[173] published a history of Liberia. You mentioned to me some time since a work that was just published, or about to be published similar to those by Carter + Bros.[174] on Liberia or West Africa. please give me the name. + [text continued on left-hand side of page] Yours very truly Benj[a] Coates

[Written on the left-hand side of the second page:]

Any information on the prints desired will be very acceptable I would like ~~one~~ or two copies of the book on Central Africa by a Baptist Missionary[175]

❖ 113 ❖

441 Sixth street

Washington D.C. 5,22, '68

Mr Benjamin Coates

    Philadelphia,

       Dear Sir-

        Your letter of 21st inst. received this morning and for its kindly tone and encouraging spirit I thank you heartily.

        My letter of the 19th must have led you to suppose that I wanted more from your pen than I did,—your letter Sir, is all that I could wish and will I think, be of great service to me; I am very much obliged to you for it and beg leave to subscribe myself

       Very truly yr' Friend

        Eleanor J. Ketchum

H. Davis and Robert Porter), it became Davis, Porter & Coates when Coates joined in 1866. George Morrison Coates (Henry's cousin and Benjamin's nephew) entered the firm as partner in 1869, two years after Davis's retirement had made it Porter & Coates. Like most publishing businesses at the time, Coates's company sold books by other publishers, as well as published books themselves. The firm was sold to the John C. Winston Co. in 1904 after Coates's retirement. Tebbel, *A History of Book Publishing in the United States*, 422–23; Jordan, *Colonial Families of Philadelphia*, 658.

    173. Joseph Tracy (see Letter 10, Coates to McLain, October 11, 1851). Tracy does not appear to have written a history of Liberia.

    174. The publishing firm and bookseller Robert Carter & Bros. was founded in 1834 by Robert Carter (1807–1889), a Scottish immigrant who arrived in New York in 1831. Carter was a deeply religious Presbyterian who applied his religious character to his publishing choices and his dealings with customers. Tebbel, *A History of Book Publishing in the United States*, vol. 1, 325–33.

    175. Probably Bowen, *Central Africa*, published by the Southern Baptist Publication Society in 1857.

❧ 114 ❧

Sharpsburg, Washington Co., Md.,
May 23ᵈ, 1868

Ben. Coates Esqr.,

My kind Friend and Dear Sir:

With heartfelt pleasure and gratitude I received, by this evening's mail, through your attentive kindness and generosity, two copies of the American Freedman,[176] and one copy of the Freedman's Friend.[177] I have looked them all over and find them replete with interesting matter. Please accept my sincere thanks. I had the honor and pleasure of receiving a brief visit from Genl. Chal. Howard,[178] Asst. Com'r F.R. + A.S., Rev. John Kimball,[179] Supt. Edc't'n, and Capt. J.C. Brubaker,[180] Sub Asst. Com'r Bureau R.F. + A.S., on the 20ᵗʰ inst. After consultation, they concluded that this could not well be made a sufficiently large school, to allow of a teacher being permanently established here. Genl. Howard proposed to have this school closed until Fall, and remove me to a place where a larger school could be opened and to provide for my salary. This is a much safer, and more agreeable plan for me to work upon; for experience has taught me, since I have been here, that this, for several reasons, could not be made a self-supporting school for more than four or five months in the year. I have been here almost two months, and have received $4,00 and some cts. Beside the matter of pay, Mr. Coates, I do not feel that I could do as much good here among so few as were there were more to do for. My scholars are all very much attached to me, and when I informed them that it was the intention of Genl. H. to have me transferred to another locality, they were much affected. Poor creatures! For all, I dread to leave them. The few that I have, have made excellent progress for the little time they have had. I have none of the old number now in the alphabet. One little boy, six years old,

176. *American Freedman*, the journal of the AFUC.

177. *Freedman's Friend*, the journal of the Friends Freedmen's Association.

178. Charles H. Howard, younger brother of Oliver Otis Howard (commissioner of the Freedmen's Bureau). Charles Howard served on his brother's staff during the Civil War and followed his brother into the Freedmen's Bureau, taking the position of Assistant Commissioner of the Bureau in Washington, D.C. Bentley, *A History of the Freedmen's Bureau*, 215; Oliver Otis Howard, *Autobiography of Oliver Otis Howard, Major General, United States Army* (New York: Baker and Taylor, 1908), passim.

179. John Kimball. See Letter 110, Johnson to Coates, April 20, 1868.

180. Brubaker was evidently a functionary of the Freedmen's Bureau (that is, the Bureau of Refugees, Freedmen, and Abandoned Lands, hence "Bureau R. F. + A. S.," with a possible error by Johnson in the last letter, just as he seems to have transposed "F" and "R" when referring to Charles Howard).

who, a month ago, knew only A, J, and H, in the alphabet, is now reading and spelling readily and correctly in lessons of three letters to the word. I am as sorry as they are that I am obliged to leave them so soon. I do not know whether this new arrangement will go into effect befor the close of vacation or not. I suppose not, though. I should be more than happy to hear from you when convenient. I am, in sincere gratitude and respect, Yours Truly

     Ezra A. Johnson.[181]

 ❖ 115 ❖

Sharpsburg, Md., May 30th, 1868.
Benjamin Coates, Esqr.,
My Inestimable Friend and Dear Sir:

I have just received a letter from Rev. Mr. Kimball,[182] Supt. Edc't'n at Washington, D.C., containing the unhappy intelligence that Genl. Howard[183] has directed him to write me that they are unable to assist me in keeping up my school here, and that they have no other school for me at this time. They express a desire to have me remain here if I wish and can obtain propper support. I have written him that I cannot continue the school if I depend wholly on the coloured people here for its support. I received $1,00 today, making in all $6,50 I have received since I have been here, and I have been unable to collect but about half the money for the book I distributed among them from the box you sent me. I have also asked Mr. Kimball whether this school can not be opened the 1st of October, or if not, whether, if I am provided with a larger school by the close of the vacation season, I cannot re-enter upon the work upon the terms proposed by Genl. Howard while here, viz: that my salary be provided for. And that if so, I would hold myself in readiness to take a school wherever or whenever I should be called upon to go. This is a sad disappointment to the anxious ones of this place. But they do not feel able to allow board and salary. And since Genl H. and Mr. K. were here and proposed to pay salary, they are still more unwilling to accede to such terms. Now Mr. Coates, please tell me what I shall do. I cannot stay here for my mere board, and yet I have nothing to rely upon after leaving here. I must do something.— Something honest and honorable—but what shall it be? What do you say to my coming to Philadelphia and taking a traveling agency for some mercantile or manufacturing establishment during the Summer months until I get another

181. Ezra Johnson. See Letter 110, Johnson to Coates, April 20, 1868.
182. John Kimball. See Letter 110, Johnson to Coates, April 20, 1868.
183. Most likely General Charles Howard.

school? Please let me hear from you as soon as possible. I shall remain here throu' next week to hear from you and Mr. Kimball. My dilemma is quite embarrassing Mr. Coates, but fear not, my Dear Sir, come what will, I am unswervably resolved to be industrious, honest and upright henceforth. Hoping to hear from you soon and encouragingly, I remain your grateful and obedient servant

> Ezra A. Johnson

P.S.

> Please tell Coll Corson[184] not to send the money to me until he hears further from me. Will you please ask him to leave $2, with Mr. Powers to be given to Rev. John Ruth, and highly oblige me?

> Very Respectfully,

> E.A.J.

[On the back of the envelope is a note reading:]
Col. Corson will please read this—+ may send $2. to Mr Power for Mr Ruth. as requested—+ charge to me B.C

❖ 116 ❖

New York June 5th 1868[185]

Benjⁿ Coates, Esq.
> Philad^a Pa.
>> Dear Sir,
>>> Your favor of the 4th is rec^d. I am grateful for the interest you take in the Charleston matter. The importance of making use of the best colored

---

184. Probably refers to Robert Corson, a member of the Freedman's Relief Association and the AFUC. See Letter 133, Coates to Coppinger, November 17, 1868.

185. Printed on AMA letterhead, with a list of officers omitted here. The AMA was incorporated in 1846 by a multiracial group of clergymen, mostly Congregationalist and Presbyterian. Originally formed to protest existing missionary groups that accepted money from slaveholders, the AMA soon directed its focus away from overseas missionary works toward abolition within the United States. Believing education to be a key to liberation, during the Civil War it opened more than 500 schools for freed slaves. Although the focus was on providing education for black people, many of the schools for which the AMA furnished buildings, trained teachers, and paid salaries, were multiracial. After Reconstruction, the AMA turned their elementary and secondary schools over to the public school system and focused on providing a college education to black people. The AMA maintained good relations with the African Civilization Society and several people—such as Henry Highland Garnet—held offices in both organizations. Clara Merrit DeBoer, *His Truth is Marching On: African Americans Who Taught the Freedmen for the American Missionary Association 1861–1877* (New York: Garland Publishing, 1995), vii–ix, 72; Joe M. Richardson, *Christian Reconstruction: The American Missionary Association and Southern Blacks, 1861–1890* (Athens: University of Georgia Press, 1986), xi–xiv, 140, 341.

men, in the great work of elevating the race, is not overlooked by us. I can not now say what we shall do in relation to the superintendency of our schools at Charleston.[186] We have however made choice of a colored preacher to go there, and take an oversight of the Church.

If we have to send another man, to superintend the school enterprise; there will therefore be less demand for another man of color, than would otherwise have been.

Yours truly

G Whipple, Sec[187]

❖ 117 ❖

Colonization Rooms[188]

Washington, D.C. June 30. 1868

Benjamin Coates Esq
  Philadelphia, Pa.
    Dear Sir

I mail herewith to your address the Repository[189] for December, 1866, and November, 1867, containing Discourses of Prof: Blyden[190] carefully marked as per his letter to you of Jan 11. 1868, which please find enclosed.[191]

---

186. Francis L. Cardozo, a member of the Charleston black upper class, was superintendent of the AMA mission in Charleston from 1865 to early 1868, during which time he helped found the Avery Normal Institute and served as its first superintendent. After he resigned, he was temporarily replaced by Ellen M. Pierce, while Whipple sought a permanent replacement for Cardozo's. Coates may have written to Whipple to suggest that the AMA choose another black man to take Cardozo's place. "Cardozo, Francis L.," *ANB* 4:375–76; Edmund L. Drago, *Initiative, Paternalism, and Race Relations: Charleston's Avery Normal Institute* (Athens: University of Georgia Press, 1990), 48–52.

187. George Whipple (1805–1876) was the corresponding secretary of the AMA from its inception in 1846 to his death in 1876. From 1846 to 1866 Whipple, Lewis Tappan (treasurer), and Simeon S. Jocelyn (secretary) held much of the actual power in the AMA. From 1866 to 1876, after Tappan resigned, Whipple was the principle source of leadership in the AMA. As a student, Whipple was one of the "Lane rebels," a group of young men who left Lane Theological Seminary after the Board of Trustees of that institution attempted to put a stop to the abolitionist activities of the student body. Richardson, *Christian Reconstruction*, 87–92.

188. Headquarters of the ACS. See Letter 8, Coates to McLain, May 16, 1851.

189. *The African Repository*. See Letter 15, Coates to Lugenbeel, June 27, 1853.

190. Edward Wilmot Blyden. See Letter 27, Coates to Lugenbeel, October 6, 1856.

191. Letter 104, Blyden to Coates, January 11, 1868.

I hope you have received file or set of the "Colonization Herald"[192] for Liberia College.[193]

> With high regard,
> Very respectfully yours,
> Wm Coppinger[194]

❖ 118 ❖

Colonization Rooms
Washington, D.C. July 22. 1868

Benjamin Coates Esq
　Philadelphia, Pa.
　　Dear Sir

　　We are informed that the barque[195] "Thomas Pope" will sail from New York on or before the 1st —— for Liberia and the West Coast of Africa. This will be a good opportunity of communicating with and sending books to Prof: Blyden.

　　Mess'rs Yates + Porterfield, 115 Wall St. New York, will forward letters or packages for Liberia sent in their care.

> Very respectfully Yours,
> Wm Coppinger

❖ 119 ❖

New York July 30.1868

Benj Coates Esq
　Philadelphia
　　Dear Sir

　　We are in receipt of your favors of 28th + 29th inst. the latter enclosing Express receipt for One Box Books to go to by Bk. "Thos Pope" to Liberia.

192. The *Colonization Herald*. See Letter 12, Coates to McLain, January 10, 1852.
193. Liberia College. See Letter 29, Coates to Crummell, October 3, 1857.
194. William Coppinger. See Letter 10, Coates to McLain, October 11, 1851.
195. Variant of bark, a small sailing ship.

The Box has arrived and is on board and we enclose Bills Lading for it. The freight including stamps is $2.37 The Bark will go to sea morning of Augs 5th wind and weather permitting,

Very truly yours
Yates + Porterfield[196]

❖ 120 ❖

[Aug[t]] 4. 1868

My dear Sir.

You needed not to have enclosed the 25 cent stamp as I shall take the letter with me and all parcels committed to my care.

My voyage has no terrors to me being over a track well known in former years.[197] By God's blessing I hope to bring back some valuable information about all the interests of the Republic. Missions, Education, College, population commerce agriculture +c +c.

Your apprehensions about our country are such as have occupied many of my thoughts, + but for rolling all burthens[198] over to the Almighty friend I should be very sad. There is danger of a class war of extermination.

May God interpose + stay the wrath of man. fare well.

Your obliged friend

J.B. Pinney[199]

Benj[n] Coates Esqr

196. See Letter 118, Coppinger to Coates, July 22, 1868.
197. Pinney was in Liberia during the 1830s as a missionary and as temporary governor, and it appears that in 1868 he returned there.
198. Variant of burdens.
199. John B. Pinney. See Letter 8, Coates to McLain, May 16, 1851.

❖ 121 ❖

BENJAMIN COATES.[200]   GEO. MORRISON COATES.
GEO. M. COATES JR.   WILLIAM M. COATES.[201]
    COATES, BROTHERS,   127 Market Street,
COMMISSION MERCHANTS,   PHILADELPHIA, Augt 5th 1868
For the Purchase and Sale of
WOOL

W^m. Coppinger Esq.[202]

My dear Sir

I am <u>very</u>, <u>very</u> much obliged to you for the information of the sailing of "Thos. Pope" which I should not probably have known of otherwise in time to send both <u>books + letters</u> as I <u>have done</u>. + have since learned that our good friend Mr Pinney[203] goes out in <u>her</u> <u>today</u> (this is her day of sailing).

Only a few days since (last week) I received the enclosed letter, + "plan" from President Roberts[204] with the preface, on which I want your opinions. My nephew to whom I have just shown them likes the "Plan" very much, but thinks the "Preface" rather ego<u>tist</u>ical, the pronoun "I" being repeated too often. I did not send the file of "The Colonization Herald,"[205] not having applied for it in time. But Mr Malcolm[206] thinks there can be no doubt but that the Board will presend a <u>bound</u> copy or bound file, to the College.

Now respecting the other book that I have talked of getting up, who can I get to attend to it for me? to <u>select</u>, <u>revise</u>, correct, + put the book in shape. I am [page break, and the letterhead is repeated] not competent [in] the work myself, and I believe there are very few that are. The <u>two</u> names that have occurred to me who would know what was wanted and could appreciate the value of a book of this kind both in showing the ability of the Negro race, + also the instrumentality of Liberia in developing the talent, are William

---

200. ACS Papers 102:192:1A:105. The first six lines constitute the Coates brothers' printed letterhead, with the exception of the month, day, and last digit of the year.

201. George M. Coates Sr., George M. Coates Jr., and William M. Coates.

202. William McLain. See Letter 10, Coates to McLain, October 11, 1851.

203. John Brooke Pinney. See Letter 8, Coates to McLain, May 16, 1851.

204. Joseph Jenkins Roberts. See Letter 1, Roberts to Coates, July 8, 1848.

205. The *Colonization Herald*. See Letter 12, Coates to McLain, January 10, 1852.

206. Probably refers to Thomas Shield Malcom (1821–1886), a Philadelphia clergyman who was secretary of the Pennsylvania Colonization Society from 1866 to 1877. *Appleton's* 3:181.

Coppinger + ED Bassett,[207] the principal of the "Institute for Colored Youth"[208] of this city, who is at present in New Haven spending his vacation, and therefore has I presume some weeks of leisure on his hands which could be devoted perhaps to selecting, revising, + writing a <u>preface</u> or introductory. one great advantage ~~that would be~~ in getting Bassett at this work, would be, that it would interest him in the work, in Africa, but my friend Mr Coppinger understands the <u>whole thing</u>, + knows what is <u>wanted better</u> than <u>any other man</u>. If I could get <u>him</u> to put the matter in shape for me I would gladly get him to do so, with the understanding however, that he would not object to accepting a <u>moderate</u> compensation for his time + trouble, which of course I would expect to pay to Bassett or any one else who should undertake it. I did not think it best to send to Liberia for this work, altho' if Crummell[209] or Blyden[210] were here, I might get their aid. If you think it best I might <u>first</u> get Bassett to look over the matter + perhaps write something as introductory, before getting you to have the matter ready for publication. I do not know whether it would be worth while. Bassett has never been in favor of Colonization, as it is generally understood but he does not object to my views of the case. Recognizing the perfect equality of all men in American, + not <u>limiting</u> my sympathy for the colored to <u>either</u> <u>Africa</u> or <u>America</u>

Please return Robert's letter + the <u>Plan</u> for the History, with your views, + oblige [me]

Yours very truly

B Coates

---

207. Ebenezer Don Carlos Bassett (1833–1908). Bassett, the son of a light-skinned black and an Indian, was born in Litchfield, Connecticut, and studied at the Wesleyan Academy in Massachusetts, the Connecticut State Normal School, and Yale University. In 1857, he was made principal of the ICY in Philadelphia, where he also taught and was the school librarian. He gave up this position to become the United States' first black diplomat in 1869, when President Grant appointed him minister to Haiti and the Dominican Republic, where he served until 1877. In 1879, the Haitian government recognized his ability by making him its consul-general to the United States. He held this position until 1888, and in 1889 he became Frederick Douglass's secretary and interpreter when Douglass was appointed minister to Haiti and the Dominican Republic. In the early 1900s, the Haitian government again employed Bassett for a few years. He spent his final years in Philadelphia. Heinl, Nancy Gordon; "Basset, Ebenezer Don Carlos," in *Dictionary of American Negro Biography*, ed. Rayford W. Logan and Michael R. Winston (New York: W. W. Norton and Company, 1982), 32.

208. The ICY. See Letter 42, Douglass to Coates, May 2, 1859.

209. Alexander Crummell. See Letter 28, Coates to Gurley, May 2, 1857.

210. Edward Wilmot Blyden. See Letter 27, Coates to Lugenbeel, October 6, 1856.

✣ 122 ✣

142 [Grove] St.

New Haven, Aug. 12, 1868

Esteemed Friend

Benjamin Coates: Your very interesting letter has just reached me. It and the spirit it breathes give me great pleasure and satisfaction. I must say too, that I feel myself somewhat flattered by the compliment you pay me, in asking my assistance and that of Mr. Coppinger[211] in your proposed literary undertaking.[212] I honor you for the noble sentiment which lies at the basis of the work.

I am sorry however to say, that, while I feel all interest in the enterprise, I <u>sincerely feel incompetent</u> to perform the part you would assign me. This would be a sufficient reason for declining the proffered responsibility. But I am, besides, in poor health, and have on hand already more than I can with reasonable diligence accomplish during the three weeks left me of my vacation.

My esteemed friend and pastor John B. Reeve,[213] 1219 Rodman St., Phil[a], is a gentleman whom I should judge fully competent for the work you propose. I do not know what his engagements are. But I should like it, if he could be acquainted with the fact of your proposed undertaking.

Please excuse my brevity. I am suffering from an incessant pain in the knee joint caused by a fall from a buggy recently, or rather ~~from~~ by a horse running and pitching me headlong to the ground.   With much esteem, I am

Sincerely Your friend,

E.D. Bassett[214]

211. William Coppinger. See Letter 10, Coates to McLain, October 11, 1851.

212. Coates was investigating the possibility of publishing a collection of addresses by various Liberian notables. He wrote to William Coppinger on May 20, 1868, announcing his intentions. He wrote Coppinger again on August 5 to ask him to "put the book in shape" and raise the possibility that Bassett might take charge of the work. Evidently, Coppinger and Bassett declined, and because the work was apparently never published, it seems likely that Reeve also did not undertake this task.

213. John B. Reeve was a pastor at Philadelphia's Central Presbyterian Church, a black church founded in 1844. He studied at Union Theological Seminary and taught for four years at Howard University. Roger Lane, *William Dorsey's Philadelphia and Ours: On the Past and Future of the Black City in America* (New York: Oxford University Press, 1991), 240–41.

214. Ebenezer D. Bassett. See Letter 121, Coates to Coppinger, August 5, 1868.

❖ 123 ❖

New York, <u>Aug 27.</u> 1868[215]

Benj[n]. Coates Esq
   127 Market St. Phil<u>a</u>.
   Dear Sir. Please find enclosed a receipt for the money forwarded in your favor of 25 + 26th. Our magazine[216] will be sent to the names you give, only a few of which are on the books. We have the name W[m]. Evans Jun, on our books. You give us the name W—— Evans. Are these the same?
   Our mailing agent sends you a dozen extra copies, this month.
   I thank you for your thoughts on the Col. Soc.[217] You make a great mistake, if you think we were ever opposed to aiding such men as you name in their efforts to reach Africa. We thought we saw, in official positions, an effort to compel men to go, ~~and~~ a willingness to send most unfit men, and a set purpose to discourage emancipation. This we did not regard as "good fruit," and therefore were possibly too willing to have the tree cut down. We rejoice in the planting of the Republic of Liberia, we wish its prosperity, we have one missionary there, and in a small way <u>aid</u> others. "May its shadow never be less."
   I assure you that I regard it as not the least of my blessings that I can now labor shoulder to shoulder with christian friends, who for years have been anti slavery men, the colonizationists. It was a cross to differ with them in times past, and I thank God, that in his kind providence, he has, by the overthrow of slavery, broken down the barrier between us. The expression of your interest in our work among the colored people of the South encourages me. I never doubted that Benj[n] Coates' heart and soul would go out towards those who were so lately victims of oppression, and I rejoice that <u>our part</u> of the great work excites his interest.
   We shall be glad to send one paper to any officer of the Penn[a]. B. of the A.F.U. Com.[218] I once had the honor to be elected by that Branch, to represent it on the Executive Committee of the Union Com., and communicated to the B. my acceptance of the service. I was constrained however, by a sense of duty, to resign my office, on the appearance of Mr. Frothinghams

215. Printed on AMA letterhead, with a list of officers omitted here. See Letter 116, Whipple to Coates, June 5, 1868.
216. Presumably the *American Missionary*, the journal published by the AMA.
217. The ACS. See Letter 8, Coates to McLain, May 16, 1851.
218. The Pennsylvania Branch of the AFUC (see Letter 84, Coates to Coppinger, May 24, 1866) consisted of the former Pennsylvania Freedman's Relief Association. See Letter 82, Clark to Coates, July 15, 1865.

letter[219]. I ~~greatly~~ fear that the "Union" has not added greatly to the efficiency of its parts. If I can, at anytime serve the Penn[a] B: or the F.C. Soc. of Penn. please command me.

Yours truly G. Whipple[220] sec.

❖ 124 ❖

Box 968 P. O.
New York Sep[e] 18/68

Benjamin Coates Esq
   Philadelphia
      Dear Sir

      I am in receipt of your esteemed favor of yesterday. I observe with satisfaction that you admit the success and beneficial results to both countries which would attend a business between the United States and Liberia—properly conducted by <u>experienced business men</u> with ample means—Your objection in general to joint stock companies is shared by myself. It is doubtful in the present case whether my own worldly interests would be promoted by surrendering the knowledge and facilities I have in this business to an association of persons who would have the power at any time of removing me from its control. The diversities of opinion in the many, the selfishness and obstinacy of a few act, I know, to hinder in a company that wise and energetic application of means to an end which pertains to individual enterprize. But without reading a positive conviction which could only come after I had made an attempt, I did think it might be possible to interest in the undertaking a sufficient number of gentlemen upon whom I could rely, either from their acknowledged position in the colonization work or from their regard for myself to give the company harmony of action and secure to myself such permanence of direction as my ability might be found to deserve. I should have

---

219. Probably an article by Octavius Brooks Frothingham (1822–1895) published in the *Independent* on July 12, 1866, that addressed the need for education in the South to be shorn of its religious character, as it had been in the North. Frothingham was a major spokesman for the AFUC in its debate with the AMA. His article was published with the AFUC's position statement, and AMA took it as an official AFUC position. It sparked a series of responses and counter-responses that worsened relations between the two groups and would have made it difficult for Whipple, as a leader of the AMA, to continue to hold a position in the AFUC. Rev. Octavious Brooks Frothingham, "Education and Religion," *Independent* 18 no. 919 (July 12, 1866), 1; Morris, *Reading, 'Riting, and Reconstruction*, 59–64.

220. George Whipple. See Letter 116, Whipple to Coates, June 5, 1868.

labored many years in vain and been proof against the discipline of disappointments and reverses in business if I could not justly lay claim to at least enough experience to entitle me to confidence while I should ~~I~~ have enough sense of deficiency to make me glad to avail myself of the advice of older and wiser business men. I doubt if there are any colored men at present to be found with sufficient business experience in both countries and sufficient means to successfully conduct a business of any magnitude Johnson ——— + Dunbar[221] with good prospects in many respects failed from utter want of judgment. Augustus Washington[222] who is one of my oldest correspondents and friends in Liberia is only an instance—unhappily a too solitary one—of what the farmers of the St Pauls[223] might be if judicious aid ~~who~~ were afforded them to overcome the difficulties of their position. If Mr. Washington were less occupied in his legislative duties he would have done ——— better on his farm. E. J. Roye[224] amassed his means by sharp trading and uses them for himself. Spite of some wealth he is of no benefit in my judgment to Liberia. Ex Pres^t. Roberts whom I know and esteem highly has not been as successful I think pecuniarily as his friends could wish. Jesse Sharp is the best instance of honest and successful industry owing its rapid growth to judicious and timely assistance. What Mr Schiefflin[225] did for one worthy man I would do in an organized effective way for many. In twenty years how few of these men we can select—how many like them who will never rise—Admirable as is self dependence and excellent the prudence and caution in business which risks nothing "the mournful truth stands everywhere confirmed—slow rises worth by poverty oppressed" and the world and Christs kingdom suffer because christian enterprize flags—I shall probably do nothing more about a company but accomplish what good I can alone   with much respect

      Yours very truly   Martin W Roberts

221. Unknown. Possibly Liberian emigrants.
222. Augustus Washington. See Letter 21, Coates to McLain, May 22, 1855.
223. The St. Paul's River in Liberia, along which were located several settlements, including Monrovia.
224. Edward J. Roye. See Letter 18, Roberts to Coates, August 26, 1854.
225. Henry M. Schieffelin. See Letter 46, Pinney to Coates, June 16, 1859.

❖ 125 ❖

Philadelphia Sept. 26ᵗʰ 1868²²⁶

William Coppinger Esq²²⁷
My dear Sir

Please accept my thanks for a copy of the
History of the Republic of Liberia,²²⁸ just recᵈ I had previously received
through my nephew²²⁹ 25 copies, which I am putting in the Libraries of the
Colored Schools in the Southern States established by the two Societies of
which I am a member. Mr Bassett²³⁰ called at the store this morning + I gave
him the copy just recᵈ from you, + also a copy of "The Memorial of the Semi-
centennial Anniversary of the Am. Col. Society,"²³¹ both of which he was
much pleased to have. I have succeeded in interesting him in the cause of
Africa, + African colonization, connected with the nationality [page break] of
the African race, as developed in Liberia. I took Ex President Roberts²³² to
The "Institute for Cold Youth."²³³ he addressed the pupils, + all were naturally
interested. Ex President R. + wife also took tea with me, with a few friends I
had a letter from him yesterday from "Marlboro Hotel" Boston.

I gave to Mr Bassett to day a copy of the Memorial Vol. you sent for
the "Institute Library" which is a large + well selected one, + open to all the
colored people of this city. Free. I also gave a copy to William Whipper²³⁴ +
one to Jnᵒ B Reeve,²³⁵ pastor of one of the colored Presbyterian churches of
this city + a particular friend of Mr Bassetts, + a man of education + ability. I
intend also to give a copy to O V Catto²³⁶ also one of our teachers and one

226. ACS Papers 102:192:290.

227. William Coppinger. See Letter 10, Coates to McLain, October 11, 1851.

228. It is unclear what work Coates means here. Assuming that it was recently published, he may have meant G. S. Stockwell, *The Republic of Liberia, its Geography, Climate, Soil and
Production, with a History of its Early Settlement* (New York: A. S. Barnes, 1868).

229. Probably Henry Troth Coates.

230. Ebenezer D. Bassett. See Letter 121, Coates to Coppinger, August 5, 1868.

231. *Memorial of the semi-centennial anniversary of the American Colonization Society.*

232. Joseph Jenkins Roberts. See Letter 1, Roberts to Coates, July 8, 1848.

233. The ICY. See Letter 42, Douglass to Coates, May 2, 1859.

234. William Whipper. See Letter 35, Wagoner to Coates, January 8, 1859.

235. John B. Reeve. See Letter 122, Bassett to Coates, August 12, 1868.

236. Octavius Valentine Catto (1839–1871) most likely was born free in Charleston,
South Carolina, to a Presbyterian minister and the daughter of one of Charleston's leading
mulatto families. When he was five his family moved to Philadelphia, where he received a comprehensive education, attending several schools in Philadelphia, including the ICY. After a year
of private tutoring in Washington, D.C., he returned to Philadelphia to teach at the ICY. During the 1860s he was involved in various movements for increased black rights, the National Equal

[page break] of the most talented + promising colored men we have among us. I think therefore that I am putting them all in the <u>very best</u> hands, + where they will be appreciated, + most likely to <u>tell</u>.

I enclose herewith $10. out of which please pay for the History of Liberia just sent to me. + the balance please, either keep + appropriate to any similar matter you may have occasion to send to me, or pay the bal. for the "African Repository"[237] as you prefer.

Yours very truly
Benj[a] Coates

❖ 126 ❖

Colonization Rooms[238]
Washington, D.C. September 28. 1868

Benjamin Coates Esq
127 Market St. Philadelphia.
Dear Sir

I am obliged by your favor of the 26th inst with its enclosure of <u>Ten Dollars</u>—$10.—at hand this morning. The copy of "The Republic of Liberia"[239] being intended for your acceptance I have turned the <u>greenback</u> for $10. over to Rev Dr M[c]Lain[240] for the "African Repository."[241]

No one but yourself could have made so excellent a distribution of our "Memorial" Volume:[242] and we shall be glad to furnish you with as many more copies for the same class of readers or for the libraries of prominent colored schools in the Southern States.

Rights League, an organization supporting black suffrage, and the desegregation of Philadelphia's street cars. Catto's leadership skills soon made him a significant force in the Philadelphia black community, and his prowess at the newly popular game of baseball made him popular with lower-class black people. Unfortunately, his prominence may have made him a target. During a riot in Philadelphia in October 1871 over black voting, Catto was shot and killed. Harry C. Silcox, "Nineteenth Century Philadelphia Black Militant: Octavius V. Catto (1839–1871)," *Pennsylvania History* 44, no. 1 (January 1977): 53–76.

237. *The African Repository.* See Letter 15, Coates to Lugenbeel, June 27, 1853.
238. The headquarters of the ACS. See Letter 8, Coates to McLain, May 16, 1851.
239. Stockwell, *The Republic of Liberia.*
240. William McLain. See Letter 1, Roberts to Coates, July 8, 1848.
241. *The African Repository.* See Letter 15, Coates to Lugenbeel, June 27, 1853.
242. *Memorial of the Semi-Centennial Anniversary of the American Colonization Society.*
See Letter 111, Gurley to Coates, May 8, 1868.

In a letter first received from Pres: Roberts[243] he refers to your kind attentions to him and your hospitality to him and his wife in Philad[a]. I wish we were housekeeping so that we might entertain them in this city I suppose you have seen Hon Aug: Washington[244] ere this as he left here on Wednesday for Philad[a].

Very respectfully Yours, W[m] Coppinger[245]

❈ 127 ❈

Marlboro Hotel
Boston Sept.28.1868

Benjamin Coates Esqr
  My dear Sir

      I drop a line to say, we arrived here safely Monday evening last. Mrs Roberts and myself tolerably well. We spent four days in New York very pleasantly; visiting several of our old friends. They insist that we must spend a week, at least, there on our return. As to this, I cannot say—I apprehend I shall have to remain here several days longer than I expected. Mr Fearing[246] and one or two other members of the Board of Trustees are very much engaged, and Mr. Tracy[247] is uncertain as to what time he will be able to convene a meeting; probably not earlier than the middle of next week. They think that I should spend as much time as I conveniently can in Boston. Well, be it so; and should the weather continue favorable I shall not object.

      Mrs Roberts sends kindest regards to yourself, and Mrs Coates[248]— whom we met on the evening of the 11,[th] at your house, and the young gentlemen, your nephews, who were also present on that occasion—and she begs that, when writing, you will remember her most kindly to your sisters—of course, in all this I unite with her.

    243. Joseph Jenkins Roberts. For more information, see Letter 1, Roberts to Coates, July 8, 1848.

    244. Augustus Washington. See Letter 21, Coates to McLain, May 22, 1855.

    245. William Coppinger. See Letter 10, Coates to McLain, October 11, 1851.

    246. Albert Fearing (March 12, 1798–May 24, 1875), a native of Massachusetts, was politically active, serving as the president of the ACS and in the state senate in the 1840s. Retiring from his ship-chandler business in 1868, he distributed more than $200,000 to various causes, including $30,000 to Liberia College. He was also on the Board of the Trustees of Donation for Education in Liberia, the New England group that largely funded Liberia College. *Appleton's*.

    247. Joseph Tracy. See Letter 10, Coates to McLain, October 11, 1851.

    248. As Coates apparently never married, it is likely that Roberts is referring to his brother's wife.

I made a "memo" of the name of the gentleman you desired me see here, but cannot now put my hand upon It—he who wrote a pamphlet on the Culture of Cotton,[249] I think you remarked, in Africa. Please send me his name.

During the evening of the 11th, Mr. Hunter[250] expressed a desire to obtain a few Liberia Postage stamps. I happen to have two or three which I herewith enclose, with the request that you will please hand them to Mr. Hunter.[251] Now, I am not quite sure that I am correct in the name; you will, however, conclude at once that I intend the gentleman who devoted himself so earnestly and efficiently in behalf of the Colored people on the question of the <u>Car</u> privilege.[252]

> With kind regards to your Brother
>
> I remain
>
> My dear Sir
>
> Yours very truly
>
> J. J. Roberts

249. Given Roberts's uncertainty about the author of the pamphlet, it is difficult to determine which of the many cotton pamphlets Coates wanted him to read. There are three likely candidates. Francis William Lorring published *Cotton Culture and the South: Considered with Reference to Emigration* in 1869. Though Lorring's work deals with Africa, it was probably too late to be the material Roberts referred to in 1868. Joseph Bardwell Lyman wrote *Cotton Culture* in 1868. And David Christy, an agent of the ACS in Ohio, wrote *Cotton is King, or, The Culture of Cotton, and Its Relation to Agriculture, Manufactures & Commerce; to the Free Colored People; & to Those Who Hold that Slavery is in Itself Sinful*. Christy's work is an attractive possibility because it contains the phrase Roberts uses in the title; however, it was written in 1855 and is a book rather than a pamphlet.

250. Probably to Benjamin Hunt.

251. The three stamps Roberts used remain in the envelope with the letter. One is a twelve cent stamp with the word twelve crossed out and the number six written in. The second stamp is a twelve cent stamp. The third is twenty-four cents.

252. In the years after the Civil War, nineteen streetcar companies operated in Philadelphia. Of these, eleven did not allow black passengers at all and the other eight only permitted them to stand on the open platform with the conductor. Black people and their white allies fought against the discriminatory practices of the companies. In 1866, Benjamin Bacon, a white Quaker, published anonymously a pamphlet entitled *Why Colored People in Philadelphia are Excluded from the Street Cars*. The next year, the *Report of the Committee Appointed for the Purpose of Securing to Colored People in Philadelphia the Right to the Use of the Street Cars* was published. The list of names associated with the pamphlet includes Benjamin Coates, Dillwyn Parrish, B. P. Hunt, and J. Miller McKim. The pamphlet outlines the actions taken by the Philadelphia community to remedy the situation, including a prior appeal to the companies themselves. The list of members of the committee includes B. P. Hunt (treasurer), J. M. McKim (secretary), Robert R. Corson, and John H. Towne. In 1867 the Supreme Court of Pennsylvania declared that the companies could not ban any passengers according to race or ethnicity, but the races could be separated in their own best interests. Reginald H. Pitts, "Let Us Desert This Friendless Place: George Moses Horton in Philadelphia, 1866," *Journal of Negro History* 80, no. 4 (Autumn 1995): 145–56;

❖ 128 ❖

Boston, Sept 30, 1868

B. Coates Esq

Dear Sir. Your favor of 28 inst. is most welcome.

President Roberts[253] and lady have been here more than a week, and are, I think, improving in health. He is today attending a County Agricultural Exhibition at Hingham, of which Mr. Fearing,[254] President of our Trustees, is President. Yesterday P.M. he was to meet the Presidential Committee of the American Board for Foreign Missions, to talk of a plan for training missionaries in the College,[255] and of other matters. We hope that he will be able to make arrangements with them and elsewhere, that will greatly strengthen the College.

I do not find that there is much need of more common schools in Liberia. The several missions have established them in almost, if not quite, every place where one is needed. The want is, a greater number of competent teachers; and for the supply of these, we must look to the College. Teachers educated there will cost less and be worth more than those educated here and sent over. The College needs endowing, and perhaps we shall want one more good man for a professor, to take the place of Prof. Johnson,[256] who may resign.

The question of emigration is a difficult one. It seems hard to refuse a passage to the multitudes who wish to emigrate. Making selections will be a very difficult matter, and to do it so as to be of much use, would be expensive. We could not do it by comparing recommendations. Nor do I see how any great amount of "material aid" can be given advantageously. Judging from experience, such aid would be mostly wasted. Like other people generally, they

---

Frederick W. Speirs, *The Street Railway System of Philadelphia: Its History and Present Condition* (Baltimore: 1877); *Report of the Committee Appointed for the Purpose of Securing to Colored People in Philadelphia the Right to the Use of the Street Cars* (Philadelphia: Merrihew and Sons, 1867).

253. Joseph Jenkins Roberts. See Letter 1, Roberts to Coates, July 8, 1848.

254. Albert Fearing. See Letter 127, Roberts to Coates, September 28, 1868.

255. Liberia College. See Letter 29, Coates to Crummell, October 3, 1857.

256. Hilary W. Johnson (1837–1901). Johnson was the son of Elijah Johnson, a prominent Liberian settler. Educated at Alexander High School, he assumed Alexander Crummell's professorship at Liberia College when Crummell was dismissed. However, Johnson had differences with President Roberts and resigned. After holding the offices of president of Liberia College, Secretary of the Interior, and Secretary of State, in 1883 he was elected president of Liberia. In 1885 he successfully ran for reelection against Edward Blyden. He left the presidency in 1892, was appointed postmaster general, and held that position until his death. *HDL* 95–96; Lynch, *Edward Wilmot Blyden*, 41, 148, 156, 160.

must learn how to use money, by the discipline of earning it. The question has occurred to me, whether we ought to refuse to give gratuitous passages, and take none who cannot pay their fare and have something left. I am not yet ready to take that ground. It would give us few passengers now. The whole subject needs to be studied anew, and apparently, it will be.

But our most pressing necessity just now seems to me to be, the consolidating and harmonizing of our own forces at home. We have suffered for years, and still suffer, for want of it. New York wants to have a policy of its own, and to execute it by its own action, and not through the Parent Society.[257] Philadelphia, much the same. New Jersey has nearly recovered from this disease. Instead of this, all the auxiliaries should contribute all their strength to Washington,[258] and then send Delegates to Washington who would, if there should be need, compel Washington to do right. Their contributions would entitle them to votes enough to control the Parent Society. Can they be persuaded to do it?

> Very truly yours,
> Joseph Tracy[259]

[Written vertically along left-hand side of page:]
Pres. Roberts was to see Mr. Atkinson yesterday.

❧ 129 ❧

> Monrovia, October 10. 1868

Benjn Coates, Esq.

Dear Sir,

Your very interesting letters by "Thomas Pope" and the books you had the kindness to send me have been duly received. Please accept my sincere thanks.

The volumes of Robertson's Sermons[260] I consider invaluable though if some of my stiff orthodox friends who think the life of religion to consist

---

257. Presumably the ACS. See Letter 8, Coates to McLain, May 16, 1851.
258. Washington, D.C., was the site of the headquarters of the ACS.
259. Joseph Tracy. See Letter 10, Coates to McLain, October 11, 1851.
260. Frederick William Robertson (1816–1853), a British minister, preferred to remain independent, although not uncommitted, in the various doctrinal issues of the day, and therefore came into frequent conflict with other members of the clergy. When, after his death, his sermons were published, they met with widespread popularity. Hensley Henson, *Robertson of Brighton: 1816–1853* (London: Smith, Elder, 1916); "Robertson, Frederick William," *ANB* 16:1290–93.

in unbending forms and theological buckram,[261] were to know how greedily I devoured them, I <u>should</u> be ostracized in their estimation as a bad man, as, alas! some regard me now, because I am not content to go in the beaten track. I tell them that we have been living here for years under false pretences—professing to be engaged in the upbuilding of a Negro nation to embrace the aborigines of the country, when, in fact, we have been directing our efforts to the erection of a rotten aristocracy on the coast, whose distinguishing mark should be large brick houses fine furniture and fine farms. We have been professing to be engaged in the work of christianizing the heathen- while in reality we have done nothing for the native. But thank God the people's eyes are opening. Robertson's views please me much., as they must please any man who is anxious for the progress of <u>truth</u>, and in earnest for <u>reality</u>, and not merely for the ascendancy of stereotyped forms of thought and expression, because they come to us supported by the authority of the influential. Give me the essence and I care not for the accidents.

I have often felt within me the yearnings which Robertson has so beautifully and in so many places expressed. Ah! those sermons make a man think. How few persons really understand Christianity, and fewer still really practice it. The "world spirit"—this is Robertson's favorite expression and it conveys a good deal—the world spirit seeks after the great and the noble + the rich +c "Have the rulers and scribes believed in him"-? The spirit of the Gospel seeks the poor and needy—the lowly—the ignorant. I have often felt that if it were not for my ties and connections I would get right up and go out among the natives and preach the gospel as I understand it, and as Robertson appears to have understood it. He has well and finely remarked—"He who seeks Truth must be content with a lonely, little-trodden path. If he cannot worship her till she has been canonized by the shouts of the multitude, he must take his place with the members of that wretched crowd who shouted for two long hours, Great is Diana +c".

The natives around us, Mohammedan and pagan are eagerly crying for instruction. Some Vey[262] men called upon me a few months ago to ask me to procure for them copies of the scriptures in their own language. They had heard that Mr. Koelle,[263] a German missionary, who some years ago, was at

261. Buckram is a coarse cloth of linen or hemp, stiffened with sizing or glue, used in hats or garments to keep them in shape. The word was also used to indicate stiffness, precise formality, or starchiness of manner.

262. Probably the Vai tribe, which was concentrated in the western part of Liberia, near Cape Mount. *HDL* 182.

263. Sigismund W. Koelle (1823–1902), a German linguist who went to Sierra Leone in 1843 under the auspices of the Church Missionary Society (CMS), wrote *Polyglotta Africana*, a

Cape Mount[264] studying the Vey language had translated some portion of the Bible into that language. I at once wrote to a friend in England for assistance in the matter. My friend made application to Mr. Venn[265] of the Church Missionary Society[266] but was informed that no portion of the scriptures had been translated into Vey; and Mr. Venn suggested that Professor Blyden might do something towards performing so desirable a work. I had already begun the study of the Vey language, of which you are aware the Alphabet was invented by the natives themselves, who keep up constant correspondence among themselves in that language, which they also teach in schools established in every considerable village.

I continue to devote what spare moments I have to the study of this interesting language. I would not like to see this indigenous literature fall into disuse, because it is a standing vindication of the Negro against the charge of incapacity for invention with which he has been branded; and it is capable of further development into a very respectable language It is to be deeply deplored that the number of those in Liberia who feel really interested in this work is as yet very small. But the work of God does not depend upon numbers.

I have ordered from England some standard English works to assist me in the prosecution of my labor on the history.[267] Works published in

---

comparative study of 160 different African languages. In 1849 Koelle returned to Africa to study the written language of the Vai, but he did not translate the Bible into their language. Neither, it seems, did Blyden. Philip D. Curtin, *The Image of Africa: British Ideas and Action, 1780–1850* (Madison: University of Wisconsin Press, 1964), 393–96; "Koelle, Sigismund Wilhelm," *Dictionary of African Historical Biography*, 111.

264. Cape Mount. See Letter 21, Coates to McLain, May 22, 1855.

265. Henry Venn (1796–1873) was secretary of the CMS from 1841 to 1873, and son of John Venn, the founder of the CMS. "Venn, Henry," *ANB* 20:208.

266. The CMS, a British evangelical organization established in 1799 by Anglican clergy, sent its first two missionaries to Sierra Leone in 1804. After a slow start—only fifteen missionaries were sent by 1813—the society gained momentum and by 1849 it had dispatched 400 missionaries, although only 127 of those were still serving, the rest having died or resigned. Most were sent to Africa, but the CMS was also active in India, New Zealand, and the Middle East. Most of the society's early work was done in Sierra Leone, but after some converted recaptives (natives rescued from intercepted slave vessels) returned to their homelands further west, the CMS expanded into the Yoruba region, making their first settlement in 1845. The CMS played a large role in the early administration of Sierra Leone and, like the Liberians, attempted to slow and stop the slave trade. Jocelyn Murray, *Proclaim the Good News: A Short History of the Church Missionary Society* (London: Hodder and Stoughton, 1985).

267. In 1867 Coates offered to support Blyden to write a history of Liberia and. Blyden, however, had already written to Coppinger in 1865 that he was "trying to prepare a School History of Liberia" (Lynch, *Selected Letters of Edward Wilmot Blyden*, 68). Coates now offered to supply Blyden with the necessary reference materials. Blyden continued to work on the book for many years, but it was never published. He did publish several shorter works on Liberia's history. Livingston, *Education and Race*; Lynch, *Selected Letters of Edward Wilmot Blyden*, 408.

England are very expensive. I have this day drawn on you in favor of Messrs. Dalton + Lucy, Booksellers,[268] for fifteen pounds in gold, which I trust you will settle, in accordance with your generous offer to assist me to get some books. The amount is much greater but I could not tax your liberality any more. The draft is drawn at ten days sight payable in gold. This is the only condition on which I can get English booksellers to honor my orders. My expenses for books are very great. My salary, owing to the high price of gold, is not sufficient to raise one above the most ordinary necessities, under such circumstances the full play of mind is impeded.

Notwithstanding this pressure however, I am endeavoring to prosecute my studies and to write the History. Were it not for the friendly aid and countenance that the few of us who are laboring for Africa receive from our friends abroad, we should be tempted to abandon everything and remove to other scenes where our cares would be simplified and reduced to the simple anxiety for self. But we cannot let white men feel more and do more for the Negro than we. To me life would lose all its charms if I were not permitted to labor in this cause. I am only anxious to go further into the interior and spend my life in direct efforts to evangelize the people. The idea of a Negro nationality is subordinate with me to that of the evangelization and regeneration of the continent—"Liberia is only a means—not the great end." This is the idea which I labor to hold up to the people continually. But in forming your estimate of Liberians you must constantly bear in mind that as a general thing we are only one generation from debasing slavery; and one generation is not sufficient thoroughly to set aside the habits of the slave and mature the character of the Christian freeman.

Very respectfully + gratefully yrs.

Edward. W. Blyden[269]

P.S. Could you procure me a set of the African Repository[270] and of Hours at Home[271] to be owned as my personal property. My house is a mile from the college.[272]

---

268. Dalton & Lucy Booksellers had a prior relationship with Blyden, who amassed a sizable library and visited England several times. Lynch, *Selected Letters of Edward Wilmot Blyden*, 77.

269. Edward Wilmot Blyden. See Letter 27, Coates to Lugenbeel, October 6, 1856.

270. *The African Repository*. See Letter 15, Coates to Lugenbeel, June 27, 1853.

271. *Hours at Home* was a monthly journal published from May 1865 to October 1870 by Charles Scribner & Co. James Manning Sherwood, a Presbyterian clergyman, was the journal's editor. He also published several books and served as editor to several other religious periodicals. *Hours At Home*; "Sherwood, James Manning," *Appleton's* 5:508.

272. Liberia College. See Letter 29, Coates to Crummell, October 3, 1857.

❖ 130 ❖

New York Oct 21. 1868

Benj Coates Esq
711 Sansom St
    Philada- Dear Sir
        Yours of yesterday is at hand
      The price of Abbeokuta[273] is 90¢ +
            Africa's M Valley[274] 75 ¢
But we are very anxious to co-operate with you in their circulation, among a
class ~~they are~~ that needs instruction + so we put them at the mere nominal
price of 45 + 40 cents –
        You may send us your cheque for the amt. at your convenience
            Yours truly
                Rob. Carter + Bros[275]
[Attached to Letter 130, Carter to Coates, November 2, October 21, 1868, is
the following receipt:]

New York October 21 1868

Benj Coates Esq

               To Robert Carter & Brothers, Dr.
for Gratuitous Distribution   530 Broadway, Corner of Spring Street
    25 Abbeokuta 11   25
    24 Africas M Valley 9   60 $20   85

❖ 131 ❖

Caldwell, ——: Monrovia, Liberia, W.A.[276]
Nov² 1868

Dear Sir
    I have already answered yr two letters, and since the departure of the
mail yr favour of Aug 2 concerning schoolbooks comes to hand. Thanks. Yr

273. A.L.O.E., *Abbeokuta; or, sunrise within the tropics: an outline of the origin and
progress of the Yoruba Mission.* See Letter 37, Wagoner to Coates, January 31, 1859.
    274. Johnson, *Africa's Mountain Valley.* See Letter 37, Wagoner to Coates, January 31,
1859.
    275. Robert Carter & Bros. See Letter 112, Coates to Coppinger, May 20, 1868.
    276. Caldwell was a settlement a short way up the St. Paul's river. Crummell moved
there in August 1867. *Spirit of Missions* 33 (January 1868): 62.

letter makes me breathe a deal freer than I have for a long time. Last year I wrote + wrote and wrote to our Com^ee for books; and at last I had to send ahead, with my own money + purchase. You can judge how hard this was for me when my salary is worth but little more than half its ostensible value $850.- ~~and when, as I have already told you the [Col^r.] Com^ee. told their —— and not have thrown me into pecuniary~~ [entrapment? ~~embarrassment?~~]. But schools must have books, or else they must be closed.

Please advise me how to avail myself of the $50. you kindly offer me. I will tell Dr. Pinney[277] what I need; + perhaps that will do [written at bottom of first page:] Benj. Coates Esq [page break] My school[278] is not a very large one; it numbers about 30 scholars; but I think I may without vanity that it is the best taught school in the rural districts, and such indeed is the estimation in which it is held in this neighborhood that parents are constantly making applications for the admission of their children, notwithstanding the opposition of their ministers to their sending to a school outside of their own denomination. My desires and my wishes are a deal larger than my means + my ability, or otherwise I w^d make it a first rate grammar school, + and a training institution for native boys. The anxiety ~~for~~ of the natives for schooling cannot be exaggerated, all thro the country they are asking for schools and letters. If we had but the means we c^d Establish a hundred schools among the natives within a month; + derive a very considerable portion of their support from the natives themselves. And these native children have great capacity. One of my school boys is a Kroo boy,[279] the equal of the foremost of my scholars, in every branch; and spurred on by an egerness for learning which is like a flame. Alas how shamefully neglected have these natives been by us Liberians! But thank God this neglect can no longer be continued. Never more in the future will any man or party be tolerated here who dares to show spite or contempt for those benighted people. Never have I seen such a revolution in public sentiment as has taken place in this country within the last 18 mos: all of our foremost, best cultivated, most enlightened men, now come forward and demand a better treatment and a high cultivation of our aboriginal population. Much of this we owe to the sagacity and the persistence

---

277. John B. Pinney. See Letter 8, Coates to McLain, May 16, 1851.

278. As part of his missionary work, Crummell oversaw several schools in his district. The particular school referred to here as "[his] school" may be one in Caldwell. He moved there in August 1867 and "immediately opened a parish school" in which his daughter taught. In September 1867 it served eighteen pupils, with more expected. Moses, *Alexander Crummell*, 169–71; Oldfield, *Alexander Crummell*, 103; *Spirit of Missions* 33 (January 1868): 62.

279. The kroo, or kru, were indigenous people of Liberia skilled as boatmen.

of Dan[l] B. Warner.[280] The crowning acts of his administration was of uniting native chiefs and announcing oneness + brotherhood with them + for organizing schools for Congoes[281] + natives. I am sorry to say that immediately on his going out of office Mr Warners schools were broken up But we will have them going again in less than three years. We are determined that this wise + saving + gracious policy shall not be crushed out

I must thank you again for Robertsons[282] sermons They are most masterly, and a deal more refreshing and edifying than his life. I read the latter some time ago, and put it aside with a painful sense of the man's excessive self: consciousness, and almost harassing morbidity. He was indeed a great man; but I have seen + known of far greater men who had a deal more modesty. But one does not see much of this fault in his sermons, which are, for the most part, healthy, vitalizing and full of solace. In much pain + sadness, I read one of them last night = "Realizing the Second Advent" and I c[d] not help thanking you, audibly for it. It gave me refreshment, both spiritually + intellectually. The figure—the —— "world is mined," is as grand as any thing I have seen in Burke or [Canning? Channing?] or Webster:[283] while the spiritual truths evolved out of the subject gave me much cheer and no little assurance

   I am Dear Sir,
    Very gratefully,
     Yr obliged servt
      Alex Crummell.[284]

280. Daniel Bashiell Warner. See Letter 10, Coates to McLain, October 11, 1851.

281. "Congo" was the term used to refer to Africans who were taken off intercepted slave ships by the Navy and deposited in Liberia.

282. Frederick William Robertson. See Letter 129, Blyden to Coates, October 10, 1868.

283. For a very similar passage, see Moses, *Alexander Crummell*, 147. Crummell, *The Future of Africa*, 42.

284. Alexander Crummell. See Letter 28, Coates to Gurley, May 2, 1857.

❖ 132 ❖

WOOL[285]
COATES BROTHERS
127 Market Street
PHILADELPHIA, Nov. 17 1868

Wm Coppinger Esq.[286]
  My dear sir
     I rec^d today the two no^s. of the "Repository"[287] for 1851. for which accept my thanks.

  I think it possible, that we may get up a quite a Banquet to Presd Roberts[288] at the "Union Leage."[289] such at least is the prospect. Here are a few whom I wish to post up in regard to Liberia's present condition, commerce +c +c, any statistics will be desirable. Can you send me any no^s of the "Repository" containing such, or annual reports. Also if you have any of the "Memorial Vol. of the Semi Sentenial Anniversary"[290] as gotten up + published by Mr Tracey,[291] I can make good use of them. I want [page break] one copy especially for Thomas Webster who has taken hold in earnest. + I believe will push it through. if successful it may be a "big thing," + give a new start, new life to African colonization. It is propose to have some of our most influential men to participate in it.

  Where will a letter reach Augustus Washington?[292] He should be here by all means. The matter as Webster has taken it up, is so different from what I first contemplated that I shall probably leave all the work and detail in his hands as it getting too heavy for me, but I want to push him up, + give the matter shape and direction which perhaps I can do better than some

---

285. ACS Papers 103:193:146. The first four lines constitute the Coates brothers' printed letterhead, with the exception of the month, day, and last digit of the year.

286. William Coppinger. See Letter 10, Coates to McLain, October 11, 1851.

287. *The African Repository.* See Letter 23, Coates to Lugenbeel, October 27, 1855.

288. Joseph Jenkins Roberts. See Letter 1, Roberts to Coates, July 8, 1848.

289. The Union League, organized in Philadelphia in 1862, dedicated itself initially to publishing and distributing pamphlets supporting the Union cause. Its members distributed 125 million copies of its pamphlets on patriotism, Lincoln, the presidency, law, and economics. The league also turned its attention to recruitment, enlisting approximately 10,000 men in its first effort, and then to organizing eleven regiments of black troops. After the war, it created an employment bureau to help reintegrate returning soldiers into civilian life. Barth and Gillam, *Invisible Philadelphia,* 1168–71.

290. *Memorial of the semi-centennial anniversary of the American Colonization Society.* See Letter 125, Coates to Coppinger, September 26, 1868.

291. Joseph Tracy. See Letter 10, Coates to McLain, October 11, 1851.

292. Augustus Washington. See Letter 21, Coates to McLain, May 22, 1855.

others. Our colored people here will be likely to know who has <u>done this</u> if it succeeds, [page break]+ if not Webster will have the trouble himself. Fred[k] Douglass[293] + others however will very likely think that Mr Coates has "come it" over[294] Webster. He is not a man that I admire by any means, + do not care to act with him publicly, but he is a man of great executive ability. + so that the good is accomplished I care not who does it, + am perfectly willing that all such men shall have the honor + glory, if such there shall be.

> Yours very truly
> Benj: Coates

We are sending of our Libraries for the schools in the South. + this in my particular line, + to my taste. + in this I can work <u>effectively</u> altho quietly. I had a letter from Blyden[295] yesterday, + one from Crummell[296] to day. So you see I have not entirely given up Liberia + am not forgotten by my Liberia friends.

❖ 133 ❖

WOOL[297]

COATES BROTHERS

127 Market Street

PHILADELPHIA, Nov. 17 1868

Mr William Coppinger[298]

> Dear Sir,

I wrote to you yesterday, for some documents + referred to our <u>proposed</u> banquet to Ex Presid[t] R.,[299] but as this matter is as yet only in embryo, + may not come off please <u>do not speak of it</u>. I had intended to request it should be <u>confidential</u>. If it does come off, which I think probable, we have reason to expect some very good men, such as Rev[d] Rich[d]

293. Frederick Douglass. See Letter 3, Coates to Douglass, June 27, 1850.

294. To "come it over" is to try to impose on someone. Adrian Room, *Brewer's Dictionary of Phrase and Fable*, 16th ed. (New York: Harper Resource, 1999), 266.

295. Edward Wilmot Blyden. See Letter 27, Coates to Lugenbeel, October 6, 1856.

296. Alexander Crummell. See Letter 28, Coates to Gurley, May 2, 1857.

297. ACS Papers 103:193:147. The first four lines constitute the Coates brothers' printed letterhead, with the exception of the month, day, and last digit of the year.

298. William Coppinger. See Letter 10, Coates to McLain, October 11, 1851.

299. Joseph Jenkins Roberts. See Letter 1, Roberts to Coates, July 8, 1848.

Newton[300] D.D. Revd Phillips Brooks[301] + +c + I <u>want</u> Stephen Colwell[302] or Bishop Simpson[303] to <u>preside</u>. But I know that Webster has invited some others that are not such favorites with me. I want Revd Albert Baines, but do not want Wendell Phillips,[304] + I want Augustus Washington [page break] Revd Stephen Smith, Wm Whipper, E.D Bassett, + O.V. Catto, and <u>no more</u> of the same complexion except perhaps Fred^k Douglass.[305] all these are to be invited, + I want it to stop there. I am a little afraid that it will be <u>overdone</u>. Still perhaps I am too cautious, as the world is moving fast, and public opinion is being fast revolutionized. But do not mention the subject until you hear from me again. If we <u>must</u> admit such men as Phillips into the Colonization ranks, we shall no doubt also have a good many better men with him. It is possible we may inaugurate a new era, + infuse new life into the cause of African Civilization. I shall try to guide + direct it, until it gets too large for my grasp. I would like a <u>few</u> of the Memorial Vol.[306] or a least one copy. Webster is full of

300. Richard Heber Newton (1840–1914), born in Philadelphia, son of an Episcopal clergyman, became a clergyman himself. He was a well-known leader in several religious movements, including the Social Gospel movement, Broad Church movement, and the use of literary criticism to enhance understanding of the Bible. *ANB* 16:364–65.

301. Phillips Brooks (1835–1893), a prominent Episcopal clergyman who was widely known for the quality of his preaching, was an opponent of slavery and an advocate of racial equality. He argued for removing the racial qualifications for the vote and was involved in the Philadelphia movement to make the city's streetcars available to black passengers. *ANB* 3:623–25.

302. Stephen Colwell (1800–1871), who began a career as a lawyer, gave up his practice to become an iron manufacturer, a business that led him to become an economic theorist with particular interest in the intersection of government and business. Among his many activities, Colwell was active in the ACS, the Union League, and the Freedmen's Aid Society. *ANB* 4:327.

303. Matthew Simpson (1811–1844), a Methodist bishop, put his powerful oratorical skills into antislavery arguments, gaining a national reputation for his opposition to the Fugitive Slave Act. During the Civil War he preached loyalty to the Union cause and was an advisor to President Lincoln and his cabinet. After the war, he supported the Radical Republicans and was offered command of the Freedmen's Bureau, which he declined. *ANB* 20:21–22.

304. Wendell Phillips (1811–1884), an energetic opponent of slavery, enjoyed a close relationship with William Lloyd Garrison, but the two, differing on some aspects of strategy, wound up on opposite sides of the split in the abolition movement that occurred after the Civil War. Before the war he sided with Garrison in the belief that the Constitution and the Union were tainted by slavery and that the nation had to dissolve them and start afresh. With the passage of the Fifteenth Amendment in 1870, Phillips decided that his work on behalf of the former slaves was complete. He then turned his attention to worker's rights. *ANB* 17:454–56.

305. Augustus Washington (see Letter 21, Coates to McLain, May 22, 1855); Stephen Smith (see Letter 48, Garnet to Coates, July 17, 1859); William Whipper (see Letter 35, Wagoner to Coates, January 8, 1859); Ebenezer Don Carlos Bassett (see 121, Coates to Coppinger, August 5, 1868); Octavius Valentine Catto (see Letter 125, Coates to Coppinger, September 26, 1868); and Frederick Douglass (see Letter 3, Coates to Douglass, June 27, 1850).

306. *Memorial of the semi-centennial anniversary of the American Colonization Society.* See Letter 125, Coates to Coppinger, September 26, 1868.

the African [page break] Steam Ship project. he is a warm admirer, + personal friend of John Hickman, + they will work together strongly for this project. Col Corson[307] who has also taken hold of this work, I mean the banquet to Mr Roberts remarked to me yesterday that we three—this is Webster, himself, + myself were each working for different objects. While I was desirous to promote African Civilization + Colonization, + to bring all the true friends of the African race to work together, that Webster was working especially for the Steam Ship Line which he understands, + has been his business, + he may want to control, while he, Col Corson, was working to infuse new life into the Union League,[308] make it more progressive and, anti-slavery, [or] to take higher ground in behalf of the African + to promote universal suffrage. Still we are [page break] all working together + probably shall continue to work together. I think I can readily educate them all up to my views, altho Webster if takes an obstinate fit is hard to move. but just now he is getting exceedingly interested in Africa. + in African Colonization + I want some document to interest him. He asks me what were the best books for him to read + really I did not exactly what to say. but if I could get a copy of Bowens' Central Africa[309] for him I would give double price for it. Is it possible to get a copy?

Yours very truly

B.C

Your notice of "No Slavery in Liberia" did not appear in the North Am.
[Written vertically on the left-hand side of the last page:]
Did you see Watson of the "N° Am" + what did he say?

307. Robert Rodgers Corson (May 3, 1831–February 19, 1904), born in New Hope, Pennsylvania, moved to Philadelphia in 1856, where he established himself as a coal merchant. During the Civil War, Corson helped to found the Union Volunteer Refreshment Saloon and became its corresponding secretary. He also made many visits to Union soldiers in hospitals and published a pamphlet, *A Soldiers' Guide*. Corson also recruited fourteen thousand black soldiers for the Union army. After the Civil War, he served as the corresponding secretary of the Freedmen's Relief Association, and was treasurer of the Association for the Prevention of Cruelty to Animals. Towards the end of his life, Corson was involved with the project that brought electric lights to Luray Caverns, Virginia. *ANB* vol. 4.

308. The Union League. See Letter 132, Coates to Coppinger, November 17, 1868.

309. Bowen, *Central Africa*. See Letter 52, Smith to Coates, August 27, 1859.

❖ 134 ❖

WOOL
COATES BROTHERS
127 Market Street
PHILADELPHIA, Nov. 21ˢᵗ 1868[310]

Wᵐ Coppinger Esq.[311]

My dear sir

I received your package, for which accept my thanks. I think I can make very good use of the books. I gave one to Mr Webster, who is becoming deeply interested in Colonization. But the two articles in the "Nᵒ. American"[312] + "New York Tribune"[313] have had a damaging effect. I am surprised that Presᵗ. Roberts[314] has not published an explanation in reply to them. Mr Webster wrote to him yesterday propounding several questions relating to slavery in Liberia, or among the natives subject to Liberian authority, or with whom they have treaties, which I presume Mr Roberts will answer as fully as the case demands. Webster [page break] was much taken aback with these articles in the paper. He is a great worker, otherwise not a man of my choice. And as to Wendall Phillips, I have no patience with him. he is one peculiarly ~~distast~~ distasteful to me. I do not think at all likely that he + I could work together, + do not think there is any probability of his wishing to become a Colonizationist, or desiring to honor President Roberts. if so I should be ready to exclaim indeed "Is Saul among the prophets?" However I am very much in hope that we can in some way give African Colonization a new start, + impart new life. I am sending books for the Libraries, of ^ nearly all our schools belonging to the "Pennᵃ. Freedmans Aid Socy"[315] also to Friends

310. ACS Papers 103:193:158. The first four lines constitute the Coates brothers' printed letterhead, with the exception of the month, day, and last digit of the year.

311. William Coppinger. See Letter 10, Coates to McLain, October 11, 1851.

312. Most likely "Bondage in a Strange Place," *North American and United States Gazette*, November 11, 1868, 2. This article suggests that the Liberian government "protect[ed] or allow[ed]" slavery among the nearby tribes and brings J. J. Roberts to task for his statement—apparently misquoted—that the sons of slaveholding chiefs were educated at Liberia College for no charge.

313. Here Coates is referring to a small item in the *New York Daily Tribune* (Wednesday, November 18, 1858, 4) that criticized the Liberian government for making "conquests" of the nearby tribes and allowing their practice of slavery to persist. The article cites statements by J. J. Roberts to support its accusations. For Roberts's responses to these two articles, see Letter 136, Coppinger to Coates, November 30, 1868.

314. Joseph Jenkins Roberts. See Letter 1, Roberts to Coates, July 8, 1848.

315. The Pennsylvania Freedmen's Relief Association. See Letter 82, Clark to Coates, July 15, 1865.

Asso[n316] (orthodox) + to some of the Hicksite Friends schools + to each I am sending a copy of the History of Liberia by Stockwell,[317] + also one or two copies each of "Abbeokuta"[318] + "Africa's Mountain Valley"[319] besides other paper + books referring to Africa, some of which we have rec^d from England. I may send you a sample. I tell my friends in both associations that it is my intention to have them all working for Africa very soon, as soon as our work among the freedmen is finished. this will probably be during the coming year, or partially so. The new state governments we hope will provide ample educational facilities for all their people black and white, + thus relieve us of much of our present work. I have heretofore read portions of the Memorial Vol.[320] but last eving I finished the greater part of it + was exceedingly interested. if I was a Younger Man I should work in earnest, + to some purpose, modestly believing that but few men if any could influence our colored population more than I can. But as it is I shall probably have to give the laboring over to younger + more vigorous men, satisfied if I can hold on to the helm awhile to guide the movement but am very doubtful if I can do that when the vessel fairly gets underweigh + under full sail. I do believe however that the civilization of Africa is not far distant.

Yours very truly

B. Coates

Will send you a list of the schools + Teachers soon.

---

316. Probably the Friends Freedmen's Association. See Letter 134, Coates to Coppinger, November 21, 1868.

317. Stockwell, *The Republic of Liberia.*

318. *Abbeokuta.* See Letter 37, Wagoner to Coates, January 31, 1859.

319. Johnson, *Africa's Mountain Valley.* See Letter 37, Wagoner to Coates, January 31, 1859.

320. *Memorial of the semi-centennial anniversary of the American Colonization Society.* See Letter 125, Coates to Coppinger, September 26, 1868.

❖ 135 ❖

WOOL[321]
COATES BROTHERS
127 Market Street
PHILADELPHIA, Nov. 28ᵗʰ 1868

Wᵐ Coppinger Esq.[322]

Dear Sir

I enclose herewith Mr Blyden's[323] last letter. I forgot to send it when I wrote to you last + Mr Malcolm retained it longer than I expected. If there is any portion of it you want for publication please copy it + return the letter to me. Mr Crummell's[324] letter refers more to matters of a private nature + is not intended for publication + would not interest other than myself.

The contemplated Banquet to Prest Roberts[325] has fallen through. Mr Webster is a man of great energy + very enthusiastic + will I doubt not prove very useful in the cause of African colonization, if [page break] his work can be well + prudently directed. he has also a large grasp of mind, + I should not be surprised if he shall prove to be the most effective worker that the cause has ever had. But I have been so accustomed "to make haste slowly" that his railroad speed almost frightens me. he carries such a very heavy head of steam. I therefore withdrew from the work intending to leave it all in his hands, but it seems my note to him has given offense + hurt his feelings + he has therefore decided to give it up for the present. I will see that he has interview with Presᵗ Roberts when he comes here and perhaps at another time perhaps later in Oct. or in Jany he may get up a large affair. Well I shall regret any disappointment to any + especially regret to have hurt the [page break] feelings of any one, but really I think I am getting too old to undertake, what I might have done with much zeal when I was a young man. Webster's intuition was to have had a banquet inviting all classes, some of our most influential men, colonizationists + abolitionists, white + black to have all the speeches + letters recᵈ reported for the paper + published in longer pamphlet to the extent of <u>30.000</u>! (Thirty thousand!!) to be distributed to <u>all</u>

321. acs Papers 103:193:170. The first four lines constitute the Coates brothers' printed letterhead, with the exception of the month, day, and last digit of the year.

322. William Coppinger. See Letter 10, Coates to McLain, October 11, 1851.

323. Edward Wilmot Blyden. See Letter 27, Coates to Lugenbeel, October 6, 1856.

324. Alexander Crummell. See Letter 28, Coates to Gurley, May 2, 1857.

325. Joseph Jenkins Roberts. See Letter 1, Roberts to Coates, July 8, 1848.

the members of <u>every</u> state legislature + all the members of Congress. The fact is I was rather alarmed at the largeness of his views, + yet it may have been just the thing, to give new life to the Colonization cause.

Yours very truly

B. Coates.

[Written on the back of the third page:]

I suppose you have seen Pred Roberts letter[326] to the "Nᵒ Am." + also to the "Tribune" of yesterday

❖ 136 ❖

Colonization Rooms[327]

Washington, D.C. Nov: 30. 1868

Dear Sir

I am greatly favored by your letters of the 21ˢᵗ + 28ᵗʰ inst and Mʳ Blyden's communication to your of Oct: 10.[328] Having copied that part of the letter touching the Vey language I beg to hand it to you herewith with tender of my thanks for its perusal and use.[329]

The proposed Banquet to President Roberts[330] as you intended it and Mʳ Webster desired were very different affairs. The first could result in good only; the latter, I fear, would have done the Society and Liberia much harm— as it would have given a political cast to the work which it is important to avoid. The time too for such a demonstration has not come—the temper of the country being to keep the colored man here as a laborer and a voter, and Liberia is not prepared to receive a large emigration of our very best blacks.

I have received the very dignified and satisfactory letters[331] of Presᵗ Roberts in the Philadᵃ North American and the New York Tribune, meeting

326. These two letters ("Bondage in a Strange Place," *North American and United States Gazette*, November 26, 1868, 1; "No Slavery in Liberia," *New York Daily Tribune*, November 27, 1868, 4) are very similar in content, as are the earlier articles to which they respond (see Letter 134, Coates to Coppinger, November 21, 1868). Roberts's purpose in writing them was to respond to misinterpretations of his own statements regarding the population of Liberia and the presence of slavery among nearby tribes.

327. The headquarters of the ACS.

328. All three letters are in this collection. See Letter 134, Coates to Coppinger, November 21, 1868; Letter 135, Coates to Coppinger, November 28, 1868; and Letter 129, Blyden to Coates, October 10, 1868.

329. The portion of Blyden's letter was published in the *African Repository* 45 (January 1869): 28.

330. Joseph Jenkins Roberts. See Letter 1, Roberts to Coates, July 8, 1848.

331. Roberts's letters. See Letter 135, Coates to Coppinger, November 28, 1868.

and refuting the cruel and unjust charge that Slavery exists in Liberia. It is my intention to give place to both in the next Repository.[332]

I notice that Prof: Blyden desire a set of the African Repository[333] for his own use and benefit. We cannot do this, but can furnish him the last twenty or twenty five volumes. Shall I get them out for him? If so, they ought to be firmly bound, for the African climate is very severe on books. The Liberia College Library[334] has the Repository and our Reports as complete as they can be made, and it seems to me he might be content to go "a mile" to them. The $25. Or $30. which it would take to pay for binding such as we can spare him, might be applied to a more deserving and vital purpose.

Very gratefully Yours,
Wm Coppinger[335]

❖ 137 ❖

Benj: Coates Esq.
127 Market St.
Philadelphia, Pa.

Philadelphia Jany 8th 1869[336]

William Coppinger Esq:[337]
My dear sir,

I have been thinking a good deal within the past year as to the future of the African race in America, and in Africa: for the interests are the same, and cannot be separated. You are aware that I have taken a deep interest in the work in both hemispheres, not especially in sending shiploads of ignorant men to Africa, who can find profitable employment, + be better educated here, nor in bringing shiploads of ignorant savages to this country to be educated, But in promoting the education, + elevation of the people both there and here, and in the diffusion of of the blessings of Christian Civilization, on each continent. The problem of the best method of increasing this work, is one that it seems to me should at this time [page break] claim the serious attention of all the true friends of the negro

332. These letters were published in the *African Repository* 45 (January 1869): 14–16.
333. *The African Repository*. See Letter 15, Coates to Lugenbeel, June 27, 1853.
334. Liberia College. See Letter 29, Coates to Crummell, October 3, 1857.
335. William Coppinger. See Letter 10, Coates to McLain, October 11, 1851.
336. ACS Papers 103:194:22.
337. William Coppinger. See Letter 10, Coates to McLain, October 11, 1851.

race. And as the abolition of slavery in the United States has well nigh terminated the work of the the different antislavery societies, and in the opinion of
many also the special work of the Colonization Society, while most of the
freedman's aid associations are anticipating the close of their labors within the
present year, Is it not well that some of the earnest friends of this long neglected people should consult together as to the best method of keeping alive a
public sympathy on their behalf? Whether a union of the most earnest and
progressing men in the ~~different~~ various associations who have heretofore
labored in different spheres, can be effected for this object, bringing together
people of different creeds or religious denominations, to do on a larger field
what is now being done by the "American Missionary Ass°."[338] would seem a
desirable matter to consider. [page break] Do you suppose, or do any of the
friends of the "Am: Col. Society"[339] believe, that ~~sufficient~~ funds can be raised
to transport a sufficient number of our industrious + working population to
Africa to fill the "Gulconda" regularly, or to <u>one half</u> her capacity? As the
political affairs in the Southern states become settled, + business with all the
industries revive, (the agricultural interests especially) will there not be an
indisposition among the laboring people to emigrate? If such should be the
case, will not the question arise, whether it is not expedient to give up the
present organization altogether, or to make such changes as may be required
by the times, + the different circumstances in which the country has been
placed by the War. When the "Am: Col. Socy" seemed near its ~~its~~ end in 1832,
1833 having lost its hold on the sympathies + the interests of the people, "The
Young Men's Colonization Socy of Penn^a"[340] was formed to create new life in
the cause by the infusion of [page break] of young blood. The experiment was
successful, the activity of the young men who formed the Board of Managers
in Philad^a ~~who~~ and soon after formed a union with the New York Society,
started ~~the~~ a new settlement[341] + began the work anew. when in a short time
afterwards the old board of the "Penn^a Col. Socy."[342] having a charter from the
Legislature withdrew from the work altogether, electing the young men of the
New Society in their places. In this way the cause was resuscitated, and went
forward for some years with increased energy. This was what was needed <u>then,</u>

---

338. The AMA. See Letter 116, Whipple to Coates, June 5, 1868.
339. The ACS. See Letter 8, Coates to McLain, May 16, 1851.
340. The Young Men's Colonization Society of Pennsylvania. See Letter 9, Coates
to Lugenbeel, June 18, 1851.
341. Buchanan, Liberia. See Letter 8, Coates to McLain, May 16, 1851.
342. The Pennsylvania Colonization Society. See Letter 8, Coates to McLain, May
16, 1851.

does not this experience throw some light on what may be needed <u>now</u>? But even with the change indicated, it it would probably prove an exceedingly difficult matter to convince the christian public, that it is of sufficient importance <u>at this time</u> for us to send thousands of laborers to Africa, many of whom cannot read, [page break] or write (+ who need an education in all the affairs of life which they can better acquire in the United States) to to induce them to contribute largely of their means, when there are so many other demands for their charity. But for the education of the ignorant, both in Africa, + in America, many may be induced to contribute, and will not the advancement of the educational interests of Liberia, the support of Liberia College,[343] the extension of good schools throughout the Republic + among the natives of the interior, tend not only to create an interest among those feel the importance of spreading a high christian civilization through that continent, but also tend to develop the material wealth + interest of Africa, so as to <u>attract</u> + <u>induce</u> the <u>immigration</u> of many of our most enterprising and capable colored men from America with capital, and skilled labor, who will make valuable citizens of that country + while advancing their own interests prove [page break] a blessing to the World. In this view of the case, could not a reorganization be effected by the withdrawal of most of the old members + directors not only of the parent ass[n] but of the different State Societies, + elect in their places younger + more active men, generally those are engaged in the work of education among the freedmen in the Southern States. It strikes me that Gen[l]. O. O Howard[344] and John M Langston[345] would both be excellent members of the executive Comm: at Washington. Two or three intelligent + educated Negro gentlemen, in the boards of each state society would have the effect of interesting our colored population very much in the work, such men for instance as William Whipper, ED Bassett, + O.V. Catto. in Philadelphia, + Henry Highland Garnett,[346] + a few others who could be found in other localities of like stamp would popularize the movement and [page break] if all, or nearly all the old members of the Penn[a] Society should withdraw probably the requisite number could be found from among the most active + effective men now engaged in the educational work among the freedmen to take their places, to work with a few of the most interested of the old members

343. Liberia College. See Letter 29, Coates to Crummell, October 3, 1857.
344. Oliver Otis Howard. See Letter 93, Coates to [Coppinger], April 7, 1867.
345. John Mercer Langston. See Letter 87, Coates to Coppinger, June 6, 1866.
346. William Whipper (see Letter 35, Wagoner to Coates, January 8, 1859); Ebenezer Don Carlos Bassett (see Letter 121, Coates to Coppinger, August 5, 1868); Octavius Valentine Catto (see Letter 125, Coates to Coppinger, September 26, 1868); and Henry Highland Garnet (see Letter 3, Coates to Douglass, June 27, 1850).

who would prefer to remain + give the benefit of their experience to the younger + newer members. In this way by retaining Mr Tracy[347] in Boston with some of his best co-laborers, Mr Pinney[348] to continue in the New York office with Mr Schiefflin[349] + a few others, Dr Hall[350] in Balt., Mr Coppinger in Washington a great work might be effected.

Possibly Mr Whipper might be induced to go to Liberia, as consul general from this govenment. If so, I do not think that a better man could be found in the <u>United States</u>. He has the entire confidence of all who know him + there is not another [page break] among the colored population of this city who is so universally respected or is so much looked up to. A most excellent practical business ———* Now with some such change as ——— could not this Colonization Society go on under its old charter without a change of name even for I must confess, that while I have sometimes felt like starting entirely a new with a new name, such as the "African Aid Union," I do not feel quite satisfied to give up the old name, that has done so much for Africa.

The work need not be exclusively confined to literary education but promising young men in America might be aided in acquiring knowledge of various kinds, as machinists, artists, the sciences, +c. + also aided in <u>getting</u> to Africa in special cases. For altho' the principles of the dominant part the genius of our government, and the [page break]

[Written vertically on the left-hand side of the previous page:]
*I doubt whether his equal for sound practical good sense is to be found among the colored population of the United States.

true spirit of Christianity shall soon abolish all distinctions of color or race, recognizing in its fullest sense the Fatherhood of God + the brotherhood of man, in all the laws + institutions of all the States. Yet I believe that Christians of all professions + denominations believe that the gospel of the New Testament is to be spread over the whole world, and my own expression is that Protestant Christianity + the English language are destined to go together. And we are not to forget that the laws of nature which are the laws of God point to the colored race, as the missionaries + civilizers of the Tropics, where climate debars the entrance, or the continuance, of the white man, while the

347. Joseph Tracy. See Letter 10, Coates to McLain, October 11, 1851.
348. John Brooke Pinney. See Letter 8, Coates to McLain, May 16, 1851.
349. Henry M. Schieffelin. See Letter 46, Pinney to Coates, June 16, 1859.
350. James Hall. See Letter 18, Roberts to Coates, August 26, 1854.

colored man thrives + flourishes, as he does <u>no where else</u>. We see already our colored population <u>gradually gravitating</u> southward, and what with the increased emigration from Europe, + in a year or two as soon as the Pacific Rail Road is finished we shall [page break] probably have half a million of Chinese rushing in as laborers to be followed rapidly by others, they too to be <u>educated</u> in the <u>English langue</u> and in <u>Christian</u> Civilization, to carry back with them at some future day to their fatherland. This will be another problem for us to solve, but it will probably ~~tend to~~ hasten the education of the black man and to tend to push him towards the Tropics. My theory is that we shall absolutely absorb a considerable portion of the <u>black</u>, the native <u>red men</u>, + also of <u>yellow men</u> from China, ~~but~~ but that a still larger portion of both the black, + yellow races will find their way back to Africa + China, while numbers of both will settle in the West Indies + Mexico. But I will not indulge further in my <u>theories</u> or what some may think my <u>vagaries</u>. Still I think it necessary to take a broad + comprehensive view of the [page break] subject so as to rightly understand its bearings and our own duties in attempting its solution.

I have taken the liberty of making these suggestions for you to think over prior to the meeting of the Col. Socy on the 19th inst. I have written hastily as I did to our friend President Roberts[351] on the same subject, a few days since. You may show this letter to Prest Roberts + to Mr Pinney, or any one else who may dare to read so long a letter of crudities, but if some one can mature a good + practical plan to continue + increase the work for Africa's civilization, from any of the crude ideas here expressed, there will be few more gratified than myself. My laboring days are well nigh ~~ended~~ ended but I shall be glad to see the work go forward in younger + abler hands. I had a letter from Mr Crummell[352] yesterday, that interested me.

Yours very truly Benjª. Coates

---

351. Joseph Jenkins Roberts. See Letter1, Roberts to Coates, July 8, 1848.
352. Alexander Crummell. See Letter 28, Coates to Gurley, May 2, 1857.

❖ 138 ❖

127 Market St
Philadelphia Jany 12
1869[353]

Wm Coppinger Esq[354]
Colonization Rooms
        Washington D.C.
            Dear Sir
                    I have your favor of yesterday. If you think proper you
may read my letter of 8th inst to your Board of Directors at their meeting
on the 19th inst. Perhaps some of the views there expressed may be rather pre-
mature. But I do think that if a portion of our most intelligent and best educated colored men of the race for whom we are working should be brought
into our councils, it will have a very happy effect in making the cause popular
with them, and especially if the educational work shall receive a much larger
degree of attention than it has had heretofore. And if Genl. O. [page break]
Genl. O.O Howard,[355] + Jno M Langston[356] should be made members of the
Executive Committee, I feel very certain that they will prove very valuable
auxiliaries, + aids, and in this ^ way much new strength, and new life may be
given to the cause. But I do not wish to press my views too strongly. still I
would like you to confer, with Revd Jon. Tracy Dr Pinney, Dr Hall, + Ex President Roberts[357] on the subject and would be glad if you will show my letter
to them + to any others or to the Board as you may think best. I trust it can
do no harm, if it does no good.
                    I have also written to President Roberts expressing some of the views
I did to you, + since then have written to Mr Tracy in regard to the importance of education in Liberia + among the [page break] natives, + have given
him an extract from a letter received a few days since from Mr Crummell[358]
in regard especially to the education of the natives, which I think important.
If Dr Tracy does not take it to Washington I would like to send you a copy. I
am sure the Board will be interested in it.

353. ACS Papers 103:194:39.
354. William Coppinger. See Letter 10, Coates to McLain, October 11, 1851.
355. Oliver Otis Howard. See Letter 93, Coates to [Coppinger], April 7, 1867.
356. John Mercer Langston. See Letter 87, Coates to Coppinger, June 6, 1866.
357. John Tracy (see Letter 10, Coates to McLain, October 11, 1851); John Brooke Pinney (see Letter 8, Coates to McLain, May 16, 1851); James Hall (see Letter 18, Roberts to Coates,
August 26, 1854); and Joseph Jenkins Roberts (see Letter 1, Roberts to Coates, July 8, 1848).
358. Alexander Crummell. See Letter 28, Coates to Gurley, May 2, 1857.

Give my regards to Mr + Mrs Roberts. I have not heard from them —— directly since they have been in Washington. I trust they both keep well, through this cold + disagreeable weather.

Yours very truly

Benj\. Coates

❖ 139 ❖

Philadelphia Jany 15ᵗʰ 1869.

William Coppinger Esq[359]
        Washington City, D.C.
My dear Sir,

I wrote to you the other day that you might read my letter (to you) of the 8ᵗʰ inst.[360] at your annual meeting on the 19ᵗʰ if you thought proper to do so. While I feel a great hesitation in saying my own views too strongly, or in assuming to teach those who whose province it is to view the whole field of operations + to judge of the feasibility, or expediency of continuing the old system, yet I am so firmly of the opinion that the change of circumstances that our country has undergone within the past few years, necessitates ^ ᵃ different policy to be adopted by the real friends of Africa, + the African race, that I should be glad to have my friends see as I do, + would even venture to present my views to [page break] to them even in a very crude shape, in the hope that they might see the matter in the same light, and be able to evolve a policy in harmony with the times, + that will secure the earnest + hearty support of the American people. That Africa is to be civilized and Christianized, + that right speedily, + by her own educated sons + daughters I have not a doubt, and that hundreds + perhaps thousands are at this time, being engaged in the educational work of the freedmen in the United States, who are soon to become missionaries to Africa, without being aware how far spread will be the results of their present labors. And it seems to me that the Question before the friends of the Am: Colonization Socy.[361] is whether they will take up the work here + carry it forward to its destined results in the Civilization + Christianization [page break] of Africa, or to leave this duty to others, but that it will go forward, must go forward, I think scarcely admits of a doubt. What I

---

359. William Coppinger. See Letter 10, Coates to McLain, October 11, 1851.
360. See Letter 137, Coates to Coppinger, January 8, 1869.
361. The ACS. See Letter 5, Coates to McLain, July 9, 1850.

wish is to blend the two works + let them go together for ^ the good of both continents. And I should not be surprised if your board should be prepared to adopt substantially the views I have expressed. Public opinion is changing rapidly, + ^ it will not do to judge of men's present views, by what they have been. You are aware how bitterly prejudiced our colored population have been, not only against the Colonization Society, but have been very jealous of every effort in behalf of Africa, fearing that some unjust + proscriptive laws will follow and this feeling possibly may to some extent prevail in the Colored Convention now sitting in Washington, gotten up by that man <u>Nesbit</u>[362] who published [page break] many years since a book[363] containing the <u>largest untruths</u> in regard to Liberia, to be found anywhere. Yet I do not know of a single educated + respectable colored man in this city, + very few if any in the United States who would object to my plan for extending civilization through Africa, + such men as William Whipper,[364] + Henry Highland Garnett,[365] are in hearty sympathy. Mr Bassett[366] who has gone to the Convention ^ at Washington 367 is growing in that direction as fast as could be expected. [There are seven crossed-out lines here which are mostly unreadable, and two similarly inscrutable lines written vertically on the left side of the page.] Indeed both whites + blacks have almost forgotten the Society altogether, + if brought to their remembrances ~~only~~ [page break] only think of it as a thing of the <u>past</u>, an <u>obsolete idea</u> that once had an existence in the days of Slavery. Still I cannot help thinking that it may be revived with glorious results. as the real Anti Slavery Socy of the World, reviving at this day the Spirit of its founder, and as a Society that shall go down in history, known by its works, while the <u>froth</u> of such men as Wendell Phillips shall have passed away + have been forgotten. The Republic of Liberia soon probably to become one of the "<u>United States</u>

362. William Nesbit. See Letter 23, Coates to Lugenbeel, October 27, 1855.

363. William Nesbit, "Four Months in Liberia: or African Colonization Exposed," in Moses, *Liberian Dreams*, 79–126. See Letter 23, Coates to Lugenbeel, October 27, 1855.

364. William Whipper. See Letter 35, Wagoner to Coates, January 8, 1859.

365. Henry Highland Garnet. See Coates to Douglass, June 27, 1850.

366. Ebenezer Don Carlos Bassett. See Letter 121, Coates to Coppinger, August 5, 1868.

367. Colored Citizen Conventions were held all over the nation in January 1869, including one in Saint Paul, Minnesota, to celebrate the anniversary of emancipation earlier that month. The convention in Washington commenced on January 14, 1869, and ended four days later. General Oliver O. Howard and George T. Downing were among the participants at the convention. One resolution discussed at the convention was an official thanks for the efforts made to educate freedmen. Another endorsed universal suffrage, and a third requested that black soldiers who had been slaves before the war receive the same salaries as free black men. *The Press*, January 15 and 18, 1869.

of <u>Africa</u>" rivalling in good works, true greatness, its foster parent the United States of America, will for all time be recognized as the fruit of its labors, "a tree is known by its fruit." Is the work so well begun having such a good [page break] foundation laid to build upon to be abandoned now? If the work is to be prosecuted, is there any other possible way, than by educating the African race in <u>America</u> + in <u>Africa</u>, to secure the desired end? I think not. Just at <u>this</u> <u>time</u>, <u>especially</u> will it be difficult to raise money to transport our laborers from out of the United States. But the time may come, + at no <u>very</u> <u>distant</u> <u>day</u> when those who are now being educated in this country will seek a home in their father land, and as the vast resources of Africa become known, + are being developed the interests of convenience may <u>necessitate</u> a Steam Ship Line between the two countries. While however we should all look to the future, is it not the <u>present,</u> that needs <u>immediate</u> action? One of the most effective agencies for [page break] Spreading a knowledge of Africa, + creating an interest in the regeneration of that continent, among both blacks + whites, is "The <u>African Repository</u>"[368] if that could be sent to <u>all</u> the teachers of every freedman's school in the United States, and to the most interested members of the different freedmen's aid associations, If its present circulation could be quadrupled, I think the public mind could be aroused to the importance of African civilization to an extent that has heretofore been thought impracticable. In addition to this if every freedman's School, or every freedman's Library was furnished with a copy of a history of Liberia, + other interesting + instructive books relating to Africa. + some of the most intelligent and highly educated colored men should be induced to take part with us in this work as associates, + co-laborers, would not [page break] an active interest soon be aroused, or stimulated into action among the colored people themselves ᵗʰᵃᵗ ᶜᵒᵘˡᵈ insure the success of the enterprise with the aid + sympathy of all classes which ˢᵘᶜʰ interest would naturally create? If this portion of the work, the large circulation of the "<u>Repository,</u>" + + securing the cooperation of influential colored men, such as Langston,[369] Whipper, Basset +c is vigorously prosecuted for the next year, even supposing that nothing should be done in aid of Liberia College,[370] or to promote the educational interest in Liberia + if not a single emigrant should be sent during the whole year, it seems to me that more real good will be accomplished,+ more progress made, than in any former year since the existence of the Society. If in <u>addition</u>, the

368. *The African Repository.* See Letter 23, Coates to Lugenbeel, October 27, 1855.
369. John Mercer Langston. See Letter 87, Coates to Coppinger, June 6, 1866.
370. Liberia College. See Letter 29, Coates to Crummell, October 3, 1857.

valuable aid, and [page break] + co-operation of Gen¹ O.O. Howard[371] could be secured it would add be greatly to the success of the enterprise, and I feel sure that his sympathies would be enlisted in the educational work if properly presented to him. But I fear I shall tire you with my long letters. On this subject I scarcely know where to stop, + have not the power of <u>concentration</u> that is desirable. I am exceedingly glad however that the Board will have the valuable aid of Ex President Roberts.[372] there are few men, <u>if any</u> in my opinion so well qualified to advise and direct as to the future policy of the Socy. + the needs of Liberia as he is. I should myself defer to his great experience + sound judgement in most matters, that come within his observation. His views will no doubt have great weight with the Board.

Yours very truly Benjª: Coates [page break] Extract of a letter from Alex Crummell[373] recᵈ a <u>few days</u>. dated Novʳ 1868[374] at Caldwell,[375] Liberia W.A. After speaking of his own school, he says.

"The anxiety of the natives for schooling cannot be exaggerated, all through the Country they are asking for schools and letters. If we had the <u>means</u> we could establish a hundred schools among the natives within a month, and derive a very considerable portion of their support from the natives themselves. And these native children have great capacity. One of my school boys is a Kroo boy, the equal of the foremost of my scholars in every branch; and spurred on by an eagerness, for learning which is like a flame. Alas how shamefully neglected have these natives been by us Liberians! But thank God this neglect can no longer be continued. Never more in the future will any man, or party be tolerated here who dares to show despite or contempt for these [page break] benighted people. Never have I seen such a revolution in public sentiment as has taken place in this country within the last 18 months: All of our foremost, best educated most enlightened men, now come forward and demand a better treatment and a high cultivation of our aboriginal population. Much of this we owe to the sagacity and the persistence of Danl. B Warner.[376] The crowning act of his administration was visiting native chiefs and announcing oneness + brotherhood with them, + organizing schools for Congoes + Natives."

371. Oliver Otis Howard. See Letter 93, Coates to [Coppinger], April 7, 1867.
372. Joseph Jenkins Roberts. See Letter 1, Roberts to Coates, July 8, 1848.
373. Alexander Crummell. See Letter 28, Coates to Gurley, May 2, 1857.
374. See Letter 131, Crummell to Coates, November 2, 1868.
375. Caldwell, Liberia. See Letter 131, Crummell to Coates, November 2, 1868.
376. Daniel Bashiell Warner. See Letter 10, Coates to McLain, October 11, 1851.

I am glad that Mr Crummell should do honor + justice to DB Warner who is a most excellent man, + made a good president, but Ex President Roberts is I believe equally interested in this good + noble work, and recognizes its importance to Liberia, to Africa, and to the World, as much as any one. .B.C.

❖ 140 ❖

Philadelphia. Jany 16th 1869[377]

William Coppinger Esq:[378]
    My dear Sir.
        I received this morning, a short but very interest-ing letter from Mr Blyden,[379] which I have just handed to Rev^d Dr Schenck to be read at the at the Board, as <u>all</u> will doubtless be interested in reading it. You may take a copy of it, if you wish for the "Repository."[380] I requested Dr Schenck to return it to me, which he promised to do, yet if you wish to retain it for a day to take a copy you may do so. The extract I sent to you yesterday from Crummell's letter,[381] will also probably interest many members of the Board.
Yours very truly
Benj^a: Coates

❖ 141 ❖

Jany 28.th/69

My Dear Coates,
        Thanks for your friendly letter just come. H.M. Schieffelin[382] came in + read it, enquired if you wrote it + remarked it was good + showed state-men like ideas.
        Our Board[383] will have some important measures to attend to—to-morrow + may require an adjourned meeting.

377. ACS Papers 103:194:56.
378. William Coppinger. See Letter 10, Coates to McLain, October 11, 1851.
379. Edward Wilmot Blyden. See Letter 27, Coates to Lugenbeel, October 6, 1856.
380. *The African Repository*. See Letter 23, Coates to Lugenbeel, October 27, 1855.
381. The extract, from Letter 131, Crummell to Coates, November 2, 1868, can be found in Letter 139, Coates to Coppinger, January 15, 1869.
382. Henry M. Schieffelin. See Letter 46, Pinney to Coates, June 16, 1859.
383. Pinney was on the board of the New York Colonization Society.

I write to ask what sort of proposition did [Willis] make to you. Do send me his letter or make an extract of the whole he wrote relating to his land.

I hope you have not offered yet to purchase it + will not, till I have this information.

I have no settled plans for the future. Mr Erdman[384] has not yet replied to the Morristown[385] call + may conclude to go West instead of coming East.

I have a letter from Agnes today. She has had a dreadful cold but is a little better Her heart yearns for N.Y. and its neighborhoods, but she will cheerfully follow "her Albert" any where.

    Yours Truly
       J.B. Pinney[386]

❖ 142 ❖

                    Washington D.C.
                    January 30 1869

Benjamin Coates Esqr
    My dear Sir
        I presume you have had from Rev. Mr [Maleium] an outline at least of the proceedings of the late annual Meeting of the American Colonization Society.[387] Business was hurried through very rapidly; and I can but think that some matters of grand importance to the future of Colonization and of Liberia, did not receive such attention as, in my judgment, their merits seemed to demand. I have reason to believe that certain members of the Board apprehended somewhat of a stormy time, and to avoid which, as appeared to me, some things that would otherwise have been freely discussed were permitted to go over to another year with but a remark or two respecting them. Whether this was wise or not time must determine.

    Mr Maynard[388] M. C. from Tenn. called on me a few evenings ago, and inquired, during our conversation, as to the desirableness of having the

384. Unknown. See also Letter 143, Pinney to Coates, February 4, 1869.
385. Moorestown, New Jersey.
386. John Brooke Pinney. See Letter 8, Coates to McLain, May 16, 1851.
387. The ACS. See Letter 8, Coates to McLain, May 16, 1851.
388. Horace Maynard (August 30, 1814–May 3, 1882) was born in Massachusetts. After graduating from Amherst College in 1838, he became a professor at the University of East Tennessee, where he was admitted to the bar and began practicing law in 1844. In 1853 he ran for

U.S. government represented in Liberia by some prominent colored man of this Country with a view to encourage emigration. I would not of course discourage the proposition; but I confess I am not clearly satisfied as to the favorable results anticipated—if indeed such an appointment could be secured. I must talk with you further on this subject when we meet.

Soon after reaching here I had a conversation with Mr. Seward[389]— indeed he sent to request me to meet him—on the subject of a reciprocity treaty with Liberia. He thought it desirable, and that the U. S. government ought readily to entertain it; but remarked that it would not be advisable to press it just at this time—especially as such a treaty is now before the Senate in respect to the Sandwitch Islands[390]; which he thought would be ratified, and in that case there would be no difficulty in regard to Liberia. Mr Sumner[391]—with whom I dined a few evenings ago, and had a long talk in regard to Liberian matters—concurred in this view. So for the present we must be content to allow matters to remain as they are.

You have heard I presume that I was ignored by Colored Citizens Convention,[392] held in this city a few weeks ago. Quite gratuitous! Gives me no concern whatever.

Congress as a Whig and lost. Four years later he was elected as a Unionist and served six years until becoming attorney general of Tennessee in 1863. Two years later he was reelected to Congress as a member of the Unconditional Unionist Party, and two years later as a Republican, continuing to hold his seat in Congress until 1875. After an unsuccessful attempt to become governor of Tennessee, Maynard served as ambassador to Turkey, and later as U.S. Postmaster General. *Biographical Directory of the American Congress, 1774–1996* (Alexandria, Va.: CQ Staff Directories, 1997), 384.

389. William H. Seward. See Letter 84, Coates to Coppinger, May 24, 1866.

390. The Sandwich Islands are the historic name for Hawaii. The slow process of annexation of Hawaii began in the 1840s, when the United States extended the Monroe Doctrine policy to the islands. Hoping to prevent European powers from ruling Hawaii, the United States encouraged a policy of self rule. After several false starts, a treaty allying the United States and the islands passed in 1876. Seward optimistically believed that the treaty would be passed, but most Americans did not share his interest. Seward and Sumner believed that once the stumbling block of acceptance of an ethnically diverse Hawaii was overcome, U.S. relations with Liberia could be more easily forged. Interestingly, just as U.S. recognition of Liberia before the Civil War had been blocked by Southern politicians who did not want a black diplomat in Washington, D.C., the reciprocity treaty with Hawaii was blocked in 1856 "largely on account of the opposition of Senators Benjamin and Slidell of Louisiana, on the grounds that his free sugar would injure the sugar-growing interests of the Southern States." Chalfant Robinson, *A History of Two Reciprocity Treaties* (New Haven, Conn.: The Tuttle, Morehouse and Taylor Press, 1904), 133; Roger Bell, *Last Among Equals: Hawaiian Statehood and American Politics* (Honolulu: University of Hawaii Press, 1984).

391. Charles Sumner. See Letter 84, Coates to Coppinger, May 24, 1866.

392. Roberts is referring to the Colored Citizens Convention held in Washington, D.C., from January 14 to 18. See Letter 139, Coates to Coppinger, January 15, 1869.

After consulting with Rev. Dr Tracy[393] on the subject, I have concluded to defer the matter of a circular, which you suggested in regard to the College,[394] until I return to [Boston].

I am glad to say the weather here continues fine: so far we have experienced no inconvenience on that score.

Please accept thanks for several news papers, and for the circular of the Pennsylvania Freedmen's Association, you kindly sent to me.

I cannot write more just now. Mrs Roberts unites with me in kindest regards to yourself and sisters, and please remember us to all the family

I remain

My dear sir

Very truly yours

J. J. Roberts

❖ 143 ❖

New York February 4.th/69

Dear Coates

I return Crummells[395] letter having made a copy for my future use.

I have not heard as to Mr Erdmans[396] decision but think he will go to Morristown.[397] I leave my future to be directed by him who leads us day by day. To-morrow! Well each day shall have its duties + strength for them. I leave for Clinton[398] tomorrow [D.V.] shall rest a while at home. Whenever my future course is clear to me you may expect an early letter.

Mr. Schieffelin[399] has a very severe cold, probably taken in waiting on his eldest daughter who has been sick for some time. I have just enough cold in my head to make me too stupid to write, so I finish: with much regard,

Yours J.B. Pinney[400]

393. Joseph Tracy. See Letter 10, Coates to McLain, October 11, 1851.
394. Liberia College. See Letter 29, Coates to Crummell, October 3, 1857.
395. Alexander Crummell. See Letter 28, Coates to Gurley, May 2, 1857.
396. Unknown. See also Letter 141, Pinney to Coates, January 28, 1869.
397. Moorestown, New Jersey.
398. Probably Clinton, New Jersey.
399. Henry M. Shieffelin. See Letter 46, Pinney to Coates, June 16, 1859.
400. John B. Pinney. See Letter 8, Coates to McLain, May 16, 1851.

144

Clarendon[401]

February 7th.

1869

Mr. Coates,

It is with pleasure that I acknowledge your bundle of seeds. I judged that it came from you, before I heard from Mr. Corson.[402] The people are very grateful for them, and I only regret that you cannot, personally, receive their thanks.

Yours Respectfully

Annie Heacock.[403]

[The envelope is addressed to:]

Mr. Benjamin Coates, Freedmen's Rooms, No 127 Market St. ~~711 Sansom St~~, Philadelphia[404]

 145

Washington D.C. 15 Feby.

1869

Benjamin Coates

Philadelphia

Penn

My Dear Sir;

I owe you thanks for several favors you have done me lately in sending me reports of the Pennsylvania Freedman's Relief association,[405] and of the Executive Board and Ladies Board of Managers of the Union Benevolent

401. Clarendon Plantation is on the northwest corner of Port Royal Island, South Carolina.

402. Probably Robert Rodgers Corson. See Letter 133, Coates to Coppinger, November 17, 1868.

403. Annie Heacock, a member of Abington Friends Meeting, went with her sister Gayner to Port Royal to teach in 1863. Their brother John was already the superintendent there, and Heacock remained in South Carolina until 1869 when she returned to Pennsylvania to teach at Friends Central School. Heacock was also active in the women's suffrage movement and served as the secretary of the Pennsylvania Suffrage Society when the organization was founded in 1869. *Friends Intelligencer* 89, no. 3 (1932): 157; Annie Heacock, *Reminiscences* (n.p., April 1926).

404. The *American Freedmen*, the journal of the AFUC, and Gopsill's Philadelphia City Directory for 1869 all list 711 Sansom Street as the address of the Philadelphia branch of the AFUC. Coates Brothers Merchants, the wool business of Benjamin Coates and his brother, George Morrison Coates, was located at 127 Market Street on the north side of Market, between First and Second.

405. The Pennsylvania Freedmen's Relief Association. See Letter 82, Clark to Coates, July 15, 1865.

association,[406] also a copy of the "Press" containing an article you had marked on "the labor Problem".[407] The latter was very interesting to me not merely by reason of its style and sentiments, but because it was sent, and it may be, written by your hand. However the latter may be the fact that it was you who sent it, lends me to infer that your mind has been aroused to a consideration of this, the most interesting, the most urgent, the most complex and the most difficult problem that can be offered to investigations of the human mind.

Every act of man which modifies the rude materials supplied by nature, so as to render them suitable for man's use, is an act of labor, and in this sense of the word,—I believe its full and true one—every man must live by labor, his own, or anothers; hence labor is the primordial temporal destiny of man upon this planet, and if under any circumstances it is avoided or not performed, individual and general discomfort and unhappiness must be the result, as we see it is in our own country, which is however the most favored of all others in so many respects.

The fact that some perform labor under moral or physical compulsion, while others, while others refuse, avoid or neglect it, either from want of energy, untoward circumstances, or the possession of wealth, has created inborn selfishness on the part of the rich and a feeling of meanness amounting to hate on the part of the laborers, which I saw strongly manifested by that class on my recent attendance upon the "Labor reform convention" at Boston, and which I fear exists more generally throughout the country than the rich are disposed to believe. It is a feeling which may become dangerous.

I would be glad if those reflection minds in our country who have turned attention towards the conditions under which labor is performed, and their results upon individuals and society, could unite themselves together for the purpose of studying the principles which must guide all reformatory measure. Such apreciation would, I think, produce good.

    I am

        Yours very truly

        Thos. J Durant.[408]

406. The Union Benevolent Association. See Letter 84, Coates to Coppinger, May 24, 1866.

407. The article, which appeared in *The Press* (Philadelphia) Monday, January 4, 1869, notes that the number of paupers in the United States increased dramatically between 1831 to 1851 and that paupers were a higher percentage of the general population than in Europe. The article also mentions that the rise in immigration to the United States in the same time period does not seem to be connected to the number of poor. While not suggesting a remedy for the problem, the article emphasizes the need to acknowledge it.

408. Thomas Jefferson Durant (August 8, 1817–February 3, 1882), born in Philadelphia, moved to New Orleans at the age of fourteen. There he studied law and was admitted to the bar.

❖ 146 ❖

388 Twelfth Street
Washington D.C.
February 22.1869

Benjamin Coates Esqr.

Dear Sir

Thursday last your friend Thomas J. Durant Esqr.[409] called, as you requested, to hand me the pamphlet—"Hayti and the Mulatto,"[410] by our friend Benjm P Hunt Esqr.[411] I was glad to meet Mr. Durant; and very much enjoyed an hour's conversation with him in regard to matters relating to his experience in New Orleans—and to hear his sanguine opinion respecting the future prospects of the people of color in Louisiana and other Southern States.

I have read Mr. Hunt's pamphlet with a great deal of satisfaction. It indicates much patient research and investigation in regard to the subject of

---

In 1846 he became a U.S. district attorney and a member of the Louisiana State Senate. During the Civil War, Durant, a slaveholder, fought for the Confederate army, but by 1862 he came to support black suffrage. After the Civil War, Louisiana's Reconstruction governor appointed Durant attorney general and commissioner of voter registration. When elections were held in the state under the old state constitution, Durant resigned because he felt the war had nullified the document and that it had to be rewritten. He moved to Washington, D.C., in 1866 and began to practice law. His most famous case in front of the Supreme Court was *Slaughter House* in 1873. In this case, Durant argued that the Fourteenth Amendment only applied to federal rights, not rights given to individuals by the states. The majority decision of the court sided with Durant. Garraty and Carnes, *American National Biography*, vol. 7, 339.

409. Thomas Jefferson Durant. See Letter 145, Durant to Coates, February 15, 1869.

410. *Hayti and the Mulatto* is the cover page title of the pamphlet *Remarks on Hayti as a Place for Settlement for Afric-Americans and on the Mulatto as a Race for the Tropics*. The thirty-six–page document begins with a summary of economic opportunities on the island. Hunt explains that tailors, shoemakers, and bakers are successful in Haiti, while native carpenters fare less well. Hunt goes on to note that there is little industry on the island, too much trade, and not enough agriculture. Although the cost of living in Haiti was lower than in the United States, Hunt discouraged African Americans from emigrating. He cited the lack of freedom of the press, the absence of successful African American emigrants, and the lack of industry as reasons that Haiti is not an ideal location. Hunt did not suggest an alternative to Haiti, but he did express his belief that the tropics will be conquered by a new mulatto race. He dismissed the notion that mulattos are unhealthy and expressed his belief that when white people and black people lived together, prejudice would gradually fade away.

411. Roberts either misremembered Hunt's name or confused him with another Hunt. Benjamin Peter Hunt was actively involved in the efforts to end segregation on the Philadelphia street cars and was the chair of the committee which produced the pamphlet *Report of the Committee Appointed for the Purpose of Securing to Colored People in Philadelphia the Right to the Use of the Street Cars*.

which it treats—as well the history of Hayti as the development of the physical and intellectual capacity of the Mulatto. His opinion, however, that "the final purpose"—if he intend a Divine purpose—"of negro slavery was to furnish the basis of a free population for the tropics of America" is, according to my view entirely too limited: nor do I quite agree with him that the white race and the black race must go together, or meet together within certain latitudes to fulfill the purpose for which the tropics were made. I confess, that I am not yet prepared to admit the theory of an amalgamation of the races to improve the physical powers of one or the intellectual capacity of the other, either within or without the tropics. Climate, doubtless, has much more to do with these developments than the commingling of races. However, I am not disposed to controvert the question. His remark, of <u>1860</u> on the subject of slavery—considered in connexion with subsequent events in the United States—are not only interesting but truly remarkable; and show very conclusively that he had carefully considered the whole subject; and had arrived at conclusions, in regard to the future of the African race, after emancipation, well deserving further careful consideration.

I regret that the fourteenth amendment[412] to the Constitution of the United States is, now, not likely to be adopted by the present Congress; in consequence of amendments by the House to the Senate's propositions which I have reason to believe will not be accepted: and if accepted, would in all probability be defeated by a nonratification of the States.[413]

412. The Fourteenth Amendment consists of five sections. Section 1 states that all persons born in the United States are citizens and cannot be deprived of their rights without due process of the law. Section 2 states that representation in Congress is based on the number of people residing in a state, but when men over the age of twenty-one are denied the right to vote, the number of people requiring representation will be reduced. Section 3 states that no person who rebelled against the United States can hold federal or state office without a two-thirds vote of Congress. Section 4 states that the United States will not pay the Confederate government's debts. Section 5 gives Congress the right to enforce the previous four sections.

413. The ratification process of the Fourteenth Amendment is particularly confusing. In 1866, representatives from the ex-Confederate states were not admitted to Congress. This Congress, composed of Northern, Western, and border states and passed the Fourteenth Amendment in the summer. Then the amendment was sent to the states to be ratified. However, Congress made it a condition that the Southern states had to ratify the amendment before they would be readmitted to the Union. By the summer of 1868, approximately twenty-one states had ratified the amendment. Many Congressmen believed this gave the amendment the required three-fourths vote it needed to be in effect, because many of the Southern states had not been readmitted to the Union at this time. The confusion over the vote total did not arise only from the ambiguous position of the ex-Confederate states. Other states, such as Maine, had been omitted from some lists of the state ratification total while others lists included them. In addition, local elections in Ohio and New Jersey changed the political makeup of the respective state legislatures, and both bodies voted to rescind the ratification of the amendment. To make matters

Mrs Roberts and I keep pretty well—we are wonderfully blessed in having so mild a winter, and are thankful. Should the weather remain open, I think of leaving here in a few days after the inauguration. While in Philadelphia, coming South, Mr John W. Price—the restaurant keeper near Chestnut where we dined together once—intimated that he would be pleased to accommodate me on my return to Philadelphia: Please do me the favor to inquire of him whether he can conveniently accomadate us a week or ten days about the Middle of March.

Mrs Roberts desires to be affectionately remembered to your Sisters, to whom please make my kindest regards—as also to your brother and nephews

And believe me

My dear Sir

Very truly Yours

J. J. Roberts[414]

I am at No. 388—not 338. Mr Durant had quite a walk to find me.

 147 ❖

New York March 6th 1869

My Dear Sir.

Thanks for the article about Whipple + by Whipple.[415] I think it would do a great deal of good to Liberia + Africa, if he could be our National Representative in Liberia, He would be able to see Liberia in all her advantages + faults + if a real lover of his race his letters to friends + correspondents would excite much interest + favour.

<hr />

worse, Georgia had ratified the amendment, but its state legislature's decision to expel black congressmen had caused Congress to revoke its readmission to the Union, leaving many in doubt that Georgia's ratification of the amendment was valid. On July 21, 1868, Secretary of State William Seward proclaimed that thirty of the thirty-seven states had ratified the amendment and that it was now officially part of the Constitution. Within a week, both chambers of Congress voted to accept the state ratification process and declare the Fourteenth Amendment part of the Constitution. The mass confusion over the ratification process of the Fourteenth Amendment led many to question is legitimacy. In the fall of 1868 the state of Oregon revoked its ratification of the amendment to signal protest over the whole process. By the summer of 1869, however, when Roberts wrote his letter to Coates, much of the controversy over the passage of the amendment had calmed. It is therefore unclear why Roberts doubted that the amendment would pass, since technically it had passed six months earlier. Joseph B. James, *The Ratification of the Fourteenth Amendment* (Macon: Mercer University Press, 1984).

414. Joseph Jenkins Roberts. See Letter 1, Roberts to Coates, July 8, 1848.

415. This does not refer to George Whipple.

If however he is very light colored the acclimation might be severe and if fatal his —— death might operate disastrously.

I went to Connecticut last Monday to visit a dying friend. While at Guilford I found a very promising colored man at the Academy. I was very much pleased with him. He is hungry for leaving. Say his only desire is to be of use to his race. I think he had better go to Lincoln College.[416] Mr Tracy[417] thinks he had better go to Liberia College.[418] Wherever educated he needs + deserves aid.

Similar cases will occur often + we could well employ a good fund for preparing them to fill there place in Africas elevation.

The best educated and most solid colored man of our Pres. Ch. in Brooklyn, has had some difference with those around him, I think growing chiefly out of envy.

He was in our office to day + would be glad to be employed in lecturing + raising money for our educational movement. I think if the A.C.S.[419] or its Ex. Com. refuse to have Mr Orcutt leave N.Y. it will result in the separation of our society at the Annual Meeting + the carrying out of your + Malcom[420] ideas. Will Penn[a] unite with us in such a movement?

Yours Truly

J.B. Pinney[421]

❖ 148 ❖

Boston, March 8. 1869

B. Coates Esq

Dear Sir.—I have this morning received the paper you sent me, containing Mr. Whipper's[422] article, for which please accept thanks. Some one had sent me a copy before, and I had been studying what to do about it. I was inclined to write to him; but as he does not know me, and for other reasons, it might not be expedient. Has he our Memorial Volume?[423] Would it be well

416. Lincoln College was originally the Ashmun Institute.
417. Probably Joseph Tracy. See Letter 10, Coates to McLain, October 11, 1851.
418. Liberia College. See Letter 29, Coates to Crummell, October 3, 1857.
419. The ACS. See Letter 8, Coates to McLain, May 16, 1851.
420. Possibly Howard Malcolm. See Letter 9, Coates to Lugenbeel, June 18, 1851.
421. John Brooke Pinney. See Letter 8, Coates to McLain, May 16, 1851.
422. William Whipper. See Letter 35, Wagoner to Coates, January 8, 1859.
423. *Memorial of the semi-centennial anniversary of the American Colonization Society.* See Letter 111, Gurley to Coates, May 8, 1868.

to send him a copy? It might give him some new views of the origin and intent of our society. But as he is all right in respect to the present and the future, perhaps it is not best to disturb his ideas of the past.

In a former letter, you suggested his appointment as U.S. Minister to Liberia. His present article goes to confirm what you said of his fitness.

I understand that he and President Roberts[424] are acquainted Has Roberts seen this article? If so, perhaps he will say all that needs to be said about it.

I suppose that Mr. Whipper is a man of some wealth, and that there are other colored men of wealth in your city and state. It would be a very handsome thing, and would exert an excellent influence, if they would endow a professorship in Liberia College,[425] or even found a few scholarships. Would it be advisable to suggest it to Mr. Whipper, or to some other of them? If so, who should do it? You have such a hold upon their confidence, that you could do it to advantage. Could any body do it better? And if any, who?

—— If the Recorder[426] represents the views of a majority of its patrons, there must be many influential colored persons who feel and think much as Mr. Whipper does. If so, it seems desirable that their views should be embodied practically in some public act such as aiding the College. I say the College, because it needs help just now, and not much can be done for lower schools, till the College furnishes better teachers than can now be found.

Very truly yours,
Joseph Tracy[427]

❖ 149 ❖

Boston, March 10, 1869

B. Coates Esq
    Dear Sir
        Accept thanks for yours of 10 inst. Educating the colored people in giving was one motive for my proposal. White men have to be educated to it by being induced to give, and it makes better men of them. It raises

---

424. Joseph Jenkins Roberts. See Letter 1, Roberts to Coates, July 8, 1848.
425. Liberia College. See Letter 29, Coates to Crummell, October 3, 1857.
426. Probably the *Christian Recorder*, a religious weekly first published by the AME Church and carried extensive information on the situation of black Americans throughout the country from 1861 to 1902.
427. Joseph Tracy. See Letter 10, Coates to McLain, October 11, 1851.

them into a higher rank in the scale of being, the rank of benefactors. Dr. Chalmers[428] was philosophically correct, when he divided all mankind into two classes, givers and receivers, and argued that, by elevating any one from the class of receivers to that of givers, you make a very beneficial change in his character, you invert him with a respectability which he feels bound to maintain, and fill him with thoughts and feelings which increase his power, and enable him to maintain it. So "it is more blessed to give, than to receive."

Circumstances have, to a great extent, placed our colored people in the class of receivers. If they would take hold of the work of giving civilization and Christianity to Africa, they would find in themselves a power which they have never been conscious of; which, indeed, they have never had, and never can have, till they engage in some such great and good work of giving. They need to take hold of something as high above their present position as they can reach, and lift themselves up by it. But enough of this preachment

We are aware of the Avery Fund,[429] and have been for some years endeavoring to obtain some aid from it for the College,[430] but so far without success. It is in the custody of the American Missionary Association[431] ~~Society~~, at New York. Mr. Whipple,[432] one of the secretaries, seems disposed to aid us, and has encouraged us to hope for something, but nothing has come. I think he is over-ruled by others. That society is engaged in extensive and costly operations among our "Freedmen", and is in debt about $90,000. But this ought not to have any influence on their management of the fund for

428. Thomas Chalmers (March 17, 1780–May 31, 1847), an early nineteenth-century religious philosopher, was born in Scotland, where he attended the University of St. Andrews. He was the minister of Kilmeny in Fife in 1803 and held that position until 1815, when he became the minister of a parish in Glasgow. Chalmers then served as minister to St. John's parish from 1820 until he became a professor at St. Andrews. In 1828 Chalmers became the chair of theology at the University of Edinburgh and remained there until 1843. He then became a professor of divinity at the New College of the Free Church. That same year Chalmers was among 470 ministers who joined the Free Church of Scotland. *ANB* 3:358–63.

429. The Avery Fund was established by Charles Avery, a Pittsburgh cotton merchant. In 1849 Avery founded the Avery Institute (later College) for black people in Allegheny, Pennsylvania. In 1858 he gave $150,000 to Christian missionaries in Africa. Money from this fund also was used to found the Avery Normal Institute for black people in Charleston, South Carolina, in 1878. *BAP* 3:337 and 5:178.

430. Tracy is probably referring to Liberia College (see Letter 29, Coates to Crummell, October 3, 1857); he was one of the college's trustees (see Letter 25, Roberts to Coates, May 15, 1856).

431. The AMA. See Letter 116, Whipple to Coates, June 5, 1868.

432. George Whipple. See Letter 116, Whipple to Coates, June 5, 1868.

Africa. Can you touch any spring which will set that machine into the right motion?

Very truly yours
Joseph Tracy[433]

 150 ❖

[Letter 150 was sent to Coates by John Pinney, the original addressee, along with Letter 151, Warner to Pinney, March 13, 1869, and Letter 155, Pinney to Coates, April 19, 1869.]

Monrovia, March 12./69

Rev. John B. Pinney[434]

My dear sir,

Your kind letter dated Jan 24. by "Jasper" has just been received. We are all gratified to hear of your safe arrival. Many a prayer was offered for your safe and prosperous journey across.

I have visited Boporo,[435]—could get no further than eight miles beyond for want of means. I have lectured twice since my return to crowded houses I have condensed my lectures and sent them for publication to Mr. Schieffelin[436]—will you try and urge him to publish them before the May meetings—and send me a copy to arrive here by the middle of June.

Our Presbytery met at Clay-Ashland[437] in December last. We had a harmonious time. The difficulty between myself and Mr. Amos amicably arranged.

A few weeks after Presbytery, while I was at Boporo, Mr. James died. Mr. Amos has been confined to his bed since the adjournment of Presbytery. He is now down the coast for his health, and between Mr. Herring + myself we keep his pulpit supplied in his absence. He speaks of returning to the U.S. to remain if his health gets no better. You know what I think of the physical ability of men of his class. Young Evans, one of our college graduates is also down the coast for his health. He is dropsical—will hardly recover the Doctors think—This young man was for over ten years a beneficiary on your funds. Now is it wise to persist in educating such unhealthy persons at so great

433. Joseph Tracy. See Letter 10, Coates to McLain, October 11, 1851.

434. John Brooke Pinney. See Letter 8, Coates to McLain, May 16, 1851.

435. Boporo, Liberia. See Letter 104, Blyden to Coates, January 11, 1868.

436. Henry M. Schieffelin. See Letter 46, Pinney to Coates, June 16, 1859.

437. A settlement on the St. Paul's river a short way upstream from Monrovia.

expense? Is not this an instance of what is technically called "unproductive expenditure"?—wasteful preparations for a result that will never arrive— planting a tree that is never to bear fruit? Can Liberia afford this? The caste question[438] is dying out. I hear nothing of it now. The ladies have applied to me recently to reorganize for them the Reading Society,[439] which I conducted some years ago—More anon—

Respectfully yrs.

Ed. W. Blyden[440]

P.S. I trust you will do what you can to relieve me of my debts in England, so as to leave my mind free to engage in the labors which are before me. The school has been taken from Mr. Gibson the faithful teacher we saw at Crozerville and given to one [Browne]—now that the Board is given a small salary for teachers. This is unfair to Gibson though he bears it patiently and goes quietly to his farm—I hope you will be able to do something for him. The reward of a self-sacrificing spirit in this world is often ingratitude and persecution.

❖ 151 ❖

[Letter 151 was sent to Coates by John Pinney, the original addressee, along with Letter 150, Blyden to Pinney, March 12, 1869, and Letter 155, Pinney to Coates, April 19, 1869.]

Monrovia, Mar. 13. 1869

Revd Doct Pinney[441]

Dear Sir,

I can do nothing more by this mail than to acknowledge the receipt of your several favours, dated, January 17.th 23^{d} + 25.th and did not know I could do this much before I saw Prof. Blyden,[442] who informed me that the

---

438. Blyden, a man of pure-blooded African descent, harbored an intense dislike for mulattos. This attitude sometimes posed a significant obstacle to his efforts. The men to whom he refers here were probably mulattos, who he believed were less suited for the Liberian climate. Although he tells Pinney here that the problem is "dying out," the presence of mulattos in Liberia's government and other positions of power was to remain an irritating issue for Blyden.

439. Perhaps the Athenaeum Club (see Letter 103, Coates to Crummell, October 14, 1867), which he and Alexander Crummell founded in Monrovia, or the "Book Concern," which Blyden mentions Letter 72, Blyden to Coates, October 9, 1862.

440. Edward Wilmot Blyden. See Letter 27, Coates to Lugenbeel, October 6, 1856.

441. John B. Pinney. See Letter 8, Coates to McLain, May 16, 1851.

442. Edward Wilmot Blyden. See Letter 27, Coates to Lugenbeel, October 6, 1856.

mails would not be closed before 12 O clock to-day. I had closed and mailed all my letters on the 10th.

You have our grateful thanks for your valuable memorials sent us by the "Jasper," which we hope to get and have the pleasure of enjoying as soon as that vessel arrives here from Bassa. Be assured Dear Friend that I shall use my best endeavours to carry out the wishes and intentions of the worthy Donors of the school Books +c +c, sent to my care, by distributing the books among the several counties in such manner as shall seem most likely to secure the object aimed at by those donors.

Doubtless, it will be more satisfactory to yourselves,—it will certainly be to myself—If I would seek and obtain the advice and co-operation of one or two others in carrying forward this benevolent work.

I am glad that ex President Roberts[443] found it to be within the sphere of, and in harmony with, his own views and experiences to be able to corroborate all your important statements made at the Directors Meeting, touching matters and things in Liberia as they appeared to you during your recent visit to this country. Also, I am gratified at the Resolution of the Directors, a copy of which you have so kindly sent to me, and which, should it be deemed best, I shall have inserted in the columns of "The True Whig". It would have been well, had our friends here pretended to as much ignorance of your remarks at Clay Ashland, as our friends in the Colonization office have done respecting that letter which it was said by certain high authorities here, they had received from America in reference to yourself. I have now said about as much as I need—in fact can, say, just now. I am in good health, but Teage[444] is quite sick to-day. I have long since dedicated him to the Lord, and have brought my mind to regard him as already lost to us.

To have let <u>this</u> child get a strong hold upon my affections, would have been to let him cause me to measure my steps back to earth again.

I am, Dear Mr Pinney, as ever

Yours D.B. Warner[445]

---

443. Joseph Jenkins Roberts. See Letter 1, Roberts to Coates, July 8, 1848.

444. This is not Hilary Teage, who died in 1853. Perhaps Warner refers to one of his own children.

445. Daniel Bashiell Warner. See Letter 10, Coates to McLain, October 11, 1851.

� 152 ✧

Boston, March 18, 1869

B. Coates Esq
    Dear Sir
        Mr. Fearing,[446] President of the Trustees of Donations, has just
left me. We have been holding a consultation over your letter of 13 inst.—
which was none too long.

I was not aware that a visit to Pittsburgh could be of any use, supposing that the whole control of the Avery fund[447] was at New York, in the hands
of the American Missionary Association.[448] We agree that, if any thing can be
accomplished by such a visit, it certainly ought to be made. I suppose President Roberts[449] is in Philadelphia by this time, or will be there soon. Please
consult him about visiting Pittsburgh. Avery's will seem to me to give the
Executive Committee of the Association at New York, full power to dispose
of the fund for Africa, principal and interest. It clearly gives them the right
to pay over $50,000, or any other amount, for the endowment of Liberia
College,[450] where they please. If there is no power at Pittsburgh which can
control them, there may be one which can exert an irresistible influence; and
in that case, it would seem that Pittsburgh should be visited first, and the association afterwards. But you probably know, or can easily ascertain, all about it.

As to allowing them to appoint a Trustee, perhaps that matter can
be arranged. The Trustees of the <u>College</u>, you know, are in Liberia. They are
a corporation, created by an act of the legislature of Liberia. Their number is
fixed by law. They fill all vacancies in their own body, except that the President of the Republic appoints one from each county, and they must be from
the several counties in a proportion fixed by law. They have the immediate
management of the College. There is no power in the United States that can
appoint a member of that Board of Trustees; nor can any person not a Liberian be made a member of it, without an act of the Legislature of that Republic. amending the Charter of the College.

The Trustees of Donations for Education in Liberia are also a Corporation, but created by an act of the Legislature of Massachusetts. It has now,
by the Charter of the College, the appointment of the President and Professors;

446. Albert Fearing. See Letter 127, Roberts to Coates, September 28, 1868.
447. The Avery Fund. See Letter 149, Tracy to Coates, March 10, 1869.
448. The AMA. See Letter 116, Whipple to Coates, June 5, 1868.
449. Joseph Jenkins Roberts. See Letter 1, Roberts to Coates, July 8, 1848.
450. Liberia College. See Letter 29, Coates to Crummell, October 3, 1857.

which, however, the Trustees of the College can take from it into their own hands whenever they think fit. By its control of the Donations on which the College depends for its support, it can exert much influence on ~~to~~ its management. But it has never been obliged to resort to that power, as the Trustees of the College have always been disposed to treat its advice with all due respect.

This Board also fills its own vacancies, as provided by its Act of Incorporation. It could not, without a legislative amendment of its charter, authorize any other body to appoint any of its members; but it is not limited by law, in respect to the number of its members, or their residence. But as the law requires a majority to be present at any meeting, to form a quorum for the transaction of business, it is obviously most convenient to have a small number, residing in the same vicinity. The present number, fixed by the Bylaws, is seven, all residing in Boston and Cambridge. Some years ago we selected three excellent men in New York, to be added to the seven; but they all were unwilling to be members of a Board of Trustees, whose meetings they could not usually attend.

Among the seven members, one is a member of the Advisory Committee of the American Missionary Association. At least, he has been, and I suppose is still. Among the Nine Presidents of that Association are several residing in Massachusetts, all of them, so far as I know, men with whom the present Trustees would like to be associated. We should be glad to elect members from New York, and from Philadelphia, if we could get over the difficulty about a quorum. Business requires us to meet quarterly, and sometimes oftener.

You see just how the matter is about Trustees. I think any thing reasonable can be done, to the satisfaction of all reasonable men.

Please let me know when President Roberts arrives and oblige

> Yours, very truly
> Joseph Tracy[451]

❖ 153 ❖

Clinton[452]

Mar 26th '69

Dear Mr Coates -

Your <u>good</u> letter came a few moments ago and Mother wishes me to answer it in Fathers[453] absence. He has gone to Nebraska on an exploring expedition and is to decide the "fatal question" while there. How much both

451. Joseph Tracy. See Letter 10, Coates to McLain, October 11, 1851.
452. Probably Clinton, New Jersey.
453. Probably John Brooke Pinney. See Letter 8, Coates to McLain, May 16, 1851.

Mother and I wish your kind letter could have reached here before his departure! It is too hard for us to think of going way off there Mr Coates and what is more I don't believe Father would be satisfied there more than one year if he was that long. The life he would lead there is so entirely opposite to that he has led so many years that it would never content him. Then too if Colonization should ever revive or he should think there was a chance for him to do anything in the cause, off he would come and leave Mother alone in a strange land. It would be just like him. But I don't worry for him; for he has been knocking about from place to place so long he would scarcely feel it. It is Mother that I am most troubled about. She is only just recovering from a severe attack of her rheumatism and is only able to sit up part of a day. It seems more than cruel after working as she has done to take her at her time of life, to a new place and start life over again. And it is not only the work I dread for her (though I think she would not stand that but a short time) it is more the breaking up of old associations and going such a distance from all her relations, especially her parents who are very feeble and old. The very thought of going there helped greatly to bring on her rheumatism and retards her recovery <u>very</u> much. This climate is too severe for her I know + Father says that, but there are warmer places much nearer home that she would love dearly to go to especially near Phila. Then too Father says he has hardly <u>money enough</u> to <u>get</u> us <u>out there</u>. Can you explain if that is the case, <u>how</u> he can stock a farm and build a house &c! He says he will <u>build a barn for the cattle and a mud house for us</u>!! Isn't that like him? How could Mother live in a house without plastering or carpets? as he threatens we will have to! I don't understand his visions of a "farmers paradise" or his enthusiasm on the subject, especially under his pecuniary disadvantages. I hope to be married in the ~~spring~~ fall Mr Coates and so will be one out of his way, provided he can furnish me a new dress for the occasion. The children are another <u>strong</u> objection to his going out there. Ella would finish school in another year and <u>wants</u> to <u>teach</u>. Fanny would finish in two years and is so attractive that I don't think she would burden him long. Then there is Bernie—Ought he to go west and spend the best part of his life on an experimental farm! HE could soon go into business and earn his board as he is bright enough. I fear Mr Coates you will tire of this long harangue, but I indeed I cannot stop when on the subject, if talking to a true friend as you are. Mother has often said "O if I only could see Mr Coates." Hoping I have not troubled you too much

   believe me
     Yours truly
     Annie F. Pinney

❖ 154 ❖

WOOL[454]
COATES BROTHERS
127 Market Street
PHILADELPHIA, March 27th 1869

W[m]. Coppinger Esq.[455]
     Dear Sir
                         at the request of Ex Pre[d] Roberts[456] I enclose here-
with check to your order for $5.9[5]
               Yours very truly
                    B Coates

❖ 155 ❖

New York April 19th 1869
My Dear Coates
     Your letter to me at Clinton[457] did my poor wife much good as it
exactly expressed her feelings. Still she is not well + I left her in bed last Friday when I came down to the city. Her sickness is the severest she has had
since we lived in Philadelphia. I think when warm weather comes she will get
better, but never well.
     Our Board meets Tuesday, so I have come down to see what they
would have me do.
     The lands in Nebraska are very rich + if I was over there in a a cabin
("hollow tree" + liberty") I should feel like a prince, now I am a beggar, +
bound.
     I enclose E.B.[458] + D.W.[459] letters[460] just received. Poor Blyden—got
in debt £100 in England for Arabic Sanscrit +c +c Books.
     No Drunkard ever had a more uncontrollable thirst for ~~Book~~ Rum
than B has of books.

454. ACS Papers 103:194:283. The first four lines constitute the Coates brothers' printed
letterhead, with the exception of the month, day, and last digit of the year.
     455. William Coppinger. See Letter 10, Coates to McLain, October 11, 1851.
     456. Joseph Jenkins Roberts. See Letter 1, Roberts to Coates, July 8, 1848.
     457. Probably Clinton, New Jersey.
     458. Edward Wilmot Blyden. See Letter 27, Coates to Lugenbeel, October 6, 1856.
     459. Daniel Bashiell Warner. See Letter 10, Coates to McLain, October 11, 1851.
     460. See Letter 150, Blyden to Pinney, March 12, 1869; and Letter 151, Warner to
Pinney, March 13, 1869.

I shall make an attempt to-morrow to get our friends here to devote $250 or half the sum to his relief, but have some doubts whether their indignation that he gets in debt will not overpower their pity for his embarrassment.

This letter is the most encouraging I have received from him, as it shows a calming of the color controversy + that he is again reconciled to his Brother Presbytery Amos. I think Edward has learned the bitterness of debt so that if aided now he would avoid future involvement.

Mr J.T. Smith called in this morning to show me a letter from Mr Horn stating that the Clinton mine was sold for taxes. Those taxes were due last Autumn and while I was in Africa. I have to day written to Mr. J.S. Slanson to enquire about it + whether the mine can be redeemed. It will be sad if the mine is lost.

> Yours
> J.B. Pinney[461]

❖ 156 ❖

4 mo. 29th. 1869. -

My dear friend,

> Benjamin Coates,

Thy very acceptable note referring to a variety of subjects in which we are mutually interested came duly to hand,—I have not had the opportunity of becoming acquainted with their friend Charles Hartshorne but I feel sure that any one whom those can commend so highly must be a good man for a manager in a board like that of the Institute and I for one should be glad to have him appointed in the place of C.Y.-

As regards the meeting held on 3rd Day evg. I fully unite with what thou says, and I was both glad and surprised that we could unite with so much harmony upon the plan adopted. During the progress of the discussion I thought, if only I could whisper to J.S. Hilles[462] and others that the minute adopted gave all the authority that even he could wish and that the wording of it to which they objected, had no peculiar significance but nevertheless made it much more acceptable to such men as Dr. Evans, A.C. Wood etc.

It was a matter in which we were obliged to move as though walking barefoot over eggs;—and though our action was rather informal and

---

461. John Brooke Pinney. See Letter 8, Coates to McLain, May 16, 1851.
462. See Hilles, *Memorials of the Hilles Family.*

unparliamentary, and the minute necessarily very vague and general in its wording, I was glad that the meeting could <u>unite</u> upon any course.

Affectionately
thy friend
<u>John E. Carter</u>

I think it very important that the Institute Com. should take early action in the matter of E D Bassett[463] etc.

❖ 157 ❖

WOOL[464]
COATES BROTHERS
127 Market Street
PHILADELPHIA July 1st 1869

Wm Coppinger Esq[465]
My dear Sir

Your favor of Yesterday is just received. In reply I would say, cert<u>ainl</u>y, by all means have <u>both</u> pamphlets <s>copies</s> <u>leaded</u> like that of Ex President Roberts[466] or <u>better if possible</u>. I want it got up in the <u>best style</u> <u>regardless</u> of the expense, but you suggested in former letter that it would be leaded. I am quite willing however that the publisher, or printer, should be <u>paid</u> a <u>full</u> + <u>fair</u> price for his work, but I want it <u>leaded</u>, on good paper, + as attractive in style as is usual with the <u>best</u> productions of this kind. I have made an alteration as you will see, enclosed [page break] in the last paragraph to the <u>Note</u> which I think makes the meaning clearer, but you may make any change in wording, or in punctuation that you may think necessary, or desirable after seeing it in print. It will not be necessary to send it to me again. Use your own good judgment, + I will be satisfied. You will see the point I wished to make, that while asking for the rights and opportunities for the black man in America, I want the <u>black man here</u> to <u>see</u> to <u>how much</u> his brethren in Liberia, under their own <u>nationality</u> (their own free Republic) <s>is</s> are already in advance of them.

463. Ebenezer Don Carlos Bassett. See Letter 121, Coates to Coppinger, August 5, 1868.

464. ACS Papers 104:196:1. The first four lines constitute the Coates brothers' printed letterhead, with the exception of the month, date, and last two digits of the year.

465. William Coppinger. See Letter 10, Coates to McLain, October 11, 1851.

466. Joseph Jenkins Roberts. See Letter 1, Roberts to Coates, July 8, 1848.

Teage[467] was a pure Negro. So I have always considered him, + so I believe he always considered himself. I knew him well <u>personally</u> and altho' he [page break] was not <u>quite</u> so <u>black</u> as either Benson, Crummell, or Blyden,[468] yet I believe he was of pure African extraction. a totally different looking man from President Roberts. he was <u>much darker</u> than Basset, + darker than most of the black men I know. So was his father Colin Teage. I have seen them both and if they were not both Negros I should be very much at a loss to know who are. I have no <u>hesitation whatever</u> in the absence of proof to the contrary, in saying that Hilary Teage was a <u>pure</u>, <u>full blooded</u> <u>Negro</u>, and that the negro race have a right to the benefit of this <u>fact</u> and this information, for he was a very superior man. superior to either Crummell or Blyden, or Benson, or Warner, or Fred. Douglass, or Saml Ward, or Henry Highland Garnett,[469] or any other black man in America. [page break] of course I do not claim Fred. Douglass as a black man. I must name him as one of the most notable + distinguished <u>colored men</u>.

Please have <u>both</u> <u>pamphlets</u> printed in the <u>very best</u> manner. <u>150 of Each seperately</u> + <u>100</u> of <u>Each</u> <u>together</u> in <u>one</u> <u>cover</u>, <u>without</u> <u>regard to the cost</u>. Since I have undertaken to do it I want to do it well.

Yours very truly

Benj^a Coates

WOOL[470]

COATES BROTHERS

127 Market Street

PHILADELPHIA Septr. 20th 1871

W^m. Coppinger Esq.[471]

Colonization Rooms, Wash.

My dear Sir

I received a letter from you, while at Conway N.H. this summer that was forwarded from Philad^a, requesting me

467. Hilary Teage. See Letter 10, Coates to McLain, October 11, 1851.
468. Stephen Allen Benson (see Letter 8, Coates to McLain, May 16, 1851); Alexander Crummell (see Letter 28, Coates to Gurley, May 2, 1857); and Edward Wilmot Blyden (see Letter 27, Coates to Lugenbeel, October 6, 1856).
469. Daniel Bashiell Warner (see Letter 10, Coates to McLain, October 11, 1851); Frederick Douglass; Samuel Ringgold Ward; and Henry Highland Garnet (see Letter 3, Coates to Douglass, June 27, 1850).
470. ACS Papers 108:204:218. The first four lines constitute the Coates brothers' printed letterhead, with the exception of the month, date, and last digit of the year.

to forward to EW Blyden,[472] at London, or to yourself, I forget which a number of copies of his pamphlet[473] containing his address, "The Negro in Ancient History," + "Liberia, its Past, Present, + Future." I felt very doubtful whether I had any on hand, and if so was pretty sure that no one could find them but myself. I returned a few days since from my summer sojourn among [page break] the mountains, + in ransacking among my books + pamphlets find about ten copies of each say 10 of "Negro in Ancient History," + 10 of "Liberia its Past, Present, + Future." if they will be of any service to Mr Blyden in the cause, I shall be pleased to forward them to yourself, or to Mr Blyden's address, wherever he may be. I suppose they had better go by mail.

Please let me know if you wish them. If you think I had better send them to Mr Blyden in England,[474] give me his address, + the best way of sending them. I see it suggested that Mr B Should locate at Timbuctoo,[475] or at some of the large towns of the interior of Africa among the Mohamedans. this seems to be his mission, + in that, may do much good, Sincerely yours,

Benj Coates

I will very willingly pay any expenses on the pamphlets if sent to you, or myself, or would contribute a portion of the expenses if Mr B. and yourself think either or both them should be republished in England.   B.C.

This mission work of Mr Blyden is to my mind a very interesting + important one.

471. William Coppinger. See Letter 10, Coates to McLain, October 11, 1851.

472. Edward Wilmot Blyden. See Letter 27, Coates to Lugenbeel, October 6, 1856.

473. The two addresses were published under the title *The Negro in Ancient History* (Washington, D.C.: M'Gill and Witherow, 1869).

474. After Blyden was forced to flee from Liberia in May 1871, he went first to Sierra Leone and then to England. He remained in England until August, when he returned to Sierra Leone, having been hired as a linguist by the CMS. He was soon removed from this post, however, because of rumors of adultery that had resulted in his expulsion from Liberia three months earlier. Instead he spent the first part of 1872 exploring the interior of Sierra Leone in the hope that he could forge a relationship between Sierra Leone and the tribes in the hinterland. Lynch, *Edward Wilmot Blyden*, 87–92.

475. Timbuktu. Its nineteenth-century spelling was not as standardized as it would become, so various writers spelled it any of several ways, including "Tombouctou."

❖ 159 ❖

WOOL[476]
COATES BROTHERS
127 Market Street
PHILADELPHIA Octr. 7th 1871

William Coppinger Esq[477]

My dear Sir

I enclose herewith Adams' Express Compy's rect for a package for you of pamphlets + African cotton, as you requested, trusting that you may be able to use them to advantage. I am glad to learn that you have so good a company of Emigrants for the next expedition. I trust that Blyden[478] may do well in his new position,[479] if he is not guilty of the charges against him it is a great outrage. if he is guilty he is a much worse man than I took him to be. They write to me from N.Y. to get them a man for the Arthington School[480] to fill his place, which I fear will be difficult to accomplish.

Yours very truly

Benj Coates.

476. ACS Papers 109:205:35. The first four lines constitute the Coates brothers' printed letterhead, with the exception of the month, date, and last digit of the year.

477. William Coppinger. See Letter 10, Coates to McLain, October 11, 1851.

478. Edward Wilmot Blyden. See Letter 27, Coates to Lugenbeel, October 6, 1856.

479. Coates is probably referring to the recent appointment of Blyden to the position of linguist in Sierra Leone for the CMS. However, on November 16, 1856, Blyden was suspended from this position because of the lingering rumor that he had had an affair with Ex-President Edward Roye's wife. Lynch, *Edward Wilmot Blyden*, 88–89.

480. Robert Arthington, a Quaker cotton manufacturer, pledged to aid Blyden in establishing a preparatory school at Vonswah, a native town in the interior of Liberia. Blyden gave up his position at Liberia College to devote his attention to this school, but before his work could begin he was expelled from Liberia. The New York Colonization Society also had a part in supporting this school. Lynch, *Edward Wilmot Blyden*, 48; Livingston, *Education and Race*, 79–80.

❖ 160 ❖

WOOL[481]
COATES BROTHERS
127 Market Street
Philadelphia April 11th 1873

Revd Alexr Crummell[482]

> Dear Sir

I duly received your favor of 24th February saying you had delivered to Revd George Whipple,[483] Twenty five copies of "Future of Africa"[484] on my account with rect from Mr. Whipple for the same, and would have remitted to you at once, but I thought it probable that Mr Whipple would need more of them to enable him to fully carry out my views. And I think it probable that he will require more yet. But I had a letter from him today saying you needed the money requesting me to remit it to you, which I hasten to do, and herewith enclose check to your order for twenty five dollars- $25. in payment of same. If Mr W. thinks he can use a <u>few more</u> to advantage please furnish them to him, + oblige.

> Yours very truly
> Benjamin Coates.

481. Courtesy HSP. The first four lines constitute the Coates brothers' printed letter-head, with the exception of the month, day, and last digit of the year.
482. Alexander Crummell. See Letter 28, Coates to Gurley, May 2, 1857.
483. George Whipple. See Letter 116, Whipple to Coates, June 5, 1868.
484. Alexander Crummell, *The Future of Africa*. See Letter 64, Coates to Crummell, January 13, 1862.

WOOL

COATES BROTHERS

127 Market Street

PHILADELPHIA *April 11th* 1873

Rev d Alex Crummell

Dear Sir

I duly received Your favor of 24th February saying You had delivered to Rev George Whipple, Twenty five Copies of Future of Africa, on my account with view from Mr Whipple for the same. And Would have remitted to You at once — but I thought it probable that Mr Whipple would need more of them to enable him to fully carry out my views. And I think it probable that he will require more. Yet But I had a letter from him to day saying You needed the money, & requesting me to send it to You — which I hasten to do, and herewith enclose Check to You order for twenty five dollars — $25. in payment of Same. If Mr W. thinks he can use a few more to advantage please furnish them to him — & oblige

Yours very truly Benjamin Coates.

Letter 160, Coates to Crummell, April 11, 1873

❊ 161 ❊

American Missionary Association[485]
56 Reade St., New York.

Rev. G.D. Pike[486], Dist Sec.

New York, <u>April 8</u>th 1880

Mr. Benj. Coates
    Philadelphia Pa.
    My Dear Brother
        Your very welcome letter reached me this day. Please accept our most grateful acknowledgments.- We have now $1650. of the $5000.[487] needful, pledged; and if responses come in as promptly for the next fortnight as they have for the last, we shall be able to give out the contract for finishing the three lower stories, during this month.
        Very truly Yours
        G.D. Pike

485. Printed on AMA letterhead, with a list of officers omitted here. See Letter 116, Whipple to Coates, June 5, 1868.

486. Reverend Gustavus D. Pike, D.D. (1831–1885), a Congregationalist pastor from 1862 to 1867, became a land purchase agent for the AMA as part of its program to provide free black people with homesteads. He held the position of district secretary of that organization from 1870 to his death. He became known as a local expert on Africa, even though he not traveled there extensively. He was also editor of the *American Missionary*, the journal of the AMA, and contributed several articles to it. "Death of Rev. G.D. Pike, D.D.," *American Missionary* 39, no. 3 (March 1885): 68–69; DeBoer, *His Truth is Marching On*, 105.

487. Coates contributed to the AMA on more than one occasion, and he left the association $500 when he died. It seems likely that Pike is referring to a $100 donation Coates made in January 1880 towards the establishment of the Tillotson Collegiate and Normal Institute in Austin, Texas. Tillotson was the AMA's first school in Texas and was originally founded to train teachers who would then be able to educate the black community. Land for the institute was provided by Rev. George J. Tillotson in 1876, and the first class entered after the completion of the college's first building in January 1881. It was for the construction of this building that Pike and other members of the AMA were raising money. William E. Brooks, "Tillotson Normal and Collegiate Institute," *American Missionary* 35, no. 6 (June 1881): 161–62; "Receipts," *American Missionary*, 1878, 1880, 1887; "Tillotson Collegiate and Normal Institute, Austin, Texas," *American Missionary* 34, no. 2 (February 1880): 35–36.

❖ 162 ❖

[This note is written on a postcard and addressed to "Benj Coates, Phila. Box 121." The postmark is September 29.]

Dear Friend

Your favor was rec^d yesterday Accept my thanks and the gratitude of the dear oppressed people who will receive its benefits

We will use it to the best of our judgment and notify you soon.

Perhaps the Society will grant us the books. Dr Rhodes will do something I hope.

Resptfly S.B [Darnell? Dannell?]

Jacksonville Florida

Benjamin Coates's will, originally created in 1872, was amended four times in 1874, once in 1878, and again in 1880. The original will and its amendments are separated by asterisks.

In view of the changes made by time since my last will was made on Jany 20ᵗʰ 1870 I desire to make some changes of the bequests ~~heretofore~~ made, <u>then</u> and therefore hereby revoke, and cancel all wills heretofore made by me, and to leave this, as my last Will and Testament.

    After the payment of all my debts and obligations, except two notes of Ten thousand dollars <u>each</u>, given to ~~my~~ each of my three sisters, viz Beulah Coates $20.000, Mary Coates $20.000 & Sarah H Coates $20.000, In lieu of which, I hereby give, and bequeathe to my sister Beulah Coates the sum of twenty thousand dollars, ($20.000.) To my sister Mary Coates the sum of Twenty thousand dollars, ($20.000.) and to my sister Sarah H Coates the sum of Twenty thousand dollars, ($20.000), to <u>them</u> or <u>their heirs and assigns</u>, also to my brother George Morrison Coates the sum of ten thousand dollars ($10.000.) to his heirs and assigns. To my nephew Henry T. Coates the sum of ten thousand dollars (say $10.000.) to his heirs + assigns, and to my ~~five~~ four nephews, viz William M Coates, and Joseph H Coates, George M Coates Jr + Edward H Coates, the sum of Five thousand dollars <u>each</u>, their heirs or assigns, that is to say to William $5.000. to Joseph $5.000. sone of my brother Geo. Morrison Coates, and to George M Coates Jr $5.000. + to Edward H. $5.000. (son of my deceased brother Joseph P H Coates their heirs and assigns. [page break] I give and bequeathe to my —— —— —— the sum of $5000., say <u>Five thousand dollars</u>. To my cousin John W Hornor, I give + bequeathe one thousand dollars say $1.000. to him or his heirs + Assigns, and to his four daughters the sum of one thousand dollars <u>each</u> viz to

Jane W Hornor $1000. to Ellen W. Hornor $1000., to Rasalie $1.000, and to Cornelia $1.000, their heirs + assigns, + to his son Jnº West Hornor five hundred dollars, say $400, + to Benj Hornor $1000. To Anne Pickering, Mary Paxson, Alice Pickering, + Charles W Pickering Five hundred dollars <u>each</u> say $500, <u>Each</u>. To Benjamin Coates Potts I devise + bequeathe the sum of one thousand dollars -($1000) and to his brother Jos. Collins Potts the sum of five hundred dollars-($500.) or his heirs + assigns. I give and bequeathe to "The Union Benevolent Assⁿ" of this city the sum of Two thousand dollars-($2.000) for the purchase of stoves to be loaned to the poor, and to "The Institute for Colored Youth" of this city I give + bequeathe the sum of two thousand dollars -($2,000.)- To Sarah M Douglass I give + bequeathe one hundred dollars. To the Trustees of Donations for Liberia College of which Jos. J Roberts is President + Revᵈ Joseph Tracy of Boston Mass. is Secy, or agent of the Board, I give and bequeathe the sum of one thousand dollars -$1.000- I also give + bequeathe <u>(one thousand dollars)</u> for general educational purposes in Liberia through my friend Joseph J Roberts and Daniel B Warner, if living, or either of them, or if both should be deceased, to be expended at the discretion of my executors for educational or missionary purposes in Africa. I give and bequeathe to "The Bible + Tract Distributing Socy" [page break] of which I am a member, the sum of Two thousand dollars-$2.000.

I also give + bequeathe to my sister Beulah to be expended by her, at her discretion within three years after my death, the sum of three thousand dollars-($3000.) for charitable purposes, either to the destitute poor, or to Institutions for their aid + relief. The balance and residue of my property I wish divided into five equal parts, which I give, devise, and bequeathe as follows. To my sister Beulah Coates, I give, devise + bequeathe one equal fifth part. To my sister Mary Coates, I give, devise + bequeathe one equal fifth part. To my sister Sarah H Coates, I give, devise + bequeathe one equal fifth part. To my brother Geo. Morrison Coates, I give, devise + bequeathe one equal fifth part. And the other fifth part I wish should be divided equally between my sister Eliza H. Coates widower of my deceased brother Joseph P. H Coates, and her two sons George M Coates Jr. and Edward H Coates, each to have <u>one third of the fifth part</u> of the residue of my property, which would have been devised to my brother Joseph P H Coates had he been now living.

And to carry out + execute the foregoing Will and Testament, I hereby appoint my sister Beulah Coates, and my brother Geo. Morrison Coates as my executors. Or in case of the death of the latter before the execution of this <u>will</u>, then I wish my three nephews, viz Henry T Coates, George M Coates Junior and William M Coates or the survivor or survivors of them to act in [page break] the premises and execute <u>this will</u> in accordance with the views here expressed. And for the services so rendered in execution, they shall receive <u>one thousand dollars each, no more, and no less.</u>

In ~~the~~ case of the decease of my brother George Morrison Coates before the execution of this Will, I devise that the portion devised to him shall go his wife and children, say <u>one third</u> to the <u>former</u>, and <u>two thirds</u> to the <u>latter</u>. The said <u>two thirds</u> to be equally divided between his three sons, Henry, William, and Joseph. And in case of the decease of either of my three sisters, Beulah, Mary, + Sarah, before the execution of this Will, then the portion that has been devised to said deceased sister shall be <u>equally divided</u> between the other <u>two surviving</u>. Or in case of the decease of two of my sisters before the will is executed one half shall go to the remaining sisters, + the other half, to the other residuary legatees, or in the case of the decease of <u>all these</u> before the execution of this will then I wish their portions should ~~go~~ be divided between the other residuary legatees <u>Unless</u>, said sisters shall have made Will, or Wills devising and bequeathing the same themselves. Which I <u>would much prefer they should do</u>. I wish that the amount devised to my sisters should be (as <u>soon as practicable</u>) <u>invested for them, and in their name</u>, in good stocks or real estate, or such good + safe securities as may be <u>approved by them</u>.

This my last Will + Testament made this 16th day of <u>December 1872</u>, One thousand eight hundred and seventy two [is] supercede all other wills by me made

Witness Present   Benj Coates   [seal]
Geo. M. Coates Jr.
    O. J. Nice
    <u>Philadelphia Decr 16th 1872</u>
[Written vertically on the left side of the last page:]
<u>Note</u> or <u>codicil</u> to the foregoing - Any + all additions of words omitted [are] made at the present writing, this 16th of Decr 1872 [on] part + parcel of this will + to be of full effect including the sum of $1000. say One thousand dollars bequeathed to Benjamin Hornor, son of Jos P. Hornor.   Signed this Decr 16, 1872
    Benj Coates

Philad^a Jany 13th 1874
Being desirous of making some changes in my last Will made the 16th of Decr 1872, in regard to the apportionment to my ~~sisters~~, Brother and

Nephews I make this as a supplement or codicil thereto, hereby <u>ratifying</u> and <u>confirming</u> all those portions not indicated in the present changes of amount willed + bequeathed to nephews, brother + Sisters.

I will + bequeathed to my sister Beulah Coates the amt stated in my will of $20.000, to Mary Coates $20.000, + to Sarah H Coates $20.000, making in this regard no change from my last will. I give + bequeathe to my brother Geo. Morrison Coates the sum of $<u>15.000</u> in lieu of the amt named in my will and to my five nephews, <u>instead</u> of the amount named in my will I now give and bequeathe the sum of $<u>15.000</u> <u>Each</u>. that is to say the sum to my sisters remains the <u>same</u>, while the amounts [page break] now given to my nephews and to my brother are increased and now stand as follows. To

Beulah Coates	$20.000
Mary Coates	$20.000
Sarah H Coates	$20.000
Geo. Morrison Coates	$15.000
Henry T Coates	$15.000
George M Coates Jr.	$15.000
William M Coates	$15.000
Edward H Coates	$15.000
Joseph H. Coates	$15.000
Making a total of ————	$150.000.

The other bequests in my will of Dec 1872 both to relatives or friends as well as to Charitable + Benevolent Institutions, are hereby approved + confirmed, with the appropriations + divisions of the residuary estate, after foregoing changes are made, are to remain as directed in my will of <u>Decr 16.</u> <u>1872</u>   Benjamin Coates

Signed in presence of
Mary Coates   Jany 14th 1874
Sarah H Coates

❖ ❖ ❖

I also bequeathe to my great nieces Hetty M Coates, daughter of William M Coates, + <u>Bessie</u> ——— Eliza H Coates, Jr, daughter of George M Coates, Jr. the sum of one hundred dollars, Each, say $<u>100</u>. Ea. to be invested for them by their parents until they severally reach the age of <u>18 years</u>.   Benj Coates
       Jany 14, 1874

❖ ❖ ❖

Also to the <u>first</u> child of Henry T. Coates, Ed. H Coates, +
Joseph H Coates the sum of $<u>100</u>. Ea
Jany 14, 1874   B. Coates
Witness
 Sarah H Coates
 Mary Coates

In the foregoing Codicil my <u>intention</u> <u>was</u>, and <u>now is</u>, to make the bequests
to my sisters, brother and nephews severally, to themselves, or in case of their
death to their heirs, and assigns
Signed this 24th day of Jany 1874   Benj^a Coates
in presence of Mary Coates
            Sarah H Coates

Philad^a June 4th 1874

      Second
            —— <u>Codicil</u> to my Last Will made in 1872.
To My Executors,
            Since making a Codicil in January last (1874) to my last Will
made in 1872 my property has somewhat increased in amt. I desire therefore
to make some changes in the sums bequeathed to my brother G.M.C. + my
five nephews, viz.
To my brother Geo. Morrison Coates I now give + bequeathe the sum of
$20.000 instead of the amt named in the codicil of my will of $15.000 and the
same change of amounts to <u>Each</u> of my five nephews. Instead of the amt of
$<u>15.000</u> therein named, I give + bequeathe to <u>each</u>, the sum of $20.000. That
is to say Twenty thousand dollars
          to George Morrison Coates ---$20.000
          " George M Coates Jr--------$20.000
          " William M Coates ---------$20.000
          " Edward H. Coates ---------$20.000
          " Joseph H Coates -----------$20.000
[page break] The amount to my sisters to remain the same, as in last Will +
Codicil, and I hereby confirm all the other bequests made in said last will, and
codicil thereto. The amount to my brother, sisters and nephews to stand thus.
          Geo. Morrison Coates --------$20.000.
          Beulah Coates ---------------$20.000.

Mary Coates------------------$20.000.
Sarah H Coates--------------$20.000.
Henry T Coates -------------$20.000.
George M Coates Jr.---------$20.000.
William M Coates-----------$20.000.
Edward H Coates -----------$20.000.
Joseph H Coates-------------$20.000.
Making a total of --------------------$180.000
given to my brother, sisters + nephews, besides their respective <u>shares</u> of the
<u>residuary</u> estate as provided for in my Will, to them, their heirs + assigns.
Witness present | Benj^a Coates
Geo. A. Haas |
Wm M [Gate] June 4th 1874

It was my <u>intention</u> at the time of making my <u>Will</u> and the several
Codicils <u>thereto,</u> and is still my wish, that my Executors shall <u>in all cases</u> pay
over the <u>full amounts,</u> <u>donated</u> and <u>bequeathed,</u> <u>without</u> <u>deducting</u> the [col-
lateral] inheritance tax. Leaving the balance of the estate to pay that.
                    Benjamin Coates
June 4th 1874

                                        March 4th 1878
I hereby authorize my executors to give or dispose of five thousand dollars to
such persons or purposes as they may think best before the distribution of my
property, leaving it entirely on their opinion.
                    Benjamin Coates
Witnesses present
Mary Coates
Sarah H Coates

In my will I have left to my great nieces Hettie M Coates and Bessie
Coates and to my great nephew George M Coates the sum of One hundred
dollars each, as a little remembrance of their uncle. I wish also to give the
same ($100) to each of my other great nephews and great nieces who shall be
living at the time of my death.

To Andrew McBride, my faithful attendant for the past four years (or nearly), I give the sum of Five hundred dollars

For James M. Curry, who has been with me two years and is also faithful and attentive I give the sum of three hundred dollars.

[written at the bottom of the page:] (over) [page break]

To Nancy Stewart and Mary Jane Smylie I give One hundred dollars each.

If however James M Curry, Nancy Stewart, or Mary Jane Smylie should not be living with us at the time of my death I leave it to the discretion of my sisters to give them the money or not.

Benjamin Coates

Philad^a April 6th 1880

Witness

    Sarah H Coates

APPENDIX 2: CATALOG OF LETTERS

This appendix is split into three sections: a complete chronological listing of the letters contained in this volume, a list of letters sent to Benjamin Coates, and a list of letters written by Benjamin Coates. Each entry contains the letter number, sender and/or recipient information, and the date.

COMPLETE CHRONOLOGICAL LISTING

1. Antebellum Years, 1848–1860

1. Roberts to Coates, July 8, 1848
2. Coates to McLain, June 23, 1850
3. Coates to Douglass, June 27, 1850
4. Douglass to Coates, June 27, 1850
5. Coates to McLain, July 9, 1850
6. Coates to McLain, September 5, 1850
   contains a copy of Roberts to Coates, July 18, 1850
7. Coates to Douglass, January 16, 1851
8. Coates to McLain, May 16, 1851
9. Coates to Lugenbeel, June 18, 1851
10. Coates to McLain, October 11, 1851
11. Coates to Lugenbeel, November 6, 1851
12. Coates to McLain, January 10, 1852
13. Bethune to Coates, January 10, 1852
14. Coates to McLain, February 28, 1852
15. Coates to Lugenbeel, June 27, 1853
16. Roberts to Coates, May 26, 1854

17. Coates to McLain, June 8, 1854
18. Roberts to Coates, August 26 and October 9, 1854 (combined)
19. Roberts to Coates, October 16, 1854
20. Coates to Lugenbeel, May 3, 1855
21. Coates to McLain, May 22, 1855
22. Coates to Gurley, June 15, 1855
23. Coates to Lugenbeel, October 27, 1855
24. Coates to Lugenbeel, November 17, 1855
25. Roberts to Coates, May 15, 1856
26. Coates to Lugenbeel, September 29, 1856
27. Coates to Lugenbeel, October 6, 1856
28. Coates to Gurley, May 2, 1857
29. Coates to Crummell, October 3, 1857
30. Coates to McLain, December 19, 1857
31. Coates to McLain, March 2, 1858
32. Coates to Gurley, May 28, 1858
33. Coates to Gurley, October 21, 1858
34. Cary to Coates, November 20, 1858
35. Wagoner to Coates, January 8, 1859
36. Coates to Gurley, January 13, 1859
37. Wagoner to Coates, January 31, 1859
38. Pinney to Coates, February 9, 1859
39. Whipper to Coates, February 24, 1859
40. Hobbins to Coates, March 2, 1859
41. Garnet to Coates, April 27, 1859
42. Douglass to Coates, May 2, 1859
43. Wagoner to Coates, May 27, 1859
44. Harris to Coates, June 7, 1859
45. Bibb Cary to Coates, June 14, 1859
46. J. B. Pinney to Coates, June 16, 1859
47. Campbell to Coates, July 14, 1859
48. Garnet to Coates, July 17, 1859
49. Morris to Coates, August 8, 1859
50. Garnet to Coates, August 17, 1859
51. Benson to Coates, August 22, 1859
52. Smith to Coates, August 27, 1859
53. Freeman to Coates, August 29, 1859
54. [Harper?] to Coates, September 6, 1859
55. Morris to Coates, September 8, 1859

56. Garnet to Coates, September 9, 1859
57. Holly to Coates, September 13, 1859
58. Morris to Coates, September 15, 1859
59. Hamilton to Coates, September 19, 1859
60. J. B. Pinney to Coates, September 28, 1859
61. Tucker to Coates, October 12, 1859
62. Smith to Coates, December 27, 1859
63. Prince to Coates, September 6, 1860

2. *Civil War Years, 1862–1865*

64. Coates to Crummell, January 13, 1862
65. Coates to Crummell, February 3, 1862
66. Coates to Crummell, February 20, 1862
67. Mitchell to Coates, April 8, 1862
68. Chase to Coates, April 10, 1862
69. Coates to Crummell, April 14, 1862
70. Kelley to [Coates], April 24, 1862
71. [L. R. M. Say?] to Coates, October 6, 1862
72. Blyden to Coates, October 9, 1862
73. Blyden to Coates, October 15, 1862
74. Coates to Gurley, February 10, 1863
75. Allen to Coates, April 23, 1863
76. Coates to McLain, April 7, 1864
77. Coates to Coppinger, October 13, 1864
78. Coates to Coppinger, November 1, 1864
79. Plummer to Coates, January 28, 1865
80. Coates to Coppinger, February 6, 1865
81. Stearns to Coates, February 13, 1865
82. Clark to Coates, July 15, 1865
83. Coates to Coppinger, October 31, 1865

3. *Reconstruction Years, 1866–1880*

84. Coates to Coppinger, May 24, 1866
85. Coates to Coppinger, May 26, 1866
86. Coates to Coppinger, June 1, 1866
87. Coates to Coppinger, June 6, 1866
88. Young to Coates, July 25, 1866
   contains two newspaper articles

89. Young to Coates, July 31, 1866
    contains one newspaper article
90. Tomlinson to Coates, March 29, 1867
91. Welsh to Coates, April 1, 1867
92. Coates to Coppinger, April 6, 1867
93. Coates to [Coppinger], April 7, 1867
94. Rhoads to Coates, May 17, 1867
95. McKim to Coates, May 24, 1867
96. McKim to Coates, June 4, 1867
97. Rhoads to Coates, June 28, 1867
98. Hartshorne to Coates, July 18, 1867
99. Hilles to Coates, August 15, 1867
100. Evans to Coates, August 27, 1867
101. Cope to Coates, October 11, 1867
102. Coates to [Cope], [October?] 1867
103. Coates to Crummell, October 14, 1867
104. Blyden to Coates, January 11, 1868
105. Blyden to Coates, January 23, 1868
106. Hilles to Coates, February 25, 1868
107. Schofield to Coates, March 12, 1868
108. Varner to Coates, March 17, 1868
109. Gurley and Gurley to Coates, April 7, 1868
110. Johnson to Coates, April 20, 1868
111. Gurley to Coates, May 8, 1868
    contains text of address given by Dr. Smith
112. Coates to Coppinger, May 20, 1868
113. Ketchum to Coates, May 22, 1868
114. Johnson to Coates, May 23, 1868
115. Johnson to Coates, May 30, 1868
116. Whipple to Coates, June 5, 1868
117. Coppinger to Coates, June 30, 1868
118. Coppinger to Coates, July 22, 1868
119. Yates and Porterfield to Coates, July 30, 1868
120. Pinney to Coates, August 4, 1868
121. Coates to Coppinger, August 5, 1868
122. Bassett to Coates, August 12, 1868
123. Whipple to Coates, August 27, 1868
124. Roberts to Coates, September 18, 1868

125. Coates to Coppinger, September 26, 1868
126. Coppinger to Coates, September 28, 1868
127. Roberts to Coates, September 28, 1868
128. Tracy to Coates, September 30, 1868
129. Blyden to Coates, October 10, 1868
130. Carter to Coates, October 21, 1868
131. Crummell to Coates, November 2, 1868
132. Coates to Coppinger, November 17, 1868
133. Coates to Coppinger, November 17, 1868
134. Coates to Coppinger, November 21, 1868
135. Coates to Coppinger, November 28, 1868
136. Coppinger to Coates, November 30, 1868
137. Coates to Coppinger, January 8, 1869
138. Coates to Coppinger, January 12, 1869
139. Coates to Coppinger, January 15, 1869
140. Coates to Coppinger, January 16, 1869
141. Pinney to Coates, January 28, 1869
142. Roberts to Coates, January 30, 1869
143. Pinney to Coates, February 4, 1869
144. Heacock to Coates, February 7, 1869
145. Durant to Coates, February 15, 1869
146. Roberts to Coates, February 22, 1869
147. Pinney to Coates, March 6, 1869
148. Tracy to Coates, March 8, 1869
149. Tracy to Coates, March 10, 1869
150. Blyden to Pinney, March 12, 1869
151. Warner to Pinney, March 13, 1869
152. Tracy to Coates, March 18, 1869
153. Pinney to Coates, March 26, 1869
154. Coates to Coppinger, March 27, 1869
155. Pinney to Coates, April 19, 1869
156. Carter to Coates, April 29, 1869
157. Coates to Coppinger, July 1, 1869
158. Coates to Coppinger, September 20, 1871
159. Coates to Coppinger, October 7, 1871
160. Coates to Crummell, April 11, 1873
161. Pike to Coates, April 8, 1880
162. [Darnell?] to Coates, n.d.

LETTERS TO BENJAMIN COATES

1. Antebellum Years, 1848–1860

1. Roberts, July 8, 1848
4. Douglass, June 27, 1850
13. Bethune, January 10, 1852
16. Roberts, May 26, 1854
18. Roberts, August 26 and October 9, 1854 (combined)
19. Roberts, October 16, 1854
25. Roberts, May 15, 1856
34. Cary, November 20, 1858
35. Wagoner, January 8, 1859
37. Wagoner, January 31, 1859
38. Pinney, February 9, 1859
39. Whipper, February 24, 1859
40. Hobbins, March 2, 1859
41. Garnet, April 27, 1859
42. Douglass, May 2, 1859
43. Wagoner, May 27, 1859
44. Harris, June 7, 1859
45. Bibb Cary, June 14, 1859
46. Pinney, June 16, 1859
47. Campbell, July 14, 1859
48. Garnet, July 17, 1859
49. Morris, August 8, 1859
50. Garnet, August 17, 1859
51. Benson, August 22, 1859
52. Smith, August 27, 1859
53. Freeman, August 29, 1859
54. R. A. H. [Robert A. Harper?], September 6, 1859
55. Morris, September 8, 1859
56. Garnet, September 9, 1859
57. Holly, September 13, 1859
58. Morris, September 15, 1859
59. Hamilton, September 19, 1859
60. Pinney, September 28, 1859
61. Tucker, October 12, 1859
62. Smith, December 27, 1859
63. Prince, September 6, 1860

2. Civil War Years, 1862–1865

67. Mitchell, April 8, 1862
68. Chase, April 10, 1862
71. [L. R. M. Say?], October 6, 1862
72. Blyden, October 9, 1862
73. Blyden, October 15, 1862
75. Allen, April 23, 1863
79. Plummer, January 28, 1865
81. Stearns, February 13, 1865
82. Clark, July 15, 1865

3. Reconstruction Years, 1866–1880

88. Young, July 25, 1866
89. Young, July 31, 1866
90. Tomlinson, March 29, 1867
91. Welsh, April 1, 1867
94. Rhoads, May 17, 1867
95. McKim, May 24, 1867
96. McKim, June 4, 1867
97. Rhoads, June 28, 1867
98. Hartshorne, July 18, 1867
99. Hilles, August 15, 1867
100. Evans, August 27, 1867
101. Cope, October 11, 1867
104. Blyden, January 11, 1868
105. Blyden, January 23, 1868
106. Hilles, February 25, 1868
107. Schofield, March 12, 1868
108. Varner, March 17, 1868
109. Gurley and Gurley, April 7, 1868
110. Johnson, April 20, 1868
111. Gurley, May 8, 1868
113. Ketchum, May 22, 1868
114. Johnson, May 23, 1868
115. Johnson, May 30, 1868
116. Whipple, June 5, 1868
117. Coppinger, June 30, 1868
118. Coppinger, July 22, 1868

119. Yates and Porterfield, July 30, 1868
120. Pinney, August 4, 1868
122. Bassett, August 12, 1868
123. Whipple, August 27, 1868
124. Roberts, September 18, 1868
126. Coppinger, September 28, 1868
127. Roberts, September 28, 1868
128. Tracy, September 30, 1868
129. Blyden, October 10, 1868
130. Carter, October 21, 1868
131. Crummell, November 2, 1868
136. Coppinger, November 30, 1868
141. Pinney, January 28, 1869
142. Roberts, January 30, 1869
143. Pinney, February 4, 1869
144. Heacock, February 7, 1869
145. Durant, February 15, 1869
146. Roberts, February 22, 1869
147. Pinney, March 6, 1869
148. Tracy, March 8, 1869
149. Tracy, March 10, 1869
152. Tracy, March 18, 1869
153. Pinney, March 26, 1869
155. Pinney, April 19, 1869
156. Carter, April 29, 1869
161. Pike, April 8, 1880
162. [Darnell?], n.d.

LETTERS FROM COATES

1. Antebellum Years, 1848–1860

2. McLain, June 23, 1850
3. Douglass, June 27, 1850
5. McLain, July 9, 1850
6. McLain, September 5, 1850
7. Douglass, January 16, 1851
8. McLain, May 16, 1851

9. Lugenbeel, June 18, 1851
10. McLain, October 11, 1851
11. Lugenbeel, November 6, 1851
12. McLain, January 10, 1852
14. McLain, February 28, 1852
15. Lugenbeel, June 27, 1853
17. McLain, June 8, 1854
20. Lugenbeel, May 3, 1855
21. McLain, May 22, 1855
22. Gurley, June 15, 1855
23. Lugenbeel, October 27, 1855
24. Lugenbeel, November 17, 1855
26. Lugenbeel, September 29, 1856
27. Lugenbeel, October 6, 1856
28. Gurley, May 2, 1857
29. Crummell, October 3, 1857
30. McLain, December 19, 1857
31. McLain, March 2, 1858
32. Gurley, May 28, 1858
33. Gurley, October 21, 1858
36. Gurley, January 13, 1859

2. *Civil War Years, 1862–1865*

64. Crummell, January 13, 1862
65. Crummell, February 3, 1862
66. Crummell, February 20, 1862
69. Crummell, April 14, 1862
74. Gurley, February 10, 1863
76. McLain, April 7, 1864
77. Coppinger, October 13, 1864
78. Coppinger, November 1, 1864
80. Coppinger, February 6, 1865
83. Coppinger, October 31, 1865

3. *Reconstruction Years, 1866–1880*

84. Coppinger, May 24, 1866
85. Coppinger, May 26, 1866

86. Coppinger, June 1, 1866

87. Coppinger, June 6, 1866

92. Coppinger, April 6, 1867

93. [Coppinger], April 7, 1867

102. [Cope], [October?] 1867

103. Crummell, October 14, 1867

112. Coppinger, May 20, 1868

121. Coppinger, August 5, 1868

125. Coppinger, September 26, 1868

132. Coppinger, November 17, 1868

133. Coppinger, November 17, 1868

134. Coppinger, November 21, 1868

135. Coppinger, November 28, 1868

137. Coppinger, January 8, 1869

138. Coppinger, January 12, 1869

139. Coppinger, January 15, 1869

140. Coppinger, January 16, 1869

154. Coppinger, March 27, 1869

157. Coppinger, July 1, 1869

158. Coppinger, September 20, 1871

159. Coppinger, October 7, 1871

160. Crummell, April 11, 1873

BIBLIOGRAPHY

ARTICLES AND THESES

Bacon, Margaret Hope. "The Heritage of Anthony Benezet: Philadelphia Quakers and Black Education." In *For Emancipation and Education: Some Black and Quaker Efforts, 1680–1900*, ed. Eliza Cope Harrison. Germantown, Pa.: Awbury Arboretum Association, 1997.

———. "The Motts and the Purvises: A Study in Interracial Friendship." *Quaker History* 92, no. 2 (Fall 2003): 1–18.

Blackett, Richard. "Martin R. Delany and Robert Campbell: Black Americans in Search of an African Colony." *Journal of Negro History* 62, no. 1 (1977): 1–25.

Davis, David Brion. "The Emergence of Immediatism in British and American Antislavery Thought." *Mississippi Valley Historical Review* 49, no. 2 (September 1962): 209–30.

Frost, J. William. "Years of Crisis and Separation: Philadelphia Yearly Meeting, 1790–1860." In *Friends in the Delaware Valley*, ed. John M. Moore, 57–102. Haverford, Pa.: Friends Historical Association, 1981.

Harris, Robert L., Jr. "H. Ford Douglas: Afro-American Antislavery Emigrationist." *Journal of Negro History* 62, no. 3 (July 1977): 217–34.

Jaquette, Henrietta Stratton. "Friends' Association of Philadelphia for the Aid and Elevation of the Freedmen." *Bulletin of Friends Historical Association* 46, no. 2 (Autumn 1957): 67–83.

Landry, Harral E. "Slavery and the Slave Trade in Atlantic Diplomacy, 1850–1861." *Journal of Southern History* 27, no. 2 (May 1961): 184–207.

Lapsansky, Emma J. "'Since They Got Those Separate Churches': African Americans and Racism in Jacksonian Philadelphia." In *African Americans in Pennsylvania: Shifting Historical Perspectives*, ed. Joe William Trotter Jr. and Eric Ledell Smith, 93–120. University Park: Pennsylvania State University Press, 1996.

Leavitt, Judith Walzer. "A Note on Medical Education in Wisconsin." In *Wisconsin Medicine: Historical Perspectives*, ed. Ronald L. Numbers and Judith Walzer Leavitt, 186–87. Madison: University of Wisconsin Press, 1981.

Lindhorst, Maria J. "Sarah Mapps Douglass: The Emergence of an African American Educator/Activist in Nineteenth Century Philadelphia." (Ph.D. diss., Pennsylvania State University, 1995).

Loveland, Anne C. "Evangelicalism and 'Immediate Emancipation' in American Anti-slavery Thought." *Journal of Southern History* 32, no. 2 (May 1966): 172–88.

MacMaster, Richard. "Henry Highland Garnet and the African Civilization Society." *Journal of Presbyterian History* 48, no. 2 (Summer 1970): 95–112.

Merlinger, Louis R. "The Attitude of the Free Negro Toward African Colonization." *Journal of Negro History* 1, no. 3 (June 1916): 276–301.

Morton, Richard L. "'Contraband' and Quakers in the Virginia Peninsula, 1862–1869." *Virginia Magazine of History and Biography* 61, no. 4 (October 1953): 419–29.

Murray, Alexander L. "The Provincial Freeman: A New Source for the History of the Negro in Canada and the United States." *Journal of Negro History* 44, no. 2 (April 1959): 123–35.

Omu, Fred I. A. "The Anglo-African, 1863–65." *Nigeria Magazine* no. 90 (September 1966): 206–12.

Perkins, Linda Marie. "Fanny Jackson Coppin and the Institute for Colored Youth: A Model of Nineteenth Century Black Female Educational and Community Leadership, 1837–1902." Ph.D. diss., University of Illinois, 1978.

Pitts, Reginald H. "Let Us Desert This Friendless Place: George Moses Horton in Philadelphia, 1866." *Journal of Negro History* 80, no. 4 (Autumn 1995): 145–56.

Qualls, Youra. "'Successors of Woolman and Benezet': The Beginnings of the Philadelphia Friends Freedmen's Association." *Bulletin of Friends Historical Association* 45, no. 2 (Autumn 1956): 82–104.

Risse, Guenter B. "From Horse and Buggy to Automobile and Telephone: Medical Practice in Wisconsin, 1848–1894." In *Wisconsin Medicine: Historical Perspectives*, ed. Ronald L. Numbers and Judith Walzer Leavitt. Madison: University of Wisconsin Press, 1981.

Schor, Joel. "The Rivalry Between Frederick Douglass and Henry Highland Garnet." *Journal of Negro History* 64, no. 1 (Winter 1979): 30–38.

Silcox, Harry C. "Nineteenth Century Philadelphia Black Militant: Octavius V. Catto. (1839–1871)." *Pennsylvania History* 44, no. 1 (January 1977): 53–76.

Smith, Ann Bustill. "The Bustill Family." *Journal of Negro History* 10, no. 4 (1925): 638–44.

"Tillotson Collegiate and Normal Institute, Austin, Texas." *American Missionary* 34, no. 2 (February 1880): 35–36.

"Tracy, Joseph." In *Appleton's Cyclopaedia of American Biography*, ed. James Grant Wilson and John Fiske, vol. 6, 152. New York: D. Appleton and Company, 1889.

"Treaty of Kanagawa." In *Japan: An Illustrated Encyclopedia*, ed. Edwin O. Reischauer, vol. 1, 732. Tokyo: Dodansha, 1993.

Westcott, Timothy C. "'No Message but Peace': The Utopian and Abolitionist Encounters of John Otis Wattles." Unpublished article, June 2004.

Wiggins, Rosalind Cobb. "Paul and Stephen, Unlikely Friends." *Quaker History* 90, no. 1 (Spring 2001): 8–27.

Wilson, James Grant, ed. *Appleton's Cyclopaedia of American Biography*, 10 vols. New York: D. Appleton, 1887–1924.

Wish, Harvey. "The Revival of the African Slave Trade in the United States, 1856–1860." *Mississippi Valley Historical Review* 28, no. 4 (March 1941): 569–88.

BOOKS

Bacon, Margaret Hope. *The History of the Pennsylvania Society for Promoting the Abolition of Slavery; the Relief of Negroes Unlawfully Held in Bondage; and for Improving the Condition of the African Race.* Philadelphia: Pennsylvania Abolition Society, 1959.

———. *Valiant Friend: The Life Of Lucretia Mott.* New York: Walker, 1980.

Barbour, Hugh, and J. William Frost. *The Quakers.* Richmond, Ind.: Friends Union Press, 1988.

Barbour, Hugh, Christopher Densmore, Elizabeth H. Moger, Nancy C. Sorel, Alson D. Van Wagner, and Arthur J. Worrall, eds. *Quaker Crosscurrents: Three Hundred Years of Friends in New York Yearly Meetings.* Syracuse: Syracuse University Press, 1995.

Bell, Howard H. *Search for a Place: Black Separatism and Africa, 1860, M. R. Delany and Robert Campbell.* Ann Arbor: University of Michigan Press, 1969.

———. *A Survey of the Negro Convention Movement, 1830–1861.* New York: Arno Press and the New York Times, 1969.

Bell, Roger. *Last Among Equals: Hawaiian Statehood and American Politics.* Honolulu: University of Hawaii Press, 1984.

Benjamin, Philip S. *The Philadelphia Quakers in the Industrial Age, 1865–1920.* Philadelphia: Temple University Press, 1976.

Bentley, George R. *A History of the Freedmen's Bureau.* Philadelphia: University of Pennsylvania Press, 1955.

Beyan, Amos J. *The American Colonization Society and the Creation of the Liberian State.* Lanham, Md.: University Press of America, 1991.

Biographical Catalog of the Matriculates of Haverford College, 1833–1922. Philadelphia: Haverford College Alumni Association, 1922.

Biographical Directory of the American Congress, 1774–1996. Alexandria, Va.: CQ Staff Directories, 1997.

Biographical Encyclopedia of Pennsylvania in the Nineteenth Century. Philadelphia: Galaxy Publishing Company, 1874.

Blackett, R. J. M. *Building an Anti-Slavery Wall: Black Americans in the Atlantic Abolitionist Movement, 1830–1860.* Baton Rouge: Louisiana State University Press, 1983.

Bloom, Robert Louis. *The Philadelphia North American: A History, 1839–1925.* New York: n.p., 1952.

Blue, Frederick J. *Charles Sumner and the Conscience of the North.* Arlington Heights, Ill.: Harlan Davidson, 1994.

Bronner, Edwin. "A Time of Change." In *Friends in the Delaware Valley, 1681–1981,* ed. John M. Moore, 103–137. Haverford, Pa.: Friends Historical Association, 1981.

Brown, Thomas, ed. *American Eras: Civil War and Reconstruction.* Detroit: Gale, 1997.

Bullock, Penelope L. *The Afro-American Periodical Press, 1838–1909.* Baton Rouge: Louisiana State University Press, 1981.

Butchart, Ronald E. *Northern Schools, Southern Blacks, and Reconstruction: Freedmen's Education, 1862–1875.* Westport, Conn.: Greenwood Press, 1980.

Campbell, Penelope. *Maryland in Africa: The Maryland State Colonization Society, 1831–1857.* Urbana: University of Illinois Press, 1971.

The Civil War Dictionary, ed. Mark Mayo Boatner III. New York: David McKay Company, 1988.

The Columbia Encyclopedia. Ed. William Bridgewater and Elizabeth J. Sherwood. New York: Columbia University Press, 1950.

Conyers, Charlene Howard. *A Living Legend: The History of Cheyney University, 1837–1951*. Cheyney, Pa.: Cheyney University Press, 1990.

Crouthamel, James L. *James Watson Webb: A Biography*. Middletown, Conn.: Wesleyan University Press, 1969.

Curtin, Philip D. *The Image of Africa: British Ideas and Action, 1780–1850*. Madison: University of Wisconsin Press, 1964

Dabbs, Edith M. *Sea Island Diary: A History of St. Helena Island*. Spartanburg, S.C.: Reprint Company, 1983.

Danky, James P., ed. *African-American Newspapers and Periodicals: A National Bibliography*. Cambridge: Harvard University Press, 1998.

Dean, David M. *Defender of the Race: James Theodore Holly, Black Nationalist Bishop*. Boston: Lambeth Press, 1978.

DeBoer, Clara Merrit. *His Truth is Marching On: African Americans Who Taught the Freedmen for the American Missionary Association 1861–1877*. New York: Garland Publishing, 1995.

Delpar, Helen, ed. *The Discoverers: An Encyclopedia of Explorers and Exploration*. New York: McGraw-Hill Book Company, 1980.

Dillon, Merton L. *Benjamin Lundy and the Struggle for Negro Freedom*. Urbana: University of Illinois Press, 1966.

Directory of the American Congress, 1774–1996. Alexandria, Va.: CQ Staff Directories, 1997.

Drake, Thomas E. *Quakers and Slavery in America*. New Haven: Yale University Press, 1950.

Drago, Edmund L. *Initiative, Paternalism, and Race Relations: Charleston's Avery Normal Institute*. Athens: University of Georgia Press, 1990.

———. *Hurrah for Hampton: Black Red Shirts in South Carolina During Reconstruction*. Fayetteville: University of Arkansas Press, 1998.

Dunn, D. Elwood, and Svend E. Holsoe, eds. *Historical Dictionary of Liberia*. Metuchen, N.J.: Scarecrow Press, 1985.

Dyson, Walter. *Howard University: The Capstone of Negro Education: A History: 1867–1940*. Washington, D.C.: Graduate School, Howard University, 1941.

Fitzhugh, George. *Cannibals all! or, Slaves Without Masters*. Ed. C. Vann Woodward. Cambridge: Belknap Press, 1960.

Foner, Philip S. *History of Black Americans: From the Compromise of 1850 to the End of the Civil War*. Westport, Conn.: Greenwood Press, 1983.

———, ed. *The Life and Writings of Frederick Douglass*, 5 vols. New York: International Publishers, 1950.

———. *Lift Every Voice: African American Oratory, 1787–1900*. Tuscaloosa: University of Alabama Press, 1998.

Foner, Philip, and George E. Walker, eds. *Proceedings of the Black National and State Conventions, 1865–1900*. Philadelphia: Temple University Press, 1986.

Foray, Cyril P., ed. *Historical Dictionary of Sierra Leone*. Metuchen, N.J.: Scarecrow Press, 1985.

Forde, Daryll. *The Yoruba-Speaking Peoples of South-Western Nigeria.* London: International African Institute, 1969.

Frost, J. William. *The Quaker Family in Colonial America.* New York: St. Martin's Press, 1973.

Gailey, Harry A., ed., *Historical Dictionary of the Gambia.* Metuchen, N.J.: Scarecrow Press, 1987.

Garraty, John A., and Mark C. Carnes, eds. *Dictionary of American National Biography,* 24 vols. New York: Oxford University Press, 1999.

Giesberg, Judith Ann. *Civil War Sisterhood.* Boston: Northeastern University Press, 2000.

Gifford, William Logan Rodman. *George Howland, Junior.* New Bedford, Mass.: privately printed, 1892.

Gilpin, Drew. *The Ideology of Slavery: Proslavery Thought in the Antebellum South, 1830–1860.* Baton Rouge: Louisiana State University Press, 1981.

Goodman, Paul. *Of One Blood: Abolitionism and the Origins of Racial Equality.* Berkeley and Los Angeles: University of California Press, 1998.

Gradwohl, David M., and Nancy M. Osborn. *Exploring Buried Buxton: Archaeology of an Abandoned Iowa Coal Mining Town with a Large Black Population.* Ames: Iowa State University Press, 1984.

Greenwood, Janette Thomas. *Bittersweet Legacy: The Black and White "Better Classes" in Charlotte, 1850–1910.* Chapel Hill: University of North Carolina Press, 1994.

Griffin, Farah J., and Cheryl J. Fish, eds. *A Stranger in the Village: Two Centuries of African-American Travel Writing.* Boston: Beacon Press, 1998.

Groves, C. P. *The Planting of Christianity in Africa,* vol. 2. London: Lutterworth Press, 1954.

Gummere, William F. *Old Penn Charter.* Philadelphia: William Penn Charter School, 1973.

Haggerty, Richard, ed. *Dominican Republic and Haiti: Country Studies.* Washington, D.C.: Federal Research Division, Library of Congress, 1991.

Hamm, Thomas D. *God's Government Begun: The Society for Universal Inquiry and Reform, 1842–1846.* Bloomington: Indiana University Press, 1995.

Harrison, Eliza Cope. *The Diary of Thomas P. Cope, 1800–1851.* South Bend, Ind.: Gateway Editions, 1978.

———, ed. *For Emancipation and Education: Some Black and Quaker Efforts 1680–1900.* Philadelphia: Awbury Arboretum Association, 1997.

Heller, Charles E. *Portrait of an Abolitionist: A Biography of George Luther Stearns, 1809–1867.* Westport, Conn.: Greenwood Press, 1996.

Henries, A. Doris Banks. *The Life of Joseph Jenkins Roberts (1809–1876) and His Inaugural Address.* London: Macmillan and Company, 1964.

Henson, Hensley. *Robertson of Brighton: 1816–1853.* London: Smith, Elder, 1916.

Holdsworth, John Thom. *Financing an Empire: History of Banking in Pennsylvania,* 4 vols. Chicago: S. J. Clarke Publishing, 1928.

Howard, Oliver Otis. *Autobiography of Oliver Otis Howard, Major General, United States Army.* New York: Baker and Taylor, 1908.

Hutton, Frankie. *The Early Black Press in America, 1827 to 1860.* Westport, Conn.: Greenwood Press, 1993.

Ingle, H. Larry. *Quakers in Conflict: The Hicksite Reformation*. Knoxville: University of Tennessee Press, 1986.

James, Joseph B. *The Ratification of the Fourteenth Amendment*. Macon: Mercer University Press, 1984.

Johnson, Ludwell H. *Division and Reunion: America 1848–1877*. New York: John Wiley and Sons, 1978.

Jones, Rufus Matthew. *Eli and Sybil Jones: Their Life and Work*. Philadelphia: Porter and Coates, 1889.

Jordan, John W., ed. *Colonial Families of Philadelphia*. Chicago: Lewis Publishing, 1911.

Katz, William L., ed. *The Anglo-African Magazine, vol. 1, vol. 2, #1–3, January 1859–March 1860* (reprint, New York: Arno Press, 1968.

Kinshasa, Kwando M. *Emigration vs. Assimilation: The Debate in the African American Press, 1827–1861*. Jefferson, N.C.: McFarland and Company, 1988.

Krapf-Askari, Eva. *Yoruba Towns and Cities*. Oxford: Clarendon Press, 1969.

Lane, Roger. *William Dorsey's Philadelphia and Ours: On the Past and Future of the Black City in America*. New York: Oxford University Press, 1991.

Liebenow, J. Gus. *Liberia: The Quest for Democracy*. Bloomington: Indiana University Press, 1987.

Lief, Alfred. *Family Business: A Century in the Life and Business of Strawbridge and Clothier*. New York: McGraw-Hill Book Company, 1968.

Lindhorst, Maria J. "Sarah Mapps Douglass: The Emergence of an African American Educator/Activist in Nineteenth Century Philadelphia." Ph.D. diss., Pennsylvania State University, 1995.

Livingston, Thomas W. *Education and Race: A Biography of Edward Wilmot Blyden*. San Francisco: Glendessary Press, 1975.

Logan, Rayford W. *Howard University: The First Hundred Years, 1867–1967*. New York: New York University Press, 1969.

Logan, Rayford W., and Michael R. Winston, eds. *Dictionary of American Negro Biography*. New York: W. W. Norton and Company, 1982.

Lynch, Hollis R. *Edward Wilmot Blyden, Pan-Negro Patriot, 1832–1912*. New York: Oxford University Press, 1967.

———, ed. *Selected Letters of Edward Wilmot Blyden*. Millwood, N.Y.: KTO Press, 1978.

Mayer, Henry. *All on Fire: William Lloyd Garrison and the Abolition of Slavery*. New York: St. Martin's Press, 1998.

McFarland, Daniel Miles, ed., *Historical Dictionary of Ghana*. Metuchen, N.J.: Scarecrow Press, 1985.

McFeely, William S. *Frederick Douglass*. New York: W. W. Norton and Company, 1991.

McPherson, James. *The Negro's Civil War: How American Negroes Felt and Acted During the War For the Union*. New York: Pantheon Books, 1965.

Meigs, Cornelia. *What Makes a College? A History of Bryn Mawr*. New York: Macmillan Company, 1956.

Merrill, Walter. *Against Wind and Tide: A Biography of William Lloyd Garrison*. Cambridge: Harvard University Press, 1963.

Miller, Floyd J. *The Search for a Black Nationality: Black Emigration and Colonization, 1787–1863*. Urbana: University of Illinois Press, 1975.

Morris, Richard, ed. *Encyclopedia of American History*. New York: Harper and Row, 1970.

Morris, Robert C. *Reading, 'Riting, and Reconstruction*. Chicago: University of Chicago Press, 1976.

Moses, Wilson Jeremiah. *Alexander Crummell: A Study of Civilization and Discontent*. New York: Oxford University Press, 1989.

Murray, Jocelyn. *Proclaim the Good News: A Short History of the Church Missionary Society*. London: Hodder and Stoughton, 1985.

Nash, Gary B. *Forging Freedom: The Formation of Philadelphia's Black Community, 1720–1840*. Cambridge: Harvard University Press, 1988.

Nelson, Harold D., ed. *Liberia: A Country History*, 3rd ed. Washington, D.C., Department of the Army, 1985.

Nesbit, William. "Four Months in Liberia: Or, African Colonization Exposed." 1855. Reprinted in *Liberian Dreams: Back-to-Africa Narratives from the 1850s*, ed. Wilson Jeremiah Moses, 79–126. University Park: Pennsylvania State University Press, 1998.

Nevins, Allan. *The Evening Post: A Century of Journalism*. New York: Boni and Liveright, 1922.

Nuermberger, Ruth Ketring. *The Free Produce Movement: A Quaker Protest Against Slavery*. Durham: Duke University Press, 1942.

Oldfield, J. R. *Alexander Crummell (1819–1898) and the Creation of an African-American Church in Liberia*. New York: Edwin Mellen Press, 1990.

Oyewole, A., ed., *Historical Dictionary of Nigeria*. Metuchen, N.J.: Scarecrow Press, 1987.

Parker, Franklin. *George Peabody: A Biography*, rev. ed. Nashville: Vanderbilt University Press, 1995.

Pease, Zephaniah W., ed. *The Diary of Samuel Rodman: A New Bedford Chronicle of Thirty-Seven Years, 1821–1859*. New Bedford, Mass.: Reynolds Printing, 1927.

Pride, Armistead S., and Clint C. Wilson II. *A History of the Black Press*. Washington, D.C.: Howard University Press, 1997.

Quarles, Benjamin. *Black Abolitionists*. New York: Oxford University Press, 1969.

Quillin, Frank U. *The Color Line in Ohio: A History of Race Prejudice in a Typical Northern State*. Ann Arbor, Mich.: George Wahr, 1913.

Rhodes, Jane. *Mary Ann Shadd Cary: The Black Press and Protest in the Nineteenth Century*. Bloomington: Indiana University Press, 1998.

Richardson, Joe M. *Christian Reconstruction: The American Missionary Association and Southern Blacks, 1861–1890*. Athens: University of Georgia Press, 1986.

Rigsby, Gregory U. *Alexander Crummell: Pioneer in Nineteenth-Century Pan-African Thought*. Westport, Conn.: Greenwood Press, 1987.

Ripley, C. Peter, ed. *The Black Abolitionist Papers*, 5 vols. Chapel Hill: University of North Carolina Press, 1985–1992.

Robinson, Chalfant. *A History of Two Reciprocity Treaties*. New Haven, Conn.: The Tuttle, Morehouse and Taylor Press, 1904.

Room, Adrian, ed. *Brewer's Dictionary of Phrase and Fable*, 16th ed. New York: Harper Resource, 1999.

Rose, Willie Lee. *Rehearsal for Reconstruction: The Port Royal Experiment*. Indianapolis: Bobbs-Merril Company, 1964.

Rosenfeld, Louis. *Thomas Hodgkin*. Lanham, Md.: Madison Books, 1993.

Ruchames, Louis, and Walter M. McIntosh, eds. *The Letters of William Lloyd Garrison*. Cambridge, Mass.: Belknap Press, 1971–81.

Salzman, Jack, David Lionel Smith, and Cornell West, eds. *African-American Culture and History*, vol. 2. New York: Macmillan Library Reference, 1996.

Sawyer, Amos. *Emergence of Autocracy in Liberia: Tragedy and Challenge*. San Francisco: ICS Press, 1992.

Scarborough, William, ed. *The Diary of Edmund Ruffin*, vol. 1. Baton Rouge: Louisiana State University Press, 1972.

Schor, Joel. *Henry Highland Garnet: A Voice of Black Radicalism in the Nineteenth Century*. Westport, Conn.: Greenwood Press, 1977.

Selleck, Linda B. *Gentle Invaders: Quaker Women Educators and Racial Issues During the Civil War and Reconstruction*. Richmond, Ind.: Friends United Press, 1995.

Slaughter, Thomas. *Bloody Dawn: The Christiana Riot and Racial Violence in the Antebellum North*. New York: Oxford University Press, 1991.

Smedley, Katherine. *Martha Schofield and the Re-education of the South, 1839–1916*. Lewiston: Edwin Mellen Press, 1987.

Soderlund, Jean. *Quakers and Slavery: A Divided Spirit*. Princeton: Princeton University Press, 1985.

Staudenraus, Philip J. *The African Colonization Movement, 1816–1865*. New York: Columbia University Press, 1961.

Stauffer, John. *The Black Hearts of Men: Radical Abolitionists and the Transformation of Race*. Cambridge: Harvard University Press, 2002.

Stearns, Frank Preston. *The Life and Public Services of George Luther Stearns*. Philadelphia: J. P. Lippincott Company, 1907.

Sterling, Dorothy, ed. *We Are Your Sisters: Black Women in the Nineteenth Century*. New York: Norton, 1984.

———. *Ahead of Her Time: Abby Kelley and the Politics of Anti-Slavery*. New York: Norton, 1991.

———. *The Making of an Afro-American: Martin Robison Delany, 1812–1885*. New York: Da Capo Press, 1996.

Stewart, E. S. *The Steward Family of New Jersey*. Philadelphia: Allen, Lane and Scott, 1907.

Stuckey, Sterling. *The Ideological Origins of Black Nationalism*. Boston: Beacon Press, 1972.

———. *Slave Culture: Nationalist Theory and the Foundations of Black America*. New York: Oxford University Press, 1987.

Tadman, Michael. *Speculators and Slaves: Masters, Traders, and Slaves in the Old South*. Madison: University of Wisconsin Press, 1989.

Tebbel, John. *A History of Book Publishing in the United States*, 2 vols. New York: R. R. Bowker, 1972.

Thwaites, Reuben Gold. *Joseph Hobbins, MD*. Madison, Wis.: Madison Literary Club, 1894.

The Times Atlas of the World, 10th ed. New York: Times Books Group Co., 1999).

Toll, Jean Barth, and Mildred S. Gillam, eds. *Invisible Philadelphia: Community Through Voluntary Organizations*. Philadelphia: Atwater Kent Museum, 1995.

Towne, Laura M. *Letters and Diary of Laura M. Towne*, ed. Rupert Sargent Holland. Cambridge, Mass.: Riverside Press, 1912.

Ullman, Victor. *Martin R. Delany: The Beginnings of Black Nationalism.* Boston: Beacon Press, 1971.

Von Frank, Albert. *The Trials of Anthony Burns: Freedom and Slavery in Emerson's Boston.* Cambridge: Harvard University Press, 1998.

Watson, Wilbur H. *Against the Odds: Blacks in the Profession of Medicine in the United States.* New Brunswick, N.J.: Transaction Publishers, 1999.

Webster's New International Dictionary, 2nd ed. Ed. William Allan Neilson. Springfield, Mass.: G. and C. Merriam Company, 1934.

Whittier, John Greenleaf. *Justice and Expediency.* 1833. Reprinted in *Against Slavery: An Abolitionist Reader*, ed. Mason Lowance, 149–55. New York: Penguin Books, 2000.

Wiggins, Rosalind Cobb, ed. *Captain Paul Cuffe's Logs and Letters, 1808–1817.* Washington, D.C.: Howard University Press, 1996.

Winch, Julie. *Philadelphia's Black Elite: Activism, Accommodation, and the Struggle for Autonomy, 1787–1848.* Philadelphia: Temple University Press, 1988.

———. *The Elite of Our People: Joseph Willson's Sketches of Black Upper-Class Life in Antebellum Philadelphia.* University Park: Pennsylvania State University Press, 2000.

———. *A Gentleman of Color: The Life of James Forten.* New York: Oxford University Press, 2002.

Winks, Robin W. *Blacks in Canada.* New Haven: Yale University Press, 1971.

Wolf, Edwin, II. *Philadelphia: Portrait of an American City.* Philadelphia: Library Company of Philadelphia, 1990.

Yellin, Jean Fagan. *Harriet Jacobs: A Life.* New York: Basic Books, 2004.

MANUSCRIPT COLLECTIONS

American Colonization Society Records. Library of Congress. Microfilm (331 reels). [viewed reels 41–48 (gen. correspondence); 88, 231–35 (Ralph Randolph Gurley's letterbook); 290 (Board proceedings); 299, 302]

Apprentices' Library Company of Philadelphia. Annual Reports.

Benjamin Coates Collection. Special Collections. Haverford College.

Charles Roberts Autograph Letters Collection. Special Collections, Haverford College. (Joseph Jenkins Roberts to Benj. Coates, Esq., May 26, 1854; Stephen Allen Benson to Benj. Coates, Esq., August 22, 1859).

Dictionary of Quaker Biography. Quaker Collection. Haverford College. Haverford, Pa.

Elias Hicks Papers. Miscellaneous fragments. Box 30. Friends Historical Library. Swarthmore College.

Free Library of Philadelphia. Special Collections. Miscellaneous Papers.

Friends Freedmen's Association Records. Microfilm. Special Collections. Haverford College. Reels #1 and #5.

Haverford College. Board of Managers. Minutes.

Institute for Colored Youth. Board of Managers. Minutes.

Pennsylvania Abolition Society Papers. Microfilm. Special Collections. Haverford
    College.
Philadelphia Monthly Meeting of the Religious Society of Friends. Minutes. Micro-
    film. Special Collections. Haverford College.
Philadelphia Monthly Meeting for the Western District. Minutes.
Philadelphia Yearly Meeting of the Religious Society of Friends. Indian Committee:
    Indian Aid Association, Minutebook, 1869–97. Special Collections. Haverford
    College.

PUBLISHED PRIMARY SOURCES

*Abbeokuta; or, Sunrise Within the Tropics: An Outline of the Origin and Progress of the
    Yoruba Mission*. New York: R. Carter and Brothers, 1859.
*A Brief Sketch of the Schools for Black People and Their Descendants Established by the Reli-
    gious Society of Friends in 1770*. Philadelphia: Friends Book Store, 1867.
African Repository, 43 vols. Washington, D.C.: American Colonization Society, 1850–
    1892.
Alexander, Archibald. *A History of Colonization on the Western Coast of Africa*. 2nd ed.
    Philadelphia: W. S. Martien, 1849.
American Baptist Missionary Union. *The Missionary Jubilee: An Account of the Fiftieth
    Anniversary of the American Baptist Missionary Union*. New York: Sheldon and
    Company, 1871.
American Colonization Society. *Thirty-sixth Annual Report of the American Coloniza-
    tion Society, with the proceedings of the Board of Directors and of the Society; and
    the addresses delivered at the annual meeting, January 18, 1853*. Washington, D.C.:
    C. Alexander, 1853.
American Freedman. 3 vols. New York: American Freedmen's and Union Commission,
    1866–1869.
Apprentices' Library Company of Philadelphia. *Annual Reports, 1823–1880*. Philadel-
    phia: Author.
———. *Annual Reports, 1870–1892*. Philadelphia: Author.
Barth, Heinrich. *Travels and Discoveries in North and Central Africa*. New York: Harper
    and Row, 1857.
Bible Association of Friends in America: Reports, 1855–1891. Philadelphia.
Blyden, Edward W. *Liberia's Offering: Being Addresses, Sermons, etc*. New York: John A.
    Gray, 1862.
———. "Liberia as a Means, not an End." *African Repository* 43 (November 1867): 321.
———. *Liberia: Past, Present, and Future*. Washington City: M'Gill and Witherow,
    1869.
———. *The Negro in Ancient History*. Washington City: M'Gill and Witherow, 1869.
Bowen, Thomas Jefferson. *Central Africa: Adventures and Missionary Labors in Several
    Countries in the Interior of Africa, from 1849 to 1856*. 1857; reprint, New York: Negro
    Universities Press, 1969.
Brooks, William E. "Tillotson Normal and Collegiate Institute." *American Missionary*
    35, no. 6 (June 1881): 161–62.

Campbell, Robert. *A Pilgrimage to My Motherland.* Philadelphia: Thomas Hamilton, 1861.

Childs, Maria. *Isaac Hopper: A True Life.* Boston: John. P. Jewett and Company, 1853.

Clarkson, Thomas. *History of the Rise, Progress, and Accomplishment of the Abolition of the African Slave Trade by the British Parliament.* New York: John S. Taylor, 1836.

Coates, Benjamin. "Cotton Cultivation in Africa." *Friends' Intelligencer* 15, no. 32 (1858): 505–6.

————. *Cotton Cultivation in Africa: Suggestions on the Importance of the Cultivation of Cotton in Africa, in Reference to the Abolition of Slavery in the United States, Through the Organization of an African Civilization Society.* Philadelphia: C. Sherman and Son, 1858.

Coates, Mary. *Family Memorials and Recollections, or Aunt Mary's Patchwork.* Philadelphia: Author's Family, 1885.

Crummell, Alexander. *The Future of Africa: Being Addresses, Sermons, Etc., Etc., Delivered in the Republic of Liberia.* New York: Charles Scribner, 1862.

Cuyler, Theodore Ledyard. *Recollections of a Long Life.* New York: Baker and Taylor, 1902.

"Death of Rev. G. D. Pike, D. D." *American Missionary* 39, no. 3 (March 1885): 68–69.

Delany, Martin Robison. *The Condition, Elevation, Emigration, and Destiny of the Colored People of the United States.* 1852; reprint, New York: Arno Press, 1968.

Douglass, Frederick. *My Bondage and My Freedom.* With an introduction by Dr. James M'Cune Smith. New York: Miller, Orton, and Mulligan, 1855.

Ellis, William. *Three Visits to Madagascar in the Years 1853-1854-1856.* New York: Harper and Brothers, 1859.

Friends Intelligencer and Journal.

Friends' Review.

Frothingham, Rev. Octavius Brooks. "Education and Religion." *Independent* 18 no. 919 (July 12, 1866): 1.

Geldart, Mrs. Thomas. *Memorial of Samuel Gurney.* Philadelphia: Henry Longstreth, 1859.

Griffith, Martha. *Autobiography of a Female Slave.* New York: Redfield, 1856.

Gurley, Ralph Randolph. *Life of Jehudi Ashmun, Late Colonial Agent in Liberia.* Washington, D.C.: J. C. Dunn, 1835.

Harris, J. Denis. *Summer on the Borders of the Caribbean Sea.* New York: A. B. Burdick, 1860.

Heacock, Annie. *Reminiscences.* n.p., April 1926.

Helper, Hinton Rowan. *The Impending Crisis of the South; How to Meet It.* New York: Burdick Bros., 1857.

Hilles, Samuel Eli. *Memorials of the Hilles family: more particularly of Samuel and Margaret Hill Hilles of Wilmington, Delaware, with some account of their ancestry and some data not before published; also extended references to the life of Richard Hilles or Hills, principal founder of the Merchant taylors school in London, 1561. The friend of Miles Coverdale, John Calvin, Archbishop Cranmer, Bishop Hooper and others, prominent in the early days of the reformation, together with a hitherto unpublished sonnet and portrait of John G. Whittier.* Cincinnati: Samuel E. Hilles, 1928.

History of Haverford College: The Early Years, 1830–1890. Philadelphia: Haverford College Alumni Association, Porter and Coates, 1892.

Hunt, Benjamin S. *Remarks on Hayti as a Place for Settlement for Afric-Americans and on the Mulatto as a Race for the Tropics: or Hayti and the Mulatto.* Philadelphia: T. B. Pugh, 1860.

Hunt, B. P. *Why Colored People in Philadelphia are Excluded from the Street Cars.* Philadelphia: Merrihew, 1866.

Institute for Colored Youth. *Objects and Regulations of the Institute for Colored Youth; ; With a List of the Offices and Students, and the Annual Report of the Board of Managers.* Philadelphia: Merrihew and Thompson, 1859–1884.

———. *Objects and Regulations of the Institute for Colored Youth; With a List of the Offices and Students, and the Annual Report of the Board of Managers.* Philadelphia: Board of Managers, Institute for Colored Youth, 1885–1901.

Jacobs, Harriet. *Incidents in the Life of a Slave Girl, Written By Herself,* ed. L. Maria Child. 1861; reprint, Cambridge: Harvard University Press, 2000.

Johnson, William Augustine Bernard. *Africa's Mountain Valley, or, the Church of Regent's Town, West Africa.* London: Seeley, Jackson, and Halliday, 1856.

The Liberator. Boston, Mass.: William Lloyd Garrison and Isaac Knapp, 1831–1865.

Lugenbeel, J. W. *Sketches of Liberia: Comprising a Brief Account of the Geography, Climate, Productions, and Diseases of the Republic of Liberia.* Washington, D.C.: C. Alexander, 1850.

McElroy's Philadelphia City Directory. Philadelphia: A. McElroy and Company, 1835–1859.

Meeting in Mother Bethel Church. *Resolutions and Remonstrances for the People of Colour of Philadelphia, Against the Colonization on the Coast of Africa.* n.p., 1818.

Memorial of the semi-centennial anniversary of the American Colonization Society, celebrated at Washington, January 15, 1867. With documents concerning Liberia. Washington, D.C.: American Colonization Society, 1867.

Memorial Minute respecting our late friend, James E. Rhoads, adopted by the Monthly Meeting of Friends of Philadelphia for the Western District, the twenty-fourth of Fourth month, 1895, and directed to be printed for distribution among the families of its members. [n.d.]

Moon, R. C. *The Morris Family of Philadelphia: Descendants of Anthony Morris, born 1654–1721 died.* Philadelphia: Author, 1898–1909.

Nesbit, William. "Four Months in Liberia: Or, African Colonization Exposed," with an introduction by Dr. Martin R. Delany. 1855. Reprinted in *Liberian Dreams: Back-to-Africa Narratives from the 1850s,* ed. Wilson Jeremiah Moses, 79–126. University Park: Pennsylvania State University Press, 1998.

Oberlin College. *General Catalogue of Oberlin College, 1833–1908: Including an Account of the Principal Events in the History of the College, with Illustrations of the College Buildings.* Oberlin, Ohio: Author, 1909.

Park, Mungo. *Travels in the Interior Districts of Africa.* London: n.p., 1799.

Penn, William. *No Cross, No Crown,* ed. Ronald Selleck. 1669; reprint, Richmond, Ind.: Friends United Press, 1981.

The Pharmaceutical Era, vol. 1. New York: D. O. Haynes and Company, 1887.

The Press

[Pugh, Sarah.] *The Memorial of Sarah Pugh: A Tribute of Respect from Her Cousins.* Philadelphia: J. B. Lippincott, 1888.

Purvis, Robert. *Appeal of Forty Thousand Citizens Threatened with Disenfranchisement, to the People of Pennsylvania.* Philadelphia: Merrihew and Gunn, 1838.

Report of the Committee Appointed for the Purpose of Securing to Colored People in Philadelphia the Right to the Use of the Street Cars. Philadelphia: Merrihew and Sons, 1867.

Scharf, J. Thomas, and Thompson Westcott. *History of Philadelphia, 1609–1884.* Philadelphia: L. H. Everts and Company, 1884.

Speirs, Frederick W. *The Street Railway System of Philadelphia: Its History and Present Condition.* Baltimore: Johns Hopkins Press, 1897.

Stockwell, G. S. *The Republic of Liberia, its Geography, Climate, Soil and Production, with a History of its Early Settlement.* New York: A. S. Barnes, 1868.

Stowe, Harriet Beecher. *Uncle Tom's Cabin: or, Life Among the Lowly.* Boston: J. P. Jewett, 1852.

———. *A Key to Uncle Tom's Cabin: Presenting the Original Facts and Documents Upon Which the Story is Founded, Together with Corroborative Statements Verifying the Truth of the Work.* Boston: J. P. Jewett, 1853.

Van Nest, Abraham Rynier. *Memoir of Rev. George W. Bethune, D.D.* New York: Sheldon and Company, 1867.

Webb, Frank J. *The Garies and Their Friends.* With an introductory preface by Harriet Beecher Stowe and an introduction by Robert Reid-Pharr. 1857; reprint, Baltimore: Johns Hopkins University Press, 1997.

Weekly Anglo-African. New York: Thomas Hamilton, 1859–1861.

SUBJECT INDEX

This subject index is organized into five separate categories, each containing entries ordered alphabetically. The entries contain the alternate spelling (if different from proper), letter number, sender and recipient, and letter date. The five categories are (1) People; (2) Organizations, Businesses, and Meetings; (3) Publications and Books; (4) Places; and (5) Ships.

I. PEOPLE

Abbott, Lyman
    Letter 95, "Lyman Abbott, Gen Sec," McKim to Coates, May 24, 1867
    Letter 96, "Lyman Abbott, Gen Sec," McKim to Coates, June 4, 1867
Adams, [?]
    Letter 19, "Captain Adams U.S.A.," Roberts to Coates, October 16, 1854
African tribes
    Letter 104, "the Mandingoes," Blyden to Coates, January 11, 1868
    Letter 129, "The natives around us, Mohammedan and Pagan," Blyden to Coates, October 10, 1868
    Letter 129, "Vey men," Blyden to Coates, October 10, 1868
    Letter 131, "Congoes + natives," Crummell to Coates, November 2, 1868
Alexander, Archibald
    Letter 12, Coates to McLain, January 10, 1852
Allen, George N.
    Letter 75, "Geo. N. Allen, Treas. ——," Allen to Coates, April 23, 1863
Amos, [?]
    Letter 150, "Mr. Amos," Blyden to Pinney, March 12, 1869
    Letter 155, "Brother —— Amos," Pinney to Coates, April 19, 1869
Anderson, ——
    Letter 33, Coates to Gurley, October 21, 1858
    Letter 36, Coates to Gurley, January 13, 1859
Andrew, John A.
    Letter 81, "Gov. Andrew," Stearns to Coates, February 13, 1865

Arthington, Robert
    Letter 159, Coates to Coppinger, October 7, 1871
Ashmum, J.
    Letter 111, "the immortal Ashmum," Gurley to Coates, May 8, 1868
[Atherbury?] [Dr. Atterbury?]
    Letter 1, "Mr. [Atherbury?]," Roberts to Coates, July 8, 1848
Atkinson, Edward
    Letter 52, "Edward Atkinson Esq," Smith to Coates, August 27, 1859
    Letter 128, "Mr. Atkinson," Tracy to Coates, September 30, 1868 (same Atkinson?)

Bacon, Leonard
    Letter 15, Coates to Lugenbeel, June 27, 1853
Baines, Rev. Albert
    Letter 133, Coates to Coppinger, November 17, 1868
Barbour, ——
    Letter 33, Coates to Gurley, October 21, 1858
Barnes, Albert
    Letter 42, "The discourse of Dr. Barnes," Douglass to Coates, May 2, 1859
Barth, Heinrich
    Letter 42, "Doctor Barth's travels," Douglass to Coates, May 2, 1859
Bassett, Ebenezer Don Carlos
    Letter 121, "ED Bassett," Coates to Coppinger, August 5, 1868
    Letter 122, "E.D. Bassett," Bassett to Coates, August 12, 1868
    Letter 125, Coates to Coppinger, September 26, 1868
    Letter 133, Coates to Coppinger, November 17, 1868
    Letter 137, Coates to Coppinger, January 8, 1869
    Letter 139, Coates to Coppinger, January 15, 1869
    Letter 156, "the matter of E D Bassett etc.," Carter to Coates, April 29, 1869
Beecher, Henry Ward
    Letter 41, "Henry Ward Beecher," Garnet to Coates, April 27, 1859
Bell, ——
    Letter 8, Coates to McLain, May 16, 1851
    Letter 9, Coates to Lugenbeel, June 18, 1851
Bell, Philip A.
    Letter 3, Coates to Douglass, June 27, 1850
Benedict, Samuel
    Letter 69, Coates to Crummell, April 14, 1862
Benson, Stephen Allen
    Letter 8, Coates to McLain, May 16, 1851
    Letter 9, Coates to Lugenbeel, June 18, 1851
    Letter 10, Coates to McLain, October 11, 1851
    Letter 12, Coates to McLain, January 10, 1852
    Letter 14, Coates to McLain, February 28, 1852
    Letter 21, Coates to McLain, May 22, 1855
    Letter 22, Coates to Gurley, June 15, 1855
    Letter 29, Coates to Crummell, October 3, 1857

Grinnell, Joseph
    Letter 99, "Jos. Grinnell," Hilles to Coates, August 15, 1867
Gurley, E. M.
    Letter 109, Gurley and Gurley to Coates, April 7, 1868
    Letter 111, Gurley to Coates, May 8, 1868
Gurley, I. McD. [E. M. and R. R. Gurley's son?]
    Letter 109, "I McD. Gurley," Gurley and Gurley to Coates, April 7, 1868
    Letter 109, "our son," Gurley and Gurley to Coates, April 7, 1868
Gurley, Ralph Randolph
    Letter 10, Coates to McLain, October 11, 1851
    Letter 15, Coates to Lugenbeel, June 27, 1853
    Letter 20, Coates to Lugenbeel, May 3, 1855
    Letter 23, Coates to Lugenbeel, October 27, 1855
    Letter 24, Coates to Lugenbeel, November 17, 1855
    Letter 26, Coates to Lugenbeel, September 29, 1856
    Letter 27, Coates to Lugenbeel, October 6, 1856
    Letter 28, Coates to Gurley, May 2, 1857
    Letter 32, Coates to Gurley, May 28, 1858
    Letter 33, Coates to Gurley, October 21, 1858
    Letter 36, Coates to Gurley, January 13, 1859
    Letter 74, Coates to Gurley, February 10, 1863
    Letter 109, "Mr Gurley" and "Husband," Gurley and Gurley to Coates, April 7, 1868
    Letter 111, "My Husband" and "Ralph Randolph Gurley," Gurley to Coates, May 8, 1868
Gurney, Samuel
    Letter 5, Coates to McLain, July 9, 1850
    Letter 17, Coates to McLain, June 8, 1854
    Letter 18, "S. Gurney Esqr.," Roberts to Coates, August 26, 1854
    Letter 40, "the Gurneys," Hobbins to Coates, March 2, 1859

Hall, George W. S.
    Letter 18, "G.W.S. Hall," Roberts to Coates, August 26, 1854
    Letter 60, "George Hall," Pinney to Coates, September 28, 1859
Hall, James
    Letter 18, "his [G. W. S. Hall's] father the Doctor," Roberts to Coates, August 26, 1854
    Letter 137, Coates to Coppinger, January 8, 1869
    Letter 138, Coates to Coppinger, January 12, 1869
Hamilton, Thomas
    Letter 59, "Thos. Hamilton," Hamilton to Coates, September 19, 1859
Hampton, Wade
    Letter 90, "Wade Hampton + co," Tomlinson to Coates, March 29, 1867
Hanson, Augustus W.
    Letter 18, "Hanson's character," Roberts to Coates, August 26, 1854

Williams, Samuel
    Letter 21, Coates to McLain, May 22, 1855
"[Willis?]"
    Letter 141, Pinney to Coates, January 28, 1869
Wilson, David Agnew
    Letter 25, "D.A. Wilson," Roberts to Coates, May 15, 1856
Wood, A. C.
    Letter 156, Carter to Coates, April 29, 1869
Worth, [?]
    Letter 88, "Gov. Worth," Young to Coates, July 25, 1866
Wriston, M. L.
    Letter 88, Young to Coates, July 25, 1866
    Letter 89, Young to Coates, July 31, 1866

Y., C.
    Letter 156, "C.Y.," Carter to Coates, April 29, 1869
Yates, Beverley Page
    Letter 25, "B.P. Yates," Roberts to Coates, May 15, 1856
Young, John A.
    Letter 88, "J.A. Young," Young to Coates, July 25, 1866
    Letter 89, "J.A. Young," Young to Coates, July 31, 1866

2. ORGANIZATIONS, BUSINESSES, AND MEETINGS

"the Academy [in Guilford, Conn.]"
    Letter 147, Pinney to Coates, March 6, 1869
African Civilization Society
    Letter 36, Coates to Gurley, January 13, 1859
    Letter 35, "your enterprise," Wagoner to Coates, January 8, 1859
    Letter 41, "The Board," Garnet to Coates, April 27, 1859
    Letter 42, "The African Civilization Society," Douglass to Coates, May 2, 1859
    Letter 48, "Bible House," Garnet to Coates, July 17, 1859
    Letter 49, "The African Civilization Society," Morris to Coates, August 8, 1859
    Letter 50, "The Board of Directors," Garnet to Coates, August 17, 1859 [?]
    Letter 50, "[Constantine elected] to the office of —— s.cty of our society," Garnet to Coates, August 17, 1859
    Letter 51, Benson to Coates, August 22, 1859
    Letter 63, Prince to Coates, September 6, 1860
    Letter 69, Coates to Crummell, April 14, 1862
American Colonization Society (ACS)
    Letter 5, Coates to McLain, July 9, 1850
    Letter 8, Coates to McLain, May 16, 1851
    Letter 13, "the Board at Washington," Bethune to Coates, January 10, 1852
    Letter 14, Coates to McLain, February 28, 1852
    Letter 30, Coates to McLain, December 19, 1857

3. PUBLICATIONS AND BOOKS

"Gambia"
     Letter 48, Campbell to Coates, July 17, 1859
"Mr. Garnets Church"
     Letter 42, Douglass, May 2, 1859
"Geneva"
     Letter 46, Pinney to Coates, June 16, 1859
Germantown, Pennsylvania
     Letter 94, Rhoads to Coates, May 17, 1867
     Letter 97, Rhoads to Coates, June 28, 1867
"Government House [Monrovia]"
     Letter 18, Roberts to Coates, August 26, 1854
Guilford, Connecticut
     Letter 147, Pinney to Coates, March 6, 1869

Haiti
     Letter 19, "Hayti," Roberts to Coates, October 16, 1854
     Letter 77, Coates to Coppinger, October 13, 1864
     Letter 146, "Hayti," Roberts to Coates, February 22, 1869
"Halifax"
     Letter 71, [Say?] to Coates, October 6, 1862
Haverford, Pennsylvania
     Letter 67, Mitchell to Coates, April 8, 1862
     Letter 68, Chase to Coates, April 10, 1862
Hingham, Massachusetts
     Letter 128, Tracy to Coates, September 30, 1868

"John's"
     Letter 90, Tomlinson to Coates, March 29, 1867

"Lagos"
     Letter 48, Campbell to Coates, July 17, 1859
Liberia
     Letter 2, Coates to McLain, June 23, 1850
     Letter 6, Coates to McLain, September 5, 1850
     Letter 7, Coates to Douglass, January 16, 1851
     Letter 15, Coates to Lugenbeel, June 27, 1853
     Letter 17, Coates to McLain, June 8, 1854
     Letter 18, Roberts to Coates, August 26, 1854
     Letter 19, Roberts to Coates, October 16, 1854
     Letter 27, Coates to Lugenbeel, October 6, 1856
     Letter 36, Coates to Gurley, January 13, 1859
     Letter 51, Benson to Coates, August 22, 1859
     Letter 55, Morris to Coates, September 8, 1859
     Letter 58, Morris to Coates, September 15, 1859
     Letter 59, Hamilton to Coates, September 19, 1859
     Letter 60, Pinney to Coates, September 28, 1859

Letter 69, Coates to Crummell, April 14, 1862
Letter 72, Blyden to Coates, October 9, 1862
Letter 73, Blyden to Coates, October 15, 1862
Letter 75, Allen to Coates, April 23, 1863
Letter 76, Coates to McLain, April 7, 1864
Letter 77, Coates to Coppinger, October 13, 1864
Letter 83, Coates to Coppinger, October 31, 1865
Letter 84, Coates to Coppinger, May 24, 1866
Letter 87, Coates to Coppinger, June 6, 1866
Letter 104, Blyden to Coates, January 11, 1868
Letter 109, Gurley and Gurley to Coates, April 7, 1868
Letter 111, Gurley to Coates, May 8, 1868
Letter 112, Coates to Coppinger, May 20, 1868
Letter 117, Coppinger to Coates, June 30, 1868
Letter 118, Coppinger to Coates, July 22, 1868
Letter 119, Yates and Porterfield to Coates, July 30, 1868
Letter 123, Whipple to Coates, August 27, 1868
Letter 124, Roberts to Coates, September 18, 1868
Letter 126, Coppinger to Coates, September 28, 1868
Letter 127, Roberts to Coates, September 28, 1868
Letter 129, Blyden to Coates, October 10, 1868
Letter 131, Crummell to Coates, November 2, 1868
Letter 133, Coates to Coppinger, November 17, 1868
Letter 136, Coppinger to Coates, November 30, 1868
Letter 137, Coates to Coppinger, January 8, 1869
Letter 139, Coates to Coppinger, January 15, 1869
Letter 142, Roberts to Coates, January 30, 1869
Letter 147, Pinney to Coates, March 6, 1869
Letter 148, Tracy to Coates, March 2, 1869
Letter 150, Blyden to Coates, March 12, 1869
Letter 152, Tracy to Coates, March 18, 1869

"Madeira"
Letter 18, Roberts to Coates, August 26, 1854
"Madison, Wis."
Letter 40, Hobbins to Coates, March 2, 1859
Massachusetts
Letter 152, Tracy to Coates, March 18, 1869
"McCarthy's Island"
Letter 48, Campbell to Coates, July 17, 1859
"a medical school"
Letter 40, Hobbins to Coates, March 2, 1859
Mendi Mission
Letter 61, Tucker to Coates, October 12, 1859
miscellaneous place
Letter 13, "the new city," Bethune to Coates, January 10, 1852

5. SHIPS